DISLOYAL
A MEMOIR

DISLOYAL
A MEMOIR

THE TRUE STORY OF THE FORMER PERSONAL ATTORNEY
TO THE PRESIDENT OF THE UNITED STATES

MICHAEL COHEN

Skyhorse Publishing

Skyhorse Publishing books may be purchased in bulk at special discounts for sales promotion, corporate gifts, fund-raising, or educational purposes. Special editions can also be created to specifications. For details, contact the Special Sales Department, Skyhorse Publishing, 307 West 36th Street, 11th Floor, New York, NY 10018 or info@skyhorsepublishing.com.

Skyhorse® and Skyhorse Publishing® are registered trademarks of Skyhorse Publishing, Inc.®, a Delaware corporation.

Visit our website at www.skyhorsepublishing.com.

10 9 8 7 6 5 4 3 2 1

Library of Congress Cataloging-in-Publication Data is available on file.

ISBN: 978-1-5107-6469-9
eBook: 978-1-5107-6470-5

Cover design by Brian Peterson
Cover photographs by Getty Images
All interior photos © 2020 Michael Cohen

Printed in the United States of America

Dedication

I dedicate this book to the love of my life, my wife Laura, and to my wonderful children, Samantha and Jake. The three of you endured so much during my years with Donald Trump and in the years since then. You have been subjected to harassment, insults and threats; you have seen me get arrested and charged and put in prison (twice). But the deepest suffering must have come as you watched me play an active role in the despicable acts of Mr. Trump. For this, I am deeply sorry. I feel unimaginably grateful that the three of you stuck by me through it all. My greatest desire in life is to do whatever I can to make up for the pain I have caused you and to bring happiness, pride, and a feeling of safety to the rest of your lives.

Acknowledgments

Due to the divisive nature of this memoir, I have decided not to acknowledge individual people. Let me just say this: to those who have helped and supported me while I wrote this book, I thank you from the very bottom of my heart.

Contents

Foreword: The Real Real Donald Trump   11

Chapter One: The Apprentice   25

Chapter Two: The Fixer   45

Chapter Three: The El Caribe   61

Chapter Four: Laura   73

Chapter Five: Catch and Twist   81

Chapter Six: Trump For President (Part One)   103

Chapter Seven: Stormy Weather (Part One)   137

Chapter Eight: That's What Friends Are For   145

Chapter Nine: The End of the World   165

Chapter Ten: How to Fix a Poll   187

Chapter Eleven: Trump For President (Part Two)   201

Chapter Twelve: Russia (Part One)   243

Chapter Thirteen: Russia, If You're Listening (Part Two)   261

Chapter Fourteen: Hurricane Stormy (Part Two)   271

Chapter Fifteen: Election Night   307

Chapter Sixteen: Typhoon Stormy (Part Three)   331

Chapter Seventeen: The Conviction Machine   349

Chapter Eighteen: Otisville Federal Satellite Camp   357

Epilogue: Retaliation   361

Appendix: Documents, Tweets, and Photos   369

"I hope he hasn't bitten off more than he can chew."
Fred Trump

Foreword: The Real Real Donald Trump

The President of the United States wanted me dead.

Or, let me say it the way Donald Trump would: He wouldn't mind if I were dead. That was how Trump talked. Like a mob boss, using language carefully calibrated to convey his desires and demands, while at the same time employing deliberate indirection to insulate himself and avoid actually ordering a hit on his former personal attorney, confidant, consigliore, and, at least in my heart, adopted son.

Driving south from New York City to Washington, DC on I-95 on the cold, gray winter morning of February 24th, 2019, en route to testify against President Trump before both Houses of Congress, I knew he wanted me gone before I could tell the nation what I know about him. Not the billionaire celebrity savior of the country or lying lunatic, not the tabloid tycoon or self-anointed Chosen One, not the avatar @realdonaldtrump of Twitter fame, but the real real Donald Trump—the man very, very, very few people know.

If that sounds overly dramatic, consider the powers Trump possessed and imagine how you might feel if he threatened you personally. Heading south, I wondered if my prospects for survival were also going in that direction. I was acutely aware of the magnitude of Trump's fury aimed directly at my alleged betrayal. I was wearing a baseball cap and sunglasses and I kept the speedometer at eighty, avoiding the glances of other drivers. Trump's theory of life, business, and politics revolved around threats and the prospect of destruction—financial, electoral, personal, physical—as a weapon. I knew how he worked because I had frequently been the one screaming threats on his behalf as Trump's fixer and designated thug.

Ever since I had flipped and agreed to cooperate with Robert Mueller and the Special Counsel's Office, the death threats had come by the hundreds. On my cell phone, by email, snail mail, in tweets, on Facebook, enraged Trump supporters vowed to kill me, and I took those threats very seriously. The President called me a rat and tweeted angry accusations at me, as well as my family. All rats deserve to die, I was told. I was a lowlife Judas they were going to hunt down. I was driving because I couldn't fly or take the train to Washington. If I had, I was sure I would be mobbed or attacked. For weeks, walking the streets of Manhattan, I was convinced that someone was going to ram me with their car. I was exactly the person Trump was talking about when he said he could shoot and kill someone on Fifth Avenue and get away with it.

My mind was spinning as I sped towards DC. For more than a decade, I had been at the center of Trump's innermost circle. When he came to my son's bar mitzvah, a generous gesture that I found touching, he told my then thirteen-year-old boy that his dad was the greatest and that, if he wanted to work at the Trump

Organization when he grew up, there would always be a position for him.

"You're family," Trump said to my son and me.

And I fucking believed him!

Pulling over at a service plaza, I gassed up and headed inside for a coffee, black no sugar. I looked around to see if I was under surveillance or being followed, a sense of dread consuming my thoughts. Who was that FBI-type in the gray coat or the muscle-bound dude a few paces behind me? The notion that I was being followed or stalked may have seemed crazy, but it was also perfectly logical. I wasn't just famous—I was perhaps the most infamous person in the country at the time, seen by millions upon millions as a traitor. President Trump controlled all the levers of the Commander in Chief and all the overt and covert powers that come with the highest office in the country. He also possessed a cult-like hold over his supporters, some of them demonstrably unhinged and willing to do anything to please or protect the President. I knew how committed these fanatics were because I'd been one of them: an acolyte obsessed with Donald J. Trump, a demented follower willing to do anything for him, including, as I vowed once to a reporter, to take a bullet.

On the eve of my public testimony, lying in the still of the night in my hotel room, taking a bullet assumed a completely different meaning. That was the level of ruination I had brought upon myself—complete and total destruction. I closed my eyes, wishing the nightmare would end. When I started working for Trump, I had been a multi-millionaire lawyer and businessman, and now I was broke and broken; a convicted, disgraced, and disbarred former attorney about to testify against the President on live television before an audience of more than 15 million Americans.

"Hey, Michael Cohen, do your wife and father-in-law know about your girlfriends?" GOP Representative Matt Gaetz tweeted at me that night, to cite just one example of the juvenile idiocy and menace aimed in my direction. "I wonder if she'll remain faithful when you're in prison. She's about to learn a lot . . ."

> **Matt Gaetz** ✓
> @mattgaetz
>
> Follow
>
> Hey @MichaelCohen212 - Do your wife & father-in-law know about your girlfriends? Maybe tonight would be a good time for that chat. I wonder if she'll remain faithful when you're in prison. She's about to learn a lot...
>
> 1:12 PM - 26 Feb 2019
>
> **1,115** Retweets **2,278** Likes
>
> ⬜ 7.5K   ⟲ 1.1K   ♡ 2.3K   ✉

Sitting in the green room on the morning of my testimony before the House Oversight Committee, I began to feel the enormous weight of what was about to happen. For some reason, after all that I'd been through, and all I'd put my family and the country through, waiting in that room was the moment when the gravity of what was about to happen truly hit home. The United States was being torn apart, its political and cultural and mental well-being threatened by a clear and present danger named Donald Trump, and I had played a central role in creating this new reality. To half of Americans, it seemed like Trump was effectively a Russian-controlled fraud who had lied and cheated his way to the White House; to the other half of Americans, to Trump's supporters, the entire Russian scandal was a witch hunt invented by Democrats still unable to accept the fact that Hillary Clinton had lost fair and square in the most surprising upset in the history of American presidential elections.

Both sides were wrong. I knew that the reality was much more complicated and dangerous. Trump had colluded with the Russians, but not in the sophisticated ways imagined by his detractors. I also knew that the Mueller investigation was not a witch-hunt. Trump had cheated in the election, with Russian connivance, as you will discover in these pages, because doing anything—and I mean *anything*—to "win" has always been his business model and way of life. Trump had also continued to pursue a major real estate deal in Moscow during the campaign. He attempted to insinuate himself into the world of President Vladimir Putin and his coterie of corrupt billionaire oligarchs. I know because I personally ran that deal and kept Trump and his children closely informed of all updates, even as the candidate blatantly lied to the American people saying, "There's no Russian collusion, I have no dealings with Russia . . . there's no Russia."

The time to testify nearing, I asked the Sergeant at Arms for a few minutes of privacy and the room was cleared. Sitting alone, my thoughts and heart racing, I had the first panic attack of my life. I struggled to breath and stand. The pressure was too much; I had contemplated suicide in recent weeks, as a way to escape the unrelenting insanity. Reaching for a seat, I started to cry, a flood of emotions overwhelming me: fear, anger, dread, anxiety, relief, terror. It felt something like when I was in the hospital awaiting the birth of my daughter and son, with so many powerful and unprecedented emotions welling up in anticipation. Only now, I was that child being born, and all of the pain and blood were part of the birth of my new life and identity.

Trying to pull myself together, I went to the private bathroom and checked my eyes to see if they were bloodshot or puffy. To my relief, they weren't. I splashed my face with cold water and felt a calm coming over me, and then a surge of confidence and adrenaline. I had pled guilty to multiple federal crimes, including lying to Congress, but I was there to tell the truth, the whole truth, and nothing but the truth. I knew that Trump and the Republican House members would want me to hesitate, falter, show weakness, even break down. They wanted me to look unreliable, shifty, and uncertain about the truth and myself. This was blood sport and they wanted me to cower. I wasn't going to give them the satisfaction, I decided. I was going to nail it.

"Show time," the Sergeant at Arms called out, opening the door. "You're on, Mr. Cohen."

One deep breath and I stepped into the hallway, into a crush of photographers and TV cameras and the craziness of wall-to-wall national obsession. I made my way alone through the jostle and shove of the surging crowd as I experienced the out-of-body sensation of seeing myself on television screens walking in to testify. It was truly bizarre to be at the epicenter of American history at that moment, to personify so many fears and resentments, to be the villain or savior, depending on your point of view, to speak truth to power in an age when truth itself was on trial. There I was, watching myself on TV, the Michael Cohen everyone had an opinion about: liar, snitch, idiot, bully, sycophant, convicted criminal, the least reliable narrator on the planet.

So, please permit me to reintroduce myself in these pages. The one thing I can say with absolute certainty is that whatever you may have heard or thought about me, you don't know me or my story or the Donald Trump that I know. For more than a decade, I was Trump's first call every morning and his last call every night. I was in and out of Trump's office on the 26th floor of the Trump Tower as many as fifty times a day, tending to his every demand. Our cell phones had the same address books, our contacts so entwined, overlapping, and intimate that part of my job was to deal with the endless queries and requests, however large or small, from Trump's countless rich and famous acquaintances. I called any and all of the people he spoke to, most often on his behalf as his attorney and emissary, and everyone knew that when I spoke to them, it was as good as if they were talking directly to Trump.

Apart from his wife and children, I knew Trump better than

anyone else did. In some ways, I knew him better than even his family did, because I bore witness to the real man, in strip clubs, shady business meetings, and in the unguarded moments when he revealed who he really was: a cheat, a liar, a fraud, a bully, a racist, a predator, a con man.

There are reasons why there has never been an intimate portrait of Donald Trump, the man. In part, it's because he has a million acquaintances, pals, and hangers on, but no real friends. He has no one he trusts to keep his secrets. For ten years, he certainly had me, and I was always there for him, and look what happened to me. I urge you to really consider that fact: Trump has no true friends. He has lived his entire life avoiding and evading taking responsibility for his actions. He crushed or cheated all who stood in his way, but I know where the skeletons are buried because I was the one who buried them. I was the one who most encouraged him to run for president in 2011, and then again in 2015, carefully orchestrating the famous trip down the escalator in Trump Tower for him to announce his candidacy. When Trump wanted to reach Russian President Vladimir Putin, via a secret back channel, I was tasked with making the connection in my Keystone Kop fashion. I stiffed contractors on his behalf, ripped off his business partners, lied to his wife Melania to hide his sexual infidelities, and bullied and screamed at anyone who threatened Trump's path to power. From golden showers in a sex club in Vegas, to tax fraud, to deals with corrupt officials from the former Soviet Union, to catch-and-kill conspiracies to silence Trump's clandestine lovers, I wasn't just a witness to the President's rise—I was an active and eager participant.

To underscore that last crucial point, let me say now that I had agency in my relationship with Trump. I made choices along the way—terrible, heartless, stupid, cruel, dishonest, destructive choices, but they were mine and constituted my reality and life.

During my years with Trump, to give one example, I fell out of touch with my sisters and younger brother, as I imagined myself becoming a big shot. I'd made my fortune out of taxi medallions, a business viewed as sketchy, if not lower-class. On Park Avenue, where I lived, I was definitely *nouveau riche,* but I had big plans that didn't include being excluded from the elite. I had a narrative: I wanted to climb the highest mountains of Manhattan's skyscraping ambition, to inhabit the world from the vantage point of private jets and billion-dollar deals, and I was willing to do whatever it took to get there. Then there was my own considerable ego, short temper, and willingness to deceive to get ahead, regardless of the consequences.

As you read my story, you will no doubt ask yourself if you like me, or if you would act as I did, and the answer will frequently be no to both of those questions. But permit me to make a point: If you only read stories written by people you like, you will never be able to understand Donald Trump or the current state of the American soul. More than that, it's only by actually understanding my decisions and actions that you can get inside Trump's mind and understand his worldview. As anyone in law enforcement will tell you, it's only gangsters who can reveal the secrets of organized crime. If you want to know how the mob really works, you've got to talk to the bad guys. I was one of Trump's bad guys. In his world, I was one hundred percent a made man.

Before I could read my opening statement to the Oversight Committee on the day of my public testimony, the Republicans started to play procedural games. It was clearly an attempt to rattle me, I thought, a spectacle that only demeaned them and the institution itself. As I started to answer questions, it was evident that the Republicans didn't want to hear a word I had to say, no matter how true or how critical to the future of the country. For all the hard truths I spoke about Trump, I wasn't entirely critical of him, nor will I be in these pages. I said I know Trump as a human being, not a cartoon character on television, and that means I know he's full of contradictions.

"Mr. Trump is an enigma," I testified to the committee. "He is complicated, as am I. He does both good and bad, as do we all. But the bad far outweighs the good, and since taking office, he has become the worst version of himself. He is capable of behaving kindly, but he is not kind. He is capable of committing acts of generosity, but he is not generous. He is capable of being loyal, but he is fundamentally disloyal."

"Liar, liar, pants on fire," one of the Republicans taunted me, perfectly expressing the stupidity and lunacy of his party's antics. To drive this point home, they actually made a sign with a picture of me on it. In bold letters, the sign proclaimed, "Liar, Liar Pants on Fire."

Sign at my Congressional Testimony. © 2020 Michael Cohen

I recognized the childish games, replete with a Trump-like slogan, because I had played them myself. In the pitiful sight of

Republicans throwing aside their dignity and duty in an effort to grovel at Trump's feet, I saw myself and understood their motives. My insatiable desire to please Trump to gain power for myself, the fatal flaw that led to my ruination, was a Faustian bargain: I would do anything to accumulate, wield, maintain, exert, exploit power. In this way, Donald Trump and I were the most alike; in this naked lust for power, the President and I were soul mates. I was so vulnerable to his magnetic force because he offered an intoxicating cocktail of power, strength, celebrity, and a complete disregard for the rules and realities that govern our lives. To Trump, life was a game, and all that mattered was winning. In these dangerous days, I see the Republican Party and Trump's followers threatening the Constitution—which is in far greater peril than is commonly understood—and following one of the worst impulses of human-kind: the desire for power at all costs.

"To those who support the President and his rhetoric, as I once did, I pray the country doesn't make the same mistakes as I have made or pay the heavy price that my family and I are paying," I testified to Congress, exhorting them to learn from my example.

"Given my experience working for Mr. Trump, I fear that if he loses the election in 2020 that there will never be a peaceful transition of power," I concluded. "This is why I agreed to appear before you today."

Representative Elijah Cummings had the final word, as chair of the Oversight Committee. I sat in silence, listening to this now deceased man with decades of experience in the civil rights move-ment and other forms of public service, who as a lawyer had represented disgraced lawyers like me. He understood that even the least of us deserve the opportunity to seek penance, redemp-tion and a second chance in life. Cummings was the lone politician I encountered in all my travails who took an interest in me as a human being. When I reported to serve my sentence, he even took steps to ensure my security in prison. It was a selfless act of kindness for which I will always be grateful.

"I know this has been hard," Cummings said to me and the nation, his words hitting me like a kick in the gut. "I know you've faced a lot. I know that you are worried about your family. But this is a part of your destiny. And hopefully this portion of your destiny will lead to a better Michael Cohen, a better Donald Trump, a better United States of America, and a better world. And I mean that from the depths of my heart."

Representative Cummings concluded by saying, "We are better than this."

Amen, I thought.

Now, sitting alone in an upstate New York prison, wearing my green government-issued uniform, I've begun writing this story longhand on a yellow legal pad. I often wrote before dawn so as not to be disturbed in my thoughts when my fellow inmates awoke. I had to report to the sewage treatment plant where some of us worked for a wage of $8 a month. As the months passed by and I thought about the man I knew so well, I became even more convinced that Trump will never leave office peacefully. The types of scandals that have surfaced in recent months will only continue to emerge with greater and greater levels of treachery and deceit. If Trump wins another four years, these scandals will prove to be only the tip of the iceberg. I'm certain that Trump knows he will face prison time if he leaves office, the inevitable cold Karma to the notorious chants of "Lock Her Up!" But that is the Trump I know in a nutshell. He projects his own sins and crimes onto others, partly to distract and confuse, but mostly because he thinks everyone is as corrupt and shameless and ruthless as he is; a poisonous mindset I know all too well. Whoever follows Trump into the White House, if the President doesn't manage to make himself the leader for life, as he has started to joke about—and Trump never actually jokes—will discover a tangle of frauds and scams and lawlessness. Trump and his minions will do anything to cover up that reality, and I mean *anything*.

Watching Trump on the evening news in the prison rec room, I almost feel sorry for him. I know him so well and I know his facial tics and tells; I see the cornered look in his eyes as he flails and rants and raves, searching for a protector and advocate, someone willing to fight dirty and destroy his enemies. I see the men who have replaced me and continue to forfeit their reputations by doing the President's bidding, no matter how dishonest or sleazy or unlawful. Rudy Giuliani, William Barr, Jared Kushner, and Mike Pompeo are Trump's new wannabe fixers, sycophants willing to distort the truth and break the law in the service of the Boss. All this will be to no avail. Trump doesn't want to hear this, and he will certainly deny it, but he's lost without his original bulldog lawyer Roy Cohn, or his other former pit bull and personal attorney, Michael Cohen.

During my testimony, Republican House members repeatedly asked me to promise that I wouldn't write a book. I refused, repeatedly. It was another way of saying I shouldn't be permitted to tell my story, in essence giving up my First Amendment rights. It was a clear sign of desperation and fear. I have lost many things as a consequence of my decisions and mistakes, including my freedom, but I still retain the right to tell this story about the true threat to our nation and the urgent message for the country it contains.

One last thing I can say with great confidence, as you turn the page and meet the real real Donald Trump for the first time: this is a book the President of the United States does not want you to read.

Michael Cohen
Otisville Federal Prison, Otisville, New York
March 11, 2020

DISLOYAL

A MEMOIR

Chapter One

The Apprentice

Donald Trump's seduction began the way it would continue for years, with flattery, proximity to celebrity and power, and my own out-of-control ambitions and desires. For me, it started on a nondescript day in the fall of 2006. At the time, I was a successful, if little-known, middle-aged midtown Manhattan attorney and businessman on the make, sitting in a tidy nondescript office with two of everything arranged before me on my desk, a function of my obsessive nature: two staplers, two tape dispensers, two phones, two cups with sharpened pencils. I was thirty-nine and I worked for the mid-sized white-shoe law firm Phillips Nizer. As a lawyer I'd long had a busy practice in personal injury and medical malpractice, but my real passion and talent was in dealmaking, and I had accumulated a multi-million dollar fortune in the rough-and-tumble taxi medallion industry. Wealthy, with a beautiful wife and two healthy, happy young children, I had just purchased an apartment in the Trump Park Avenue building for $4.9 million and I tooled around the city in a Bentley and considered myself semi-retired.

I had it made, in other words, but I didn't know that I was on the precipice of a mid-life crisis that would lead to an all-consuming fixation and my downfall.

On this fall day, in 2006, sitting at my desk doing the paper-pushing drone work of practicing the law, my secretary buzzed on the intercom.

"It's Donald Trump, Jr. on line one," she said.

I was half expecting the call. I knew the younger Trump from my recent purchase of three units in the new Trump Park Avenue, a project then under construction to be converted into my family home; two one-bedroom units and a two-bedroom apartment on the 10th floor of what had been the high-society Delmonico Hotel were being consolidated into a single residence with sweeping views of the iconic avenue from the living room running half the length of the building. Don Jr. was handling the construction job on behalf of the Trump Organization, so we talked often.

I picked up the call—news about the Trump Park Avenue, or TPA as insiders knew it, was a welcome distraction from my routine legal work. Besides, I'd become friendly with the younger Trump and enjoyed our banter and shared New York real estate tough guy personas. I had long cultivated the image of a hard-ass, the kind of lawyer who could solve any and every kind of problem, not necessarily through my legal acumen, but as a hyper aggressive, take-no-prisoners fixer—kind of a knock-around version of the TV character *Ray Donovan*, but in real life.

"Hey, D, what's up? How are things going at TPA?" I said.

"I'm not calling about TPA," Trump, Jr. said. "Can you meet with me and my dad at his office? It's about something else and very important. My dad thinks you could be very helpful."

Everything with the Trumps was always "very," I would learn, but I didn't hesitate. A meeting with Donald Trump? Hell, yeah. I'd met Trump once before a few years earlier, at a political fundraiser for a Republican candidate for New York Attorney General, but that had only been in passing.

Within minutes, I was walking excitedly up Fifth Avenue towards Trump Tower. To me, the elder Trump wasn't just a celebrity and billionaire real estate developer. As an undergraduate at American University, in Washington, DC, I'd read *The Art of the Deal* when it was published in the 1980s not once but twice, and I considered the book a masterpiece. Ruthless, relentless, insatiable, brilliant, innovative, hard-edged, hard-driving, above all always a winner—the self-portrait of Trump contained in those pages, however fictional and far from the truth, had enthralled me. Secretly, in my heart of hearts, I thought I possessed some of Trump's best qualities. I saw myself as deal-driven, relentless, a hard worker, never afraid, prepared to be brutal and heartless in pursuit of my ambitions. I already had wealth but I wanted it all: power, the good life, public acclaim, fame, big deals, fast cars, private planes, the excess and glamor and zest for life that Trump appeared to personify so effortlessly.

Walking up Fifth Avenue, I had an inkling what the meeting might be about. In recent weeks, as Don Jr. and I had discussed progress on the renovation of my TPA apartment, he'd told me about a fight that was brewing at another Trump property in midtown near the United Nations, this one called Trump World Tower, or TWT. I also owned an investment unit in TWT, which I rented out for $15,000 a month, and I'd encouraged my parents and mother- and father-in-law to also buy into the building, meaning that together my family owned more than half a dozen apartments in the East Side skyscraper that had boasted celebrity residents like Harrison Ford and the New York Yankee Derek Jeter. The 72-story tower (which claims to have 90 floors on the elevator push button, classic Trump) was in turmoil because the condo's board of directors had gotten into a blood feud with Trump, the elder, about disputed fees and who should get the benefit of a city tax abatement of $100 million.

Both the board and Trump had engaged lawyers as the fight grew more and more bitter and personal, the younger Trump had told me. Now the board was trying to remove the Trump name from the building, on the grounds that it was more valuable to the owners without the association with *The Apprentice* reality TV star. The threat was not only an affront to the elder Trump but also a real and serious threat to the brand—and the Trump name was basically all that the Trump Organization had left to sell by 2006. If the TWT disassociated itself from Trump, what would happen next? Who else might see the name as a liability? The name Trump was attached to a seemingly endless string of golf courses and products, and any threat to the brand was taken to be existential.

I'd sympathized and expressed outrage at the offense to the Trumps, even offering assistance, if desired. I believed in the Trump brand and the value it brought to real estate and that he was rightfully due a payment of nearly $15 million for securing the tax abatement. Don Jr. knew of my reputation as a tough-guy attorney, so I figured that was why I'd been called.

Entering the revolving doors of Trump Tower, with an appointment with the proprietor, I was in awe at the majesty of the famous atrium: the grand escalator, the pink marble walls, the brass of the place, literally and metaphorically. The sheer scale and class of the building were incredible, at least to my way of thinking. The building had been designed to create such an impression, of course, but it worked on me.

Presenting myself at the security desk, I was told that Mr. Trump was expecting me. This acknowledgement of my existence by the great man provided a jolt of excitement. Escorted to the

26th floor, headquarters of the Trump operation, I was greeted by a beautiful young blonde woman who also said that Mr. Trump was expecting me—giving me another moment of pleasure. I was immediately ushered through glass doors into a large office with a sweeping view of Fifth Avenue and Central Park.

Sitting behind a large, cluttered desk was the elder Trump, talking loudly on a call on speakerphone. To me, the hulking Trump was even larger in life than he appeared on television. His presence filled the room, as I surveyed the office, an homage to Trump, with a vanity wall boasting scores of magazine covers with Trump's image, along with shelves packed with glass awards and deal mementoes and sports memorabilia, including a garish and glittering version of Mike Tyson's heavyweight world champion belt. Three red-velvet executive Egg chairs were arranged in front of Trump's desk, with Don Jr. seated in one and the Chief Financial Officer of the Trump Organization, Allen Weisselberg, in the other. I was directed to sit in the middle seat, where I waited as Trump conducted what seemed to be a private conversation with us all listening in.

The call over, Trump yelled out for a Diet Coke, stood, and offered his hand to me. Like all New Yorkers, I had followed Trump in the tabloids for years and knew about his foibles and idiosyncrasies, but as an ardent fan and true believer, I knew more than most, including reports that Trump was a germophobe, so I reluctantly offered my hand in reply as he gave me his power grip.

"Don tells me great things about you," Trump said, as half a dozen employees of the company filed into the office and arranged themselves behind me, standing at attention. "You do know I gave you a great deal on your new apartment," Trump continued.

I blinked. I didn't know what to say in reply. This was Trump's first tell, if I'd had the ability to see what was unfolding, but events were moving so fast and in such a tantalizing way that I didn't have the presence of mind to consider what had just occurred. I had paid the asking price on the Park Avenue apartment; there had been no discount or special consideration—it had never even come up. But there it was: within the first few seconds of our meeting, Donald Trump had lied to me, directly, demonstrably and without doubt. What was I supposed to do, if I had possessed the where-withal to gather my wits and take on the implications? Call Trump on it? The lie seemed silly, harmless, and childish, the kind of fib that was pointless to contest; it occurred to me that Trump might actually believe it, too. In a matter of a couple of sentences, with no conscious thought or understanding of what was actually hap-pening, I had given my unspoken consent to start to play along in a charade that I would come to learn was all-devouring and deadly serious.

For now, I parried with a joke, of a kind. "Would you like to buy the units back?" I asked.

"No, no," Trump said quickly. "You made a great decision to buy at TPA, just like you did at TWT."

The blonde assistant entered with Trump's Diet Coke, and she offered me one. Trump took a sip of his soda and revealed what the meeting was really about.

"There is an issue I would like your help with," he said. "I have a rogue board at TWT. We're in litigation and they're looking to take the Trump name off the building."

Trump smiled.

"You more than anyone understand the value of the Trump brand, as you own apartments in a few of my buildings. You had your parents and in-laws and friends buy as well, and you all have made a lot of money."

"Yes, yes, that is true," I replied. "Tell me why the board is doing what it's doing at TWT."

Trump replied by way of introducing me to the employees now

crowding into his office. The top executives and lawyers for the Trump Organization were all in the room and, it seemed, astonishingly, that they were now to be put at my disposal—a perfect stranger to Trump, a relatively small-time attorney, and someone with no apparent connection to the matter other than my unit in Trump World Tower and whatever Don Jr. had said to recommend me.

"All of these individuals will walk you through whatever questions you may have and will provide you with any support you need," Trump said.

I was incredulous, excited, overwhelmed. I was a graduate of the University of Western Michigan's Thomas M. Cooley Law School, perhaps the least-prestigious institution in the nation from which to receive a legal education, and I was being asked to assess a serious situation and determine strategy on a critical business matter on behalf of billionaire celebrity Donald J. Trump? Don Jr. had evidently suggested that I might be able to help, but it appeared that I was being put in charge of a project that clearly was of great importance to the older Trump. I sensed that the issues involved had to be much larger than I'd anticipated, just as the opportunity appeared to be much larger, a chance I wasn't going to let pass me by. I had my own work to do back at my office, but all that could wait for now, however long this new venture took. Internally I resolved that I was going to succeed for Trump, come what may.

"I will let you know my thoughts after I review the materials," I told Trump in a serious tone. Turning to the staff, I said, "Is everyone ready to get to work?"

Trump glowered at his team, leaning back in his chair, as my question hung in the air.

"I mean right now," I said.

The yes-sir executives leapt into action. I was taken to a conference room and I was soon reviewing invoices from Trump World Tower to see if there was any substance to the allegations of wrongdoing by the Trump Organization leveled by the condo board. With the Trump team at my disposal, I spent six hours that day, and then the next four days in succession, doing nothing but intensively searching the financial records; I was an attorney with an hourly rate, but payment was never mentioned, and I knew better than to rock the boat by raising the question of my fees. I calculated that working for free was a way to ingratiate myself and offer Trump no reason to complain or get rid of me.

After researching the issues, I concluded that the board had indeed wrongly accused Trump, and I recorded that conclusion in a three-page memorandum outlining the allegations, the controversial issues, and the way to proceed, as I saw it. The board was alleging false, petty, and disingenuous infractions, I wrote, and the real victims were the owners of the condos who were being forced to pay exorbitant legal fees to pursue a pointless feud. Worse, I concluded, the board had awarded sweetheart deals to landscapers for their own benefit.

Finishing reading my memo the next day in his office as I watched in anticipation, Trump looked up, elated, as if he had finally been vindicated and now he had proof that he was in fact the true victim. I knew I was trying to please Trump, but in this dispute the billionaire really was being wronged, I believed. Over time, as Trump became a patriarchal figure to me and I fell under the trance-like spell of the real estate tycoon, I would come to understand that questions of right and wrong didn't matter to Trump in the slightest—all that counted to him, and then to me, was winning and displaying blind loyalty.

"This bullshit can't stand," I said, Trump's chin tilting and chest swelling with self-righteous delight and I, in turn, puffing out my chest in indignation. "I will lead a coup to take over the board of directors and rid the building of these animals."

Trump leapt to his feet, exclaiming, "Michael, you're great. Whatever you need in terms of help, you got it. Go get 'em."

Let me stop for a moment to point out that I'm not making up Trump's nearly constant use of the word "great" to make myself look good. That was how he talked. Hyperbole was his instinctual method of communication, exaggerating his own talents and wealth and physical characteristics and achievements, as if by enlarging things he could make them real. The same was true for those around him, if you remained on his good side. I called it the "flatter lie," the untruth aimed at inflating my ego, which I knew really wasn't entirely true but that he knew I wanted to be true, so the dynamic was circular in nature and mutually reinforcing. I saw this all the time in Trump, as he sought praise and then offered praise in return, as if the act of bestowing his half-true approval lent the observation more gravitas. Huuuggeee, great, fantastic, the best—that's how he talks, and thinks, like he's starring in his own ongoing major motion picture.

With access to the Trump Organization's records, I had the contact information for all of the more than 300 owners in Trump World Tower. A small group of Trump's advisors and owners started circling the names of the owners we knew, including my parents and in-laws, and we started an underground campaign to gather signatures and proxy voting rights, the process rippling out as more and more residents heard our version of events and quietly agreed to support our effort to oust the board. Some of the residents were prominent, like the lawyer George Conway, the husband of President Trump's future spokesperson Kellyanne, but the effort was covert in the beginning, in order to blindside the board in the forthcoming condo board meeting. As the effort proceeded, the elder Trump displayed an intense interest in the matter, as he viewed the peril to his brand to be serious, and a variety of advisors and attorneys got involved, but I was the most avid and active advocate and point man.

The turnout for the condo meeting in March of 2006 was expected to be so large it was moved to the Church of the Holy Family opposite the United Nations on East 47th Street. More than 300 people attended the meeting, with beefy security guards hired by the board of directors checking IDs at the door to ensure that no outsiders were able to enter. The room bristled with tension and animosity.

Stepping outside, with the line stretching down the block, I grinned in appreciation as Trump glided up in a black limousine right on cue, as if he were in the middle of an episode of *The Apprentice*, with his executive team in two trailing SUVs. Also accompanying Trump was a gang of muscle-bound men, looking like the forward line of an NFL team as the namesake of the building waved a hand and the bodyguards parted the sea of people, sweeping away the supposedly tough security guards the board had hired to prevent precisely such a show of intimidation. I was delighted by the performance.

Watching the spectacle, all I kept thinking was that this guy's got game. For weeks the board had planned for that moment, only to be completely destroyed by their opponent. That was real power, I thought. Not just physical power, but the cash type of power, and the ability to mentally dominate your adversary. For me, this wasn't some event I was watching as a spectator. I was right in the thick of it. It was irresistible, intoxicating, thrilling.

Inside, Trump saved me a seat in a pew next to him, a small gesture that defied belief to me, like I was becoming part of his intimate circle. Trump was agitated, angry that he'd been put to all this trouble by this ungrateful board of directors who understood nothing about real estate or the value Trump brought to the project, he told me. He waved his arms and expressed red-faced outrage as he stood and shouted out his indignant reasons for the board to be replaced and his fee to be paid, aiming his worst contempt for the chairman, a former executive with US Airways—before it went bankrupt.

"What does he know!" Trump bellowed. "He ran his airline into the ground!"

The crowd gasped in shock at Trump's aggression, but I loved it. It incited me to go even further. As I rose to speak, all eyes were on me, but the only pair that I really cared about was Trump's. The allegations against Trump were false, I thundered, as the room began to stir in even deeper partisan division. I had prepared my speech in great detail, outlining the perfidy of the former airline executive and exonerating Trump. We had a stack of proxy votes we had the power to exercise, and the outcome of the vote was a foregone conclusion, but I poured myself into the speech. I had run twice for office, once for New York City council and once for state senate—both attempts dire failures, I'm sorry to say—but I had a taste for public speaking and the spotlight, especially with the admiring gaze of Donald Trump looking up at me.

Then it came: the applause.

"What a great speech," said Trump, offering the praise that I was quickly learning had an aphrodisiacal impact on me. "Man, you are a great speaker."

Still worked up, I sat and took my printed speech from my breast pocket, autographed it and handed it to Trump with a flourish. "Here, Mr. Trump, now you will remember me forever," I said.

"I will," Trump said, pocketing the speech. "I will."

A few days later, I received a package containing my speech, now in a gilt gold frame, with a note from Trump in his usual dense handwriting on the page saying, "You are a great speaker and a great friend. Donald."

After the excitement, days and weeks passed quietly as the renovations on Trump Park Avenue continued and I wondered if I'd ever again have the chance to work for Mr. Trump. Then, one day, Trump's longtime assistant and occasional *The Apprentice* co-star Rhona Graff called asking if I had time to talk to Trump. I did—of course I did. I could think of nothing better than talking to Trump, helping Trump, pleasing Trump.

"Michael, my man, did you get my gift?" Trump boomed on the speakerphone a second later.

"I did," I replied, thanking him profusely for such a thoughtful gesture.

We congratulated each other and ourselves on our glorious victory, the mutual reinforcement serving as a way for our newly forming bond to strengthen.

"Listen, I need you to handle another issue for me," Trump said. "Actually, it's cleaning up a mistake Don made. Are you free to stop by today, at around noon, say?"

"For you, I will make myself available," I replied, again giddy at this further indication of Trump's belief in me, inviting thoughts of where this might eventually lead for someone who'd occupied the role of fan and onlooker to Trump, but was now on the way to becoming an advocate and intimate.

"Donald Trump just called me again for another project," I called out proudly to my younger brother, Bryan, also an attorney with an office next door, as I pulled on my jacket.

"Very nice," Bryan replied, sardonically. "But maybe this time see if he intends on paying you for your time."

As I headed out the door, I had absolutely no intention of charging Trump for my time, no matter how many billable hours were consumed. I'd spent weeks on the Trump World Tower dispute and received no money in return, but I'd been compensated in an intangible way that was more valuable. I believed that I had to succeed completely and utterly to remain in Trump's good graces, and I knew I had to be on time as I again hustled up Fifth Avenue to the gilded golden tower. Trump hated tardiness, I knew, and I was going to do nothing to displease him.

Walking into the fabled concourse for my new assignment, I was again greeted warmly at reception and on the 26th floor, now as a potential regular, a feeling I enjoyed immensely. Shown into Trump's office once more, I sat in the middle red-velvet Egg executive chair, next to Don Jr. and an attorney named George Sorial, another young lawyer who had become one of the new members of the board of directors at Trump World Tower, like me. The Trump Organization's Chief Operating Officer, Matt Calamari, was also in attendance, signaling that a consequential matter was at hand.

I was given a rundown of the situation. Trump Mortgage Services had been founded in 2003, at the suggestion of Don Jr., and its name had been changed to Trump Mortgage LLC in 2005. But the enterprise hadn't proved successful, despite the housing boom then zooming along at supersonic speed. In Trump's telling, the whole fiasco was his son's fault. Don Jr. had brought him a "shit" deal, he said, and introduced him to a supposedly highly qualified mortgage broker named E.J. Ridings. Don Jr., who oversaw development and acquisitions for the Trump Organization, sat quietly as his father demeaned him. Over time, I would come to learn that his father held him in extremely low esteem.

"Don has the worst fucking judgment of anyone I have ever met," Trump would often tell me, adding that he'd been reluctant to bestow his first name on his first-born son. He didn't want to share his name with a "loser," if that was what his son turned out to be.

Trump Mortgage appeared to be an example of exactly that: a losing proposition that was tarnishing the Trump name. When

Trump re-launched the company in April 2006, with a gala in the concourse of Trump Tower, he had predicted huge success. CEO E.J. Ridings claimed he had fifteen years' experience as a broker and promised $3 billion in mortgages originated in the first year alone. Trump Mortgage would "own New York," Trump had said, and that in time it would dominate the country and the world.

"I think it's a great time to start a mortgage company," Trump had told Maria Bartiromo on CNBC only months before the global financial crisis struck, collapsing the market. Supposedly a great prognosticator, Trump had predicted, "the real estate market is going to be very strong for a long time"—only days before the global economy crashed.

I learned that the company didn't actually lend money; it was a brokerage that aimed to find clients and match them to banks willing to take on the loans. Hiring a group of aggressive salespeople, some rejects from other brokers, with little background checking, the company operated out of 40 Wall Street, another Trump property. The Trump Mortgage floor was divided in two: On one side were salespeople devoted to high-end residential and commercial mortgages; on the other was a boiler room filled with high-pressure hustlers making cold calls to unsuspecting home owners trying to convince them to refinance their mortgages—the kind of liar loans and sub-prime borrowers that were rapidly turning the mortgage industry into a toxic pit.

According to what Trump now told me, Ridings had inflated his credentials, as revealed in a *Money* magazine article that had just been published. Ridings wasn't "a top professional at one of Wall Street's most prestigious investment banks," as he'd claimed. Instead, he had had a three-month run at Morgan Stanley, with only six days working as an actual broker. But Ridings had fooled the gullible Don Jr., and, in turn, the elder Trump. The company didn't broker $3 billion in mortgages in 2006, nor did it manage the downwardly revised estimate of $1 billion; only $25 million in loans had been originated. Brandishing the magazine, Trump again cast himself as the victim of other people's failings, particularly his son and his pal E.J. Ridings.

I honestly didn't consider the possibility of Trump's own gross negligence and incompetence contributing to the collapse of the company as I sat in the red Egg chair and listened to Trump, believing every utterance, or, more accurately, not caring about the truth. Trump told me he had a job for me to do, and that was all I cared about. It was a strong-arm operation, it appeared. Trump told me I was to go downtown to 40 Wall Street unannounced and shut down Trump Mortgage. I was tasked with throwing Ridings out of the office, closing the business, and collecting all the files so that Trump's lawyers could start liquidating the company.

Trump looked me directly in the eye. "Michael, this is really important," he said. "This guy is damaging the brand, and you of all people appreciate the Trump brand. Go do this for me and be rough. Be rough. And I mean really rough."

Slipping downtown in Trump's ultra-luxury limo, along with the attorney George Sorial and COO Calamari, I considered what Trump meant by "rough." It was something like a mobster order, it appeared, an instruction for me to take matters under control and make it crystal clear to Ridings that the decision was final, nonnegotiable, an offer he couldn't refuse. I also believed I'd been told to do it in as humiliating a way as possible. Not for a business purpose, of course, but for the pleasure of inflicting harm and exercising raw power—a cocktail I would come to find alluring.

In fact, Trump didn't actually own Trump Mortgage. Like many of "his" businesses, there was a licensing agreement, paying Trump royalties for the use of his name, a structure which shielded him from liability, but also meant he had no equity in the business. But I wasn't going to let legal niceties bother me.

Arriving at 40 Wall Street, we made our way up to Trump Mortgage, where a crooked logo was hanging on a glass door. The COO Calamari was from Brooklyn, with a thick 'dems and 'dos accent, so he spoke first, instructing the receptionist to fetch Ridings immediately and tell him to come to the conference room. Now, as in: right now.

"It's show time," I said, all of us now smiling.

Ridings arrived, looking chipper and grinning. I ordered him to sit.

"Michael is Mr. Trump's lawyer, as is George, and you know who I am," Calamari said.

"What's going on, gentlemen," Ridings said, the grin disappearing.

"Nothing good," I said coldly. "Trump Mortgage is now closed. Mr. Trump wants all the files and records. You need to tell your staff to go home right now. They can take nothing, except their personal belongings. Everyone is to leave except for the computer guy. Do you understand?"

Ridings seemed stunned. "I need to call Don Jr.," he said.

"Don't bother," Sorial replied. "Don't waste your time. He already knows. Mr. Trump has directed us to do this and we don't want this to be harder than it has to be."

But I did want to make it harder—much harder. Some primal instinct reveled in the power I possessed, if only by proxy and proximity to Trump. "What are you doing still sitting there?" I demanded of Ridings, not allowing a minute for the new reality to sink it. "Get up now, tell all your employees to go home, and wait for further instructions."

As Ridings started to argue, I departed to track down the IT person. Finding him, I demanded the password and log-in details for the server, which were given over reluctantly as the techie watched Ridings and Sorial shouting in the conference room.

Fighting against an apparent *coup de grace*, much like the one I had orchestrated at Trump World Tower, Ridings again demanded to talk to the Trumps, which was agreed to.

I knew it was useless. One thing I had learned from my limited interactions with Trump was that he is not a forgiving person. Once he sours on you, you are done. Watching the staff depart in confusion and disarray, Ridings was witnessing his world collapse by the fiat of a single man and his enforcers, which included me, with no right of appeal.

The job done, riding back uptown in the limo, we giggled recalling how hard-ass we had been to an essentially defenseless man taken by surprise and literally ordered out of his own business in an extra-legal and abusive manner. These were the permission slips I was starting to issue to myself. I was an officer of the court, sworn to uphold that law, which did not include staging a raid on a company and firing all the employees immediately and posting a security guard to ensure they couldn't return. Nor did I consider the plight of someone like Jennifer McGovern, a single mother of three who was owed $238,000 in commissions she had legally earned and which she has never received to this day; the liquidation was arranged to insulate the Trump Organization, no matter the impact on the completely innocent. And I was a willing accomplice—more, I was an eager participant.

Back at Trump's office, Calamari told Trump all the supposedly glorious details about the encounter, aggrandizing how rough I had been on Ridings. Trump was beaming. Ever helpful, I then offered the password and log-in digits for the server, advising that Trump should change them to protect the data and files.

"Damn good thinking," Trump said.

Praised once again, I was walking on air as I made my way home to the now-completed Trump Park Avenue apartment, a short four-block jaunt. For a fleeting moment I felt sorry for E.J., having his company taken away from him in the blink of an eye. But that emotion was swallowed up by the recollection of the day's events, Trump's accolades, and the completion of the task. "Mission Accomplished," I thought to myself, riding the elevator up to my apartment. I confess I never really did understand why pleasing Trump meant so much to me, and others. To this day I don't have the full answer.

In a matter of a couple of months, I had started falling under the spell of Donald Trump. The question no longer was what I would do for Trump—the question was what I wouldn't do. And the short answer was that I would do and say pretty much anything. I had not only bullied a perfect stranger, without knowing the complexities or legal framework of the dispute, but I did it with gusto and an utter lack of conscience. Filled with pride, I didn't wonder what lay ahead, or what other moral and ethical and ultimately criminal boundaries I would cross. Nor did I consider that Trump was testing my fealty and submissiveness, the way a gang leader assesses a new recruit, giving the wannabe small crimes to commit to see if he will act without question or concern for his own well-being. Donald Trump was like a mafia don, in a sense, and I wanted to be his soldier in the worst way, and I was ready to pass any test put in my path.

Entering my new apartment on the 10th floor, I was greeted warmly by my wife Laura, daughter Samantha, twelve, and son Jake, seven. Eager to tell Laura about my heroic exploits, at least in my mind, I was shocked to see her face contort into a grimace as I related details of confronting and unmanning E.J. Ridings at the behest of Donald Trump. As the rush of words poured out, her face crinkled into a frown and she started to shake her head in disapproval. This mystified me as I continued to talk like a warrior returned from the field of battle, only to discover that what I thought was heroic didn't look the same way to Laura. I was at a loss for words at my wife's response; I thought for sure she would not only approve of what I'd done, but see it the way I did: as a triumph.

"Your day sounds horrible to me," Laura said, my shoulders slouching in bewilderment as I discovered there was another way to view what I'd done that day to please Trump.

Bullying people to do things was not attractive to her at all. She wasn't impressed by things like that. When I started doing work for Donald Trump, I wanted her approval, but she wasn't going to give me praise for pushing someone else around. We didn't talk a lot about business and my work, and she let me go my own way, but I wasn't going to be admired at home for the things I was doing for Donald Trump, and I knew it. As our children grew older, they came to feel the same way. They would beg me to quit working for Trump, but I didn't listen. It seemed to them that I wouldn't listen to anyone, not even the people who loved me most, as I gradually gave up control of my mind to Trump.

Chapter Two

The Fixer

Early in 2007, I received another call from Don Jr., asking for my assistance in a media relations matter that had come up. The younger Trump knew that I had a lot of connections in the press, from the *New York Post* to *Politico* from my two runs for elected office, and they needed a resident in one of their projects to provide a testimonial for an article being written about a proposed project in Jersey City, across the Hudson River from Manhattan, that I was considering investing in. I was happy to help, for no charge, as I now viewed the elder Trump as a pathway to the corridors of power in the city and beyond.

I needed no instruction from the Trumps about what to say. This was the skill I would develop over the years, as I became Trump's spokesman, thug, pit bull, and lawless lawyer. Trump viewed any representation of his name, brand, properties, or the products he endorsed to be a matter of the highest importance. He wanted all of his interactions with the press to be manipulated for maximum benefit, no matter the underlying truth, and in a post-modern society where the representation of the thing was more important than the thing itself, at least in Trump's intuitive way of seeing power and spin, that meant a relentless willingness to lie, exaggerate, mislead, and above all brag and boast and boost.

"Trump properties are solid investments," I told the *New York Post* for an article about Trump titled "Upping the Ante" that appeared in February 2007.

"Michael Cohen has great insights in the real-estate market," Trump said about me in the article. "He has invested in my buildings because he likes to make money—and he does."

Trump concluded, "In short, he's a very smart person."

This was the mutual-admiration society we were forming, or perhaps we were just metaphorically jerking each other off, to be a little coarse, but Trump knew I'd love it when he'd sent me a signed copy of the article telling me what a great job I'd done. And so I did.

Now impatient for more Trump action, it was only a matter of another few weeks before he called me again. Instead of the show-of-strength feats I had performed for him the first two times, now he wanted to draw on my legal expertise, I discovered. Trump's current lawyers had told him that the ongoing dispute with the board of directors of Trump International Resorts—what he referred to as the "casino board"—wasn't going well. The company was in Chapter 11 and faced liquidation and ruination. According to Trump's attorneys, he had no way to stop the board from continuing to limit and proscribe his ability to influence the company as liquidation closed in, yet again. The agreements that Trump had entered into were too restrictive, they said, terms drafted by white-shoe firms who had papered Trump's deal with the publicly traded company.

In many ways, Trump Entertainment Resorts—or TER—was

emblematic of Trump's career as a showman and entrepreneur. Trump styled himself as an iconoclastic businessman in Manhattan initially, but his time in Atlantic City was when he became a real fixture in the tabloids. The first crisis for the company came in the early 1990s with the collapse of the Trump Taj Mahal in Atlantic City, a potential catastrophe Trump had escaped in the short term by having his father Fred Trump buy millions of dollars' worth of chips from the casino as a way to avoid reporting a loan to the casino regulatory board. Running to Daddy and using his bank account for a bail-out didn't square with Trump's image as a swashbuckling self-made billionaire, so this desperate move was little known and never discussed by Trump.

Through Trump's years of repeated boom and bust, casinos had remained at the heart of his brand and business strategy, nearly always with the result that creditors lost money loaned to these concerns—part of the reason virtually all of the banks in the United States refused to do business with him. In 2007, the board was now trying to negotiate a buyout with different suitors, hoping to attract private firms or publicly traded companies to acquire the failed enterprise.

"Michael, what do you know about bankruptcy and Chapter 11 procedures?" Trump asked when I entered his office.

"Very little," I said. "Thankfully."

"The board is busting my balls," he said, ignoring what I'd said. "My lawyers say that there is nothing I can do about it. I want you to read these documents and give me your opinion. I want you to find something I can use to bargain with."

Trump handed me two giant documents, both more than five hundred pages, each tome an ocean of legal technicality and detail.

"Whoa," I said, "this is like *War and Peace* times two."

"Don't worry," he said. "I want you to bill me for your time on this one. Just don't take advantage of your hours."

"I value your trust in me," I said. "I would never take advantage of you."

"By the way, what is your hourly?"

"The firm bills me out at $750 an hour."

"Shit," Trump said. "You're expensive. But you gotta understand that I never pay lawyers their rack rate."

"I'm not worried. I know where you live and work."

Trump ignored my attempted joke.

I went home and started to review the documents. My education in bankruptcy law was a dim memory from distant days in law school, and I was nobody's idea of a legal scholar. But I could read the documents and cross-reference the various provisions and it was quickly evident that the odds were stacked against Trump. He'd self-evidently been negotiating from a position of weakness, which was typical for folks who are deep in debt and up against financial institutions used to getting their way. Trump was the chairman of the board, I saw, but it was really only as a figurehead. His rights as a member of the board were also basically non-existent, in substance, and all of the real decision-making power was in the hands of others. The situation seemed dire—as might be expected for a company that had clearly been run into the ground by years of what seemed to be bad leadership and poor decision-making.

It was clear that Trump wanted me to find some kind of loophole or legal technicality that he could leverage to his advantage. I was beginning to understand what Trump wanted from me. He didn't want me to be like his other lawyers, measuring the merits of a situation and providing advice based on sound legal reasoning. He had lawyers who could provide that kind of guidance. He didn't need me to be a lawyer when he was in the right. He needed a lawyer for when he was in the wrong: when he was trying to go around the law, or offer a twisted or tortured interpretation to an agreement that could be used to screw the other side.

Roy Cohn was Trump's Platonic ideal as an advocate. In the 1970s, Cohn had represented Trump when he and his father Fred were investigated by the Department of Justice for discriminating against blacks in his rental properties in New York City. The truth was simple, as I would come to learn: the Trumps were actually racist, scheming to keep African Americans out of their rental properties. But that didn't matter to Trump. He wanted a lawyer who would fight when the cause was clearly racist and illegal.

Roy Cohn had played the role of pit bull for Trump until the Boss dropped him like a hot potato in his hour of greatest need when he was dying of AIDS—a fate I should have considered as I insinuated myself into Trump's world. That night, all I kept thinking was that I didn't want to disappoint Mr. Trump. That's how I put it in my mind. Like so many now, in Congress and in the press, I was willing to say and do anything to please Trump. I was exactly like Rudolph Giuliani would become: the crazed advocate mocking others and proving my unquestioning loyalty, even as it led to ruin.

That night I obsessed over the documents. I read and reread the pages, looking for an angle, an argument, a way to give Trump an edge. *Think, you dope*, I said to myself. *Think, you dope.* I was pacing around the apartment, talking aloud to myself, getting mad at myself, finally outright yelling at myself like a demented football coach giving himself a furious halftime beat down: "Goddamn it, you can't fail," I hollered at myself. "Find something, goddamn it, *find something.*"

"Stop it, Michael," my wife Laura said to me as she watched me ranting and raving like a lunatic. "If there is something in there you'll find it. Calm down. This is his problem, not yours."

Laura insisted we go to dinner with friends that evening, as we had planned, but I was hopelessly distracted at the restaurant. She took my hand and stroked me gently, reassuringly, and my worries faded away, at least for a while.

But when we got home around midnight, I sat down with the documents and began to scour the terms again.

"How long are you going to read tonight?" Laura asked.

"I'll see you in the morning," I said. "Sleep tight."

Laura rolled her eyes. "So stupid," she said, heading to bed.

Deep in the night, sitting under my lone light in the living room overlooking Park Avenue, I stumbled upon the hook. I carefully reviewed the sections related to the "Trump Mark," as it was defined in the agreements, double- and triple-checking what looked like a potential hole in the brick wall the elite lawyers had constructed around Trump. My reading was perhaps unorthodox, and it certainly strained the underlying business intentions, in all likelihood, but it seemed like there was a defensible legal argument. Or at least enough of a suggestion of one to raise an issue for Trump to bring before the board.

The concept revolved around the licensing agreements that Trump had with the company, as they related to the Trump Mark, and his ability to remove his name from a property if he was dissatisfied with how it was being managed. Trump could claim that TER was in default and that they had failed to cure the breach, I argued. Although there wasn't, in fact and in law, really a reason to claim a breach, times were very rough in Atlantic City, yet again, and available funds were being spent on general maintenance and payroll, leaving certain elements of the Taj to fall into disrepair. Throughout all of his permutations since the early '90s, including bankruptcies and financial disaster, Trump had somehow managed to retain control of the food court and parking lot of the casino. If he alleged that both weren't properly maintained—that they were pigsties—Trump could use that as a basis to refuse the company access to those areas. A casino with no parking or food services would be in serious trouble, I knew, allowing Trump to have the upper hand as he demanded "necessary repairs"—which he would then slow walk or block from being done.

The logic of the two-page memorandum I wrote to Trump was immediately apparent to him. Trump effectively had no special rights as a board member or chairman, but this approach gave him a virtual veto over the company's activities.

"No food, and worse, no place to park the thousands of cars for staff and visitors," I said to Trump.

"Yes," said Trump. "Nice."

Trump held up the memorandum. "How much time did you put into this?" he asked.

"It took me around one hundred hours," I said. "The invoice is going to be around $100,000."

"Geez," said Trump. "I thought we were friends."

Trump eyed me, weighing what to say next.

"Look, you clearly love this shit," he said. "It's exciting here and you get to do great things. You must hate it over there, at that sleepy old firm. It's not you."

"What are you saying, Mr. Trump?" I asked.

"Would you be interested in working for me, directly, answering only to me?

I didn't know what to say—because I was dumbfounded.

"Can I have a day or two to think this over?" I asked.

"No," Trump said. "I'll send my guys over to pack up your office and bring your stuff here in the Trump Tower, to my floor. I'll set you up in Ivanka's old office."

Trump offered a lowball salary. I countered and we met in the middle, less money than I was making at my firm. But I was already wealthy, with my taxi medallions and real-estate holdings worth millions, so it wasn't the pay that most interested me. The attraction was the action: the game, the deals, the thrill of the chase.

"Don't tell anyone how much I'm paying you," Trump said. "I don't pay anyone that much."

"Okay," I said. "But what about my invoice?"

"Invoice?" he said. "You want to get fired on your first day?"

* * *

I DIDN'T THINK about the fact that I had been recording my hours at my law firm, and that Trump owed the firm the fees, not me personally, another indication of how untethered from a normal way of behaving I was beginning to act. My little brother still worked at the firm and he was soon getting harassed by the billing department for the Trump payables, the first step in our falling out of touch as I entered the hall of mirrors of Trump's world.

Sitting in my new office on the 26th floor a few days later, my new desk neatly tricked up with two phones and two staplers and two legal pads at the ready, I read about an ongoing dispute in the Trump Park Avenue development, the building where I lived. During the renovations, from its former glory as the glamorous Delmonico Hotel—the place where the Beatles met Bob Dylan, to give just one example of its storied history—the construction crew hadn't removed a ledge-like feature from one of the higher floors on the back of the building. The ledge looked like a balcony, but it didn't have railings, and thus constituted a significant danger to residents, making it impossible for Trump to obtain the necessary certificate of occupancy without its removal.

For months, Trump executive Matthew Calamari had tried to resolve the issue with the owner of the unit with the ledge, to provide access for a crew to remove the hazard, but the man had refused to cooperate; he was unwilling to put up with the dust and noise and adopted a belligerent stance. I noted the man's name, recognizing him as a fellow resident I saw in the lobby from time to time. I was filing the matter away, hoping a solution would bubble to the surface, when I went to dinner that evening with some friends who also lived in TPA. Over veal *parmigiana* at an uptown eatery called Elio's, I heard a scandalous story from our friends: the couple had been in their bedroom the night before, making love, when they were startled by the sight of a drunken teenage boy leering at them from the ledge of the apartment next door. My friends were furious, saying that the kid was about to go to college and they weren't sure what to say or do about the Peeping Tom intrusion.

This was incredible good fortune, I knew instantly: the name of the kid involved was the same as the man who had been giving the Trump Organization a hard time. The tables were about to be reversed, with prejudice, I realized with scarcely concealed delight.

The next morning I called the man, introducing myself with my new title of Executive Vice President and Special Counsel to Donald Trump, and laid out the case for allowing access to remove the ledge, as a safety hazard and a courtesy. I was patient and lawyerly.

"I'm not doing shit," the man replied.

"Is that right?" I replied.

"That's correct."

"Well, you might want to think about that," I said, my temper rising. "Because I know for a fact that your son was on that ledge a few nights ago and he did a freaking Peeping Tom act on your neighbors. The kid was drunk, with a bunch of buddies having a party at your place. So they were screwing around and intruding on the privacy of your neighbors in a way that just might be a criminal offense under New York law."

"I don't know what you're talking about," he said, now sounding uncertain and scared.

"You know that college your son has applied to?" I said. "The one you've been working so hard to get him in to? Well, how are they going to like it when I tell them that your son is a drunken pervert, spying on your neighbors? How about the police—what are they going to think? Your wife? Because that's what's going to happen."

"You can't—"

"I just did," I said, cutting him off and now talking with menace in my voice. "This is as serious as a heart attack. What you're going to do is execute the document I'm going to email you, in the next twenty minutes, or I'm going to bring hell down on your shoulders. Your choice."

Twenty minutes later, I was in Trump's office brandishing the executed permission to enter the apartment and make the necessary renovations. The issue had eaten at Trump for months, the kind of infuriating dispute that got under his skin and drove him crazy; he wanted his way at all times, and he wanted it immediately.

"No, shit, Michael, how did you get this?"

"I can't tell you," I said.

"C'mon. Why not?"

"Plausible deniability," I said. "Boss, there are some things you don't want to know about, and this is one of those."

"Wow," Trump said, contemplating the release with wonder and delight. "This is a real Roy Cohn move."

I knew there was no higher praise from the man I was starting to call Boss.

* * *

ON THE LAST day of my first week, I was summoned by a call from Trump's assistant, Rhona Graff. She told me that Trump wanted to see me.

"You called me, Boss," I said, standing at the threshold to Trump's office.

"Yeah," Trump said. "Grab your jacket. We're going to the GM building for a meeting of the Trump casino board. We're leaving in five minutes. It's only a couple of blocks, so we'll walk over."

"Yes, sir, I'll bring my file."

This was the moment Trump was going to deploy my legal strategy on the board of TER. I was dutifully waiting at the elevator when Trump arrived in his customary oversized jacket and extra-long red tie. Descending to the ground floor and the pink marble atrium, Trump walked into the crowd of people shopping in the lobby, mostly tourists come to gape at the American excess the building personified.

Stepping out of the elevator, an electric current traveled through the atrium as people turned, in disbelief, and caught sight of Trump's distinctive orange combover and hulking presence. *The Apprentice* was the most popular reality show on television at the time, making Trump a genuine celebrity, but this was more than the adulation given to an actor or a rock star, it seemed to me. Trump embodied an entire portfolio of ambitions and desires and resentments, for countless people, including me.

To an outsider, my attraction to Trump—or as I described it, my "obsession"—seemed to have its roots in money and power and my lust to possess these attributes, if even only by proxy. What other explanation was there for my starstruck, moth-to-the-flame compulsion to insinuate myself with a man so transparently problematic in myriad ways? But I knew the real answer, for me and others in Trump's world, and eventually for a significant percentage of the citizens of the United States. The answer, I was coming to see, included something deeper than the obvious lures of money and power, though those were crucial factors. It was physical, emotional, not quite spiritual, but a deep longing and need that Trump filled for me. Around Trump I felt excited, alive, like he possessed the urgent and only truth, the chance for my salvation and success in life.

It was only the beginning of my tenure with Trump, but this day was etched on my soul—even as I gave that soul over to the man I worshipped, a word that wasn't too extreme to describe the devotion I was starting to feel. Trump could have quietly exited the building through a rear entrance, or in a car from the parking lot below, but he thrived on the attention the tourists and passers-by heaped on him. What was a cheap jolt of adrenaline for Trump, and a way of showing off to his new acolyte attorney, for me represented something mystical.

"That's Donald Trump," the rumblings began amongst the midday crowd in the atrium. Growing more loud, like a wave rippling over the large space and turning to an excited din, the exclamations turned to "That's Donald Trump!" and catcalls saying, "Tell my son he's fired!" Trump stopped for selfies and signed whatever was put in front of him, from clothing to baseballs to bare skin.

The voyage from the elevator to the revolving door onto Fifth Avenue was perhaps one hundred feet, but Trump and I had barely moved a few feet when the crowd started closing in.

I remember this like it happened yesterday. Trump glanced in my direction, gave me his devilish grin and winked at me. He motioned for me to come closer as the masses started to jostle and push to get closer. When I was right next to him he whispered, "This is what Trump is all about."

The energy, the action, the chaos, it was intoxicating and I never wanted it to stop. I was a junky in need of a fix. Even though the attention wasn't for me, I didn't care. I was in the Very

Important Person section of this small, exclusive club, and I loved being there.

Finally arriving at the GM Building, catty corner from Central Park South, Trump again did selfies with the security guards, and then we went up to the meeting of Trump Entertainment Resorts.

In the boardroom, I outlined Trump's position on the buyout proposals under consideration and how he controlled the parking lot and food court and both were in a state of disrepair, putting TER in default. As Trump's designated hard-ass, I described the consequences for the board if they failed to heed Trump's directions on the matter—insolvency, chaos, disgrace; I laid it on thick and heavy.

As I spoke, Trump suddenly interrupted. I surmised that he felt that his attorney had brought the issues to a head and now it was time for the billionaire to bring down the hammer. I watched in silent admiration as Trump laid down the law to the board in a dramatic and overbearing fashion, the board likewise stunned into silence. The food court and parking lot were shit holes, he said, and the disgraceful disrepair entitled him to demand the breaches of contract be remedied. In the meantime, that gave him veto power over the company—and that meant that the board had to do what he wanted, whatever that happened to be.

Then Trump suddenly stopped talking. The meeting was far from over; it was really only just beginning, with many difficult, unresolved issues to be addressed. But Trump didn't care. He sensed he had an advantage, however transitory or weak in substance, and so this was the moment he ended the meeting, as if he were yelling cut on the set of his own personal reality television show.

"Michael—we're done, let's go," Trump said. "This meeting is over."

My head was spinning. Still high from the adoration in the atrium at Trump Tower, now I was storming out of a high-powered board meeting with hundreds of millions of dollars on the line and Trump had suddenly, unilaterally, melodramatically, called an end to the proceedings, apparently for no other reason than that he could.

Trump's supposed victory was pyrrhic, and short lived. As events emerged in the coming months and years, Trump Entertainment Resorts would fail to find a buyer. Despite Trump's histrionics, it ended up in bankruptcy again in 2009, owing in excess of $1 billion. In 2014, the company would file for bankruptcy yet again, turning union members into another class of stiffed debtors. Its assets dwindled to the pathetic specter of a hulk of an abandoned wreck once known as the Trump Plaza in Atlantic City waiting for its demolition. With blown-out windows, gilded ceilings collapsed, and giant holes in shoddy floors, the eyesore and firetrap illustrated the delusional and failed business endeavors of Trump. A blight on the boardwalk, once the epitome of Trump's wildly ambitious approach to business outlined in *The Art of the Deal* in the 1980s, the bluster and bullying that Trump displayed at the board meeting might have given me pause. But it didn't. To the contrary: I was even more ardently astounded by Trump's performance.

Walking through the lobby at the GM Building the day of the Trump Entertainment Resorts board meeting was like the experience at Trump Tower, only even more intense, with as many as a thousand people jostling for a peek, a photo, an autograph, some connection to a man so many held in awe. I felt like I belonged to something—someone—special and important. It didn't occur to me that the entire spectacle had been staged for my benefit. Not because I would actually benefit in any way, of course, but that it was part of a performance meant to draw me into Trump's centrifugal force, precisely in the way a con man draws a mark into his world. Like a confidence artist, Trump was showing me that he inhabited a different type of reality, one that he would share with me alone, a world that was filled with wonder and excitement and power and intrigue and adulation. All I had to do was do what I was told, without question or a second thought. I didn't just accept this invitation; I leapt at it. I wasn't Trump's mark as much as I was his acolyte, a willing participant in a fantasy that heightened my senses and my sense of self.

"Stay close, my man," Trump whispered to me in the lobby. "These are Trump people. Isn't this something?"

Chapter Three

The El Caribe

At the same time as I dreamt of nothing but business and money and power as a child, to the extent a small boy can comprehend such ambitions, I never dreamed that I'd be working for a billionaire real estate tycoon in the heart of Manhattan. I grew up in a very nice center hall colonial in Lawrence, one of the well-to-do suburbs known as the Five Towns on Long Island, just outside New York City. There were four bedrooms, with an extra room in the back for our live-in help, and we were a prosperous and happy family. The atmosphere in my home was very Jewish, not so much religiously as culturally. My father Maurice was a Holocaust survivor from Poland. As a kid, aged six, he'd had to hide in the woods with his family during the German occupation of the Second World War, which had a formative impact on him. My Dad wasn't hugely religiously into Judaism when I was a kid, but he was very proud of his heritage as a Jew, and that formed a big part of my identity growing up and hanging around with other Jewish kids, many of them the children of refugees from the former Soviet Union.

During the war, my father's family had the relative good fortune to wind up in a Russian internment camp instead of one of the German death camps in Poland, such as Auschwitz. His family was prosperous in Poland, though his father was only a butcher, and when they were released after the war, they traded their jewels to finance a voyage to Ellis Island and the American dream. But they were turned away in New York because they were all ill with malaria, so the family was sent to Toronto, Canada, where my dad was raised and educated. After graduating from medical school in Toronto and specializing in ear, nose, and throat medicine, along with reconstructive head and neck surgery, he came to New York in the 1960s when he was in his late twenties to teach at the Downstate Medical Center, where he met my mother, Sandy, a surgical nurse.

Living in the suburbs, I went to yeshiva for elementary school, and I was a good kid—sweet and sensitive, if you can believe it. But by middle school, another aspect of my character was emerging. I became the class clown, always joking around with my buddies and getting on the teacher's nerves. I could have been a good student, but to the frustration of my parents and a long succession of teachers, I didn't care much about grades or studying. From as early as I can remember, I was interested in business and making money. I was the kind of kid who set up a lemonade stand outside our house, with a couple of neighborhood boys, and when cars didn't stop, I went into our yard and dragged a picnic bench into the middle of the street to force them to slow down. Adults driving home thought it was adorable and hilarious that a six-year-old had such chutzpah, but we made a fortune that day and we blew it buying ice cream for all the kids we knew.

I had an older sister, Melissa, a little sister, Lori, and a younger brother, Bryan. As a kid I could have had my own room, but when Bryan was born, I volunteered to have him share it with me. He was seven years younger than me, but I'd always wanted a little brother, so Bryan became not just a sibling, but someone I wanted to mentor and protect and inspire.

For high school, I went to Woodmere Academy, a good private college-prep school filled with preppies. I hung out with the popular crowd, for the most part, but I had friends from all kinds of groups. I stood out from the crowd because I never took a drink, not even one sip of beer, so I was often the designated driver when we went out at night. I was a responsible kid, well dressed, polite to adults, but always with the quick joke to my buddies. As strange as it might sound, given how badly I got lost as an adult, in school I hated bullies, or anyone who picked on someone weaker. I started to lift weights, because I was so skinny, and I have never suffered from cowardice or feared confrontation, so I had a few fistfights— always, I believed, for a good cause.

My dad had a medical practice in Brooklyn and he worked long hours, so I grew close to my Uncle Morty Levine, my mother's older brother. He was a playboy bachelor who never had kids, and he still lived at home with my grandparents, leaving him time to hang out with me as he cruised around Brooklyn in his Bentley. Morty was also a doctor and basically a member of my nuclear family because he was at our place so much, eating meals or just hanging out. But his main interest in life was running the swanky catering hall and mob hangout he owned in Mill Basin called the El Caribe. Morty was a real ladies' man, with flashy cars and always a different woman on his arm, but he just loved consorting with the wise guys who were members of the El Caribe. To Morty, the mobsters were funny, irreverent, a little scary— maybe even a lot scary—but they had a mystique about them, and there was no question about their willingness to break the rules, or the law. This approach to life was contagious, and I caught the bug just like my uncle had.

Ever since I was a kid, I have had a strong sense of loyalty, along with its evil twin of fury at betrayal. When I was in high school, one of my teachers told my parents that I was one of the most loyal friends he had ever seen—but that I was also the worst enemy to those who didn't repay my loyalty. The teacher meant it as an insult, I knew, but I took it as a compliment.

The roots of this part of my character harkened back to my days at the El Caribe watching wise guys from the Gambino and Lucchese crime families and how they behaved. They always had a specific kind of energy around them, a charisma that I found compelling. They were constantly joking around and playing tricks and pulling pranks on each other, which I liked, and which came to be how we acted at the Trump Organization—like gangsters, but in suits and ties. At the same time, the men in the El Caribe demanded and commanded respect. They were gangsters, and the sense of fear that people felt around them—that I felt around them—was very powerful.

In the 1980s, Brooklyn was a very different place than it is now. The borough was riddled with mobsters—Italian, Russian, dirty cops on the take; it was like the whole borough was dedicated to organized crime. The El Caribe was at the white-hot heart of the scene in that era. The country club was the kind of place where a mob boss like Anthony "Gaspipe" Casso threw his daughter's wedding, a nice affair with a bottle of Moët on every table and representatives from all five families and their wives dressed to the nines. There was the Emerald Room and the Tiara Room and the Venetian Hour Room, with candlelit white linen dining with real silverware. It was classy, in a specific over-the-top Brooklyn ethnic way: Corinthian columns, giant chandeliers, garish luxury.

For me, the real action at the El Caribe was in the summer at the swim club and gym, where wise guys swam laps, worked on their biceps, and plotted murders, and I was right in the middle of it. If you believe some in the press, this somehow made me half a mobster. This was where a lot of the false speculation about my connections to organized crime came from. The allegations that I was a mobbed-up teenager are ridiculous, the fevered fantasies of journalists all swept up in conspiracy theories as crazy as the lunatic right that Trump attracts. I was a high school student: I didn't whack guys; I went to algebra class.

But there was a kernel of truth to the notion that the El Caribe did play a role in shaping my persona and teaching me the principles that I have lived by, for good or ill. The role model of the Brooklyn mobster tough guy from the '80s was definitely part of how I acted in the Trump Organization and during the 2016 election campaign. The Boss himself grew up in Queens, and he also drank from the same mob-infused waters of New York City mafia machismo. Trump's father Fred also had long experience with the wise guys of Brooklyn, who controlled the cement industry, and he had taught his son how to stay on the good side of the mafia and ensure construction projects came in on time by greasing the right palms.

The things I learned at the El Caribe were loyalty, friendship, and *omerta*—or the mafia code to keep your mouth shut. I was just a kid, but I was in close proximity to some of the biggest and toughest and most dangerous gangsters in New York, and therefore the world.

To me, even though I didn't understand what was really happening—that all the talk about loyalty and honor and the family was bullshit and that all that mattered was money and power, much like in the Trump Organization—I was attracted to the scene. Very attracted. To my young eyes, it seemed like they were answering to a higher power—not religious, of course, but a strong, ruthless tribal loyalty that gave them the courage and ambition to do precisely what they wanted, no matter the consequences.

When I was fifteen, Uncle Morty suggested I stay with him and my grandmother (as I've noted, Morty still lived at home) in Brooklyn for the summer and work for him at the El Caribe. He gave me real responsibilities, like signing up new members and collecting money from the restaurant and bar. During the slow times in the summer, I would be invited to sit with Gaspipe or gangsters like Roy DeMeo, Anthony Senter, Joey Testa, and Frank Lastorino, a kind of Murderer's Row of gangsters, like the 1950s Yankees batting lineup, only these guys really were murderers. This was when I first heard the name Roy Cohn, the infamous New York attorney who worked for Senator Joseph McCarthy during the Red Scare and later was a lawyer for many mobsters—including Donald Trump. But I was just a kid, and I didn't see any of the connections, or perils.

During the summer of 1980, at age fourteen, I got an up-close look at how the mob really operated. One glorious sunny day, the El Caribe swim club was packed, the Olympic-sized pool overflowing with members and their families, the twenty cabanas filled with Brooklyn wise guys smoking cigars and enjoying giant platters from the restaurant. The food and booze were plentiful and some folks were getting more than a little tipsy, with this one guy floating around in the pool on his back, obviously drunk, when he decided it would be hilarious to take off his swimsuit. The exhibitionist was floating around butt naked, thinking he was funny, until a short, stocky, muscular Italian-looking man wearing a white wife beater-type shirt with a huge, primitive tattoo reaching from his shoulder to his elbow took offense.

"Hey, asshole," the wise guy said. "Put your fucking pants on. My wife and kids are in the pool."

The drunken idiot just laughed and rolled over to display his lily-white bare ass. The wise guy was standing right next to me and I knew immediately that the drunk had made a major mistake. I admit I was scared because I could tell something was going to happen. Sure enough, in the blink of an eye, the wise guy pulled a handgun from his pocket and shot the drunk in the ass. Holy shit! There was pandemonium as everyone panicked and I went to the loudspeaker to tell members to get out of the pool. There was a streak of blood in the water as the drunk floated in the pool moaning and the police and an ambulance were called.

As I stood there watching the crowd disperse, another wise guy type came over to me and tapped me on the shoulder and gave me a hard look. I had been an eyewitness to the whole scene. I had seen the shooter and could identify him, of course, and that was what this tough-looking man had come to talk to me about.

"Listen kid, you're one of us," he said in a thick Brooklyn accent. "You saw nothing. You know nothing."

I nodded.

"Good boy," he said. "Remember what I said."

The man patted me on the shoulder and left with the shooter, the pair disappearing into the crowd. The NYPD turned up that afternoon and asked questions of the members who were still at the El Caribe, but they got no leads. When the detectives asked me what happened, I said I hadn't seen a thing. I didn't say a word. It was partly out of fear; no way was I going to go against Brooklyn gangsters who were obviously prepared to use violence at the slightest provocation. But mostly it was a sense of admiration I had for the men and how they lived. The drunk had stepped way out of line, pulling off his swim trunks with hundreds of women and children in the pool, and the wise guy had taken the law into his own hands, rough justice that made sense to me intuitively. I also liked how his friend watched out for him. The more I thought about what happened, the more I admired their friendship and loyalty and way of seeing the world.

A couple of days later, as I was working at the pool, a tough-looking man I had never seen before turned up at the El Caribe and caught my eye and motioned for me to talk to him. I walked over to a private area in a hallway off the pool. I knew exactly what he wanted to talk about.

"I said nothing," I said.

"I know," he said, patting me on the shoulder. "You're a good kid."

He handed me two envelopes, one thick with cash, the other less so. "One is to cover the cost of the cleanup," he said. "And this one is for you."

"For what?" I asked.

"For being loyal," he said.

With that, the tough guy left, and I never saw him again. As I counted my money—$500 in twenties, major cash to a kid—I was hooked on everything that gesture contained, in my well-off white suburban teenage boy way. I was like the young Henry Hill character in *Goodfellas,* fetching drinks and lighting cigarettes for the Lucchese crime family—which was actually the exact crew that hung out at the El Caribe and was fictionalized in Scorsese's movie. I loved the swagger and strut, the way the rules didn't apply to them, the tough talk and cursing, but most of all, how feared they were.

All through high school, I flipped pizzas during the summer at the El Caribe, or I worked by the pool, or I helped track the finances. Eventually I asked Morty if he wanted to open an ice cream stand and sell cones to the customers, splitting the profits fifty-fifty. I made a mint from that business, working long hours all summer to save for the upscale cars I started to buy and eventually import from Europe. Porsches were a particular favorite, but I would drive anything, the nicer the ride, the better.

My uncle ran a car service for members of the El Caribe, to do errands or pick up and drop off family members, partnering with a Russian gangster who hung around the club. Sometimes I would drive the Mercedes for wise guys who used the service, to pick up money as a side hustle. One day, a wise guy named Anthony Senter called me over and said he wanted me to take a ride with him. I was delighted to do so, and I followed his instructions as he guided me through Mill Basin into a commercial district where Italian-American stores and boutiques lined the streets. Anthony was part of the Gemini Lounge outfit, a crew attached to the Lucchese crime family and Gaspipe Casso that was responsible for as many as 200 murders over the years, including whacking a Russian gangster named Vladimir Reznikov, the significance of which I would learn later. In mob circles in Brooklyn, Senter was a kind of prince, one of the most lethal of the wise guys.

That day, Anthony was pure glamour to me as I followed him into a fine clothing store. It was a high-end menswear place, with thousand-dollar ankle-length leather jackets and merino sweaters starting at prices over $500 apiece. I'd never seen clothes that expensive, so I was amazed when Anthony started building up a big pile of jackets and suits and sweaters. He was a decade older than me, but a really sharp dresser who prided himself on his appearance: slicked-back hair, tight silk suit, Italian designer shoes shined to a gleam. I couldn't believe that he would spend so much money in one place on clothes, until I discovered that he wouldn't. The anxious, probably terrified owner was watching Senter carefully, fetching him different sizes and colors and making sure he was pleased, until the mobster decided he'd had enough and he ordered me to take tens of thousands of dollars in merchandise outside and put them into the trunk of the Mercedes—without pulling out his credit card or even hinting that he was going to pay.

I was standing flabbergasted on the sidewalk when Anthony told me to pick a sweater for myself; we were around the same size. Then he handed me a full-length black Armani leather jacket, worth at least a grand.

"It's a gift from me for you," Anthony said.

"I can't," I said, not sure what to do or say. Clearly there was some kind of racket going on: extortion, protection money, maybe a gambling debt, who knew? Should I take part in this shakedown, an impressionable Jewish teenager who was indeed very impressed?

Senter gave me a hard look. "Listen, kid, if someone gives you something you take it. Understand?"

I did: you couldn't say no to these men. To turn down a gift was an insult to his honor and generosity. Gestures mattered to tough guys, and they didn't want to be doubted or have aspersions cast on their conduct, particularly not by some kid. In this way, I was learning another language, one with its own grammar and syntax, not to mention pitfalls and perils.

I took the black Merino sweater and the black leather jacket, which made me look like a hit man when I wore it, and treasured these gifts for years. A couple of years later, I read in the *New York Post* that Anthony and his partner Joey Testa were convicted of murder, and he's currently serving life at Allenwood, Pennsylvania— the traditional mobbed-up federal facility that was also portrayed in *Goodfellas*. I guess there's more than a little irony in us both ending up in prison—but maybe that was predictable. At the time, Anthony seemed to me much more than just a Brooklyn tough guy taking what he wanted; the mob's rules were hard, hidden, probably hypocritical, but very attractive to me.

Around this time, my family started to notice that my mannerisms and personality were changing. I was strutting and talking in 'dems and 'dos like a Brooklyn mobster, only I was wearing polo shirts with upturned collars and sailing shoes like any other middle-class white suburban kid from a well-off family in the '80s. My parents didn't find my new affect cute or funny. To the contrary, they weren't going to tolerate a wannabe gangster strolling around the house ignoring the rules and pretending to be involved in an elaborate criminal enterprise. I was playacting, of course, but they took this seriously. My dad was a doctor and my mother cared about how the community viewed our family; the Cohens were respectable, not mob-affiliated.

One night my father called me into his bedroom.

"What are you doing?" he asked.

"I have no idea what you're talking about," I said—only I said it with an imitation wise-guy attitude, to his dismay.

"Cut it out," he said. "The whole mafia, gangster thing. You're not one of them. You'll be a surgeon like me, or a lawyer like your Uncle Ralph. Okay?"

"Sure, Pop," I said, as I kissed him on the forehead.

But, in truth, his admonition went in one ear and out the other. In my heart, I was determined to continue to be the new self that I was constructing. I would behave well around my family, and I would be a good kid who worked hard and got decent grades and went to a decent college. I wasn't sweating bullets to get into the best possible school, though, not like the worker bees in my high school; I was interested in succeeding in life, not amassing prestigious degrees and joining exclusive fraternities. I was like Groucho Marx—I didn't want to belong to any club that would have me as a member. I knew I would go to law school, just as my parents wished, a typical well-mannered Jewish boy pleasing his family. Inside, though, I belonged to another tradition: the Tough Jew. I

wanted to be like Bugsy Siegel and Meyer Lansky and Roy Cohn—
or Downtown Burt Kaplan hanging out by the pool at the El
Caribe. I liked how wise guys moved, talked, thought. I liked how
they resolved issues and commanded a room. I would practice law,
I determined as a kid, but I'd practice it like a gangster.

Chapter Four

Laura

My apprenticeship as a yuppie wannabe has sparked a sea of conspiracy theories, perhaps none more crazy or ill-founded than the imagined guilt by association because of my proximity to certain Russian criminals in the 1980s. Allow me to set the record straight.

One of the regulars at the El Caribe was a Russian gangster and businessman named Marat Balagula. He often conducted business at the El Caribe, in the health club my uncle set up on the lower level, so I saw him all the time. He was a tough-looking guy, well built, with shark-like eyes, and someone definitely not to be trifled with; he was the boss of the Russian crime syndicate in Brooklyn, a very serious force at the time. Like so many others at the El Caribe, Balagula was connected with Lucchese boss Gaspipe Casso and together they ran an illegal "tax" scam skimming two cents for every gallon of gasoline the Russian mob sold from scores of Brooklyn gas stations—one of the most lucrative swindles the mafia ever concocted, netting millions upon millions.

In those years, there were lots of kids of Jewish refugees from the former Soviet Union growing up in Brooklyn and Long Island, and they formed a part of my social group. During this time I once or twice ran across a Russian émigré kid named Felix Sater, whom I'll discuss in detail in due course, but I barely knew him as a kid, no matter the fevered speculation about our Russian real estate connections in later years. It also happened that I was friendly with Marat Balagula's daughter Malavena, a pretty Jewish girl who also lived in the Five Towns. Her family's house was in Hewlett Harbor, an expensive area by the water, and the Balagula family definitely lived in style. One evening, I was at Malavena's place with a bunch of other well-off Jewish kids for a party. By this time I was a student at American University, in Washington, DC, and I was back home for the summer break before my sophomore year, running my ice cream concession at the El Caribe and hanging out with friends. I was also unattached.

That night our gang went out to a nightclub called Sprat's on the Water, and I started talking to a young girl named Laura Shusterman. She was gorgeous, seventeen years old, a rising senior at Kew-Forest School in Queens, a prestigious prep school that had once educated a boy then called Donny Trump, until his father lost patience with his bad behavior and worse attitude and enrolled him in a military school upstate. There was nothing romantic between Laura and me at the time, but I liked her a lot. After that night, Laura's best friend called and asked what I thought of her. I told her that Laura was the kind of girl you marry, not someone you just fool around with.

As I went back to college in Washington, DC and eventually graduated from American University, I worked at the El Caribe during the summers but I always had other ways to make a buck.

Scalping tickets was one way I learned to earn serious cash. The business was simplicity itself: buy seats at face value and sell high, the higher the better. It happened that I knew the guy at Ticketmaster who had first access to the best seats for the best acts coming through New York: Michael Jackson, Elton John, the Rolling Stones. I would buy a couple dozen super-premium seats, front and center, and then wait for the show to sell out (usually very quickly). Then I set about marketing them to the high rollers and wise guys at the El Caribe, as well as anyone who wanted the most coveted seats for the most coveted shows. In short, I was an opportunist, an impulse that I took to its furthest limits in pushing for the ultimate opportunist to take over the White House.

As I've said, another business I went into was importing high-end European cars. At the time, there was a real arbitrage between European and American prices for sports cars like Porsches and Ferraris. I partnered with a buddy in college and we'd front the money to buy a couple of cars from Italy or Germany, arrange for them to be shipped to the Port of New Jersey, then sell the vehicles to wealthy folks. While other college kids were hitting frat party keggers and writing home for their allowance, I was making bank on my own.

In truth, I was an indifferent student at American University. Ever the dutiful son, I made sure that I passed and didn't burden my parents with excess tuition or the fear that I would drop out. But I wasn't motivated by literature or music or the other pursuits of a liberal arts student; I was biding my time, ticking the boxes I knew were necessary to get to the life I was imagining for myself back in New York City as an attorney and entrepreneur.

For law school, I chose the Thomas Cooley Law School—or I really should say it chose me, as it was the easiest school to get into in the entire nation, so I qualified. I figured that it didn't matter if you went to Harvard or Yale or Stanford for law school; all that mattered was that you were able to pass the bar exam. Once you passed, all admitted attorneys were given the same title: Counselor.

By the time I graduated from law school and moved back to the city, my little brother Bryan was studying at New York University and he had a new girlfriend, also an undergraduate at the college. Bryan told me that his girlfriend had a friend that I should meet; she was great, he said, very pretty and smart and she was like an older sister to his girlfriend. She was three years younger than me and she worked in fashion and lived in Queens; she was Ukrainian by birth, like Bryan's girlfriend. He gave me her number, but I didn't do anything about it. I was dating other girls and chasing around the nightclubs of Manhattan, and I was extremely busy trying to establish my law practice as a personal injury litigation expert. My business model was to accumulate as many cases as possible and settle them as quickly as possible, but what I was really doing was learning how to negotiate and conduct business in New York City, which was the equivalent of learning how to knife fight with gangsters—only these mobsters were wearing suits and ties.

The gangster reference isn't made casually: the insight is central to understanding me, but also Donald J. Trump. At the time, the fascination with the mafia, evidenced in movies like *The Valachi Papers* and *The Godfather*, had morphed into a national obsession with organized crime. Mobsters like John Gotti were in the news every day and movies like *Goodfellas* packing theaters. The tabloids were filled with stories about wise guys getting whacked— lots of them my old heroes from the El Caribe—but something more pervasive was happening in the business circles I longed to inhabit. The cultural markers of the tough New York real estate operator were shifting, with Donald Trump at the forefront, at least as he portrayed himself in *The Art of the Deal*. Business in New York has always been hard-edged, with the opening bid in negotiations typically starting with an exchange of "fuck you" and the threat of litigation. No tactic or ruse was too low, including preying on the weak or vulnerable—in fact, that became Trump's business model, perhaps because he'd gone broke so many times himself, only to be bailed out by his Daddy, that he knew just how defenseless the insolvent really are.

When I was single again, Bryan kept telling me how great this Laura girl his girlfriend knew was, so one day I dialed her digits. Before long, we figured out that we'd met years earlier, at Sprat's on the Water, and we were both friends with Marat Balagula's daughter. The connection was quick and undeniable: she was gorgeous and sweet and I was sociable and ambitious and family-oriented with a soft spot for my nieces; I liked her friends and family and was happy to spend time with them. In short order, we fell for each other, hard.

When Laura and I started dating, I naturally met her parents. She was an only child and the apple of her parents' eye, so to speak, so they doted on her, and when it became apparent that she and I were getting serious, they also took me under their wing. Laura's family had immigrated from Ukraine in the early '70s, so they were technically Ukrainian, but in reality, in the former Soviet Union, their only meaningful identity was that they were Jewish. This form of identification, religious and cultural, really defined the life of the Shusterman family, much as it was central to the Cohens.

Laura and I were married at the Pierre Hotel on October 9, 1994, with 300 guests and a really lovely ceremony, and we soon had two beautiful bouncing babies, first Samantha and then Jake. We bought an apartment on the Upper East Side of Manhattan and enrolled the kids in Colombia Grammar, the oldest non-sectarian private school in the city. I was very involved in the school, joining the board of trustees and working on countless fundraisers. As with my investment properties, where I always wanted to join the board of the condos to keep an eye on how the business was being run, I wanted to be on the board of the school, as my most precious assets were in the school's hands.

By then, I based my burgeoning legal practice out of a modest two-story building I co-owned in an industrial section of Long Island City, in Queens, above the workshop of a taxi business run by me and my business partner, a man named Simon Garber, a Ukrainian Jew with a checkered past but a good eye for how to make money on medallions. Simon had started out as a student driving taxis in New York and then Chicago, before he went into business in Moscow—yes, the mind spins at the coincidence, but that's all it was. By the '90s, Simon was running hundreds of cabs out of a garage in the famous Meatpacking District, and he and I became partners as I started to transition much of my growing net worth into the rough-and-tumble taxi industry.

I was always on the lookout for a good deal, always looking for an edge or inside scoop. At the time, I discovered that one of my personal-injury clients had to make himself scarce in a hurry, two steps ahead of the debt collectors and the law, because he'd consolidated all of his fifty taxi medallions into a single company. One of my client's cabbies had negligently run over and killed a Wall Street trader, and the damages had been set at more than $10 million, effectively bankrupting my client's company. He drained the medallion company of all the cash he could and lit out for Israel, leaving his company as a shell in the rearview mirror. Dealing directly with the liquidators, Simon and I purchased many of the fifty medallions in foreclosure, and I was on my way to getting rich.

There was really only a single problem to my partnership with Garber: Simon was a party animal. Inevitably, he started to cadge cash and grant himself advances from company accounts against future revenues so he could indulge his desires. We started to fight and it quickly got very heated, as I could see his business, and by association my business, going broke.

The solution I came up with was to go out on my own. I moved my office to Manhattan, to shared space with my younger brother Bryan in a building occupied by one of his clients, the son of the jeweler Harry Winston. At the time, the value of taxi medallions kept rising inexorably, to nearly a million dollars each, and I started to view myself as a wealthy investor who also had a legal license on the side. My real forte was doing favors for others. This included all manner of things, from help getting a doctor's appointment with a leading specialist for friends in the middle of a health scare, to arranging for reservations at a hot restaurant, or a political tip for a reporter. When Saudi royalty wanted to purchase the Harry Winston building, I was involved in the negotiations, establishing good relations with Middle Eastern rulers in charge of a multi-billion dollar investment fund. That was how I was starting to network, to move myself closer to the higher reaches of power and influence; I didn't have a specific destination in mind, but I was plenty ambitious, and very energetic, and I reveled in the sharp-edged sport of getting ahead in New York City.

My life was in excellent order as our children moved through elementary school and Laura and I shopped for a larger apartment in Manhattan. Taxi medallions were a high-leverage asset, and I used the easy finance available from banks based on the soaring valuation of the dozens of medallions I owned to acquire yet more medallions. There was risk involved, but in the early 2000s, they seemed like a safe bet. During these years, I tried a couple of other business ventures, including a gambling cruise line in Florida that didn't work out, but what I was really doing was networking and getting to know people in New York City's real estate and business circles, looking for deals and opportunities.

It was at this time that I bought into Trump World Tower,

along with my parents and in-laws, renting out the unit I purchased at a handsome return, along with a unit in the Trump
Palace that I flipped for a tidy profit. Along the way, I started to
chat with reporters for the New York daily newspapers, especially
the tabloid *New York Post*, as I toyed with the idea of going into
politics. I would feed journalists like Maggie Haberman and
Richard Johnson tidbits about deals I heard about, and in return
we'd gossip about politics and news events of the day. Along the
way, I decided to run for office, specifically for New York City
Council in 2003, standing as a Republican against the longtime
Democratic incumbent Eva Moskowitz in my uptown district; I
really had no ideological opinions, apart from being pro-business,
but the real attraction for me was the thrill of the fight and the
chance to gain power, impulses that would grow steadily and eventually lead to my ruin. I had a knack for public speaking; I was the
kind of guy who gave speeches at birthday parties, cracking jokes.

I didn't win, but it whetted my appetite for the cut and thrust
of politics, and I discovered how much I enjoyed the back-and-
forth with journalists. The persona I was developing was that of a
tough, no-nonsense but clear-eyed New York attorney and businessman who was willing to work hard but also fight hard. I had a
foul mouth and a wise-ass sense of humor, I like to think, but I was
also beginning to try to attach myself to more powerful players in
the city in the hope of rising in the ranks.

After my unsuccessful run for office, my brother and I moved
our law practice to the white-shoe firm of Phillips Nizer, as I've
said before, and I befriended a young real estate developer named
Donald Trump, Jr. when Laura and I purchased three units in the
new development, Trump Park Avenue, to consolidate into a single
unit. That was life, as I knew it, and it was a great one, until the
nondescript day in the fall of 2006 when my phone rang and the
Trump family summoned me unto my destiny and my downfall.

Chapter Five

Catch and Twist

The concept of "catch and kill" has now entered the vernacular, along with the #McToo movement and a growing awareness of the ways that wealthy and powerful men bury the truth about their predatory sexual behavior, from the rapes of Harvey Weinstein to the depredations of Trump's old friend Jeffery Epstein, who ran a sex ring for the rich and famous at his Manhattan mansion and Caribbean island—not to mention his Palm Beach cavorting with another self-styled playboy named Donald J. Trump. The root of the word *conspiracy* is literally "to breathe together," and that was precisely what rich men and publications like the *National Enquirer* did to hide the truth about exploiting and abusing women.

Those rich men included my Boss.

The reality was far more brutal and awful than has previously been revealed, as I will demonstrate. The straightforward catch and kill is only the simplest form of the true endeavor, which is to find, stop, and spin or twist any story or rumor that could harm the interests or reputation of the rich and powerful. Sex was only part of the story, as Trump viewed anything that could hurt his brand or name as a mortal threat. Saying he wasn't as rich as he pretended to be was, in many ways, worse than calling him a sexual predator; calling out his buildings or branded products as third-rate was far more damaging, in his mind, than a story about grabbing women by the pussy. The task in a catch, kill, and twist operation was to bury the truth, and if that wasn't possible, to distort it beyond recognition, to sow doubt and confusion and even fear.

I knew this all from personal experience, which started in my earliest days working for the Trump Organization. In the beginning, it was obvious that my role as Trump's personal attorney was essentially managing chaos, as he was always, always, always enveloped by crisis and teetering on the brink of disaster. It was exhausting, but also exhilarating, as I always had ninety-nine problems on my desk and a thousand things to do.

One afternoon early in my tenure, I was doing some routine work—likely cleaning up a mess made by Don Jr.—when my phone rang. It was David Pecker, the CEO of American Media, on the line. Pecker was a peculiar figure in the media, a former accountant with no journalism experience who'd parlayed a bean counter's financial ability, along with a canny sense of timing and willingness to take up projects most would consider beneath their dignity, to become a real power in the press, running the *National Enquirer* and a string of smaller publications. Pecker had a signature thick moustache he'd worn for decades, and a taste for the best tables at the restaurants that were the hardest to get a reservation at—the kind of prestige marker typical for New York players keeping score on their status.

I would discover that Pecker's considerable power emanated from a virtually complete lack of morality or basic decency or shame, compounded by a brazen willingness to cover up rapes and assaults and despicable acts of all varieties, provided he was benefitting a powerful man and that he would receive a favor in return; in a way he was like me, a fixer, but on the next level, with tabloids doing his bidding. Pecker's sly, secretive manner made him seem sphinxlike, but in private conversation, he was very matter of fact and transactional, always acting from the most reliable of motives: his own self-interest. He was a true master of the *realpolitik* of sex and scandal and power, I would discover, as he became a mentor and co-conspirator and then co-target of a federal criminal investigation.

I'd known David for years, but this was our first conversation with me ensconced in my new role with Trump. When I started to work for Trump, another element of my curiosity was the window it might give me on how the world really worked at the highest levels—and this was my first lesson for the postgraduate degree in sleaze I was embarking on at the real real Trump University, not the fake, rip-off school the Boss used to fleece the gullible, but the genuine PhD-level education in manipulation and control I was about to get.

"Michael, I need your help," Pecker said calmly. "The husband of a woman named Jill Harth is alleging that Donald forcibly kissed her after cornering her at an event at Mar-a-Lago. It was a long time ago, in the early '90s."

"What?" I blurted. "C'mon, that's got to be bullshit."

"Michael," Pecker replied patiently, like I was the naïf Grasshopper in an episode of *Kung Fu* and he was Master Po citing verses of wisdom from Taoist philosophy. "I trust you. Mr. Trump trusts you. Over time, you will learn that it's not about the truth. I have been watching his back for years. When I spoke to Mr. Trump about this, he told me to call you—that you and I will work together and handle these problems together."

Trump and Pecker had been friends since the mid-1990s, part of the chauffeur-driven class who shared each other's confidences and operated far above the lives of the little people who have jobs and pay taxes and follow the rules. Since Trump's first flirtation with running for President in 2000, with the Reform Party, Pecker had trumpeted Trump's cause in banner headlines and fawning profiles in the *Enquirer*, often citing bogus polls, and referring to him in sycophantic terms designed to thrill the real estate mogul as a "gazillionaire."

As with Trump's first lie in our first conversation, this was another moment that I might have taken a breath and given pause. The truth doesn't matter? Then what does? I assumed I was about to find out, and it shames me to say this, and this won't be the last time you'll hear me say this, but instead of wondering about the underlying morality or indeed the plight of a woman allegedly assaulted by Trump, I instantly felt excited to be included in such a small and exclusive circle. Mr. Trump trusted me? David Pecker trusted me? My chest puffed in pride as I pondered the fact that Trump only let a tiny, tiny number of his topmost executives into his inner circle and they'd worked for him for many years, some for decades. I really and truly was an insider now, I figured, with exhilaration.

"David," I replied. "Tell me the allegations."

Pecker offered a sanitized and abbreviated version of the story, in itself part of the way to avoid taking ownership of what we were really doing. According to Pecker, Jill Harth's ex-husband had done some work for Trump at one of his casinos in Atlantic City years earlier, promoting an event called Donald J. Trump's American Dream World Finals, a bathing beauty contest where the entrants had to sing and tell jokes. The judges were a panel of celebrities, including Trump, and there was also a "hottest, one-of-a-kind" car design competition, all staged in the Crystal Ballroom in the Castle Resort on the Boardwalk on Atlantic City. Trump had stiffed the ex-husband, Pecker explained, but worse, he'd continually hit on his beautiful then-wife Jill Harth, propositioning her in nightclubs in Manhattan and at a restaurant in the Plaza, culminating in offering her a tour of Mar-a-Lago in Palm Beach by herself, and, while her then-husband cooled his heels in the dining room, showing her into his twelve-year-old daughter Ivanka's bedroom and lunging at her, trying to force himself on her, pushing her onto his daughter's bed and grabbing her genitals.

Ms. Harth had managed to escape somehow, but Pecker explained that now the ex-husband wanted to sell the story to the *National Enquirer*, getting paid for dirt on the star of *The Apprentice*.

Unspoken was the fact that the ex-husband had no clue who he was dealing with at the *National Enquirer* and the real power dynamic at work. Jill Harth's former husband imagined he was talking to journalists about a potential story about a powerful figure that would be certain to get national attention; sure, it was a tabloid, the kind of publication sold at the check-out counter in grocery stores, and of course he was hoping to make money, and the whole subject was covered in the kind of slime that would make any respectable reporter run away. But even the tenuous hold the *National Enquirer* had on journalistic standards, which Trump extolled when it served his purposes, even *that* fig leaf was a sham. David Pecker wasn't going to deal fairly or seriously with the ex-husband of some nobody woman with a long-forgotten salacious claim about his old friend. The whole concept was ridiculous. That wasn't how the world worked, I was beginning to glimpse, as I realized Pecker's allegiance was to Trump, and the truth truly didn't matter. As soon as Pecker had heard about the pitch of the Harth story, he told me, he'd intervened and done what he had done for years: called Trump in order to conspire to cover it up, or catch and kill, as it's known. Trump had told Pecker to call me, and so it was that I was being knighted into this inner sanctum. Now it fell to me to solve this problem, I was told by Pecker. He wouldn't run the story, of course, but I needed to find a way to keep it under wraps.

Walking down the hallway to Trump's office that day in 2007, I dreaded what was about to happen. I had to go into the Boss's office and question him about a woman he'd in all likelihood sexually assaulted, a subject I felt certain would piss him off. I knocked timidly on the door and Trump looked up from his newspaper and waved me in. I sat in the middle red Egg chair and gulped, figuring I'd use indirection and express my gratitude instead of putting Trump on the spot—it felt like obsequiousness was necessary, as usual.

"I just heard from David," I said. "I am honored that you feel comfortable with me handling these types of matters for you."

"You know David trusts you," Trump said. "So do I. Just don't make me regret my decision."

"Never, Boss," I said. "Are the allegations true? Do we have a contact number for her?"

"I know she called Rhona a few times," Trump said, not answering my question, again par for the course. "Man, she's really great looking. She's in love with Trump. Go get the file of her emails from Rhona and then handle it with David. No stories on this. Got it?"

"Of course, Boss. I know what to do."

"Let me know how you do," Trump said as I left.

Trump's assistant, Rhona Graff, had her own office, and I was surprised that when I told her what I was after, she nonchalantly opened a filing cabinet and flicked through scores of files, finally pulling one out and handing it to me. It was like troubles such as the one I was now charged with dealing with were a matter of routine and scores of others had made similar allegations. Back in my office, I opened the file and read the emails from Ms. Harth to Trump. There were notes seeking employment as a make-up artist for Trump on *The Apprentice*, and as his personal stylist. The emails expressed admiration for the Boss and there was no mention of sexual assault or improper behavior; they were most definitely not the kind of notes that might be written by a woman who'd been attacked, or at least that was how it seemed to me. Like the letters of recommendation for Trump University, which purported to speak to a ninety-eight percent approval for the transparently worthless degree, the backstory to Ms. Harth's emails was no doubt more complicated; not many people come into contact with the fantastically wealthy and the entrée into their world and the economic benefits that come with such proximity. As I knew all too well, there was an urge to please and stay in the good graces of a man with Trump's power, and victims of sexual assault often act in ways that don't seem consistent with the aftermath of an assault, as we've all learned in recent times.

In truth, Trump had stayed in contact with her long after he stiffed her husband and the business she had run with her ex, telling her that she was married to a loser. She thought of Trump as a stalker and sued in 1997, but the case was settled out of court, along with the claim by her husband for money due for the Atlantic City event—a way to disguise the payoff to cover up the story about sexual assault, the ex-husband believed.

The embittered ex now wanted revenge, and I had to stop him. To catch and kill the story, as instructed, I picked up the phone and dialed Jill Harth's cell. A man picked up and I explained who I was, a process that I loved and that almost always had an incredible impact. My title as Executive Vice President and Special Counsel to Donald J. Trump had a hypnotic effect, I could see, especially on everyday people. I then asked to speak to Jill Harth.

"Sure," the man said, without asking why I was calling. "Hold on one second."

"Hi, this is Jill," Ms. Harth said pleasantly.

I knew right away from her tone of voice, even knowing that this was Trump-related, that she wasn't going to be a problem, so I played nice.

"I'm sure you know about the allegations being raised to media outlets by your ex-husband," I said.

"I do," she replied.

"I hope I can count on your assistance in refuting these malicious statements," I said.

I went on, "I see that you have kept in contact with Mr. Trump over the years," my subtle—or not so subtle—way of letting her know I'd read her emails and was aware of her pleas for employment.

"What I need from you is a statement emphatically denying the allegation. With both parties denying what is being said, any reporter would have to include both statements in a story, making the allegations look like a hit job on Trump or just irrelevant."

For twenty minutes, we talked about the best way to proceed. Bizarrely, perhaps, we never talked about the truth of what Trump was supposed to have done. As a woman, I guess she understood that what Pecker said was absolutely correct: the truth didn't matter. She wanted work as a makeup artist and stylist, and a man like Trump could provide her the connections that would change her life. This was the underlying bedrock truth that was actually the central reality of the exchange. Jill Harth knew that if she went along with me, there was a chance she might make money, and conversely, if she didn't, she would be fighting against forces that rendered her not just vulnerable but defenseless. Through my office, Trump could crush her like an insect—that was the subtext, and even as we talked politely, the stranglehold of money and power was on her throat.

Yes, that was what I did, and yes, I know how wrong it was—but not at the time. I had no second thoughts or scruples, and it never occurred to me that there was no way to reconcile what I was doing with how I wanted my daughter to be treated, or my son to behave. That was what depravity looked like: depraved.

"You know if I ask him to give me a job, he will," she said, a forlorn attempt to assert some version of her own purchase on power.

"I will see what I can do," I replied, not quite dismissively, then reminding her of the real power at play. "But first I must get the statement from you, so we can put this issue to rest."

"Okay," she said meekly.

We crafted a statement, by which I mean I crafted a statement that she went along with, creating a narrative that was false, as she knew, and, sorry to say, so did I. The statement was thus ready for any reporter who pursued the story. This wasn't pure catch and kill, as Trump didn't pay her for her silence and I didn't quash the story. I did something slightly different, as I learned the martial art of hiding marital infidelity. There was no media organization on the planet that was going to run a story based on unsubstantiated allegations of an aggrieved ex-husband that both his ex-wife and Trump denied, not without at least including the denials; it made no sense to publish what has been twisted into nothing more than unprintable nonsense.

The story disappeared for nearly a decade, until Trump ran for President and she tried again to get work from the Boss, which in my line of work constituted great success.

"Do me a favor," Trump told me when I presented him with a

copy of Jill Harth's phony statement. "Make a copy of this and take it upstairs to Melania. Let her know this whole thing was bullshit and the ex-husband was trying to make a few bucks."

"Will do, Boss," I replied.

Trump sighed. "She really was great-looking back then," he said, reminiscing fondly about the attractiveness of Jill Harth, and without doubt the time he'd stuck his hands between her legs and groped her.

I called Melania, as instructed, and we performed a game of kabuki theater, each of us aware of the deception but following an unspoken rule that we wouldn't acknowledge that reality. I told her about the false accusations circulating regarding Jill Harth and the story her ex-husband was trying to sell about Trump trying to force himself on her. She listened silently as I described the mutual denials, all while I could tell she knew I was lying.

"I don't care what people say or write," she said. "Thank you for letting me know."

But she knew. She knew everything, but she didn't do what most wives would do and insist on the whole story.

* * *

BACK IN MY office, back in a place I'd begun to feel comfortable, useful, and like I belonged in a way I'd never really experienced before, I waited for my next assignment. Like everyone else at the Trump Organization, I was tasked with hunting for real estate deals for the company, but I was also a businessman running my own money, and I occasionally came across an opportunity that was too small or off-brand for Trump but that fit me perfectly. That was what happened when I identified a ninety-unit rental apartment building in uptown Manhattan that was up for sale. The price was excellent and it had a stable history of good tenants, so I took a run at acquiring it and was actually able to finance and close the deal.

When I proudly told Trump about the fifty-eight-million-dollar purchase, his mood soured and he got petulant.

"Why didn't you bring the deal to me?" he asked.

"It wasn't big enough for you, Boss," I said. "It wasn't your kind of deal."

"You didn't give me a chance," he said, sulking. "Remember, you work for me first and foremost."

I was a little disheartened, mostly because I'd wanted to share the pleasure of the art of my deal with the man who'd supposedly written the book, but I knew his anger was exactly the same as the emotion he aimed at his children. Trump only cared about subjects that concerned him, and his benefit and well-being, so anything that detracted or distracted from the complete and utter focus on him and his ego was a waste of time and energy. The rejection was weirdly a kind of compliment from Trump, in that he was treating me just as he treated his children: badly.

One of the more unusual aspects of working for the Trump Organization was how an entire floor of the Trump Tower was turned into a Hollywood sound stage for episodes of *The Apprentice*. Trump would call me, in his gruff voice, like Don Corleone, and say I should come to the set to watch the proceedings. For days on end, I would sit in the control booth witnessing the antics, part of my job description that might give you a sense of how damn fun it could be working for the Trump Organization. Yes, Trump yelled and screamed and bullied, and I was one of his favorite targets for derision and insults, and yes, he asked the impossible and required that no one around him ask any questions or doubt his word, and yes, much of what I did was morally and legally and ethically repulsive and soulless. But you won't understand the full picture unless you can grasp how incredibly entertaining it was not just to watch the insane spectacle of manipulation and debasement that constituted reality television at its highest level. I was part of the action, in on the joke, the recipient of Trump's knowing winks and grins. If Trump was playing the world for a ship of fools, a common denominator of confidence artists all through the ages, then at least I was his first mate, or, maybe more honestly, lackey. It was kind of like the old joke—and I loved old jokes; I was a member of New York's legendary private comedians' club, The Friars Club, and often attended their celebrity roasts—where the circus worker is shoveling elephant shit and someone asks him why he doesn't find a better job. What, he asks, and leave show business? That was me: shoveling shit but part of the show.

Trump's older kids were co-stars on the show, and it was evident that they were thrilled at all the attention and glamour associated with performing in the top-rated reality TV show. The same was true for some employees, like Trump's assistant, Rhona Graff, who appeared occasionally. I wound up as co-president of the production company that made *The Apprentice* and *Celebrity Apprentice*, and I routinely suggested people I'd met as contestants.

But it wasn't long after I started working for Trump that the global financial crisis hit the real estate industry. Trump likes to pretend he'd foreseen the disaster, much as he liked to lie about opposing the Iraq invasion of 2003 from the start, twenty-twenty hindsight being a specialty of his, but he was as clueless as any average Joe, I can attest with absolute certainty. When I signed on to work for Trump, I assumed he was a multi-billionaire with hundreds of millions in cash on hand at all times, ready to pounce on an opportunity at a moment's notice. What I was discovering was that Trump wasn't nearly the man advertised in *The Art of the Deal*. To start with, after 2008 and the free fall in value of his various real estate holdings, including Trump Tower and his golf courses, he effectively dropped out of the building business.

"No one is going to develop properties in this market," he told me. "You'd have to be out of your fucking mind to try to sell condos in this market."

Thus did Donald Trump's supposedly triumphant career as an iconic real estate developer end: quietly, with no fanfare or acknowledgement; he still pretended to be a builder, and it played a big part in his coming political career, but the truth was that he turned virtually all of his focus to tending to his brand-licensing deals. There would be an occasional exception to this rule, like the acquisition of the Doral golf course in 2011, but Trump spent his waking hours chasing money from endorsements for products like Trump Steaks and Trump Vodka and, infamously, Trump University. He'd endorse pretty much anything, as long as he had a piece of the action and didn't have to put up any money. This hardly was the expected activity of a billionaire investor, of course, and I often wondered about the truth of his net worth. Trump certainly fixated on my growing wealth from my real estate holdings and taxi medallions. He frequently commented on the amount of money I had as a way to throw it in my face that he was so much richer than me. It was like water off a duck's back to me, but it fed his need to demean people around him who had the temerity to get ahead in life; success was always a zero-sum game for him, and he and he alone had to be the winner.

Calculating Trump's real net worth was one of the strangest and most telling aspects of life in the Trump Organization. When *Forbes* and *Fortune* and the other publications that measured wealth were compiling the list of the richest people on earth, Trump would go into a frenzy. He would have CFO Allen Weisselberg and me concoct the highest possible number, inflating the valuation of his buildings and golf courses by using the absolute most optimistic comparable properties, and then we'd juice that number and juice it again and again until the Boss had a number that satisfied the requirements of his ego. Conversely, as you'll see in later pages with potential criminal consequences, when it came time to pay taxes—an obligation Trump didn't minimize or avoid, but rather almost certainly illegally evaded—the same properties would be deemed essentially worthless, or better yet the subject of giant capital losses which he could then deduct. I remember sitting in Trump's office on the 26th floor when a tax refund check for $10 million from the government arrived. He held the check up for me to see, flabbergasted but also delighted.

"Can you believe how fucking stupid the IRS is?" Trump asked. "Who would give me a refund of ten fucking million dollars? They are so stupid!"

But the biggest thing that was happening in these early years was that I was becoming fluent in Trump's secret language of silences, nods, and signals, to the degree that I was turning into his alter ego.

In the 1980s, Trump had had a fake spokesperson named John Barron, who would call tabloid reporters to boast about the Boss's sexual prowess and all the beautiful women he'd dated; it has always seemed more than a little odd that his youngest son's first name is Barron, though whatever that might indicate, I'll leave to the shrinks. In the 1990s, the avatar was named Johnny Miller, and he would shamelessly brag about Trump's wealth and sexual conquests, in a voice that was uncannily like the Boss's—because it was his voice. These semi-comical charades were transparent to most every reporter, but they served a mutually useful purpose: providing lazy journalists with easy headlines, and also shoveling coal into the always red-hot furnace of Trump's ego.

In the 2000s, Trump came up with an even better idea. Instead of using a fake character, he developed a real, live double who could speak to the press on his behalf and shamelessly extoll his truly incredible, mind blowing, unique and huge talents. That person was me: I was his John Barron and Johnny Miller. In that capacity, I kept up a constant stream of calls with journalists at the *New York Post* and the *Daily News*, as well as *The New York Times*, the *Wall Street Journal*, and the *National Enquirer*. In truth, my most important task was learning to channel the voice of Donald Trump and to convey his thoughts on any subject without having to ask him what he wanted to say; I was like Howdy Doody or Charlie McCarthy, a ventriloquist doll speaking for the Boss and faithfully saying precisely what he would say, no matter how crass or stupid.

In many ways I wasn't really a lawyer for Trump so much as a surrogate and attack dog with a law license. Along the way, I got involved in all of the wacky business ideas that Trump got involved in, many of them of the white trash and violent variety—one of the little-appreciated ways that he connected with the white working-class people in the Midwest who propelled him into the White House and remain his base of so-called deplorables. Professional wrestling was one of Trump's earliest connections with the tastes of baseball-cap wearing, pickup-driving men who otherwise would seem a million miles away from Trump's pampered and gilded gold existence. Fast food, trash TV, leering at attractive women—Trump channeled blue-collar white men because that was part of how he saw life, but also because he knew he could make a buck that way.

In 2009, Trump made a deal with his friend Vince McMahon of World Wrestling Entertainment to appear in a WWE Raw stunt. In this charade, McMahon would sell WWE Raw, only to later learn that it was his nemesis, Donald Trump, who was the purchaser. I was tasked with reviewing the Agreement and making sure that Trump received the agreed-upon fee. Trump had a long-standing relationship with McMahon and loved the bread and circus aspect of wrestling, with the phony plot lines known as "kay-fabe" pretty much exactly matching the nutball narrative he carried around in his head about life, politics, and the intelligence of his audience.

One afternoon, Vince McMahon came to Trump Tower to go over the plot they'd stage for the event, which involved Trump slapping him in the face. To rehearse, McMahon asked Trump to stand up and slap him. Trump was reluctant.

"I don't want to slap you," he said. "I'll hurt you."

"Don't worry," said McMahon. "Give me a real slap. Not a soft one. The crowd needs a real slap."

"Really?" Trump shrugged and gave him a soft slap across the cheek.

"That's a girl slap," McMahon said. "Let me have it. Reach back and put your whole body into it."

"Really?"

McMahon nodded.

Trump was grinning now, clearly enjoying the idea of being able to slap someone around with no consequences—indeed, to get praised for it. Trump was a big man, 6'3", easily 275 pounds, and even though he was in terrible shape and flabby, I knew he was plenty strong. Trump reared back, as we all flinched in anticipation, apart from McMahon, who was also obviously enjoying schooling his new pupil in the finer points of fake violence. Then the Boss smacked him hard.

McMahon rubbed his face, while the crowd in Trump's office giggled in disbelief.

"Okay," said McMahon. "Now really let me have it."

"Oh, man," Trump said, this time really letting go and giving him a very hard five-finger *smack!* across the face and nose, the crack of skin on skin echoing into the hallway like a slapshot, and causing us all to burst out laughing as McMahon rubbed his ruby-red cheek and chuckled.

"This is going to be some show, Vince," Trump said. "We'll make it look real for them."

"Yeah," said McMahon. "Real real."

We all flew to Green Bay, Wisconsin for the event titled Trump: The New Owner of WWE Raw. All of us invited were eager to experience what we knew was going to be a wild, fun night. In the dressing room under the stadium, we could hear the mounting noise of the crowd coming in, and it was obvious that the place was going to be sold out, not to mention the huge pay-per-view audience. This was when Don Jr. spoke out of turn, at least in the eyes of his taskmaster father.

"Hey, Dad, are you nervous?" he asked.

"What did you say?" Trump asked, his face reddening. "I'm going in front of millions of people. What kind of stupid fucking question is that? Get out of here."

We all stood in awkward silence, staring at our shoes, feeling sorry for the son and his perfectly innocent question.

"God damn it," Trump said with a heavy sigh, as if his son wasn't present. "The kid has the worst fucking judgment of anyone I have ever met. What a stupid thing to say—to put that thought in my head."

Don Jr. said nothing, also inspecting his shoes, and no doubt desperate to flee. The hurt was evident in his face and demeanor, even though this was hardly the first time I'd heard Trump insult his son and remark on his supposed lack of intelligence. I often wondered why the son stayed around in the face of the abuse of his father, though I knew the answer, because Don Jr. had told me the story. A true outdoorsman who would be most at peace raising cattle and hunting buffalo in Montana, after college he'd gotten a job as a bartender and enjoyed the work and the separation from his distant father. But after a couple of years, the elder Trump presented his son with an ultimatum: work for the family business or be cut off entirely—in effect disowned and disinherited if he didn't serve at the beck and call of his father. Don Jr. hated real estate, office politics, the whole circus that surrounded his old man, but he didn't want to be exiled, so he resolved to tough out the worst parts of being a Trump, including being humiliated in front of a group of colleagues by his own father. I really felt for him in that moment, as his father fixed his tie and adopted his scowling stage presence to enter what amounted to the twenty-first century version of the Roman Forum, the roar of the crowd above now echoing in the hallways.

"Are you okay?" I asked Don Jr. as we made our way to the ring and were out of the earshot of the Boss.

"I'm all good," he replied, putting on a brave face. "We have a tortuous relationship. It's not the first time he's said that, and it won't be the last."

The location in Wisconsin was no coincidence, as an epicenter of Middle America, and I've often wondered how many swing voters Trump might have won that night at the Resch Center, with over 10,000 fans screaming and yelling like lunatics as Trump appeared walking towards the ring for the bout, dressed in a pink tie, black suit, and black knee-length overcoat, his face set in a grimace that made him look like an overgrown version of Bart Simpson. Trump loved being the heel—wrestling parlance for the bad guy—knowing that the script called for him to win, naturally, and then engage in the emasculating and mock spectacle of selling the RAW Company back to McMahon for a quick, hefty profit.

Trump slapping McMahon was supposed to get the bout off to a frenzy-making start, but the Boss got swept up in the moment as everyone watched him strut up to McMahon and then ferociously slap him in the face. Trump slapping McMahon shocked the crowd as they watched the skit play out on the jumbotron, hearing the thunderous slap while the camera zoomed in on the five finger, or Triple F, imprint on McMahon's cheek.

I'd never seen the Boss look so happy. He loved trafficking in violence, or the threat of violence, as could be seen during the election campaign, when he implored his followers to beat up a protestor at a rally in Las Vegas in 2016.

"I'd like to punch him in the face," candidate Trump said as the protestor was roughed up.

The crowd in Wisconsin went wild, as they say, and in this case that was exactly what the insane intensity of the live audience felt like as they cheered on Trump—a wealthy celebrity who viewed their form of entertainment as worthy of his attention.

So, WWE Raw was part of my job description, too, and I loved it. Life with Trump was filled with improbable, even unbelievable events that contained their own logic but mostly revolved around an ancient Roman piece of wisdom: *carpe diem*. When Trump dispatched me to Fresno, in northern California, to try to secure the right to develop a giant golf project called Running Horse, I embraced the outrageous and audacious approach of Mr. Trump and immediately started promoting our bid the way P. T. Barnum would have: I went on radio stations, extolling the awesome super-luxury nature of Trump's courses, how we would build condos and gated communities and a PGA Championship-level course on the 1,000 acre site. I set about trying to convince the Fresno City Council that they should finance the cost of the development out of a bond issuance, explaining that the Trump Organization was bringing unparalleled expertise and excellence that would lift the economy of the entire region. I checked in with Trump multiple times a day as he urged me to even greater bombastic heights, but as the weeks passed, it became evident that I wasn't going to convince the local political class, including a rising star in the Republican Party named Devin Nunes, to make the population pay for a billionaire's golf course.

Soon after the Running Horse project fell apart, I was assigned to a project in the Meadowlands in New Jersey, for the development of a 1,000-apartment golf course community to be built on a massive landfill near the Hudson River. The proposal was failing, and needed a brand name to revive it, and so entered Donald Trump's personal attorney. The idea was to create the technology to properly vent the landfill so the methane and other gases didn't cause an explosion, and then have a world-class course within easy driving distance from Manhattan, enabling Wall Street players to hit the links any time they wanted. But chasing deals was a tricky and uncertain matter with many more failures than successes, no matter what Trump claims about winning all the time, and this idea didn't pan out either.

Trump didn't take setbacks well, to put it mildly; his form of leadership revolved around anger, fury, rage, and always chaotic blaming and shaming. I was no different than the Trump children, who caught hell when they brought a deal to their father that wasn't a home run, or didn't happen at all, though that was inevitable. I had befriended a Saudi prince who wanted to invest his family's billions in the United States, so I introduced him to Trump in the Boss's office, but nothing came of that, apart from the pair of diamond-crusted sunglasses my Arab acquaintance gave me.

To be on the receiving end of a Trump tirade, in the aftermath of the financial crisis, was nobody's idea of a bargain. He belittled me and shouted and mocked the smallest aspects of my appearance or manner, in a way that would normally drive any sensible employee to seek another job. But the magnetic pull of Trump was irresistible for me: for every ridiculous rant, there was a WrestleMania, or a head of state stopping by the office, or a tabloid rumor about an *Apprentice* sexual scandal to put down, and the sheer pace and variety of life in the swirling tornado that always surrounded him was addictive. I was like a junkie, mainlining the excitement and the rush of people and money and craziness, about as far from my staid white-shoe law firm existence of recent times as can be imagined. When Trump hinted to my colleague George Sorial that I ought to quit and work elsewhere, I immediately went into the Boss's office and asked if he wanted me to go. I was fine with leaving if that was what he wanted, I said, but he backed down right away, maybe to avoid direct conflict, which he despised, but mostly because he knew he'd stumbled into a useful and effective advocate willing to do what was required, come what may, which was a rare and valuable commodity.

There was also the fact that I took on the slimiest assignments without complaint. One of the worst was cleaning up the mess in the aftermath of a clusterfuck known as the Trump Network. This brilliant idea started soon after I began to work for Trump, and essentially involved a couple of operators who sold vitamins and supposed health pills and supplements who approached the Boss about a multi-level marketing scheme. The structure was like Amway, with each commission-based salesperson paying the person above them in the pyramid, thus the pejorative term "pyramid scheme" to describe what was really a scam. The way to keep the Ponzi scheme ticking along was to have more and more salespeople signing up, to continually increase the payments being kicked up the ladder. But the problem was the most basic of any business: the products didn't sell. I'm not sure if it was quality, or whether or not the vitamins actually did anything, or bad marketing, or bad design, or the Trump brand having no earthly relevance to a health-based product, but the company was a total failure and I was tasked with exiting the Boss in a cost-effective and timely fashion.

Trump Suits, Trump Ties, on and on it went with the product lines. When the clothing company that made Trump Suits approached the company about partnering on a line of Trump-endorsed pay-per-view mixed martial arts promotions to be called Affliction Entertainment, the Boss assigned me to lead the initiative. Like Trump, I liked fighting in business but also in the ring— only in my case that meant actual combat. Muay Thai, the Thai form of boxing, is sometimes called the "art of eight limbs," referring to the elbows, hands, shins, and knees, all deployed to defeat your opponent, which was a pretty good analogy for what it was like working for and with Donald J. Trump.

As the Chief Operating Officer of Affliction Entertainment, I was charged with making sure Trump got his cut of the proceeds, even if the company fell apart, as it soon did; the Boss didn't want to share the losses, of course, but he wanted what he considered his guarantee for putting his name all over the rings used for the two promotions that actually got produced. One evening, I was in the Hamptons having a heated discussion about Trump's fees with the president of Affliction and the distribution partners who had done business with Affliction Entertainment. Things quickly got out of hand in the limo we were riding in along Montauk Highway and a fistfight broke out between us. The fact that I was willing to literally physically fight and punch another man in the face on behalf of Mr. Trump should give you a sense of the lengths that I was willing to go to please the Boss, much to the ongoing and growing disgust of my wife and kids. But I couldn't quit working for Trump, I knew—not for the money, as most think, but because by then I was obsessed with him, not as an acolyte or hanger-on, but as a way to stay close to his celebrity and glamor and power.

I was the canary in the coal mine for the millions of Americans who are still mesmerized by the power of Trump.

Chapter Six

Trump For President (Part One)

There are many ways to track the beginnings of Donald Trump's presidential ambitions, dating back to the 1980s, when he toyed with a run and started taking out full-page ads in *The New York Times* as a forum to air his public-policy positions. In those early manifestations of Trump's aspirations, he revealed an uncanny knack for channeling the fears and resentments of the age, even as he displayed a hair-trigger approach to negotiating when he advised Ronald Reagan's Secretary of State to start talks with the Soviet Union by banging his fist on the table and shouting, "Fuck you!"

Just one example was Trump's call in 1989 for the death penalty for the Central Park Five, a group of black kids convicted of the rape of a white female jogger in Manhattan's famous park. The fact that the kids were exonerated years later, when it was proven beyond doubt that they were not guilty, didn't prompt Trump to back down or admit a mistake; he'd understood instinctively that the racial anxiety and resentments then gripping New York City would provide a potent symbol that he hoped to ride to power. That was always Trump's way, learned at the feet of Roy Cohn, his first attack-dog attorney: Never apologize, and never admit to error or weakness. Never. Ever. Not even in the time of Coronavirus, as the world would discover.

In 2000, Trump again flirted with the idea of aiming for the presidency, this time as a candidate for the small and fractious Reform Party. Trump's candidacy was touted by his old friend, David Pecker, a connection I would come to increasingly lean on. The Reform Party had been founded by billionaire and failed presidential candidate Ross Perot, and it lacked a coherent philosophy, which actually suited Trump well, but it was constantly besieged by infighting and feuds and the Boss quickly dropped out.

Ever since I signed on with the Trump Organization in 2007, I had wanted the Boss to run for president, and I told him so again and again. I thought Trump was a visionary, with a no-nonsense attitude and the charisma to attract all kinds of voters. I saw many times that he had a natural ease with working-class folks, especially his fans—like those who watched *The Apprentice* and *Celebrity Apprentice* and WWE—provided they were kept at a distance.

In the years since, I have asked myself why I wanted so badly for Trump to become president. I developed a slew of answers and justifications over time: I thought he would rise to the office and it would bring out the best in him. I thought his brand of straight talk and no-bullshit honesty would rid the country of the scourge of political correctness. I thought his business acumen and way of seeing the world would offer a bracing change for the country and help fix our failing infrastructure. I thought his America First political stance would make the country stronger, and I thought his original and unique approaches to trade and taxes would transform society, for the good. I thought his aversion to the nonstop, unending wars in the Middle East would restore sanity to foreign policy.

Those were the things I told myself as I nagged and wheedled and tried to convince him to take the idea of running for the White House seriously. I knew he was a liar and a master manipulator, along with the myriad less-than-sterling characteristics I had witnessed over the years, but I believed his positive qualities outweighed the downsides and perfection shouldn't be the enemy of good.

But here's the ugly truth—a motive I share with deep and abiding regret and shame, and one only unearthed after much soul searching and reflection as I painted the walls in prison and stared at the ceiling from my bunk. The real real truth about why I wanted Trump to be president was because I wanted the power that he would bring to me. I wanted to be able to crush my enemies and rule the world. I know it sounds crazy, but look at what Trump is doing now: running the world, into the ground, but still, he literally rules. Underneath all the layers of delusion and wishful thinking and willful ignorance and stupidity, I was like Gollum in *The Lord of the Rings*, lusting after the power that would come from possessing the White House—"my precious"—and I was more than willing to lie, cheat, and bully to win. Trump was the only person I had ever encountered who I believed could actually pull off that feat, and I recognized early the raw talent and charisma and pure ruthless ambition to succeed he possessed. I saw what others didn't, what others thought was a joke, at their own peril, and that was my true motive. I knew Trump would do whatever was necessary to win. I just lacked the imagination and moral purpose to actually think about what that would mean for America, the world, for me, and for my family.

Because here's the thing: When you sell your soul, you do exactly that: sell your soul.

Although I never heard Trump use the N-word in my time spent with him, there were many times that he made racist comments. What he said in private was far worse than what he uttered in public. As an example: in September 2008, we were in Chicago for the "topping off" ceremony for The Trump International Hotel and Tower. Bill Rancic, who had won the first season of *The Apprentice* four years before, had been put in charge of the project. Trump reminisced to me about Rancic, who had been in a head-to-head with another contestant, Kwame Jackson. Kwame was not only a nice guy, but also a brilliant Harvard MBA graduate. Trump was explaining his back-and-forth about not picking Kwame.

"There was no way I was going to let this black fag win," he said to me.

* * *

THE ELECTION OF 2008 was a cataclysm for Trump, as he watched a young African American senator from Illinois defeat first Hillary Clinton and then John McCain. Barack Obama's victory in many ways was the defining event of Donald Trump's rise. There were really no words to describe Trump's hatred and contempt for Barack *Hussein* Obama—always all three names and always with a disdainful emphasis on the middle. This was when I started to witness the increasingly reactionary and unhinged Archie Bunker racism that defined Trump and his views on modern America. He was friendly with many African American people, pretty much exclusively of the celebrity variety—of course, Trump really had no friends, only interests and desires and ambitions—and he wasn't so stupid as to use the N-word, at least not in my presence. Mike Tyson, Don King, Oprah—those were the black folks he admired and embraced. Rich, famous, part of the peer group he inhabited. But, as a rule, Trump expressed low opinions of all black folks, from music to culture and politics. Africa was a hell-hole, he believed, and Nelson Mandela, to use but one example, was an object of contempt for Trump.

"Tell me one country run by a black person that isn't a shithole," he would challenge me as he cursed out the stupidity of Obama. "They are all complete fucking toilets."

When Mandela passed away, years later, Trump told me he didn't think the South African founding father and national hero was a real leader—not the kind he respected.

"South Africa was once a beautiful country twenty, thirty years ago," Trump said, endorsing Apartheid-era white rule. "Mandela fucked the whole country up. Now it's a shithole. Fuck Mandela. He was no leader."

Don't ask me how I squared this kind of racism with his qualifications to be president. I wanted power, as I've confessed, and that blinded me to just about everything awful and true and dangerous about Trump—my precious.

Watching Obama's Inauguration in 2008 with Trump, with the massive, adoring, joyful crowd on the Mall, incensed the Boss in a way I'd never seen before—he was literally losing his mind watching a handsome and self-evidently brilliant young black man take over, not only as Commander in Chief, but also as a moral world leader and guiding light. It was just too much for Trump. I thought I'd seen the worst of Trump then, but when Obama won the Nobel Prize, Trump went ballistic, as if the universe were playing some kind of trick on him to drive him out of his mind. It was almost like he was hearing voices, the way he ranted and raved about the idiotic Obama and how he was beloved by so many Americans. Trump mocked the way Obama talked, walked, even appeared, as if acting presidential was just that: an act. The shtick you see him pull at his rallies, when he mocks the idea of being "presidential" and says how easy it is to pretend to be a serious leader, walking like a robot and marching around like a fool and a phony, was first performed for yours truly in Trump's office while I sat quietly listening to him go on and on and on about Obama and caricature his mannerisms. We even hired a Faux-Bama, or fake Obama, to record a video where Trump ritualistically belittled the first black president and then fired him, a kind of fantasy fulfillment that it was hard to imagine any adult would spend serious money living out—until he did the functional equivalent in the real world.

Trump didn't despise Obama. It was much, much stronger than that. I figured that Obama was the only person on the planet whom Trump actually envied—truly, madly, deeply. Air Force One, walking the carpet to deliver the State of the Union, the way Angela Merkel and other world leaders obviously admired and listened to Obama—it drove Trump out of his mind. Then came The Speech: Obama was invited to address the German nation in front of the Brandenburg Gate, in the same place as John F. Kennedy in the early '60s, one of the indelible images of American history in the

Trump with Faux-Bama.
© 2020 Michael Cohen

twentieth century. Trump went from incandescent to sputtering, spittle-flecked fury as he watched Obama talk about freedom and ridding the world of nuclear weapons and turning back the rising seas by fighting global warming.

"You've got to admit he's a great orator," I said.

"Fuck him," Trump yelled at me, Obama on the screen before him calmly addressing untold millions of Germans thrilled to have a world leader ushering in the prospect of a twenty-first century where diversity and tolerance and peace and responsibility would become global aspirations, and maybe even realities.

"He's obviously very smart," I said, knowing I was egging Trump on, but also honestly impressed by Obama's speech and demeanor.

"Obama is a fucking phony," Trump screamed. "He's a *Manchurian Candidate*. He's not even fucking American. The only reason he got into fucking Harvard Law School and Columbia

was fucking affirmative action. He could never get into those schools on his fucking grades. Fuck him."

* * *

HERE IS THE true story behind Trump's first serious attempt to run for president and avenge the cosmic injustice that Barack Obama represented to him. In 2011, as always, part of my daily duties was to scour the newspapers for mentions of Trump, in large part to satiate his insatiable ego, and I undertook this responsibility with real pleasure and energy, especially hunting for signs that Trump's political fortunes might be making news or causing speculation about the Boss running for higher office. The prospect of a Trump candidacy was being promoted by the ever-eager and ingratiating David Pecker in the *National Enquirer*, but there were very few signs that the mainstream media was taking the idea seriously.

Then, in mid-April of 2011, Public Policy Polling released an opinion survey that stunned me as I read it sitting at my desk first thing in the morning. Barack Obama was up for reelection the following year and speculation was circulating about potential candidates for the Republican nomination. The obvious leading contenders were Mitt Romney and former Arkansas governor Mike Huckabee, but both seemed like lame choices to me. I thought Trump could eat them for breakfast, if he really committed to the campaign.

The Public Policy Poll that day had the amazing result that twenty-six percent of GOP primary voters said they would support Trump from among a slate of Republican candidates that included his name. I immediately grasped the implications as I clipped the story from the newspaper and readied it to bring it to the Boss's attention the moment he arrived at work. I knew that Trump would want to discuss the poll, not just with me and his kids but with anyone who entered his office or spoke to him on the phone; when Trump was ego-surfing, no one was exempt from his need for praise and admiration.

Trump arrived in the office soon after and I instantly walked the short distance to his office. I knocked on the door and entered.

"Hey, Boss, you have to see this," I said.

I proudly handed him the clip and took a seat in my usual middle Egg chair.

"No shit," Trump said, scanning the article, his face forming into a priceless expression, partly amazement, partly delight, partly disbelief, but mostly a kind of transcendent vindication as if he'd known the truth all along. "Wow," he said, reading on. "Michael, what do you make of this?"

"It's tremendous, Boss," I said. "Twenty-six percent is unprecedented. You aren't even a politician or even someone with political inclinations."

Trump finished the article and leaned back in his oversized, overstuffed burgundy executive chair, contemplating.

"What do you think about doing it?" he asked.

"Doing what?" I asked.

"Let's do it," Trump said. "Shit, I've done everything else. Why not? I'm bored with buildings, golf, and television. Being president would be very cool."

Trump was now in a reverie, imagining the possibilities in a way I'd never seen before. His enthusiasm was infectious, and my mind was also racing as I imagined a real Trump campaign, with me as a central part of the operation.

"Take a look at how to make this happen," Trump said to me. "I'm serious. I want to do this. It's perfect timing. I've got age, wealth, notoriety. I can do the job much better than Barack *Hussein* Obama, that's for fucking sure. Michael, go figure this out. What's the worst that happens? We lose? So what. This can be the greatest infomercial in the history of politics."

Trump smiled at the thought of the win-win proposition he uniquely possessed: the inevitable wall-to-wall ink and air time his candidacy would command would translate into one giant, free, ongoing advertisement. The logic was genius, he and I both knew, our grins spreading.

"And the best result is that we win," Trump said. "Now that would be something."

The "we" Trump was referring to was himself, of course, as he drifted into a reverie, his eyes taking on the thousand-yard-stare that I would see in action four years hence. I could see he was imagining walking into the White House, sitting down in the Oval Office, taking over as Commander in Chief.

"I would have the Marine Corps band play Hail to the Chief every morning as I got out of bed," Trump said.

* * *

How did Donald Trump come to command twenty-six percent of Republican voters in the spring of 2011? The short answer—the only honest response to that question—was one word: Birtherism. I know because I witnessed it unfold from the inside. As a way to test the waters, in the weeks before the poll, the Boss gave a speech to the Conservative Political Action Conference in February of 2011, and that was his coming-out party. In the address, Trump ticked off all of the conservative boxes: pro-gun, anti-abortion, low taxes, ready to wage a trade war with China, but his signature credential was his promise to make America great again. The room was packed for the speech as he received huge applause, and it was well-received in the right-leaning press, the media restless with an uninspiring list of candidates like Rick Santorum and Newt Gingrich. Trump was a fresh face, a reality TV celebrity with a bombastic reputation. A matchup with his archnemesis Barack Obama would be epic, it was obvious, and killer for ratings.

To liberals at the time, the idea of Trump running for president was literally a joke, and leading pollsters and pundits said so again and again in magazines like the *Atlantic*. But Trump was five steps ahead of the mainstream media, I knew, as the Trump Organization engaged with the producers of the forthcoming Comedy Central "Roast of Donald Trump." The Boss had approval over all the jokes for the roast, and he didn't really care how he was made fun of, with a few specific and very important provisos: no one was to mock his wealth, his various bankruptcies, or his hair; those subjects were strictly out of bounds, I knew, as I parsed the script on his behalf—and a script it was, with every joke vetted and requiring final approval by me.

The Trump roast was the perfect vehicle for his campaign, a judo-like way for the Boss to both embrace and deflect the supposedly hilarious idea that he would become Commander in Chief. By sitting on a stage while he was being ridiculed, Trump would prove that he could take a joke, even if he very rarely laughed—in fact, he almost never laughed, unless it was at a crude sexual comment, or at someone else's misfortune. After reviewing the proposed gags, I'd sit and watch him work over the material with his giant Sharpie, essentially dictating how the evening would play out.

Trump had been roasted before, at the Friar's Club in New York City in 2004, a comedy club I belonged to—but I didn't attend that event. I knew there had been some great zingers at that roast. "The reason Trump puts his name on all his buildings is so the banks know which ones to take back," said a comedian named Rich Vos. The comic Stewie Stone said he'd read Trump's book on how to become a billionaire and he enjoyed it. "But if your father wasn't one first, you'd be a waiter in this hotel," he said. At the time, Trump was engaged to Melania Knauss, as she was then-known, prompting the President of NBC, Jeff Zucker, to apologize for not being able to make it to the wedding. "But I'll catch the next one," he said.

Comedy Central aired the Trump roast on March 8, 2011, with Trump entering on a gilded gold golf cart, and taking to the dais with a mostly B-List group of celebrities, including Snoop Dog, Larry King, and the usual comedians hired to skewer celebrities. Finding stars willing to participate had proven difficult, even among some of Trump's supposed friends, like Mike Tyson and Don King; I guess they didn't want to associate themselves with a man pushing a conspiracy theory about President Obama's place of birth.

The term Birtherism didn't exist in the mainstream media in 2011—not until the Boss took it up. For years, conspiracy theorists had speculated about Obama's birthplace, claiming it was Kenya, not Hawaii, despite the absence of evidence to support the allegation. The idea that the President of the United States wasn't American was unprecedented, the kind of scurrilous insinuation that was transparently racist and nativist in nature.

But Donald Trump recognized a great marketing opportunity when he saw one. I don't know how he picked up on the idea, other than browsing in the press as he always did, but like an old-time carnival barker—really, like the greatest showman and promoter of all time, P. T. Barnum—Trump recognized the potential instinctively. No matter what anyone says, including Trump, I know for a fact that he didn't care if the conspiracy theory was true or not. He didn't care where Obama had been born, or the insult it was to the President and his family, let alone the crude racism lurking barely below the surface. What he cared about was identifying an issue that he could exploit to his advantage, no matter how divisive—in fact, the more divisive, the better, because it would arouse strong feelings for those who took his side.

The same was true for Trump's preposterous claim that he had seen Arabs in New Jersey celebrating on September 11, 2001, as the World Trade Centers collapsed after the terror attack masterminded by Osama Bin Laden. Trump didn't see any such celebration, obviously, nor did such a ghoulish and disgusting spectacle ever occur, it goes without saying. But Trump had the innate ability to access the deepest prejudices and fears of people and exploit them for his benefit. He divided the world into Us vs. Them, mainlining the most emotional and irrational impulses of the masses, with Arabs and Syrian refugees and the slaughter of the Kurds. He abandoned the truth in favor of falsehoods—which he knew perfectly well were false—in exchange for news-cycle soundbites, and the media has fallen for it over and over and over, to this day and beyond.

Birtherism was one of Trump's most successful early Big Lie gambits. The pattern I had witnessed so many times began to emerge, as his mind quickly traveled from naked and shameless exploitation of the birther conspiracy theory to the conviction that it was true. If Trump wanted to believe something because it served his purposes, he decided to begin to believe, a leap of the imagination that was effortless to him, even second nature. What started as a ratings extravaganza morphed into self-delusion before my eyes. The first step along the path was accumulating positive reinforcement, and Trump accomplished this by calling in executives and friends and asking them a simple question: You don't think Barack *Hussein* Obama was born in America, do you? It was obvious from the way Trump asked the question what answer he wanted, and I was stunned to see how many people were willing to feed into the Boss's personal animosity for Obama.

To spread his new marketing ploy, Trump appeared on *Good Morning America* in March of 2011, and that was when his name really entered the national conversation about the presidency. He said he was skeptical about Obama's citizenship and birthplace, hence legitimacy as president, and they gave him the air time to spread that nastiness. Even better: for free. This was quickly followed by appearances on *The View* and *CNN Newsroom,* and then in April on NBC. The polls started to register Trump as a potential candidate and I started to clip newspaper stories to show him, culminating in the Public Policy result with the Boss at twenty-six percent.

But that wasn't all there was to it. As events moved along, the story Trump was pushing took on another dimension: Not only was Obama not American, he wasn't even Christian, the Boss told me. By then, Trump was reading what he called the "populist" publications, like *Breitbart* and *World News,* every day, as he lectured me about the truth of world affairs, the tales getting taller all the time.

"Do you think Barack *Hussein* Obama was born in Hawaii?" Trump asked me one day that spring. "Bullshit. There is no record of his birth in a Hawaiian hospital. You know he's not even fucking Christian. He's a Muslim. He admitted it."

I was sitting in my red Egg chair when Trump handed me a document purporting to be from the *Harvard Law Review* stating in a biography that he had been born in Kenya.

"I can't explain why the bio states that," I said. "But I'm certain he was born in Hawaii. There is no way the Clinton machine would not have uncovered that if it was true because—"

Trump interrupted me mid-sentence. "Bullshit," he said. "He's a fraud. He's a *Manchurian Candidate.* You'll see."

"Well, if you're right, that would create the most difficult situation in American history," I replied. "Every bill passed and signed by him would have to be repealed as invalid and unlawful. It would be a complete clusterfuck."

As he listened, Trump's eyes lit up: he'd come up with an idea. He looked at me with glee as he picked up the phone and dialed one of his favorite reporters. I knew he was going to drop a head-line-making bombshell and the gullible reporter would have no clue that he or she was being played. This is a little-appreciated fact about his path to power. He screams about fake news and reporters being the enemies of the people, like a tin-pot dictator, but the truth was that the media's psychotic fascination with Trump was one of the biggest—maybe the biggest—cause for his rise to power.

"I have a team of investigators in Hawaii and elsewhere obtaining proof of Obama's birth in Kenya," Trump told the reporter from the *National Enquirer*.

The journalist was like a moth to the flame—and I knew what that felt like. The conversation was on speakerphone, so I heard him beg for more sensational leads, all the better to please his boss at the *National Enquirer*, David Pecker.

"Tell me more," the reporter said. "What agency are you using? What have they found? Are they in Hawaii and Kenya? What can you share?"

"Nothing yet," Trump said. "But soon I will make a major announcement of the findings and, trust me, you will be shocked."

"Can I get an exclusive on this when you're ready?" the reporter asked.

"Sure," Trump said. "You have been good to me. Just keep reporting that way and I will give it to you."

Trump hung up.

"We don't have anyone in Hawaii that I know of," I said. "Do you want me to put someone on that?"

"No," Trump replied. "Who fucking cares? Wait until the headlines come out. This story is going to be huuuuuge!"

He then gave me an earnest stare and exhorted me to handle the press with caution. I was his partner in crime, metaphorically speaking, and he wanted to ensure that I understood what to do next. The question of whether I would knowingly participate in a lie and a fraud had long ago been asked and answered; this was what Trump meant by loyalty, and what is still playing out nightly on the news as the Vice President and cabinet members repeat things that they know not to be true.

"Make sure that you stay on message when we get calls from other media outlets," Trump said. "We have a team of people in Hawaii and soon Trump will be making a statement on the results. Got it?"

"Yes, sir," I said.

Within days, my phone was lit up with calls from *The New York Times*, *Washington Post*, the networks, Fox, CNN, you name it, all the free publicity we wanted, courtesy of the free press. The reporters begged me for a scoop, no matter how small, a way to advance the story even an inch, to own a tiny piece of the news cycle. On background, they pled, off the record, off-off the record, please tell me more, anything at all, please, please, please . . .

As instructed by the Boss, I replied as I'd been told to: Mr. Trump will release the findings from his investigative team very soon.

The headlines were soon bannered across the nation, along with op-eds condemning Trump's allegations—just more publicity, as far as the Boss was concerned. Why did I go along with this ridiculous and racist attack? Why did the press? The truth was that I didn't just passively not protest Trump's transparently false accusations against Obama; I actively, rabidly, incessantly, insistently repeated the lies and innuendo, knowing in my heart that it was wrong—but unable to stop myself. I know that's not much of an explanation. I know it sounds like a cop out, and hardly the most likable trait a man might offer in his defense. But that is what it feels like to lose control of your mind—you actually give up your common sense, sense of decency, sensitivity, even your grip on reality. It was like having a mental illness: the reality was hard for outsiders to grasp, in all of its dimensions. The fact that I'd departed from reality, in my desire to please the Boss, meant that I really and truly had actually taken leave of my senses.

As I said at the start, I was in a cult of personality. And I loved it. I reveled in the intrigue and gamesmanship and manipulation, as terrible as that sounds. I had convinced myself I was in on the joke with the Boss, but, in truth, the real joke was on me.

After every call, I'd go to Trump's office and tell him about the network or publication that had reached out. Trump was thrilled.

"I told you this would be a monster story," Trump told me. "Fuck Obama. If you think he hates me now, just wait."

The lengths to which Trump would go to goad Obama had no bottom, as I saw when Trump started questioning his academic record, making it appear that the President had been the beneficiary of affirmative action instead of a brilliant student who had been the first black Editor-in-Chief of the *Harvard Law Review* and graduated *magna cum laude*, especially as compared to the Boss's mediocre record as a student. When cries emerged to see Trump's academic record, it was obvious to the Boss that he was in real trouble. He'd called Obama a "terrible student" and demanded that he release his transcripts—but what if Trump's grades at the New York Military Academy high school, Fordham, and the Wharton School of the University of Pennsylvania were released?

As the controversy erupted, Trump called me into his office and tasked me with putting out a fire of his own creation. He didn't say why—he never did. He told me what he wanted done, even though it was as plain as the nose on my face that he wanted his academic record suppressed because he was a middling student, at best, but it remained unspoken. I was pretty sure there would also be a history of disciplinary action in the record, which would further embarrass the Boss, to the extent that was possible.

To placate Trump, I contacted the upstate New York Military Academy, where he'd been sent by his parents as a teenager to instill some sense of discipline, and explained that all hell would break loose if they didn't immediately provide me with all of the Boss's high school academic records. I didn't ask nicely: I was blunt and brutal, as usual when on a mission for the Boss. The pressure was jacked up by using wealthy alumni to pressure the school, forcing the headmaster to scurry into the basement and remove the documents—another unprecedented event. That was Trump when it came to Obama: competitive, but in many ways afraid of actually being compared—even though he would ridicule any suggestion that he was intimidated by the President.

The White House Correspondents' Dinner was held in late April of 2011, in Washington, DC. I chose not to go, but I watched from home as President Obama took to the podium in front of hundreds of reporters and celebrities to join in the annual political joke fest. I knew the Boss was in the crowd as the guest of Lally Weymouth, daughter of the legendary *Washington Post* owner Katharine Graham, and it was easy to spot Trump's orange coif sticking out like a sore thumb in the sea of tuxedos and formal dresses, especially when Obama began to rip into the *Celebrity Apprentice* star by mocking his presidential aspirations.

Obama had released his long-form birth certificate a few days before, telling supporters that he was trying to put the controversy to rest and remind voters that politics wasn't a reality TV show—an obvious dig at Trump. But the Boss wasn't going to let the show end that easily; life was indeed a reality TV show to Trump. The Boss had turned the spurious allegation into a real political force, with forty percent of Republican voters by then believing that Obama hadn't been born in the United States, so the release of the birth certificate wasn't going to deter him. Trump had identified his base, I knew, and he viewed the release of the birth certificates as a triumph, not the end of the matter.

Unknown to the world, only a few hours earlier, Obama had ordered the operation to kill Osama bin Laden, so the fact that the President had such incredible comedic chops was amazing to me.

"Now, I know that he's taken some flak lately, but no one is happier, no one is prouder to put this birth certificate matter to rest than The Donald," Obama said. "And that's because he can finally get back to focusing on the issues that matter—like, did we fake the moon landing? What really happened in Roswell? And where are Biggie and Tupac?"

"But all kidding aside, obviously, we all know about your credentials and breadth of experience. For example—no, seriously, just recently, in an episode of *Celebrity Apprentice*—at the steakhouse, the men's cooking team did not impress the judges from Omaha Steaks. And there was a lot of blame to go around. But you, Mr. Trump, recognized that the real problem was a lack of leadership. And so, ultimately, you didn't blame Lil Jon or Meatloaf. You fired Gary Busey. And these are the kind of decisions that would keep me up at night. Well handled, sir. Well handled."

The room exploded with laughter as the celebrities turned to catch a glimpse of the reddening face of Trump. Many in the media have speculated that his animus for Obama came from that night— the humiliation in front of a room of power players—and was what made Trump want to run for the presidency. I can tell you with absolute certainty that wasn't true. Not even in the slightest. He hated Obama long before then; the hatred that would animate him in the years to come needed no further fire.

But it did seal Trump's resolve to run, I thought. To take the temperature in Iowa, the Boss and I agreed that I should fly out to

Des Moines to meet with the leaders of the GOP, but because of my schedule, it wasn't going to be possible for me to take commercial flights. For the first time ever, to my knowledge, including with Trump's kids, the Boss suggested that I use his 727 for the one-man trip. Even that came with an asterisk, though, because the 727 was up for sale and the new 757 was going to be delivered soon, so I wasn't getting the true gilded treatment he reserved for himself.

The cost of the flight was likely a campaign contribution violation, even though we didn't really even have a campaign at the time. We got around the pesky federal election laws as we usually did: by way of deceit. In this case, we used our go-to front, or beard, when Trump and I were hiding the true nature of our activities—a man by the name of Stewart Rahr. Universally known and loved as "Stewie Rah Rah" in wealthy New York circles, he was a pharmaceutical billionaire who'd divorced his wife of many years in the throes of a midlife crisis and turned himself into a party animal and big-time playboy, at least as much as a man in his late sixties could manage—and he managed very well.

Rah Rah was the straw man I would use to buy a portrait of Mr. Trump that was up for sale at an art auction in the Hamptons a couple of years later. With Trump, everything had to be the biggest and the best, most especially his public profile, and that included a nine-foot tall portrait of Trump painted by the artist William Quigley. When the Trump portrait came up for auction, Rah Rah kept bidding the price up, with the final bang of the gavel coming in at $60,000, a ridiculously high price for the run-of-the-mill portrait, but it was the highest price paid at the event, giving the Boss bragging rights—and that was all he cared about.

To reimburse Rah Rah for the painting, Trump arranged for his charity, the Trump Foundation, to cut him a check, using the charitable tax deduction as a way to reduce the cost of the portrait. This was typical of Trump's method of accounting and evading taxes; he had no regard for the niceties of actually doing real charitable work or following tax laws. The giant, smiling image of self-regard was then hung in Trump's Doral golf club, proving that it had exactly zero benefit for any charitable cause, but again, that was par for the course for the Boss: little people pay taxes, as Leona Helmsley, another wealthy New York real estate figure who committed the crime of telling the truth, once remarked. In the end, the Trumps would have to repay the back taxes on the painting, along with a substantial fine, and close the charity down when the New York Attorney General brought a case against the family for using the so-called foundation as a sham. But justice delayed was justice denied in this case, as he successfully hid the venal truth from the world long enough to become president.

For the private flight on Trump's plane, I had Rah Rah pay the cost, to be reimbursed by Trump eventually, a type of under-the-table back scratching common for the true elite. But when another candidate complained to the Federal Election Commission, the leading Republican lawyer governing the agency—an attorney named Don McGahn—cut off the investigation, proving his loyalty and usefulness to Trump, which would be rewarded when he was appointed White House Counsel after the Boss won the election of 2016.

Landing in Des Moines in the Trump-branded jet, I was greeted by scores of reporters waiting in the hangar. I did a press conference, of course: the most dangerous place in America was in between me and a camera, especially if I was extolling the virtues of the Boss. The head of the Republican Party had arranged a tight schedule for me, with fifteen-minute meetings stacked on top of each other, but the universal response was enthusiasm for a Trump candidacy. There was a $100-a-head lunch fundraiser, which was packed, and I offered the keynote address—relishing the chance to speak in public. I raved about Trump's love for the wide-open spaces of Middle America and the prairie states of Red America. But nothing could have been further from the truth: Trump couldn't locate Iowa on a map any more than he could tell the difference between the locations of Kansas and Kansas City.

I gave the Boss the download when I flew home and took his call late at night—as usual, his last call of the day.

"Tell me, what was the reception like in Iowa?" he asked.

"Off the charts," I said. "You can't imagine all the clamoring."

"Tell Melania," Trump said, passing the phone to his wife.

I gave her the whole spiel about the press and the lunch and the crowds, but I could tell she wasn't interested. She wasn't disrespectful, just disinterested, and eager to get off the phone so she wouldn't have to listen to her husband's chief enabler sing his praises.

"That's great," she said, and *click*, she was gone.

To promote Trump's run in 2012, I set up a website called shouldtrumprun.com, and soon it was getting hits. This was when Roger Stone came into the picture. Trump and Stone had met years earlier, when both were moving in Roy Cohn's libertine circles in the nightclubs of Manhattan. Stone was a longtime political consultant, or more like a political conspiracy monger, who'd worked for Richard Nixon and had a giant tattoo of the disgraced president on his back.

Stone turned up at the office wearing tiny black sunglasses and a broad-shouldered suit, his hair slicked back, and affecting the strut of a cartoon character or a clown playing one. I was taking a crash course in political campaigns, with folks like Chris Ruddy at *Newsmax* and reporters at the *Des Moines Register* sharing their contacts and insights as I worked the phones. The vibe between Stone and me was instantly not good. Stone was a sycophant to Trump, but he and I had an instant dislike for each other. Part of it was personal style: Stone was a braggart and bully and he wanted to dominate Trump's attention, traits in direct conflict with my role as the Boss's tough guy, so part of it was also structural.

Trump didn't take sides in our feud, but he ridiculed Stone behind his back, as he did most everyone, including me, no doubt. The Boss had no concern for the morality or sexual conduct of his acolytes or team members like Roger Stone, a swinger known for wearing ass-less chaps during the Gay Pride Parade in Manhattan. Trump joked about Stone and what a crazy person he was, devoid of moral purpose and willing to do anything in service of himself or a politician he supported, always and only because it would benefit him personally. To Trump, those were good qualities to possess.

"Roger's a fucking pervert," Trump said to me. "But he can help me. He's the dirty trickster. He's the best trickster money can buy."

* * *

So how did the amoral Trump come to be beloved by evangelical voters, a question that remains one of the abiding mysteries to this day? Begin with the premise that Donald Trump hadn't darkened the door of a church or chapel since the age of seven, as he would openly admit in his past incarnation. Places of religious worship held absolutely no interest to him, and he possessed precisely zero personal piety in his life—but he knew the power of religion, and that was a language he could speak.

I lived in Trump Park Avenue and one of my neighbors was an evangelical pastor named Paula White. She had known Trump for more than a decade, after he'd seen her show on TV and he'd invited her to come to Atlantic City to give him private bible studies, her version of prosperity gospel the only conceivable version of Christianity that could appeal to Trump. Self-interested, consumed by the lust for worldly wealth and rewards, with two divorces, one bankruptcy, and a Senate financial investigation—she was a preacher after Trump's heart. The fact that she was beautiful and blonde didn't hurt, either.

As part of the division of labor in the campaign, I was assigned to lead the outreach to faith communities on behalf of Trump, mostly because having Roger Stone attempt to make those connections would be a farce. It was at this time that Paula White called me and said that she wanted to put together a group of evangelical leaders to meet with Trump to discuss his potential candidacy and the spiritual and political dimensions of his campaign. The idea was for Trump to solicit their support, so I readily agreed to help put the session together. More than fifty religious leaders came to Trump Tower to meet the Boss in a conference room on the 25th floor. Some of the most famous evangelicals in the country were there, like Jerry Falwell Jr., Pastor Darrell Scott, and Dr. Creflo Dollar, an Atlanta preacher who would later be charged with choking his daughter and ridiculed for soliciting contributions from his parishioners so he could purchase a $65 million Falcon 7X private jet to "safely and swiftly share the Good News of the Gospel worldwide."

As an organizer, I went to watch the proceedings, and what I saw was amazing, to put it mildly. Sitting around the long conference room table, the group started to discuss Trump's three marriages, his views on abortion, homosexuality, family values, America's role in the world, and God's place in the Boss's heart. As a little kid, Trump's family had attended Marble Collegiate Church in Manhattan, where he listened to the sermons of Norman Vincent Peale. The Protestant preacher was the author of *The Power of Positive Thinking* and an early radio and television star, sermonizing about the materialistic advantages of American conservative religion, making him a hero to the folks meeting with Trump as a pioneer in blending or conflating wealth and Jesus in a way that somehow found the Son of God was all about the bling.

Trump milked the Norman Peale connection like a dairy farmer at dawn, not letting one drop spill. Peale's version of God's word revolved around tall tales he told that were completely unverifiable and calling for the banishment of thoughts or emotions that were negative, which must have penetrated young Donny Trump's consciousness as a boy. Trump always lived in the present tense. He never looked backwards, except in anger or to blame others, which was part of Peale's appeal to his followers. When Trump was sitting in the pews as a boy, Peale was one of the most famous pastors in the world, which had to impress the kid, but it was likely the cult-like egomania that he urged Christians to follow that seemed to have penetrated the little Donny's impressionable brain, no doubt reinforced by his taskmaster father and hyper-ambitious mother.

As the evangelicals inhaled Trump's Norman Peale horse shit, they solemnly asked to approach him to "lay hands" on him. I watched with bated breath. Trump was a massive germophobe, as I've noted, so the idea of dozens of sets of hands touching his clothing and skin would appall him, I knew. But even this didn't faze the Boss: he closed his eyes, faking piety, and gave the appearance of feeling God's presence as the assembled group called for guidance in determining the fate and fortune of Donald Trump, America, and the message of Jesus Christ.

If you knew Trump, as I did, the vulgarian salivating over beauty contestants or mocking Roger Stone's propensity for desiring the male sexual organ in his mouth, as he would say less politely, you would have a hard time keeping a straight face at the sight of him affecting the serious and pious mien of a man of faith. I know I could hardly believe the performance, or the fact that these folks were buying it.

Watching Trump, I could see that he knew exactly how to

appeal to the evangelicals' desires and vanities—who they wanted him to be, not who he really was. Everything he was telling them about himself was absolutely untrue. He was pro-abortion; he told me that Planned Parenthood was the way poor people paid for contraception. He didn't care about religion. Homosexuals, divorce, the break-up of the nuclear family—he'd say whatever they wanted to hear, and they'd hear what they wanted to hear. This was the moment, for me: the split second when I knew Trump would be president one day. It was an intuition, but it was also based on the intangibles. Trump's answers to their questions were compassionate, thoughtful, Godly, in a way that I knew in no way reflected his beliefs or way of seeing life. He could lie directly to the faces of some of the most powerful religious leaders in the country and they believed him—or decided to believe him, a distinction with a real difference. Trump was imperfect, they knew, with his multiple marriages and carefully cultivated reputation as a womanizer. But he knew what they really cared about—the core,

Evangelical leaders laying hands on Trump. © 2020 Michael Cohen

core, core beliefs. Anti-abortion laws, Supreme Court justices, opposition to gay marriage and civil rights, and the cultural war-like rhetoric aimed at godless liberals. That was Trump's rat-like cunning, and it was a talent I knew then that he would ride all the way to the White House.

The prayer over, Trump opened his eyes as if he had indeed been in deep meditation and conversation with God.

"What do you think about me running for president?" Trump asked Pastor White in a reverent tone.

There was a silence in the room, as bowed heads were raised and eyes opened. This was no longer a question about the ambitions of a billionaire celebrity—it was about the soul of the nation; the Almighty was being summoned to guide the faithful. Paula White was very serious as she talked in a low voice, addressing the assembled in a passionate but measured way, Trump listening with yet more fake piety.

"I don't think the time is right," she replied, slowly.

Evangelical leaders laying hands on Trump. © 2020 Michael Cohen

"I don't either," Trump said, also slowly, carefully, and thought-fully.

As the two-hour session broke up, another event took place that would come to have a huge impact on the 2016 election, whether God wanted it or not. The genesis of this momentous moment, as you'll see in the pages to come, was my first meeting with Jerry and Becki Falwell and the implications it would have on the future of America. With folks milling around in the hallway of Trump Tower, I fell into a conversation with the couple that would provide the first flutter of a wave to the butterfly wing flapping that rippled outward and led to the devout and undying devotion to Trump of millions of evangelicals that still mystifies so many Americans.

Justin Bieber was the catalyst.

Go figure.

Jerry Falwell Jr. was a lot like me, in many ways, I thought: an attorney who didn't practice law, a transaction-oriented person who lived in the real world even as he floated through a kind of dreamy existence of wealth and power—in his case, evangelical royalty, in mine, the moneyed corridors of Trump's Manhattan. Becki was beautiful and vivacious, with a ton of energy and life. Chatting, they told me that they were staying in New York for an extra day because their twelve-year-old daughter Caroline wanted to see Justin Bieber perform at a special show he was giving the next morning at Rockefeller Plaza for NBC's *Today Show*.

"Oh, God, it's going to be a complete madhouse," Jerry said. "The things we do for our children."

"As I would do for mine," I replied. My daughter Samantha was a little older, but I would have moved heaven and earth to give her the kind of thrill that the Falwells were seeking. This presented an ideal opening for a fixer, like me, I realized.

"I'm not sure if I can pull it off, but a close friend of mine is an executive at Bieber's record label," I continued. "Let me call him and see if I can get you into the VIP area and possibly get a meet-and-greet."

Becki's eyes lit up, like I'd offered her the chance to be a super-star in her daughter's eyes—and who wouldn't want to be that for their tween?

"Michael, thank you for even offering to try," she said.

Becki offered me a hug and peck on the cheek, as we swapped cell numbers and I told them I'd call as soon as I had news. This was the kind of thing I was put on earth to do, to be honest about my real role in Trump's circle, but also more broadly in my life. Doing favors, making connections, working my Rolodex—that was me, figuring out how to give the Falwells' daughter a lifetime memory. Not knowing where it would lead, but knowing it was likely going to be somewhere.

Back in my office, I called my buddy and asked for three tickets to the VIP area for the Bieber concert the next morning, along with the possible chance to actually meet the cherubic Canadian in person. My pal was good with the tickets, but said it would be harder to swing the personal introduction. He said he'd try. The notice was short, and the demand huge, and he didn't want to get my hopes up, so I didn't tell the Falwells about that possibility, instead calling them and saying they were good to go on the tickets. I knew my friend would be there to take great care of them, so that was all excellent, and the Falwells were beyond excited to tell their daughter she was going to have a first-class seat at the show, only a few feet from her idol—heady stuff.

"I can't thank you enough," Jerry said as I gave him directions on where to report for the tickets. "You made this trip even better than it already was. We're friends for life."

The impact this tiny favor would have on the world was the furthest thing from my mind—but it would indeed come to matter, in the way random events multiply to form a pattern that can be

Me with the Falwells. © 2020 Michael Cohen

seen to have real importance in hindsight. Part of the art to being a fixer, doing small and big things for people, was never, ever asking for anything in return—for myself, that is. For others, I was more than happy to call in a chit or IOU or however you want to describe the sense of obligation that comes from granting your tween daughter her greatest wish in life, a moment in the presence of the Biebs. This particular favor and another of greater significance would come due in 2016, to the enormous benefit not of me, but the political prospects of candidate Donald Trump.

Not that Trump deserved the admiration and support of the devout folks he'd just met. Trump's true feelings about the encounter with the evangelicals, and the laying on of hands, a supposedly sincere and pious summoning of the will of God, were revealed as I entered Trump's office at the end of the day to have a final recap of his thoughts on the laying on of hands ceremony.

"Can you believe that bullshit?" Trump said, with incredulity, referring to the ritual and the evangelicals. "Can you believe people believe that bullshit?"

* * *

IN THE END, the real real reason Trump didn't run in 2012 had nothing to do with prayer or other worldly guidance. He was ruled by worldly concerns, specifically money. He was making multi-millions (Trump would often bag as much as $65 million for each season) as the star of *Celebrity Apprentice,* and the producer, Mark Burnett, needed to know if Trump was going to sign up for the next season. Ratings were declining, but Trump was still making serious money, constituting a rare positive cash flow for the Boss with his other businesses not nearly as successful, and he said he wasn't going to just quit the show.

"You don't leave Hollywood," Trump told me, as he explained

why he was dropping the presidential bid. "Hollywood leaves you."

In the never-ending swirl of chaos at the Trump Organization, in the middle of helping Trump figure out if he was going to run for president, I was also pursuing a deal in the Eurasian country of Georgia on behalf of the Boss. I'd been to Ukraine once, in 2002 with my brother, but this was my first foray into doing business in the former Soviet Union, an experience that would morph over time into a national scandal, allegations of espionage, and my imprisonment.

This proposed transaction was for Trump to sell his name and brand to a Georgian-American businessman I knew who was going to build hotels in the cities of Tbilisi and Batumi. My friend was connected to the CEO of a large Georgian company called Silk Road that would finance the deal, so it was decided I should travel to the country for a site inspection. I arrived to a military reception at the airport and a motorcade to the hotel, followed by a press conference with the media announcing that Donald Trump was coming to Georgia. This was my first glimpse of the power of the Trump brand in the former Soviet Union. I'd learned that Trump had a certain audience in the United States, mostly not at the higher levels of taste and society, but there were many who weren't attracted to his gaudy blend of wealth, braggadocio, and machismo. Not so in Georgia, not by a long shot. The more boorish elements of Trump's shtick were directly relatable to wealthy oligarchs ripping off the resources of their countries, as if he was a universal role model.

Trump's lack of scruples and conspicuous consumption had long attracted Russian investors to buy into his condo projects in New York and Florida, using numbered companies to hide the true ownership of the properties. This dicey practice was hardly limited to the Trump Organization, though the Boss displayed a strange obsession with Russia, as I'll discuss in due course, and the attitudes about foreign oligarchs and obviously corrupt officials from Third World countries were extremely lax for the Trumps.

Learning how entwined business and government were in Georgia, that evening I found myself having a private dinner with President Mikheil Saakashvili. In the morning, I was given the use of a military helicopter for the ride to Batumi, courtesy of the President, to look at a gorgeous ten-acre site on the Black Sea. The following day, to my amazement, I was summoned to the capital of Kazakhstan, where the Prime Minister pitched me on the idea of developing a $300 million Trump-branded hotel project in anticipation of a G-7 summit that country was holding in three years. The Kazakh deal never came through, but it was another element of the pleasure of working for Trump—you never knew where you were going to go, or who you were going to meet, and there was rarely a dull moment.

For Trump, everything was ultimately about making money and obtaining power, and he could see that his presidential odds were getting longer by the day. At the time, he was also in the process of acquiring two golf courses in Ireland and another in Scotland, and he was concerned about what would happen to his various businesses if he turned his attention full time to the 2012 campaign. A lot of the junky, fast-buck branding initiatives he'd gotten involved in—Trump Vodka, Trump Steaks—were starting to fail. Trump University was beginning to become a legal and publicity nightmare, with government investigations looming, and it was evident to me that I was going to be up to my neck in troubles that needed fixing.

"The kids can't handle all of the businesses on their own," Trump finally said to me. "They're not ready for it."

Then there was the inconvenient fact that Trump's poll numbers had tanked. As a rising reporter from *Politico* named Maggie

Haberman—who was a friend of mine and would go on to cover me and Trump in *The New York Times* to this day—wrote, "The Donald went up, and then The Donald melted down." From the twenty-six percent number in April, Trump had played the birther story for millions of bucks in free press, as we'd anticipated, but Obama's release of his birth certificate had taken the wind out of the sails of that story. Trump's belligerence and refusal to let the matter drop weren't wearing well, it appeared. By May he'd dropped to eight percent and fifth place, tied with Ron Paul, and far behind the eventual nominee, Mitt Romney, which amounted to a slap in the face for the Boss.

Left unspoken was Trump's true appetite for a showdown with a politician as popular and talented as Barack Obama, no matter how much Trump boasted about defeating him. Fear was an emotion Trump would never admit to, but it struck me as more than a little convenient to snipe from the sidelines about birther conspiracies—but another thing altogether to step into the arena and face the withering wit and soaring rhetoric and the real danger of humiliation at the hands of the 44th President of the United States.

"I swear to you we'll do this in 2015," Trump said to me privately, as he prepared to announce he wasn't going to run at the "up fronts" to promote the following season of *The Apprentice*, a way to try to monetize what had clearly been a publicity stunt—or so it seemed to the world.

"If you do this, we'll do it shoulder to shoulder," I replied. "I swear to you. I'll be at your side."

"I know you will," Trump said.

Chapter Seven

Stormy Weather (Part One)

During Trump's flirtation with a presidential candidacy in 2011, I'd become his main spokesperson on cable news. I loved being on CNN and MSNBC and Fox, fighting in the Boss's corner, for the fun of the combat and how it was raising my own public profile as well. Some didn't like my pugnacious style, but my audience of one loved it when I went over the top in defending his latest racist or reactionary outbursts. In fact, I started to receive death threats, at the office and on my cell, with a level of frequency that made me apply for a license to carry a gun for self-protection. In New York City, that meant that I had to show the authorities that I had a "special need" to have a weapon on my person, so I was interviewed by an NYPD detective who came to my office to see evidence of the death threats I'd received. As we were talking, my cell phone rang and it was some lunatic ranting and raving and threatening to kill me, which was more than enough to convince the officer that I qualified. Now I was like the Boss and his son

Don Jr. or any other self-respecting New York tough guy: packing heat.

In hindsight, this was another milestone along my road to the madness of true Trump mania. Instead of wondering about the wisdom of facing the wrath of Trump haters uttering threats and risking my life, or pausing to think of the fact that I was doing all this in the service of a pathological liar, or more generally putting my increasingly crazy work duties in context as a sane person might, I purchased two Glock pistols, an ankle holster, and a waist holster that attached to my belt. Walking the streets of Manhattan with my hidden weapons giving an extra strut to my stride, I really had become what I wanted to be as a kid: a gangster lawyer, working for a New York organized crime don and Donald.

With the election ruled out, I was back in the saddle, back to the usual insanity of the Trump Organization. But I had no clue of the nature or extent of the storm, or whirlwind, heading in my direction when I received a call in October of 2011 from a lawyer in LA who identified himself as Keith Davidson, asking if I was Special Counsel to Donald Trump. I replied that I was.

"I represent an individual named Stormy Daniels," Davidson said. "Her real name is Stephanie Clifford. She's an adult entertainer."

"Okay," I said, Googling her stage name and seeing my computer screen fill with images of an extremely busty blonde. "Are you referring to the Stormy Daniels who's a porn star?"

"Yes," he said. "Do you know her work?"

Her "work", I thought?

"No, I just Googled her," I said. "What can I do for you?"

"I need your assistance," Davidson said. "There's currently a story on a website called thedirty.com that depicts an alleged sexual encounter between our clients."

"Are you kidding?" I said. "Do you know that Mr. Trump is a

germaphobe? Where and when was this supposed to have happened?"

By then I was looking at thedirty.com and an anonymous story detailing a sexual encounter between Trump and Stormy Daniels at a "golfing event," without offering details or corroboration. This was not good, I could see, as I waited for Davidson to get to the point of his call.

"The alleged encounter took place in 2006, at a charity golf event in Utah," Davidson said. "But that's not why I'm calling."

"So what can I do for you?"

"Ms. Daniels is equally upset about the story," he said. "She has retained me in part to file a cease-and-desist order forcing the website to remove the story. What I need from you is a statement from Mr. Trump denying the allegation, similar to what I already have from Ms. Daniels. With the two statements, I can accomplish this."

"Wow," I said, actually amazed that the conversation was taking this turn. I was waiting for a shakedown, of some kind, but this attorney from LA was offering to do a favor for the Boss. "Let me go in to Mr. Trump and get you the statement you need. I will call you back shortly."

I printed the article and walked down the hall to see Trump. He was on a call, as usual, so I sat in my regular middle Egg and waited patiently until he finished.

"What's up, Michael?" Trump asked.

"I just received a call from a lawyer in Los Angeles about this," I said, standing and handing him the article.

Trump leaned back in his burgundy chair and read the article, and I swear he started to chuckle.

"Not good, Michael," he said. "Not good. Is this getting any attention? I'm sure Melania isn't going to take this well. So what's this about the lawyer?"

"He represents Stormy Daniels," I said. "And she's denied the allegation. He wants you to do the same so he can file a cease-and-desist and force the site to remove the article."

"So she's denying the story?" Trump asked, his curiosity now piqued, as was mine, but for a different reason—I wondered if it was really true. I knew it wasn't the right time to ask, but I also figured he wouldn't be able to resist the temptation to brag about his conquest of a porn star if it was true; he was in his late sixties at the time and he'd want me to know, even with a wink and a nudge, that he still had game.

"Yes," I said. "And with your permission I will issue a statement on your behalf emphatically denying the allegation."

"Good, good, Michael," he said. "Are you sure she also denies the affair?"

"Yes, Boss. I'll be getting a copy of her denial for my file."

Back in my office, I called Davidson back, on the cell number he'd given me.

"Mr. Trump denies any affair with Ms. Daniels, in Utah or anywhere else," I said, even though I hadn't actually asked that question. "On behalf of Mr. Trump I will be issuing you a statement of denial. Does that work?"

"Yes," he said.

"Can you please send Ms. Daniels's denial for my file and in the event any reporters jump on this story," I asked. "I don't believe it's going to just disappear."

"Absolutely," Keith said. "Give me a few minutes and I'll send it to your email. Thanks for your help."

"No, Keith, thank you, for all you're doing," I said. "I'm sure we'll be talking further about this. I'll get you my statement after receiving yours."

I was correct about the media. I quickly did an online search and discovered that there were a bunch of articles picking up on thedirty.com's lead, including a feature in a publication called *Life & Style* with the heading "Did Donald Cheat" and two pages of photographs of Trump, Melania, and the dyed-blonde porn star, who self-evidently had breast implants.

Knowing Trump would be pissed, I started to work the phones on behalf of the Boss, calling the woman who I'd learned was peddling the Daniels story, a self-styled agent for women with dirt to sell on celebrities and wealthy men named Gina Rodriguez, and issuing a standard form threat: stop this story immediately. Then I emailed the general counsel of *Life & Style* magazine and demanded the story be retracted, but it was too late, because it had gone to press.

When Davidson sent me Daniels's denial letter I printed it out, wrote one for Trump along the same lines, and made my way to the Boss's office again. He was on the phone but I could tell he was agitated about my current mission, and keeping word from reaching his wife.

"So what do you have for me?" he asked, ending his call abruptly.

"A copy of Stormy's letter," I said, passing it to him. "Your statement will be short and mirror her denial."

"Good, Michael," he said, eyeing the document. "Let me know when the lawyer gets that article taken down, if he can. Make sure you keep this letter in case I need it to be sent upstairs. You understand."

"I do," I said, knowing he was referring to his wife. "Don't forget I'm married to an Eastern European woman too. They don't play around when it comes to this kind of stuff."

Trump nodded knowingly, sharing the male resignation to the ways of women, but I also could tell he was eager to tell me the true story. As I'd suspected, he couldn't resist taking credit for bedding a porn star; he wanted me to think he was still a stud, I could tell. Trump's meticulous caution when it came to insulating himself from getting caught in any of his many, many scams and deceptions was thrown to the wind in favor of a moment of pleasure in a sexual brag—like he'd be caught doing four years hence on *Access Hollywood*. To me, he looked like a little kid caught in a lie; I knew he'd slept with Daniels. I thought I'd give him a little nudge, but I figured his juvenile impulse would kick in regardless.

"Ok, Boss," I finally said. "What really happened here?"

"I got stuck going to a charity thing in Utah," he sighed. "I was there with Big Ben Roethlisberger," referring to the Pittsburgh Steeler quarterback and Super Bowl winner. "When these two girls came over to us. When we found out that Stormy was a porn star—can you believe they call them stars?—Big Ben was in heat. The only problem for him was that he was standing next to Trump and all they wanted was Trump. Can you believe it? Big Ben is like this big, amazing quarterback, but all she wanted was Trump."

Trump held up the photo of Daniels in the thedirty.com article and shook his head sadly. The recent image of her showed a woman in her early thirties, pretty in a vah-voom kind of way, but not exactly a study in classy restraint and style, as Trump preferred in his wife and daughters, but his taste for blue-collar pleasures apparently extended to the fairer sex.

"She didn't look like this back then," he said. "That's the problem with time. It's not good to anyone. You should've seen Big Ben going after her. But all they wanted was Trump."

I nodded in agreement. He constantly referred to himself in the third person, a trait that I saw as a quirk at the time, but in hindsight was the indication of dissociative egomania that should have served as a warning. The big point he was making, I knew, was that he'd been in a competition with an NFL star quarterback for the attention of a porn star and the reality TV star was going to win any such showdown, as least in his reckoning. Winning was always, always, always Trump's top priority, no matter the price, less a competitive streak than a compulsion that has led the nation and maybe even the world to the brink of disaster.

Trump told me that he'd offered to get Stormy Daniels on *The Apprentice*, no doubt the real reason that she'd been interested in Trump in the first place. As we all know now, Daniels was a canny operator with an eye on the main prize, so why wouldn't she be interested in networking with a network star and real estate tycoon? Porn was sex in return for money, a transaction Trump could understand, and she must've been chasing a taste of his power and prestige as she submitted to the advances of an obese and hulking married man nearly three times her age in a hotel in Lake Tahoe in 2006.

The Boss said that he'd been unable to convince NBC and Mark Burnett, the producer of *The Apprentice*, that it was a good idea to have a porn star on the show. Daniels was more than a porn star, as we've all discovered: she wrote and directed the films with a certain flair, and she'd managed to start with nothing in life and turn herself into a celebrity, of a kind, or I should say of a kind that Trump was attracted to. Pro wrestling, porn stars, Kentucky Fried Chicken—there was a consistency to his appetites.

In the days ahead, thedirty.com took down the story and it drifted into the ether. Trump wasn't a presidential candidate and his celebrity was barely B-List, truth be told, and it looked like it would stay that way forever, so the currency of the potential scandal quickly dropped in value, as I explained to the Boss. The story was irrelevant and it would quietly and quickly die, I told him. With the mutual denials, the lone remaining concern was that his wife might catch wind of what really amounted to little more than a rumor. Even then, both of us knew, the fallback position was that Mrs. Trump was like countless wives of wealthy men in America and around the world. She knew her husband almost certainly cheated on her, but she'd made her peace with the deal she'd entered into with Trump. She could know it was true, in her heart, but she didn't want to *know*. Like her husband, she relied on plausible deniability. That was where I came in, as Trump's fixer, as he and I both understood intuitively: I was the buffer, offering both the Boss and his long-suffering wife a way to live a lie.

But as Trump looked at the photo of Daniels, it was impossible not to see him reminiscing, in the same way he'd talked about Jill Harth, an aging lion recalling his conquests in the wild, knowing that those glory days were rapidly disappearing into distant memories.

"Man, she would have been great for ratings," Trump said, now with a heavy sigh. "And great for me."

"Not if Melania found out," I said.

"That's for sure," he said. "Now get out of here and go finish this. Let me know if anything new happens."

"Yes, Boss."

Chapter Eight

That's What Friends Are For

Why does Donald Trump have no friends? Perhaps the story of the Trump Winery in 2011 will shed some light on the matter of what it's like to be his "friend." For years, Trump had been friends with John Kluge, a media conglomerate billionaire in the 1980s, and once one of the wealthiest and best-known men in America; he'd topped the *Forbes* list as the richest man in the world in 1984. Kluge had accumulated the collection of independent TV stations that would eventually be put together to form the Fox network under Rupert Murdoch, and Kluge had moved in the same social circles in Palm Beach and New York that Trump inhabited.

Kluge also shared the Boss's propensity for messy divorces. By the 1980s, Kluge's third wife was named Patricia, a former nude model with a faux upper-class British accent who'd married a man nearly three decades older than her, only, inevitably, to get divorced a few years later. In the settlement, the former Mrs. Kluge took possession of a house in Charlottesville, Virginia, called Albemarle, along with a cash settlement of $100 million. The house wasn't a mansion, it was whatever was bigger and more impressive than that—more like a castle. The forty-five-room colossus was surrounded by more than 200 acres that she turned into a vineyard making fine sparkling wines, a high prestige, high-risk business. Like many divorcees or widows of wealthy men, she had expensive property and fancy jewelry and tastes, but not enough income to maintain the lifestyle she'd become accustomed to after she sold the rights to her annuity, so she ran up a mountain of debt that she couldn't sustain in the aftermath of the global financial crisis of 2008. Leveraging the vineyard to take out more and more loans, her wine company was soon forced into default by its bank.

By 2010, she'd been compelled to hold two auctions to sell jewelry and furniture, raising $15 million, but even that sum hadn't kept Patricia Kluge from having to declare bankruptcy. This was a classic example of how Trump read the newspaper, for deals and opportunities, not the news; he'd figured she had to be a billionaire, so he was amazed when he came across reports of her destitute status. When she came to Trump Tower to meet the Boss in 2011, it was instantly obvious to him that she was in deep trouble—and she was going to be in even deeper trouble in short order.

A "friend" approaching Trump for assistance in a time of need was making a mistake of epic proportions. Trump doesn't help people, he preys on them, and buying the estates of the formerly super wealthy was a specialty of his, as his purchase of Mar-a-Lago illustrated; beating down the price and taking advantage of people who'd once been wealthier than the Boss gave him a kind of existential and karmic thrill. His crocodile tears and fake empathy for the downfallen ex-wife of a recently deceased good friend were preposterous, as I could see his mind was spinning a million miles an hour trying to figure out how to acquire the property for the lowest possible number.

She was trying to sell the house and vineyard at auction for $100 million, but Trump told me there was no way he was going to pay that much, nor would anyone else. He was going to get it cheap and his method of approach to such matters was to find a point of weakness to exploit. In this case, the Kluges had an adopted son who was also in financial distress, a common occurrence in wealthy families, Trump told me; every family has a weak link, he believed. Trump learned that the land near the vineyard, including more than 200 acres that had to be crossed to get to the estate, was held in a trust for Mrs. Kluge's only son.

"Kluge's son is a complete mess," Trump told me, as he explained what he'd done. "He was desperate for money. So I bought the right of first refusal to acquire the land next to the vineyard for $500,000. Now I have a lien on the son's interest and he won't be able to do anything with the property unless it goes to me."

Holy shit, I thought: classic Trump. He'd identified the weak link in his adversary—because that's what Patricia Kluge really was to him by now—and he was going to exploit it.

"Are you serious, Boss?" I asked.

"Yeah," Trump said. "They can do whatever they want with the land but they will have to deal with me. It's complicated, but the land and house are split into separate entities, and the land is the real value. The house is worth very little without the land surrounding it. Trust me, I am going to own this property on the cheap."

Trump greedily flicked through a portfolio of photographs of Albemarle and the rolling hills of Virginia. The place really was spectacular.

"This will be my next acquisition," he said. "Trump Winery."

Applying the brutal logic of New York real estate, Trump arranged for "No Trespassing" signs to be put up all along the road to greet visitors to the estate and he let the grass go un-mowed so that anyone driving up to view the potential investment would have to wonder about the manner in which the gateway property was kept, thus damaging the valuation and functionality of the estate as a place of business.

With a lien on the adjacent land, and no takers on land at the exorbitant price, coupled with a derelict neighboring property, Trump approached the bank then holding the remaining Kluge land through bankruptcy. By then Kluge had gone bankrupt, making her even more vulnerable—as Trump knew from personal experience. Control of the land with the right-of-way easement for the only access to the estate did indeed make Trump the only possible buyer, the bank had to reluctantly admit. The bank was trapped, selling him the underlying land of the vineyard for $6.2 million, plus $1.7 million for the equipment and inventory, far less than the $16 million paid at the foreclosure auction.

This left the house, which was a separate parcel of property, and Trump had a plan for this stage of the game, as well.

"You know, Michael, I'm the only possible buyer for the house, too," Trump said.

"I agree that the house has to be part of the land," I said. "But they could sell to someone who doesn't care about the acreage in the front of the house."

"No chance," Trump barked, opening up a map of the parcels of land to show me. "You drive in from the front gate. It's a fifty-acre drive up to the house. I own all the land in front and on the sides of the house. So here's what I'm going to do. I'm going to build a wall."

"A wall?" I asked. "For what reason?"

"I'm going to build a wall right in front of the house," Trump said. "I'm going to put up a twenty-foot concrete wall with Trump Winery painted every twenty feet in massive letters. Can you imagine waking up in Kluge's mansion and looking out the fucking bedroom window and all you see is a concrete wall with my name on it?"

Trump laughed.

"Now, there's a real fucking selling point," he said.

"Holy shit," I said, out loud this time. "You just made a $50 million house worthless. Even worse for the bank, they have to maintain the house to make sure it's salable in the meantime. They're going have to spend real money."

"Exactly," Trump said triumphantly. "I'm speaking to the bank later today. By the end of the day I'll own the whole fucking thing."

And so it came to pass. Trump bought the house for $6.7 million, making the total purchase price for the entire estate less than $13 million, when the asking price had been more than $100 million. There was an undeniable kind of genius to Trump's approach, a completely amoral will to win, no matter the cost—in this case, essentially taking away the Kluges' son's inheritance in one fell swoop.

Even better, Trump bragged to me as he celebrated his victory, there were millions of dollars' worth of excellent wine in the inventory of the vineyard, which he could rebrand as Trump Wines and sell in his golf courses and hotel bars, yet another win.

"What a deal," Trump said to me. "I just stole the property. In this case someone else's loss is Trump's gain."

He pulled out a bottle of wine.

"Here's a bottle of red," Trump said. "Take it home and try it out with Laura. I hear it's the best sparkling red on the market."

The story could end there, with Trump putting his son Eric in charge of the vineyard, but that was never how things went at the Trump Organization. Because get this: Trump made Patricia Kluge think he'd done her a favor. Seriously. She was bankrupted and walked away without a penny, her son was essentially disinherited, despite once having a father who was the richest man on the planet, and somehow she was happy with the transaction. I knew Trump had hired her and her current husband to work for Eric at the vineyard, with a one-year contract for $250,000—which he terminated at the end of the year, of course. Kluge had been ripped off by the worst jackal of them all and she didn't even know it, and probably doesn't to this day. And she was grateful for being torn to shreds and devoured, a fact that boggled my mind.

"My worst nightmare and personal Armageddon are finally over," she told the *Daily Beast* at the time Trump took over her vineyard. "I'm thrilled beyond belief. Now I can finally relax, take a week off, go on vacation."

That was the real real art of the deal—or steal.

*   *   *

BUT DON'T GET the impression Trump was always or even usually a rational player. He knew how to take advantage of others, but there was an essential foolishness, even idiocy, to insisting on getting his way all the time. Let me give you an example of his ruinous and relentless need to always "win."

Later in 2011, a lawyer friend of mine in Miami called to say that he was representing the Doral golf club in Miami in its Chapter 11 bankruptcy proceedings. He wondered if this was a property that might interest the Trump Organization. I immediately knew this was a prospect the Boss would want to hear about, so I asked my friend to send me the documents related to the Doral. Two large binders arrived the following day via FedEx laying out the details and specifications for the impending sale of the property, one of the most prestigious clubs in the country and the home of the legendary Blue Monster course; it was also the site of a PGA Tournament Trump was desperate to host. I read the terms of the proposed sale with growing excitement: the project didn't just suit

Trump's portfolio of golf courses, it epitomized the themes of excellence and luxury, together with a ton of history and prestige. Doral wouldn't just be another golf acquisition, it would become one of the pearls of the Trump Organization.

I picked up the deal books, stepped over to Trump's office, and knocked on his door, as usual. He waved me in, in the familiar way that happened dozens of times a day, and I sat and told him that I'd bird-dogged a deal through a business associate that put us in the inside position to buy Doral. Trump wasn't excited—he was thrilled. The look on his face when he got a dose of deal fever was always fun to behold, a mixture of delight and aggression and determination. Hitting the intercom button on his speakerphone, he called for Ivanka to come up from the 25th floor, where the kids each had an office.

I was about to learn another lesson about treachery and Ivanka and how the Trump family operated. For years, I had been very friendly with Ivanka. She was my neighbor at Trump Park Avenue, and when she was single it wasn't unusual for her to stop over for a casual pasta dinner with my family; she loved my homemade lasagna. We joked around with each other and she enjoyed the banter of business and gossip and the media. She wasn't like one of the bros, but she was no shrinking flower or delicate debutante; she wanted to be in business with the big boys and her ambition and sharp elbows were evident. But she changed when she got involved with Jared Kushner, the scion of a New Jersey real estate family with its own history of troubles and woes. Kushner was supremely arrogant, a real snob, to be honest, with an exaggerated sense of his importance and intelligence. I would occasionally see him in the gym at Trump Park Avenue, or at the office, but for the most part he kept me at arm's length—which was more than fine with me.

As I explained the Doral deal to Ivanka, I could see her eyes widening, much like her father's had. There was a way of conducting business inside the Trump Organization, with nothing written down but an understanding that whoever brought a deal to the company got to work the deal; all deals were ultimately for the benefit and glorification of Donald J. Trump, of course, but finding attractive transactions was a way of keeping score and getting ahead, and this Doral acquisition promised to be a huge win for the company.

For the most part, Ivanka worked her own brands, including her lines of clothing and handbags, but she and the other Trump children also wanted to do deals for the main company. After a few days, wondering when I was going to get word from the Boss to proceed on Doral, my friend called to say that Ivanka had come down to Miami and started talks to buy the golf course, without so much as a word or a nod in my direction. As the deal proceeded, I was kept in the dark, with no explanation or justification or apology. That was how the Trumps worked, I was seeing, with guard rails around anything that might serve their interests. In this selfish and self-serving way, Ivanka was very much her father's daughter; my lawyer buddy commiserated, but business was business.

The final price for the Doral Hotel and Spa was $150 million, financed by a loan of $125 million from Deutsche Bank, and a complete renovation was quickly undertaken at the cost of $250 million. The plan was a "return to grandeur" for the run-down resort. The multiple golf courses were to be redone, along with the hotel and pool area, with nearly 700 guest rooms reimagined in tasteful minimalist neutral colors, but with the Trumpian touch of gilded gold accents.

"When completed, Doral will be the finest resort and golf club in the country," Trump told the press.

As the renovation continued, I discovered that despite the rhetoric, Trump was cutting corners, having "cheap attacks," and screwing the many contractors and subcontractors who were working on the project. This wasn't unusual, and a significant part of my job description involved dealing with vendors the Boss had decided to rip off. This behavior was part of what constituted "loyalty" to Donald Trump: whatever he wanted done, I would do, no matter how dishonest, or dishonorable. Trump saved the crappiest jobs for me, a fact that I took pride in; I was given the dirty work because I was willing to get dirt on my hands—and blood if necessary.

If that seems bizarre to you, think about it like being under the spell of a cult leader. I don't mean that as a cliché or an accusation: I mean literally. How did Jim Jones get his followers in Guyana to drink the poisoned Kool-Aid (actually, it was a cheap knockoff called Flavor Aid) and commit mass suicide? The answer was that Jones took control of the minds of those drawn to him, not all at once but gradually, over time, by luring them into his mind.

"Stop drinking the Kool-Aid," we would say to each other at the Trump Organization all the time.

The joke wasn't really a joke, even as we joshed around. Trump would say so many things that were illogical or just plain bullshit, as we consciously would know, but we would stay on his message, even though we knew it was nonsense. We would repeat what he said, as if it were true, and then we'd repeat the message to one another so often that we would actually begin to believe the distortions ourselves.

This mind meld is what I see every day as I sit in prison watching the nightly news from the White House. Trump's staff and advisors aren't all so stupid that they don't understand, for example, that extorting the President of Ukraine to investigate Democratic candidate Joe Biden is a terrible, terrible idea and precedent, or that downplaying a global pandemic might work for one news cycle but will only harm innocent people over time. But witness the politicians and media folks like Sean Hannity and Rush

Limbaugh making excuses for Trump, or saying he did nothing wrong. Or the pathetic spectacle of Rudy Giuliani committing *harakiri* for Trump, just like I used to do, somehow imagining that the fate that befell me and Roy Cohn won't happen to him—as if the rules of gravity have been suspended magically. Think of all the responsible and conservative and moral, even devoutly religious, Trump supporters not just rationalizing or explaining away his transparent dishonesty, but actually turning it upside down and saying it's perfectly normal.

Franz Mesmer was a German doctor in the eighteenth century who believed in a phenomenon he called "animal magnetism." He would mesmerize people using actual magnets, but Trump doesn't need any physical props to succeed in getting his followers to do what I did—virtually anything he wanted. Part of it was a function of loyalty, which led to willful blindness. There was also a fever-pitched desire to please that made me sycophantic, it's true to say. But there was another element that rarely gets discussed: Trump is a master at getting otherwise seemingly sensible people to enter into his fantasyland because of the fear that failure to do so means banishment. This explains the behavior of many members of Congress and the Cabinet, as displayed daily in the news, terrified of facing a primary or a tweet or a tantrum. It was a huge part of a process that I fell victim to and know intimately. Once the small lies and delusions pass, then it became easier and easier to swallow bigger and bigger lies and delusions.

I know this insanity up close and personal.

Take the paint job during the renovation of the Doral. One afternoon in 2014, I was summoned to Trump's office. As I walked in, Trump was on a call with David Fader, the general manager of the Trump Doral, talking on the speakerphone. The pair were discussing the paint used in the renovation of the buildings and guest rooms at the Doral. When the house staff wiped down the walls of the rooms, as part of a routine cleaning, it appeared that the fresh paint was coming off. The walls were becoming spotty and discolored and faded, only weeks after the new paint had been applied.

"We just painted the entire goddamn place," Trump said to Fader. "I hear the rooms look like shit. Get the fucking painters back and make them redo the entire job. Tell them, I'm not paying for their time or paint."

Trump turned to me.

"Michael just walked in. He will call you and the two of you better figure this out."

Trump hung up. Following orders, I went to my office and dialed up Fader to discuss a course of action to get the painters to correct the obviously poor job they had performed for the Trump Organization. I was already mustering my outrage, girding for battle, when David told me the truth.

"I told him to not use that paint," Fader said.

"What are you talking about?" I said. "What's going on here?"

"Look, Michael," Fader said. "There are levels of quality involved in the Benjamin Moore paint the Boss chose. We needed at least a level-three quality. But the Boss decided to go with the absolute cheapest level-one paint, which is pure garbage. It requires more paint to cover the wall, but it also doesn't last. So that's the explanation. It wasn't meant for this kind of commercial job."

I burst out laughing, at least initially. The situation was absurd. Trump had had a "cheap attack" and made a poor decision on the type of paint the contractor should use, which didn't surprise me in the slightest. Trump was constantly making errors, large and small, like pretty much any human being. The difference was that Trump would never acknowledge his errors. Hell, he wouldn't just deny his own mistakes, he'd blame others, circular logic that best resembled a Mexican standoff that left everyone pointing their guns at each other—but never Trump.

Does that sound familiar to you?

For all the ridiculousness of the situation, I knew Trump was pissed and that I had to come up with a plan for my sake, and for David's sake, a fact that we both understood intuitively. Going to Trump and telling him that he'd ordered the worst-quality Benjamin Moore paint available would only result in our instant dismissal or a screaming fit with blame hurled in all directions, except himself, with the net result that we would be back where we started: with a delusional proposition that had to be supported as fact, despite the blatantly obvious truth that it was a lie.

Ring a bell?

I sat at my desk and weighed the options. David emailed the contract and sure enough the Benjamin Moore paint specified in the invoice was exactly as described. Super Hide paint was well known in the industry as low-quality, and not meant to last. The Super Hide level was used to paint new houses that were going to be flipped, or by fly-by-night painters playing their customers for fools—or by clients foolish enough to cut corners.

How on earth could I blame the contractor for using the paint specified by the customer? In normal circumstances, a complaint like this would be treated for what it was: idiotic. But not in the Trump Organization, I knew. I resolved to bluff my way through the problem, like a gambler with a bad poker hand going all in.

I called the painting contractor, introducing myself as Trump's Special Counsel and Executive Vice President, credentials that usually had the effect of grabbing people's attention. When I described the situation, the contractor was amazed but also pissed that I was bringing up the quality of the paint. He explained that he had told the folks from the Trump Organization that Super Hide was inferior and not suited to a project like Doral, with high use and the inevitable wear and tear of a hotel and golf club. The contractor then raised his own issue. He said that Trump hadn't paid for the work he'd completed and he couldn't make payroll; he was barely making his costs on the job and he needed to be paid in a timely fashion. I explained that payment wasn't my issue, but I could tell that I wasn't going to get anything from this small timer struggling to keep his business alive.

I decided to up the stakes. I was going to go after Benjamin Moore directly, I decided. When I called the company and identified myself, stressing, as always, my high-level positions, I was put through to the secretary of the CEO. The executive wasn't available, the secretary said, but I explained why I was calling in detail and told her that the Trump Organization had been sold faulty paint and demanded a refund. Assured I would receive a return call, I reported back to Trump, who immediately went into a rant about the shitty paint and how I needed to rectify the problem.

"Michael, go do your thing," Trump said, "Don't disappoint me."

The words hung in the air, and then swirled around in my mind as I returned to my office. This was now on me? I didn't order the paint, Trump did, but that was how the flow chart worked in the Trump Organization. The buck didn't stop at Donald Trump's desk: it never got there. What "don't disappoint me" actually meant, I knew, was an implicit threat that I would be fired if I didn't somehow resolve a situation he had created to his satisfaction. All of the staff at the Trump Organization routinely joked about how any given day could be your last, pressure that you might think would drive us away but in fact made us all the more determined to defend Trump and do what he wanted, no matter how morally or legally dubious.

The return call from Benjamin Moore didn't come from the CEO. The Florida director of regional sales was on the line, politely offering his assistance.

"Nice to speak with you, Mr. Cohen," the director said.

"Likewise," I replied. "We seem to have a problem with the paint Mr. Trump purchased for Doral."

I read out the invoice and the detailed identification of the paint and pointed out that the paint had proved to have been of extremely low quality; the paint came off the wall when washed and failed to adhere properly.

The director promised to discuss the issue with the quality control department, but he reassured me that the company stood behind its products one hundred percent.

"I appreciate your help," I said. "I suggest you call me back this afternoon, because Mr. Trump is really angry and he has asked me to make the resolution of this issue a priority."

I knew the director was rattled. By this time I had convinced myself that the paint actually was somehow defective. I know, I know: I was sharing the Trump delusion. But that was the alchemy, and I see it traveling throughout the White House and beyond all the time. In defending the indefensible, you can't resort to reason or facts or good business practices; you can't appeal to conscience or justice or fairness. All that is left is what I resorted to, and what Trump displays so often: rage.

The next call followed that pattern. The director wanted to be reasonable. They had batch tested the paint, he said, and it was fine for the level of quality of Super Hide. He asked me to arrange for a gallon of the paint at Doral to be sent to their test lab to be assessed to see if it differed from the standard Super Hide paint. He offered to pick up the gallon, if that was easier. He wanted to find a mutually agreeable solution, which made perfect sense—but I knew it meant that the contention that the paint was flawed would be shown to be a lie. Super Hide was Super Hide, after all. The director promised that the company would be transparent in determining the quality of the paint. He pledged his word.

Enough, I screamed inwardly. The only arrow I had in my quiver was the one I fired: I lost it.

"Take your pledge, which is worthless at this point. The paint is pure shit. It doesn't stick to the walls. It wipes off when the rooms are being cleaned."

I took a breath.

"Here is what I want you to do. Go speak to whoever you need to speak to. Then take out your checkbook and overnight to me a check with a full refund of all of our costs."

The director replied that he had talked to both the contractor and the Trump representative who placed the order and they confirmed that Super Hide was the grade specified. Mr. Trump had personally made the decision, after being informed of the quality issues such a cheap paint would inevitably have. Under the circumstances, with no proof of any issues related to the paint, it was impossible to offer any compensation.

You're going to challenge me, I thought? You know who you're talking to, buddy boy, I thought. Fuck you. Game on.

"Is this your final decision?" I asked, now quaking with anger. "Let me play out the scenario for you and your entire executive team. Before close of business today I will be instructed by Mr. Trump to pursue all legal rights and remedies, in law and in equity, against Benjamin Moore for the sale of your defective product. As with every lawsuit filed with a Trump trademark attached, significant media attention sadly becomes a reality and statements from people like me and our public relations department will ensue. Are you really going to explain to your customers that you manufacture a paint that doesn't adhere to a wall? A paint that you can't maintain? A paint you can't stand behind? Or that Super Hide is such a low classification that it should only be used for things like school projects?"

I was indignant by then. Kind of like you see the President's defenders on the nightly cable talk shows: red-faced, nearly shouting, filled with righteous rage.

"I don't think so," I said, sarcastically. "I want you to explain to the public how you differentiate between products you will and won't stand behind with your Benjamin Moore one hundred percent guarantee promise. Please, don't even try to respond. First, what you say I will not buy and it will not be accepted by Mr. Trump. Second, I really don't care what you have to say. I was hoping to resolve this amicably and to be able to continue to do business with Benjamin Moore for our future needs. But now you throw this bullshit at me? No thank you. Before we hang up, tell me the name of your counsel and tell me the correct address for receipt of service of process for the company."

"Mr. Cohen, Mr. Cohen, please wait . . . " the director pleaded. "I never said I was finished. I just was telling you what corporate told me. Please give me a little time to speak with them again. I'll call you back later today, or tomorrow at the latest."

"Fine," I said. "I will need to begin drafting the lawsuit in the meantime."

Hanging up, I knew I was going to get a good resolution—I knew I was going to "win." The only question was whether the offer Benjamin Moore was now going to make, as I felt sure they would, would be enough to satisfy the Boss.

The next call began with the director defending the company's stellar reputation. He said the company disagreed with my statements and how I had characterized its business ethics, pausing and then continuing, but in these circumstances he had been instructed to find a resolution. I knew better than to make the first offer; as a personal injury and medical malpractice attorney, I learned to always let the other side shoot first; the first offer served as the floor for future talks.

After a lot more back and forth, it was agreed that Benjamin Moore would give us 10,000 gallons of paint for free, to compensate for the poor-quality Super Hide. The wholesale price for the better-quality paint was around $30 a gallon more than Super Hide, so the amount was substantial. The snag was that we had no need for so much paint, let alone anywhere to safely store several semi-trailer loads of paint. As a gesture of my generosity and reasonableness, I suggested as a solution that the company give the Trump Organization a credit for the 10,000 gallons, to be used over time. The director was thrilled with this idea and as soon as I had an email confirming the arrangement I went to see Trump.

When I walked in, Trump was on the speakerphone, which he placed on mute when I put the printed email on his desk. I told him what had happened, with a real sense of pride.

Trump chuckled. "This is great," he said. "I just wanted to see if you could get something from Benjamin Moore. I didn't expect this. Great job."

I floated back to my office, as usual after receiving his praise. This episode encapsulated my decade as Donald Trump's personal lawyer. The lie turned into a delusion turned into a supposed reality and then a grievance, followed by more lies, more bullying, and ultimately the ruthlessness of New York real estate—where lying and cheating and stealing are the order of the day—unleashed on folks with no clue about the depravity and dishonesty of the TV star and self-styled mogul.

But that wasn't the end of the Doral story, not by a long shot. The painting contractor eventually walked off the job, no doubt in frustration at not being paid in a timely fashion. Scores of small contractors have had to sue Trump over the years to try to get justice against a billionaire who has absolutely no compunction about screwing the little guy. I know because I was often the one tasked with doing such lowlife things to innocent and honest business people providing goods and services to the Trump Organization. I hated myself for what I did, even as I did it, but that didn't stop me, and I have no excuses to offer. But you might detect a theme that applies to the politics of today: Trump's version of loyalty is one way, as I famously learned, just like so many others have—indeed, like the nation has. But loyalty to Trump means the willingness to do things you know to be wrong and that are harming others.

With Trump there was always the domino effect: when he screwed one small business, he would hurt others, the impact cascading into family-owned companies struggling to make ends meet. The same thing happened in Miami, only this time one businessman fought back. After the fiasco with the Super Hide paint, the contractor quit and this, in turn, led to an unpaid local paint supplier named The Paint Spot suing and putting a lien on the entire Doral property. The claim was for $32,000 in paint that was never paid for by Trump Endeavor, the entity operating the resort. As always, Trump's litigators in Florida fought the case tooth and nail, threatening the business owner with ruinous legal costs just as he was about to give a deposition.

"Let's play ball," the owner, Juan Carlos Enriquez, said, as NBC News reported in 2017.

I wasn't shocked when I read the press report. I was still on the inside in Trump's world—more of that story down the road—but I knew as much as anyone the real truth of his business ethics, or lack thereof. The story described how Enriquez had run up huge legal bills with his own attorney, a risk that he'd dealt with by putting the lawyer on contingency—which was easy for the attorney to do because the claim for nonpayment was so obviously valid. In the end, Enriquez had incurred nearly $300,000 in legal fees, a sum he couldn't possibly pay.

"This is a company that just started," Enriquez said. "Where am I going to get $300,000? I would have gone bankrupt."

Not that Trump would have cared. That was the whole point of the Trump legal strategy: to make it impossible for the little guy to stand up for his rights. And make no mistake, the lack of ethics applied equally to his three children, despite Ivanka's carefully tended image—all them are like jackals when it comes to harming innocent businesspeople.

After winning the case, getting a judgment against Trump for nonpayment, plus the large legal bill, Enriquez said he was going to open another paint store. But there was one challenge, according to NBC News.

"I still haven't gotten my money," Enriquez told the NBC reporter.

Chapter Nine

The End of the World

Explaining exactly how Trump came to dominate my thoughts, night and day, for years on end, isn't a simple one-dimensional undertaking. The first vital ingredient was my desire to please him, which was matched by my fear of displeasing the Boss. Over and over again, these two co-equal motivations urged me further and further into the embrace of his way of seeing the world and life. But another element of Trump's gaslighting genius involved his ability to attract a certain type of person into his inner world. It's something you can recognize in the news today, with the likes of Lindsey Graham and Jim Jordan and Mike Pompeo and the other people surrounding Trump. The Boss had an unerring eye for sycophants: yes men, loyal soldiers, call them what you will. During my years at the Trump Organization, there was a small, hardcore group of executives who formed a cadre around Trump. There was Alan Garten, co-general counsel and litigation director (a full-time job in a company with a sue-first impulse), Executive Vice

President and legal counsel George Sorial, and Larry Glick, who ran the entire golf operation for Trump—plus me, as Executive Vice President and Special Counsel to the Boss. We saw each other through the good times and the bad times, becoming friends and partners in the craziness that constituted life on the 25th and 26th floors of Trump Tower.

The four of us were all different, with different skill sets and points of view, but we shared the same ultimate task: protecting and fighting for Donald Trump. In the same way the Republican party has been taken over by the President, each of us in this group of loyal soldiers had dedicated our consciousness and consciences to him.

In 2013, that meant trying to find solutions to the rolling disaster that was Trump University. Originally conceived of as a strict licensing deal, Trump had insisted on owning the vast majority of the equity in the New York company posing as an institution of higher learning by offering get-rich-quick schemes in the real estate business. Trading on his reputation as a billionaire dealmaker, Trump convinced folks to pay from $1,500 for a three-day course to as much as $35,000 for the "gold" plated degree. The fact that the "University" was little more than a mail-order diploma, with the courses consisting of receiving photocopies of boilerplate real estate basics, was part of the problem, but so was setting up an educational institution without any of the necessary legal or regulatory approvals.

The consequences of this fly-by-night approach were closing in by 2013, with the New York State Attorney General investigating Trump University and the Texas AG also making noises that he was going to look into the shadier business practices of the school's hardcore sales tactics and shoddy organization. Student complaints were proliferating, and it was only a matter of time before the terrible quality of the education offered by Trump University caught up with the Boss. Using coercive tactics, officials running the "school" urged "students" to give the University and the "teachers" great reviews, but that was solely so they could receive their "diploma," hardly a fair way to conduct market research or get real feedback. To the contrary, the ninety-eight percent approval rating best resembled Vladimir Putin's election results or Kim Jong-un's approval rating in North Korea.

The four of us in the Trump Organization were running interference in the unfolding lawsuits and government investigations. George Sorial was in charge of dealing with the many formal complaints from students and regulators, including negotiations with Texas that promised to be resolved with a mutually agreed settlement to cover the most egregious legal violations of Trump University.

"We should be able to close out the entire matter with a settlement of $500,000," George told Trump during a conference in the Boss's office.

"What?" Trump said. "I don't settle. We did nothing wrong. We have a ninety-eight percent approval rating from our students. I bet we have a better approval rating than Harvard. No settling. Get them to drop the matter."

Trump turned to me. "Michael, what are you doing to close this fucking mess down?"

"Boss, I created a spreadsheet of all the vendors and tabulated the debt at around five million," I said. "I spoke to Weisselberg, who told me there is around one million in cash in the bank for the company, so it looks like the vendors are going to have to take an eighty percent discount. Don't worry, Boss. George and I are on it and we know what you want."

"Keep me posted," Trump said.

As we walked to my office, George was despondent. "The Boss is insane," he said. "I know these people in Texas. They will never drop the inquiry."

"Do what you can," I said. "Try to get the number down. If we stick together, maybe he'll agree to settle and move on."

Screwing small businesses again, the script was the same for more than 100 vendors for Trump University. I told them that the "school" only had $1M in cash to meet all its liabilities, which came to $5M, so they had to take twenty cents on the dollar, or sue the company in bankruptcy, which would only drag out the inevitable and waste even more money and time. I explained that I understood that they deserved to be paid, but I had been directed by Mr. Trump to close the licensing deal down; it wasn't really a licensing deal, but calling it that was designed to give them pause about suing. Would they be able to go after Trump's deep pockets, or only the remaining legal entity? This doubt was my leverage. I then told them I was working on the final tax return, to permanently shutter the business, so this was their last opportunity to get paid.

"Do you understand what I'm telling you?" I'd said.

"Yes," they'd replied. "A billionaire Donald Trump isn't going to pay me, a poor person trying to earn a living. So what are you offering?"

"Twenty percent of the invoice," I would reply.

Silence ensued, as doom and the walls closed in. One after another, faced with the prospect of pouring more good money after a bad debt, they capitulated. As I accumulated the releases, I reported to Trump's office to receive his gleeful approval. To Trump, this represented winning, and I never once witnessed a glimmer of sympathy or humanity or regret or shame in his demeanor.

"Michael, my man, you're the greatest," he'd say.

I basked in the praise, like the jerk I had become. Like my testimony before Congress—the time I lied, that is, not the time I told the truth, and, yes, I know how bad that sounds—I knew what I was doing was wrong, but I couldn't stop it; I didn't want to stop it. I took a weird kind of pleasure in harming others in the service of Donald Trump, to my eternal shame. I kept this inner reality hidden from my wife and kids. I knew perfectly well that they wouldn't approve of what I was doing; to the contrary, it would disgust and dismay them. So I never discussed this kind of dirty business with them. Ever. Until one night, when Laura and I were out to dinner with acquaintances at Elio's, our favorite uptown Italian restaurant.

"I heard you spoke with my comptroller yesterday," my acquaintance said.

"What are you talking about?" I replied.

"You spoke to my comptroller to settle an outstanding invoice for Trump University," he said. "Seriously, Michael. Twenty percent, take it or leave it? My cost of goods is eighty percent, so I'm losing money. This is just wrong."

My heart rate spiked, and I grew lightheaded as Laura looked me dead in the eye, a look of cold exasperation on her face.

"What did you do now, Michael?" she asked.

My acquaintance explained to my wife how I'd ripped off his business on behalf of Donald Trump and how despicable it was to treat small businesses that way. I had no defense. I recognized the name of his business when he told me—I hadn't put one and one together—and it was undeniably true what he was telling Laura.

"I didn't know that was your company," I said. "I'm sorry. My hands are tied."

We sat awkwardly, Laura crestfallen at her husband's behavior, and not for the last time, until the businessman's wife sighed and said that they knew it wasn't my fault—as if that was some form of excuse—and we shouldn't ruin our dinner. Conversation turned to the veal *parmigiana* as I inspected my menu, feeling two inches tall. This was the price paid for working for a supposedly great businessman, the genius behind *The Art of the Deal*. The fraud.

"I'm going to enjoy this meal," the husband said. "You know why, Michael? Because dinner is on you."

"Absolutely," I replied.

* * *

In Trump World, there were two kinds of invitations that were the most coveted to his circle of friends, admirers, celebrity hangers-on, and wannabes. The first was a chance to play golf with Trump at one of his clubs. In theory, that meant the person invited had to have at least a five handicap, which severely limited the number of people eligible for this great honor (as he imagined it to be). But, as with everything Trump, the rule was more honored in the breach than in the observance. Handicaps, as anyone who has golfed with Trump knows, were an incredibly flexible concept for the Boss. Serious golfers consider themselves honor-bound to record every round they play, in order to fairly and accurately track their handicap; golf is ultimately a self-regulated sport, so a lot can be known about a man's ethics by examining how he manages his handicap; to say that Trump was economical with the truth about his golf game would be the polite way to put it.

I wasn't much of a golfer, much preferring tennis, but I witnessed Trump on the links from time to time. Despite all the cheating, and his truly godawful swing, Trump was actually a pretty good golfer. His drives were long and straight and seemingly blessed by good bounces or breaks; when he shanked or sliced a drive it seemed like it would always—well, okay, not always, but often—bounce off a tree and end up on the fairway. He was like Rodney Dangerfield in *Caddyshack*. But around the greens he routinely did things like call a chip shot a gimme—a truly ridiculous liberty—or give his ball a nudge or a kick to get a more favorable lie. I figured that was how Trump had always encountered the world, as a boy born with a silver spoon (or shovel) in his mouth:

he got special treatment, had liberties denied others, and that applied to his beloved golf game as well.

The second variety of coveted invitation was far more exclusive and elusive: the offer to accompany Trump to the Miss Universe or Miss USA pageants. These invitations were rare and highly prized, and in this regard I was a member in good standing of Trump's innermost circle. Not only was I regularly invited to these pageants; I was on the board of directors of the Miss Universe Organization, the corporation that ran both events. Trump owned fifty percent of the entity, with NBC Universal owning the other half. To reflect his equity position, the Boss had three seats on the seven-person board, to match NBC's three seats, with the seventh possessed by the president of the Miss Universe Organization, or MUO, as we called it. I knew I was for sure a highly valued and loyal Trump executive when he appointed me to the board in 2010, a honor usually reserved for himself or his kids.

"Congratulations, Michael," Trump said at the time. "You are now a board member of MUO. I hope your wife won't mind."

"Why do you say that?" I asked. "Does the board seat come with perks I'm unaware of?"

"Michael, you have no idea how beautiful these women are," he replied. "Just make sure you stay married."

"Don't worry, Boss," I said. "I'm sure my marriage will survive."

"Wait until you get backstage as these beauties are getting dressed and made up," he said. "They are the finest pieces of ass from every state and country."

Every year Trump and I would flick through the photo book containing the shots of the contestants from all over the world in bathing suits. We were like a pair of fifth graders slobbering over the images, as we flipped from page to page weighing the merits of each entrant.

"Wow, what a piece of ass," Trump would say.

"Shit, it looks like this one could kill you in bed."

"Man, she has gorgeous skin."

Trump would go on and on in wonderment as he drooled over the photos.

In 2012, the Miss Universe Pageant was to be held in Las Vegas, so Trump and I set off with a posse of executives and friends, including the omnipresent one-man security detail named Keith Schiller, a former NYPD cop who was always at Trump's side. Trump had a new Boeing 757 that year, and flying in his private jet contained a secret language, known only to initiates: where you sat on the plane demonstrated your importance and relationship to the Boss. There were three areas. In the front there was the cockpit, a private sitting area for four people, and two bedrooms. In the middle there was executive seating, including sofas and a 120-inch flat screen TV. In the rear there were a dozen first-class seats, relative Siberia on Trump's plane. I sat in the middle section, a symbol of my role as his private attorney and confidant always ready and at hand, always the eager courtier.

Landing in Vegas, there were six black SUVs waiting on the tarmac, each assigned to take part of the entourage to Trump International Hotel Las Vegas, all of us with pre-assigned rooms, room keys on hand and our luggage quickly stowed in the back—a hyper-efficient system that allowed us to concentrate on why we'd come to the city: for fun.

"Hey Boss," I called out. "The hotel or the pageant? They're doing rehearsals for the next two hours."

"Pageant," Trump declared, without hesitation. "Michael, wait until you see the production they put into this event. Depending on where they are in the rehearsals, maybe we can catch a few of them in the back getting dressed. They are truly the best of the best."

Silence was often the best response to Trump, I had learned, especially when it came to lewd remarks. There was really nothing to say, I knew, unless you wanted to confront Trump with a politically correct remark, and that would only result in ridicule and disgust and, in all likelihood, a steep decline in his regard. In this way, I could relate to Billy Bush in the "grab them by the pussies" video in which Trump boasted about how his celebrity status afforded him the privilege of being able to sexually assault women. It was offensive, to say the least, but I knew what Bush was doing when he giggled nervously and went along with Trump. The sexist swagger was part of life inside Trump's bubble, a juvenile redoubt that was proudly, defiantly, and most definitely Neanderthal about women.

Seated dead center in the auditorium, front row in the audience as the contestants rehearsed their choreographed dance sequence, Trump was rapt, as he leaned over and whispered to me.

"Holy shit, look at Miss Brazil," Trump said. "She's fucking gorgeous. Look at that face and body. Man, I would like a piece of that."

"She's definitely gorgeous," I replied, scanning the stage filled with beauties in bathing suits.

"Which one do you like?" Trump asked.

"Miss Germany," I said. "She's the full complete package. Beautiful, and man, can she dance. She's definitely professionally trained."

"Shit, you're right," Trump said. "Good call. I wonder what your parents would say if you brought her home?"

This was Trump's idea of humor, because my father was a survivor of the Holocaust and she was German. Get it? Ha, ha. Silence from me again, as Trump continued to inventory the merchandise on display as we watched the women. After an hour, he stood and announced that he was going to go on stage to greet the contestants. It was amazing to see how these young beautiful women from all over the globe blushed and giggled in the presence of Donald Trump; his power and charisma were undeniable. He took photos with the beauty queens as they clapped in excitement at getting a picture with a reality TV star and proprietor of the pageant. Then Trump called out for me and the others in his entourage to join him on stage.

"Girls, these are my executives," Trump said. "This is Michael, my killer lawyer. But sorry, girls, he's happily married, so he's out of bounds."

The women laughed, and so did I.

Back at the hotel, in the restaurant named DJT in honor of his initials, Trump was ebullient about the pageant that night.

"After the show, we have an after-party," Trump said to me. "It's crazy. I want you to bring the girls by to see me, especially Miss Germany and Miss Brazil."

"Of course, Boss," I said. "That's easy. They love you."

With Trump, flattery gets you everywhere.

"Did you see their faces when I took the pictures?" he asked. "One of them was rubbing my back and squeezing into me. You know I can have any of them, if I want. In fact, I could have all of them."

"I'm sure," I replied. "I'm sure you can, Boss."

Miss USA, Olivia Culpo, won that year, not his favorites from Brazil and Germany, but that didn't impact Trump's mood at the after party. The arrangements for the event at a club in the hotel followed the usual pattern. The place was throbbing with music and sex as scores of beautiful young women danced and drank champagne and oversexed middle-aged men tried to catch their eye. There was a cordoned off VIP section, where I sat, and inside that there was another, even more private area, also marked by a red velvet rope, guarded by Trump's bodyguard Keith Schiller and reserved for the Boss alone. As instructed, I delivered Miss Brazil and Germany's Alicia Endemann to Trump's lair, where I was thanked and dismissed. That was how things worked with Trump. I knew that there was a real likelihood that he would at least try to hook up with one of the beauty contestants, and I knew there was a decent chance he would succeed, but, as with his shady business dealings and dirty deeds, he had a preternatural way of hiding the truth of his activities. Plausible deniability wasn't just a strategy for Trump—it was his way of life.

Trump and me with Miss Germany. © 2020 Michael Cohen

I should stop here to comment on the common perception of Trump as a sleazy womanizer, constantly having sex with strangers as some kind of sex addict. That wasn't how the Boss operated, no matter the popular view he encouraged. As you will see in the pages to come, Trump did have affairs with people like a porn star and a former Playboy centerfold, and I was assigned the task of hiding those trysts from his wife and the public. But he wasn't a lothario and many, many women weren't attracted to him at all—in fact, in my experience, the most attractive and intelligent women were often both repulsed and, in a strange way, pulled towards his money and power and prestige.

When he told Billy Bush that he would grab women by their genitals, I have no doubt he literally meant what he said—that was always true of Trump—but I never saw him do such an awful thing. I did see him corner pretty women in his office and forcibly kiss them as they recoiled; he would grab the women by their cheeks and pull them towards him and kiss them plum on their lips.

In 2013, the Miss Universe pageant was to be held in Moscow, it was announced in Vegas, and thus began the sequence of events that would unravel in front of the nation over the years to come. I was there at the very beginning, and I was at the heart of the unfolding events all along, so I know the central role played by Aras and Emin Agalarov, a Russian father-and-son team. The Agalarovs were classic Russian billionaires: connected to Putin, and self-evidently able to get things done in the former Soviet Union, qualities that mattered greatly to Trump. For decades, Trump had been chasing his personal great white whale—a Trump hotel in the center of Moscow—with no success until an initiative was begun in the months leading up to the 2016 election, a potential deal that I was in charge of and that would cause a nation-shattering controversy—but that was still years away.

In June of 2013, Trump and I traveled to Las Vegas together once more to meet again with the Agalarovs for that year's Miss USA pageant and the release party of the pop star Emin's new single, the two events tied together for the promotion, with Trump appearing as himself in the video for the song. The Agalarovs were part of the promotion for the 2013 Moscow Miss Universe pageant—yes, the pee tape party, as you'll see.

Checking into the Vegas Trump Tower, I was summoned up to

Trump at the Miss USA Pageant with business associates. © *2020 Michael Cohen*

his suite to discuss the day's events. Trump was in his underwear, white Hanes briefs, and a white short-sleeve undershirt, watching cable news on television. He barely seemed to register that it was unusual for a grown man to be in a state of undress in front of an employee, but there it was. On this occasion, Trump was fresh from the shower and he hadn't done his hair yet, as it was still air-drying. When his hair wasn't done, his strands of dyed-golden hair reached below his shoulders along the right side of his head and on his back, like a balding Allman Brother or strung out old '60s hippie.

I called his plane Hair Force One, for good reason. Trump doesn't have a simple combover, as it would appear. The operation was much more involved than a simple throw-over of what was left of his hair: the three-step procedure required a flop up of the hair from the back of his head, followed by the flip of the resulting over-hang on his face back on his pate, and then the flap of his combover on the right side, providing three layers of thinly disguised balding-male insecurity. The concoction was held in place by a fog of TREsemme TRES Two, not a high-end salon product. Flip, flop, flap, and there was the most famous combover in the world.

The real reason for the extravagant and obvious overcompensation for his baldness was vanity, and the desire to appear younger and more vigorous than he was. But there was another unknown reason: he was hiding unsightly scars on his scalp from a failed hair-implant operation in the 1980s. That was the disfiguring operation that resulted in his furious "emotional rape" of his first wife Ivana, as she documented in a lawsuit in the early '90s; like Samson, Trump believed his virility and image were harmed if he was seen to be losing his hair, or, even worse, injuring himself in an attempt to disguise male-pattern balding. If Trump let strangers see the red sores on his scalp, he would appear to be vulnerable, even pitiable, not the unstoppable sex-god alpha-male billionaire he wanted to present to the world—and himself.

With Trump ready for the night's festivities in Vegas, we made our way to the party 2012 Miss Universe winner Olivia Culpo was hosting to celebrate the release of Emin's latest single, and then we all went to dinner. This was followed by an after-party at a night-club in the Palazzo known as The Act. The location for the party was selected by the Russian oligarchs the Agalarovs, an opportunity for them to show us the kind of entertainment they found amusing or arousing. Lavish debauchery was the promise of the Vegas club, which was part of chain of strip joints known as the Box that aimed to push the boundaries of decency to the breaking point and beyond. At The Act, that meant the appearance on stage of sex dolls, dildos, strap-on penises, strippers pretending to snort coke, pretending to actually take a crap on the stage—the place was truly lewd and disgusting and infantile. In a skit called "Hot for the Teacher," a man dressed as a college lecturer wrote filthy titles for his forthcoming classes on a blackboard while strippers dressed as coeds took off their clothes and stood over him, pretending to urinate. Another jewel of an act at The Act involved two strippers drinking champagne and pretending to snort coke as they undressed, while one of them simulated giving the other a golden shower as the other caught the fake urine and drank it.

Classy stuff. I have no idea what might have happened with the Boss the following year in Russia, when the Miss Universe pageant was held in Moscow, and according to the Steele Dossier, Trump allegedly had a group of prostitutes urinate on the bed in his hotel suite as a kind of symbolic insult to the Obamas, who had previously slept in that bed. I had my nephew's bar mitzvah in Florida to attend that week, and so I was spared the delights of the louche Moscow nights hanging out with the Agalarovs. But I do know that the decision to go to The Act in Vegas in 2012 was made by the Agalarovs and the Russian men certainly seemed hugely entertained in a venue that boasted golden showers and fairly bristled with the energy of sex for sale. They were the same men who hosted Trump in Moscow in 2013, so it doesn't seem entirely impossible that the amusements of a golden shower were again part of the Boss's festivities. Trump's hatred for Obama was on a level that might provoke some sort of perverse and perverted ritualistic humiliation in a hotel suite. Like the Faux-Bama he hired to express his hatred and contempt for Obama in symbolic ways, I can attest that he was entirely capable of being entertained by such an act, even if he is a germaphobe, as he claims to be. However, this claim never occurred, to the best of my knowledge and investigations, and as verified to me by the Boss's longtime head of security and attaché, Keith Schiller.

In Vegas, our gang was like a frat-bro party that night, charged with testosterone and aiming to live out the cliché: what happens in Vegas stays in Vegas. Jostling through the drunken late-night crowd at The Act, we were shown to the VIP section by security, as always, stationed front and center of the stage to fully appreciate the club's offerings. The atmosphere was electric as the club goers pointed and stared and took out their phones to take pictures of the celebrity Donald Trump in their midst, the kind of improbable turn of events that Vegas specializes in. The lights were dimmed and a short middle-aged white man came on stage wearing a gold jumpsuit. As the stage lights came up, it was revealed that he appeared to be handicapped; he seemed to be blind, and one of his arms was malformed and his hands appeared the size of a four-year-old boy's. But that wasn't what stood out. The bulge in his pants was, well, enormous, like he'd stuffed his groin with tube socks.

I was sitting next to Trump when he turned to me and the Agalarovs and said, "Now *that* guy is packing a missile."

Then a female emerged on stage. She was heavily overweight, perhaps 300 pounds, bleached blonde and wearing a postage stamp-sized American flag bikini. She started to do cartwheels across the stage, landing the routine in a full split at the center of the stage directly in front of the short man in the gold tracksuit. Within seconds, his pants were pulled off and he was wearing what is known in porn circles as a "cock sock." Yeah, I know: not exactly the Lincoln vs. Douglas debates.

As I watched in amazement, things took an even weirder turn. The man in the gold tracksuit began to sing into a microphone. The tune he belted out was *God Bless America*. As he sang the famous paean to national pride and fealty, in a voice that sounded like a professional opera singer, Trump's face was rapt in delight.

"Holy shit," Trump said to me. "This freak can really sing."

The woman in the bikini began to grind on the man's outsized penis, stroking and caressing it, stimulating a giant erection as the obese stripper acted like they were having sex on the stage.

"Holy shit," Trump said again, in disbelief and delight.

The room was now pounding with laughter and astonishment, the atmosphere rip-roaring and rudely raw. No one was going more wild than the men in our cordoned-off VIP section, with Trump and the Agalarovs and others in our *Hangover*-like posse howling as the lights came up and we all looked around in disbelief: did we just see what we think we saw?

"That's one hell of a way to make a buck," Trump declared to all.

The Act's Facebook page reported on Trump's attendance the next day, a fact that no reporter has ever discovered, to my amazement: "Even Mr. YOU'RE FIRED got caught in the Act," the post on Facebook said, with a photograph of Trump at the club.

"Did the pissing into wine glasses duo perform that night?" a poster on Facebook asked in the same post. The golden shower pair had performed, The Act's Facebook page confirmed, though I didn't catch that part of the show.

While this event has remained unknown, I was there and can tell you that Trump loved that night at The Act: there was an essential boyishness to his attitudes about sex and pornography and places like that night club. His followers imagine this to be part of his willingness to be politically incorrect, but there was something far more licentious and lurid about Trump's attitudes about women. His attitudes came from a different era, more like the Rat Pack of the 1950s, and he never took seriously the need to respect women. If he ever got caught cheating and Melania threatened to leave him, Trump told me, he wouldn't be upset or hurt at the loss, and I suspect she knew it. The relationship was just another deal, plain and simple.

"I can always get another wife," Trump told me. "That's no problem for me, if she wants to go, so be it."

Trump's grandiose sense of self-importance, his need for constant praise, his exploitation of others without guilt or shame was the classic definition of a narcissistic sociopath. One morning a friend called me with a joke that I found very funny. Later I was in Trump's office and decided to try it out on the Boss and gauge his reaction. The joke went as follows:

"Donald Trump is coming down the elevator from the 26th floor. It stops on the 20th floor and in enters a gorgeous buxom blond in a miniskirt. She takes one look at him and squeals, 'Oh my G-d. You're Donald Trump.' Trump nods his head. She continues: 'I have this recurring dream where I'm alone in an elevator with you and I pull off your pants and give you the greatest blow job of all time." Trump says: 'What's in it for me?'"

After telling him the joke, the Boss asked: "Is that a real joke?"

"I didn't make it up," I replied.

"Write it up for me."

I went back to my office, typed it up, made a few copies, and placed it on his desk.

Later that day when I went into his office, he was on the phone reading the joke to the person on the other end of the call.

As if he needed confirmation that other men were just as bad as he was, as he constantly projected his worst traits onto others, Trump often kidded me about fooling around on my wife. He wanted to know how often I cheated, and if I'd ever been caught, and all the lurid details. I always told him that I didn't fool around on Laura, but he didn't believe me; he would say I had to be lying because, of course, everyone cheats in his world.

It was around the time of the Vegas trip in the summer of 2012 that I took my wife, daughter Samantha, and son Jake to Trump's golf club in Bedminster, New Jersey, for an afternoon playing tennis and hanging out by the pool. This was one of the perks of working for the Trump Organization: access to his clubs and restaurants and spas was complimentary for a senior executive like me. This was a really hot and sticky summer day, and I was standing with Trump outside the pool area, discussing some pressing business matter, like the size of the breasts of a woman sunbathing on a lounge chair, when he whistled and pointed in the direction of the tennis courts.

"Look at that piece of ass," Trump said. "I would love some of that."

I looked over and stopped cold. My fifteen-year-old daughter had just finished a tennis lesson with the club pro and she was walking off the court. She was wearing a white tennis skirt and a tank top, with her hair pulled back in a ponytail.

I turned to Trump, incredulous. "That's my daughter," I said.

Trump turned to me, now surprised. "That's your daughter? When did she get so hot?"

I said nothing, thinking to myself, or I should say allowing myself to think: *What a fucking creep*. Who talks about a man's daughter in that way? All of the countless times I'd gone along with Trump's crude comments swirled around my mind.

Samantha waved and walked over, giving me a kiss.

"Give me a kiss, too," Trump said, and she complied with a tiny peck, glancing in my direction with unease.

"When did you get such a beautiful figure?" Trump asked Samantha. "You're really grown up."

Samantha blushed and said nothing.

Trump offered me a bro-like bumped fist, which I reluctantly accepted, as usual, not knowing how to extricate myself from the situation and spare my sweet daughter any more of this unwanted and inappropriate attention.

"You better watch out because in a few years I'll be dating one of your friends," Trump said to her.

I'm sorry to report that Samantha was used to creepy rich men behaving in sketchy ways around her, but this was going too far. When we were alone, she told me with disgust that if you're an attractive female the first thing Trump commented on was your appearance, as if he had the right to offer an opinion in your presence. Samantha said she was sick and tired of the way Trump demeaned and degraded me, as if he needed to keep me in my place. She wanted me to quit working for Trump because he was constantly doing things like threatening to cut my pay in half, as he actually did, or withhold my bonus or fire me. Our family had money independent of Trump, which he didn't like, Samantha believed, because the Boss wanted me to be subservient to him in all ways, so when I bought a nice car or had a fun vacation Trump would use it as an excuse to ridicule me and make me feel small— again, as if an insignificant speck like me had no right to enjoy the good life he led. This was part of his cult-leader persona—his slow, incremental, relentless way of saying nasty things to me about my abilities and intelligence, things that weren't true, until some part of me started to believe him.

Samantha felt like I had Stockholm Syndrome, and I'm ashamed to say she was correct; she was fifteen years old and she saw Trump much more clearly than I could, which I was unable to grasp, let alone act upon. That was the sorry truth. I can admit I was being an idiot, but what is far more painful to know in hindsight is that my daughter thought I was an idiot. In so many ways I was a hero to her; I provided for everything she wanted in life, and I would do anything for her, but this blind spot made me impervious to her pleading with me to stop working for Trump. The same was true for my wife and son, and even my mother and father and in-laws. Recognizing that reality is one of the most humbling things I have been forced to admit to myself, and confess in public, a true measure of the destructive nature of Trump's cult.

I told Laura what Trump had said and done to Samantha as soon as I saw her at the pool. She shook her head, more in sadness than shock, as it seemed like par for the course for Trump. Like Samantha and my son Jake, she wished I would leave the Trump Organization and do virtually anything else with my life. I was stunned by the crassness of Trump, at the same time as I knew it was all routine for him and he wouldn't pause for a second to think he'd acted out of line or done anything wrong. The concept was foreign to him. To Trump the narcissist, if he did something, it was by definition fine by virtue of the fact that he'd done it, an insane version of papal infallibility that would be on full display when he ascended to the Presidency.

"That's disgusting," my wife Laura said to me as I said he'd asked Samantha for a kiss. "He's disgusting."

Chapter Ten

How to Fix a Poll

By the beginning of 2014, it was apparent that Trump was seriously considering running for President, to my delight. As we prepared to make the announcement—a process I helped manage with microscopic precision—we ran into a bump in the road. The premise of Trump's candidacy would be that he was famous as a highly respected real estate developer and billionaire businessman. That was a central proposition, along with his celebrity and willingness to say and do things that were politically incorrect.

But at the time, CNBC was conducting an online poll to determine the twenty-five most influential business people alive to celebrate the twenty-fifth anniversary of the network. Trump was one of the two hundred businessmen listed as contenders. I learned about the poll when I received an email from the Boss's assistant, Rhona Graff, telling the staff of the Trump Organization that the vote was being conducted and requesting everyone to click on the hyperlink and vote for Mr. Trump. In any other business this would seem like a joke, the kind of thing David Brent would do on *The Office*, with the egomaniac boss looking like the self-aggrandizing fool he was. In Trumpland, however, this was not only perfectly normal, it was standard operating procedure. The two prime and coequal imperatives of the company were to protect Trump, usually from himself, and to feed his insatiable ego.

The CNBC poll seemed almost designed to challenge the self-regard of American business leaders. The criteria were a direct appeal—or attack—on the image of the two hundred candidates nominated for the competition, a list that included well-known moguls like T. Boone Pickens and Oprah and Steve Jobs. "The person must have been more than a good CEO," the rules said. "He/she should have altered business, commerce, management or human behavior—in other words, the person should be responsible for ushering in meaningful change, with business being the primary sphere of influence."

The premise was irresistible to Trump: he would kill to win that competition, I knew the second I read about the poll. I immediately voted on my desktop, and then I voted again on my tablet, followed by votes registered from both of my cell phones, using four different IP addresses to disguise the multiple clicks. I figured if everyone in the company did the same thing, Trump would at least make the top ten. But when I looked at the results, with the running totals available online, I discovered Trump was near the bottom of the list—around 187 out of 200. Word around the office was that Trump wasn't happy—"pissed" was the exact term—which was confirmed when one of his assistants brought a note from Trump to me. It was early in the morning, before most others had turned up for work, but Trump often woke before dawn, particularly if he was mad about something, as he frequently was. I was always an early bird myself, turning up before eight most mornings, our shared habit of waking early likely a function of our bond as teetotalers. The note consisted of a printout of the poll rankings, with the humiliating place Trump occupied highlighted by a black Sharpie circle, and in the margin in his distinctive, manic, all uppercase handwriting, "SEE ME ASAP."

I entered Trump's office carrying a notepad and pen.

"You want to see me, Boss?" I asked.

"Yeah," he said. "What can we do about this poll? I'm at the bottom of the fucking list. Check into this immediately and let me know."

"Of course, Boss, I'm on it," I said.

This was the kind of project Trump assigned to me. Trump didn't say what he wanted me to do, because he didn't have to: I knew immediately he wanted me to find a way to put the fix on the poll to increase his ranking. This wouldn't involve attracting more voters, or trying to convince others that Trump fit the criteria, because the people answering the poll obviously didn't think he was the best candidate; to the contrary, the vote made him look ridiculous. But Trump knew he could count on me to figure out a way to cheat—a reality I take no pride in admitting.

Back in my office, I called my friend John Gauger, the chief information officer at Liberty University. I'd met John in 2012 when Trump had been invited by Jerry Falwell Jr. to address the school, and I'd accompanied him to Virginia. John also had a side business called RedFinch Solutions LLC, which provided services for search engine optimization and Internet reputational management. John was younger than me, in his early thirties, and I knew from past experience that he was a flexible thinker when it came to issues like the one I was confronting on Trump's behalf.

"Do me a favor," I said, sending him a link to the CNBC site. "Check into this online poll for me. The Boss is unhappy with his current standing and I need to know if there is something we can do."

Gauger asked for half an hour, promising he'd work on a solution. I went back to Trump's office to give him an update, knowing that if something was eating at him—and the poll clearly was—he wanted to be constantly updated. I told him I had a technology consultant looking for solutions.

"Get it done," he growled.

When Gauger called back he had a plan.

"Try to follow me on this," Gauger said, rattling off a bunch of numbers and tech terms that made no sense to me.

"Stop," I said. "Please, in English."

"I can do this very easily," John said. "The algorithmic code they're using is very basic. My team and I have already cracked it. We can manipulate the voting by inserting IP addresses casting votes for Mr. Trump based on the overall number of total votes, so the votes aren't visible. That way, we will be totally undetected while we move Mr. Trump higher in the rankings. But we need to buy IP addresses since we don't own enough to make a dent in the rankings. At the same time, we'll perfect the algorithm to ensure a seamless strategy."

"How much does all that cost?" I asked.

"They aren't expensive," Gauger said. "It depends on how many we buy. Let's purchase a hundred thousand and see how that moves the needle. It'll cost $7,500."

"Give me a few minutes and I'll get back to you," I said.

When I returned to Trump's office it was evident that he had been impatiently waiting to hear from me. When he wanted something done, he wanted it done yesterday, I knew, and what could be more important than fostering his reputation as a transcendental business figure and tycoon?

"What do you have for me?" Trump asked.

"Good news," I said. "A friend of mine has already cracked

the algorithm being used by the polling company. Now we need to insert votes favorable to you."

"Really?" Trump asked. "Can we get caught?"

"Not according to my friend. What we need to do is purchase IP addresses. It'll cost $7,500. We will need more but that will give us a gauge on getting the job done."

"Wow," Trump said. "Go do it. I want to be number one."

"Boss, you don't want to be number one," I said. "That will potentially attract unwanted attention. Let's go for, say number nine. Then you're in the top ten."

"Good," Trump said, looking very pleased that he was going to be able to manipulate the poll.

All morning, I obsessively checked the poll results as Trump's ranking began to rise. I was supposed to wait until three in the afternoon to check in with John Gauger, but I couldn't stand the suspense as I watched Trump rise into the top thirty. I had other projects that I was working on—actual business matters that weren't purely throwing red meat at the caged-tiger-like ego of Donald J. Trump—but when I went to see the Boss on an unrelated and actually consequential subject, I discovered that he too was fixated on the CNBC poll.

"How are we doing?" Trump asked, without having to specify what he meant.

"We're at number twenty-nine and climbing," I said. "I have a status call with my friend at three. I will update you then."

"Man, your friend is great," Trump said. "Who is he?"

"You don't want to know," I said. "It's better that you don't even know his name. Let's just call it plausible deniability if something happens."

"Something could happen?" Trump asked, now alarmed. "I thought you said it was undetectable."

"It is," I said. "But even if there's a one percent chance that something happens, you are able to truthfully state that you don't know who was involved."

"Good," said Trump. "But one day you'll tell me who it is."

"Sure, Boss," I said.

When three rolled around, Trump was still gradually but inexorably rising in the rankings. I called Gauger excitedly.

"Holy shit," I said. "Trump is at twenty."

"It won't be moving much more tonight," he said. "We've been tracking the voting quantity over the day and it really slowed a lot, so we need to start again when the level of activity increases. We also need to buy more IP addresses so we have enough in reserve to make sure Mr. Trump gets to number nine."

"Perfect," I said. "Let's talk tomorrow."

The next morning, I was in Trump's office by 8:30 talking to the Boss about nothing but the most pressing question of the day: his fake ranking. By then he had moved up to eighteen and the volume of the voting was increasing, exactly as Gauger had said.

"We need more IP addresses to get back in the game today," I told Trump.

"Go do it," Trump said. "Keep me informed."

"I'm authorized for another $7,500?" I asked.

"Yes," Trump said. "Just make sure I make it to the top ten."

All that day, Gauger and his team of techies fed the fake IP "votes" into the poll, and all day, Trump continued his manufactured ranking rise. The poll closed at three that day, I knew, so I was constantly refreshing my search engine to monitor the results. Gauger had promised a top ten finish, predicting confidently the final result exactly at number nine.

As three o'clock neared, my intercom rang and I was summoned once more to see Trump.

"Do you know the poll closes at three today?" he asked, acting like he thought he knew something I didn't.

"Yes, I do," I said. "You are currently at number eleven. My friend has assured me that you will be number nine at closing time. He altered the algorithm and more votes will be cast for you."

"Really great," Trump said. "Good job . . . no, great job!"

When the poll closed, Trump was, as promised, number nine. I printed a copy of the poll and delivered it to Trump's office. He was on the speakerphone when I entered, so he motioned me to sit. I dropped the poll on his desk and he smiled devilishly, with delight.

"Whoa," he said to the person he was talking with on the phone. "I just got a CNBC poll that shows I'm the ninth-most-important businessman of the past twenty-five years. Not bad, huh?"

For the rest of the day the calls flooded in, praising Trump as he told everyone he talked to about his position in the polls. Like so much else with Trump, on one level he had to know the entire "accomplishment" was nothing more than a lie. He'd paid to push the poll, as any sane person would have appreciated, but Trump was unhinged in reveling in the ranking, as if it was a real achievement and a real reflection of his standing in the business community and with the general public. If Trump's insistence weren't such a dangerous delusion—if all of this rampaging egomania hadn't come to have such dire consequences for the United States and the world—it would be funny. As people repeatedly told him that he deserved the recognition and that of course the result was predictable—"What would you expect," was the sentiment, "you're Donald Trump"—his grip on reality appeared to vanish. Before long, Trump believed he really was rated in the top ten and was regarded as a profoundly important business figure. I not only enabled that belief, I actively and eagerly participated in perpetrating the myth.

The feeling was euphoric—until the following day, when the bottom fell out of the scam. During the day, Trump discovered that CNBC claimed to have reserved the right to remove anyone they wanted from the list and that they had unilaterally removed his name from the list. The network didn't say why—they didn't have to, as written in very small print on the launch page of the poll.

Trump was incandescent. "What the hell!" he screamed at me. "Michael, I want you to call the president of CNBC and tell him we will sue them if they don't restore me to my rightful slot!"

I duly did as instructed, leaving a long and very strongly worded message with the president of CNBC's secretary explaining that I was Special Counsel and Executive Vice President to the Trump Organization and that legal action would be taken if the network didn't immediately reverse their outrageous and unfounded and capricious decision. The voters had spoken, I told her in my blunt and harsh tone, and Donald Trump absolutely insisted that his right to retain his ranking was of paramount importance. The poor secretary took my dictation and promised my call would be returned, in due course. I walked thirty paces down the hall to Trump's office and reported what I had done. By then, Trump was figuring out who else had been removed from the list and it appeared that T. Boone Pickens, the Texan magnate and a Trump

---

Rhona Graff

From:	Sally Geymuller [sgeymuller@█████████]
Sent:	Thursday, February 27, 2014 11:52 AM
To:	Rhona Graff
Subject:	Boone Pickens office

FYI

Rhona,
Do your PR people have any interest in talking to our people about why Mr. Trump and Mr. Pickens were dropped off of the CNBC Contenders list after having been #8 and #9?
Sally

████████████

Sally Geymüller
Assistant to T. Boone Pickens
BP Capital
8117 Preston Road, Suite 260
Dallas TX 75225
214/█████ office
214/█████ fax

Follow Boone Pickens on Twitter

The email from T. Boone Pickens's assistant to Rhona Graff.
© 2020 Michael Cohen

acquaintance, had also been dropped. There was no indication why Pickens had been removed, but given the famously gargantuan ego of the oil tycoon and corporate raider, he was as infuriated as Trump. The only difference was that he had made the list, to the best of my knowledge, fair and square.

Pickens sent an email to Rhona Graff, Trump's assistant, suggesting the two businessmen talk, so Trump instructed me to call him about starting a lawsuit or issuing a press release. I soon had Pickens on the line, as he told me in his Texas drawl how outraged he was by CNBC's high-handed attitude; we didn't discuss the reason he'd been taken off the list. Like Trump, he was furious and insulted and he intended to do something about it, so I suggested I get Trump on the line. I patched Trump in and soon we were having a three-sided conversation bemoaning the terrible injustice of the poll. Both men praised the other, stoking and stroking each other's egos, as they considered their options.

The call was certifiably insane, but I played along, offering my advice and counsel. A lawsuit would be expensive, it was agreed, without adding that the likely outcome would be the discovery of the fraud and the humiliation of their ego trips being exposed to the public. That was a story I knew my journalist connections would eat up; nothing was quite as exciting for the press as stories revealing the egomania of self-aggrandizing rich white men.

After the Pickens call, I was summoned to Trump's office and instructed to call the reporters I knew to try to get them interested in a story about the terrible treatment Trump had received at the hands of CNBC. Trump wanted me to emphasize his ranking and make sure it was prominently discussed in any coverage.

"Do I discuss T. Boone Pickens as well?" I asked.

"No," Trump said. "Make it about just me. He will do his own. He's not my concern."

I wasn't surprised when there were no takers in the press. No one wanted to be treated like Trump's PR flak, at least not in the legitimate press; corrupt tabloids like the *National Enquirer* or biased broadcasters like Fox were another story. The general counsel for CNBC eventually called me and pointed out that there was a disclaimer on the website of the poll explicitly providing that any candidate could be removed, without cause and for any reason. When I protested loudly, channeling Trump's fury, the lawyer calmly said the Boss had been taken off the list and there would be no explanation given or apology forthcoming. It went without saying that the network might have figured out that Trump had cheated, and so I didn't push the matter further. In the end, the poll came and went and barely registered in the public consciousness. The important thing, for Trump, was the printout he had of the poll showing him at number nine. He had hundreds of copies made and he added the poll to the pile of newspaper clippings and magazine profiles of himself on his desk that he would give to visitors. That was one of the supposedly big treats about gaining entry to Trump's 26th floor office: a gift of a stack of stories about him, whether real or fantasy, with the lucky few getting a complimentary Trump Gold Chocolate Bar Bullion.

If something didn't work out for Trump to his satisfaction, he dropped the whole project instantaneously, or at least after he'd wallowed in his outrage and anger. The same went for people. Or debts. Or promises. So I wasn't truly shocked when, a week later, I walked into Trump's office and dropped John Gauger's invoice for the work he'd done on the poll on his desk. The services rendered included purchasing the IP addresses and payment for the time spent by Gauger and his team to cheat on Trump's behalf. I'd written at the bottom of the invoice "Approved," hoping that Trump would just initial the document and I could close out the entire fiasco.

"Leave it," Trump said, appraising the invoice but not signing it. "We'll deal with it later."

"No worries," I said.

Walking back to my office, I had the sinking feeling that getting payment was going to be difficult, and that's exactly how it played out. Somehow, I deduced, in Trump's mind the poll hadn't yielded the desired result, and so he'd convinced himself that he shouldn't be burdened by having to pay for Gauger's services. That was precisely what Trump said when I raised the question with him a few days later. He complained that he didn't get credit for his #9 ranking, so why should he have to pay?

Knowing Trump as well as I did, I knew he wasn't going to pay up—and he knew that I knew. That was how things worked with Trump. Many, many things—really most things—were unspoken, especially if he was doing something dishonest or unethical. I wasn't going to confront him and explain how John had done all that he'd promised, or point out that I had taken a big risk on Trump's behalf by cheating and getting John to participate, or that John was a friend and someone I relied upon for web- and tech-related advice and I didn't want to burn that bridge. No one spoke the truth to Trump, and I'm sure that is the case now that he's turned the White House into the mirror image of his office in the Trump Tower, with yes men like me doing his bidding and never, ever, ever confronting him with reality.

After failing miserably with Trump, I then tried to convince CFO Allen Weisselberg to pay the invoice, but he refused. He and Trump were like Frick and Frack when it came to stiffing vendors, so I knew that had little chance of actually working. In the end, Trump said he didn't want to pay the invoice because it would create a paper trail to prove that he had cheated in the CNBC poll. But he conceded that he would pay Gauger eventually, when enough time had passed to distance himself from the poll and make it difficult for any enterprising reporter or tax auditor to connect the payment to the questionable campaign to cheat. I told

Gauger that he'd get paid someday, without saying when, and he agreed to keep the invoice as an open receivable, which enabled me to keep using him over the years, including during the madness of the election in 2016, when I truly got swept up in the tornado that was the Trump Campaign.

But first I had another catch and kill operation to run, not for Mr. Trump but for my dear friends, more like family to me, the Falwells—and, like the Bieber favor a few years earlier, this would have a huge impact on the 2016 election, evangelicals, the Supreme Court, and the fate of the nation. This situation began with a phone call, as so many did for me as a fixer, from Jerry Falwell Jr., telling me a story that stretched back years to a visit he and his wife had taken to Miami. They'd stayed at the five-star Fontainebleau Hotel and soaking up the sun the pair had become friendly with a kid working at the pool. Jerry called him a pool boy. He said they'd stayed in touch with the pool boy and talked about helping him finance a business with an investment in real estate. Jerry didn't fill me in on all the details, only that a deal was never consummated and the relationship ended with hard feelings. The kid had filed a lawsuit, Jerry said, but that wasn't why he'd called me, as I knew. I wasn't the lawyer you called to help with litigation; I was the lawyer you called when you had a problem that needed to be solved—or made to go away.

By this time, I knew it had to be serious. The simple act of calling me to ask a favor was in itself like using up the favor, because he knew that if he asked me to do something for him I would move heaven and earth to help. Since the laying of hands ceremony in 2011, I'd stayed in steady contact with the Falwells, meeting them for dinner when they were in New York. I knew their children and shared in family news, as a close friend, much closer than Trump ever was to two of the most powerful evangelicals in the nation.

"This is personal," Jerry said.

"I will do everything I can for you," I vowed, and I meant it.

Jerry continued in a sheepish voice that somehow the pool boy had come into possession of photographs he'd taken on his phone. He said the photos weren't pornographic, or anything like that, but they were embarrassing. He said that he and his wife Becki had purchased a new tractor for their farm and Mrs. Falwell had started to pose for portraits as she climbed on to the hood of the tractor. One thing lead to another, Jerry said, now speaking like a man who knows he did something stupid that he regrets but he had to just own up to it and get it out. Becki had started to pose for photos with her top open a little bit, and then a lot, and then the top came off, then the bra, and soon she was vamping like a softcore MILF.

Pausing, as if to say, I know, I know, Jerry said that the terrible thing was that the pool boy was now threatening to shop the photographs to publications as a way to pressure the Falwells to settle the lawsuit on favorable terms. They had no idea how he'd managed to get the photos, Jerry said, although he had to have figured out a way to get into his phone, I surmised. The problem was that the Falwells had multiple children, which would make the release of the images mortifying, but their livelihoods also centered around their religious beliefs and reputations. If Becki Falwell was seen half-naked by the students of Liberty University, let alone evangelicals all over the country, it would be an unmitigated disaster. Catch and kill, I thought, but in this case it was just going to be kill.

"Send me a copy of all the pleadings and the contact information for this young man," I said. "I won't call the pool boy, I'll talk to his lawyer."

"Becki is beside herself," Jerry said. "She's afraid these images will be all over the Internet.

"Relax," I said. "Please tell Becki that I'm on it. This is personal to me as well. I will call you no later than tonight."

The lawyer's name and contact information were in the pleadings online, so I called immediately. I asked if he was still representing the pool boy and he said he was. I laid out the details of the situation, in outline, including the conversations between the parties when the pool boy had menaced the Falwells, saying he'd release the raunchy pictures of Mrs. Falwell.

Before the lawyer could speak, I went for the jugular.

"You are aware that his actions are tantamount to extortion," I said. "I am going to ask you to contact him right now, ask him where the photos are, and if they are in his possession, he needs to turn them over to me and give me the names and contact information of anyone and everyone else who he showed the photographs to. I also need to know if he made any copies.

"Go now and do this," I continued, "and call me right back. If I don't hear from you by three o'clock this afternoon I will instruct the Falwells to contact the FBI and file a complaint."

"That won't be necessary," the lawyer replied. "I'll call you right after I speak to him."

I called Becki and reassured her that the pictures wouldn't get out, but I could hear the sadness and fear in her voice. I reassured her that I wouldn't let her down, and I didn't. When the lawyer called me back, he told me he'd spoken with his client and he was sure that the matter would end there. I repeated that his client would face serious criminal charges if the pictures surfaced.

"That won't happen," the lawyer said.

"If by chance they do," I said, "I will use every resource at my disposal to see that he goes to prison."

"I assure you we will not be speaking again on this matter," the lawyer said.

There it was: my second chit with the Falwells. In good time, I would call in this favor, not for me, but for the Boss, at a crucial moment on his journey to the Presidency.

Chapter Eleven

Trump For President (Part Two)

After nearly a decade, in 2014, I started planning to leave the Trump Organization. The idea was to start a real estate hedge fund, running money with and for Mark Cuban and his family, along with my own stockpile of funds. I wasn't quite a centimillionaire on paper, but I was closing in on that number with my taxi medallions and real estate holdings, and I felt confident that I was going to continue to succeed as a businessman in my own right.

Besides, the Trump Organization was increasingly becoming a sleepy backwater, at least relatively speaking compared to other NYC developers. *Celebrity Apprentice* wasn't on the air anymore, after slowly dying with falling ratings and increasingly idiotic story lines and obscure C-level contestants, denying the Boss the revenue stream he'd long relied on. This, in turn, slowed down his now-dwindling business interests. I worked on an attempt to buy the Buffalo Bills of the NFL for $1 billion, which failed when Trump couldn't arrange financing—no banks were willing to loan him that kind of money with his long history of defaulting and declaring bankruptcy.

The only bank that would still deal with Trump was Deutsche Bank, the German financial institution with a reputation for playing fast and loose with the rules and laws, but the bank was upset at the way Trump used incredibly inflated valuations of his real estate holdings to justify his company's loans. A mansion in Westchester that he had purchased for $7M was given a value of $291M, to cite but one example (ironically, it was the very house a famous Wall Street Ponzi schemer named Sam Israel had rented from Mr. Trump as he ran his scam in the 2000s). Reducing Trump's hyped estimates by seventy percent, he could no longer command large lines of credit or the financing to play with the big boys.

In truth, I was also fed up with the taunting and teasing he incessantly inflicted on me. He didn't like that I was forming my own relationships with business icons like Mark Cuban and Carl Icahn. Trump didn't like that I was starting to run in the same social circles, and he'd let me know by way of putdowns and sarcastic remarks about my new Rolls Royce or the vacations I took at exclusive resorts. When I spent a few days on Steve Wynn's yacht, Trump took it as an affront, as if I were somehow diminishing his status by consorting with people he viewed as peers. He thought I was getting uppity, it seemed to me: I was always his personal attorney, a lackey, someone who did his bidding. As I've said, in the world of Donald Trump, success was a zero-sum game, and anyone who had the temerity to make money and get ahead in life, without bowing and scraping to the Boss, had to be kept in their place.

In effect, Trump was slowly becoming just another crotchety semi-retired rich dude who'd inherited a ton of money and spent decades playing with his family's fortune, ending up as the owner of a few buildings in Manhattan, a few golf courses in America, Ireland, and Scotland, and a reputation as a conspiracy-peddling celebrity and political wannabe. He had substantial holdings, without doubt, but he was hardly the world-beating billionaire he liked to portray himself to be, and I honestly thought I could do better with bigger players with deeper pockets and far less agitation.

By this time, my daughter Samantha was beyond desperate for me to quit working for Trump. She was tired of the entire Trump clan and all the intrigue that surrounded them. Ivanka shunned her in the lobby of Trump Park Avenue, a petty slight signifying that Trump's daughter believed the Cohen family was beneath her social stature. In this way, in the constant measure of status and snobbery, the Trumps were actually tiresome and conceited bores—something you'd never hear said about that family, but it was true.

"Did you quit today?" Samantha asked me on a daily basis, repeating herself for emphasis. "Did you quit today? Did you quit today?"

Samantha didn't like the Trumps and their incessant competitiveness and egomania, but she had become close friends with Tiffany before I even began working for Trump and at the University of Pennsylvania, where they both studied, though she'd been amazed and appalled at how Tiffany's father treated the only daughter he'd had with Marla Maples. I also really felt for Tiffany and the way she was treated. The pecking order of the kids was painfully apparent. Trump was very specific about his views on the importance of female beauty in measuring the value of women, including inside his own family. When he wanted a particular businessman to do his biddings, he would often have me send Ivanka to take the meeting with a married man who the Boss figured would be susceptible to her charms.

"They can't think straight when they're around her," Trump

told me of deploying his elder daughter to deploy her looks with lustful men twice her age. "They can't keep their eyes off her."

But the beauty myth cut both ways in the Trump family, I knew. His daughter Tiffany was referred to as the "red-haired stepchild" by the other Trump kids, just one of a million ways she was treated differently than her siblings. The casual cruelty included Ivanka, who jealously guarded her position as Trump's favorite and surrogate, even at the expense of her vulnerable younger sister, as I saw firsthand. After graduating from college, Tiffany asked her father to call Anna Wintour, the editorial director of Condé Nast, to arrange for her to get an internship with *Vogue* magazine. I was in Trump's office with Ivanka one day as he mused over the idea of supporting Tiffany pursuing a career in fashion.

"I don't think Tiffany has the look," Trump said to Ivanka and me. "She just doesn't have what you have, honey."

"I agree, Daddy," Ivanka said. That was how they referred to each other: Daddy and honey. "She just doesn't have the look is the right way to say it, Daddy."

Contrary to public perception, and in contradiction to his impossibly broad but secret roles in the administration, Trump didn't particularly like Jared Kushner, either. I don't say that from a place of envy, as might seem obvious, with the thin and callow scion seeming to bestride the globe like a colossus while I paint the walls in a prison camp in the Catskills—yes, I am aware of appearances—but really as a simple observation. The reason Trump leans on Kushner so heavily is that there's no one else he can trust, to his way of thinking, to run the back channels and side deals that the Boss deems essential to any endeavor; present or future. Jared will do as he's told, with discretion, in a way that Trump can't find in other advisors. If you doubt my word, just look at what happened when the maniac Rudy Giuliani started to freelance foreign policy in Ukraine. There were two Rudys—one batshit crazy and one clear-headed—and if you wanted to get anything sensible out of him it was like rolling the dice. By that measure, Jared Kushner was Dag Hammarskjold incarnate.

So, by the end of 2014, only one thing was holding me back from quitting the Trump Organization: the tantalizing possibility that the Boss would run for President in 2016. After chickening out in 2012, afraid of staring down Barack Obama, I knew in my gut that Trump would enter the race for this cycle. He kept a running commentary on the Republican candidates as they declared they were running, holding them all in contempt, and always bragging how he could whip them with one hand tied behind his back, and I actually agreed with him. Jeb Bush was a favorite whipping boy, with his only real claim to the office being his last name, and Marco Rubio and Ted Cruz wouldn't have a prayer in the public arena against the blast furnace of Trump's rhetoric. On and on Trump sniped at the dwarves holding solemn press conferences and affecting the manner of men who the public could imagine in the highest office in the land.

So I worked on Trump about running for President. I didn't nag him, but I didn't let him forget that I was hoping he'd run. Finally, the day after New Year's in 2015, I requested a sit-down meeting with Trump to discuss the Presidency. Trump was in a good mood that day, which was a good sign, so I cut to the chase.

"Are we doing it?"

I didn't have to say what "it" was; we were like an old couple completing each other's sentences.

"Yes," Trump said.

I didn't ask for any further confirmation, or engage in any discussions or speculation. Not wanting to push my luck, I immediately went to my office and began working the phones. This was as close as I will ever come to the rush the conductor of an orchestra must experience as they wave their baton and the strings and wind instruments and percussion all rise in unison to become a symphony. My instruments were two cell phones and two land phones, each with five lines, as I spread the word with my press contacts that the Boss was going to run—for real this time.

My first stop was Maggie Haberman at *The New York Times*. I'd known her a long time, and I knew that no publication mattered more to Trump than the *Times*, no matter what he said to the contrary. He cared more about what the *Times* said than the opinion of his wife or children. Next, I called David Pecker at the *National Enquirer*, my go-to bullshit artist. Then came Sean Hannity at Fox, contacts at CNN, MSNBC, CBS, George Stephanopoulos at ABC, Emily Jane Fox at *Vanity Fair*; my contacts list was extensive, not least because the address books in my phones were synced to Trump's—that's how connected we were, like Siamese twins. Think about the fact that our phone address lists were identical: do you do that with your spouse, or children, or anyone?

That was my relationship with Donald Trump.

The volume of incoming calls I was getting was soon insane and overwhelming. I juggled three different conversations, putting reporters on hold on different lines, all the calls on speakerphone, just like Trump. I told them we were forming an internal exploratory committee, which at first basically meant me, and I said we were examining the opportunity, given Trump's unique position as a multi-billionaire plutocrat celebrity entering politics. I talked about how we had to figure out how to potentially transfer the Trump Organization's vast enterprises to a trust, to be run by his children, and I said we were engaged in gauging the level of interest in his candidacy.

The quotes were all the same, more or less, but every reporter wanted their own quote because they didn't like citing other publications, so I just rattled off the lines over and over again. I had friends at liberal and conservative outlets, in television and print, and by the end of the day the story that Trump was going to run had gone viral.

I knew that Trump would want to be updated on the smallest of details, as he measured how much free press he was going to be able to command, as well as soaking up the sensation of ego stroking that he craved constantly, and in the coming weeks I wound up in his office offering detailed reports more than a dozen times a day.

"What about self-funding the campaign," Trump said to me one afternoon.

I knew there was no way he was going to spend his own money on politics. He was far too cheap, to begin with, and he was far less liquid than was understood by outsiders, but he appeared to be seriously contemplating the idea.

"I don't want to take money from a super PAC," Trump said. "A billionaire can't ask people for five bucks. Maybe I'll self-fund the primary but do it cheap. I don't need to spend a lot of money because we'll get all the free press we want."

Please pause over that final sentence and read it again. And again. And again. Because if you want to understand how Donald J. Trump became president, you have to grasp the essential fact that by far the most important element wasn't nationalism, or populism, or racism, or religion, or the rise of white supremacy, or strongman authoritarianism. It wasn't Russia, or lying, or James Comey, though all of those forces were hugely influential. It wasn't Hillary Clinton, though heaven knows she did all she could to lose the election.

No. The biggest influence by far—by a country mile—was the media. Donald Trump's presidency is a product of the free press. Not free as in freedom of expression, I mean free as unpaid for. Rallies broadcast live, tweets, press conferences, idiotic interviews, 24-7 wall-to-wall coverage, all without spending a penny. The free press gave America Trump. Right, left, moderate, tabloid, broad-sheet, television, radio, Internet, Facebook—that is who elected Trump and might well elect him again.

The underlying reasons were both obvious and hard to discern, and it continues to amaze me that this phenomenon isn't a central part of the conversation about the current plight of the United States of America.

Start with the proposition that Trump was great for ratings. If you're a right-wing AM radio commentator, or a lefty Brooklyn political podcaster, you were making bank talking about Trump. It's like a car crash, with people unable to avert their gaze. The Boss knew this and he knew how to exploit the greed and venality of journalists because he was (and is) an expert on the subjects. But there was something deeper and more primal in the way the media obsessed over Trump, as I did. Trump was a great *story*. He was chaos all the time. By five a.m. every day, he'd created the news cycle with his stubby fingers sending out bile-flecked tweets attacking anyone or everyone. In this way, as in so many others, he was the absolute opposite of Obama. Instead of No Drama, it was Drama All the Time.

The thing that astounded me, and still does to this day, was that the media didn't see that they were being played for suckers. They didn't realize the damage they were inflicting on the country by following Trump around like supplicants. What Trump did was transparent, once you identified it, and this remained a central fact of the campaign. If interest in Trump was waning, even just a little bit, he'd yank the chain of the media with an insult or racist slur or reactionary outrage—and there would be CNN and the *Times* and Fox News dutifully eating out of his hands. Like so much about Trump, if it weren't tragic, you'd laugh—or cry.

In the frantic days after I'd first floated the coming Trump can-didacy, I started to feel myself change. The transformation wasn't obvious to me, at first, as I just seemed like a harder and more determined version of my prior self—ready, willing, and able to please Trump no matter what. But there was a new variety of shamelessness that was emerging, a personality that seemed disembodied and disordered and floating in the ether—like a cartoon character bullyboy I was creating.

In short, I was becoming Trump.

Perhaps I can best explain this by way of analogy. In simple terms, I looked at Trump as a blank canvas that I could paint any way I wanted. For me, that meant portraying him in the most flattering light possible, with all of his flaws and weaknesses not just hidden but turned into virtues and strengths. When *Forbes* said his net worth was "only" $4.1 billion I went ballistic. The truth, I well knew, was that Trump's net worth was ridiculously inflated and he wasn't worth nearly that much money—perhaps $2 billion, absolute tops. I'd personally pumped in the helium into his balloon-like net worth to the tune of billions by adding ridiculously high estimates to his holdings. To give but one example, consider the valuation I put on the four floors of retail space in the Gucci building adjacent to Trump Tower. The revenue from the building was approximately $28 million per year, a nice earner, but to value the property I used as a comparable property the commercial space at the nearby St. Regis, which had just sold for $700M. The St. Regis had 28,000 square feet, while the Gucci building had 50,000 square feet, so I pegged the price at $1 billion—and the press bit. But here's the thing: the St. Regis retail space was all at street level, thus much, much more valuable than the four-story Gucci property. The real value of Trump's Gucci space was maybe, just maybe, $300M, but who cared?

A better way to understand what I was doing was to liken it to acting. Method acting, to be specific. I was inhabiting the character I was playing for the press, repeating lines from a script. Lying for Trump became nothing to me. In my mind, I was an actor speaking lines written for me by someone else—in this case, Donald Trump. I was reciting the agreed-upon line of nonsense, in the most realistic and convincing way I could, with complete and total commitment to the role, like Robert DeNiro in *Raging Bull*, and what I was merchandizing was indeed raging bullshit. Trump had

TRUMP
THE TRUMP ORGANIZATION

Michael D. Cohen
Executive Vice President and
Special Counsel to
Donald J. Trump
Direct Dial (212) 836-3212
mcohen@trumporg.com

May 5, 2015

BY FEDERAL EXPRESS

Rev. Joseph M. McShane, S.J.
University President
Fordham University- Rose Hill Campus
441 East Fordham Road
Bronx, N.Y 10458

Re: *Records of Donald J. Trump*

Dear Reverend McShane,

Please be advised that I am Executive Vice President and Special Counsel to Donald J. Trump.

It has come to my attention that several media outlets have asked for the release of my client's records. We have turned down these requests.

As I am sure you are aware, pursuant to applicable law, including the Family Educational Rights and Privacy Act (20 U.S.C. § 1232g; 34 CFR Part 99), the release or disclosure, in any form, of such records (or any information contained in such records) to any third party without my client's prior written authorization is expressly prohibited by law, with any violation thereof exposing the subject educational institution to both criminal and civil liability and damages including, among other things, substantial fines, penalties and even the potential loss of government aid and other funding. The criminality will lead to jail time.

Accordingly, please be advised that (i) my client does not consent to any release or disclosure of any educational records to any third parties; and (ii) if in the event any of his records are released or otherwise disclosed without his prior written consent, we will hold your institution liable to the fullest extent of the law including damages and criminality. As you are again no doubt aware, this notice applies to any and all of The College Board's employees, agents, third parties, vendors and any other person or entity acting for or on its behalf.

I thank you for your cooperation. Please guide yourself accordingly and contact me to inform me that the records have been permanently sealed.

Very truly yours,

Michael D. Cohen

P.S. Mr. Trump truly enjoyed his two years at Fordham and has great respect for the University.

725 FIFTH AVENUE · NEW YORK, NY 10022 · (212) 832-2000 · FAX (212) 935-0141

A threatening letter to the President of Fordham University. © 2020 Michael Cohen mocked Obama's education and demanded to see his academic transcripts, but when reporters began to seek the Boss's grades from the New York Military Academy, Fordham, and Wharton, I went ballistic. I threatened officials with "jail time" and forced the institutions to keep their records confidential, and I mean sealed . . . a nice piece of hypocrisy I pulled off without a second thought.

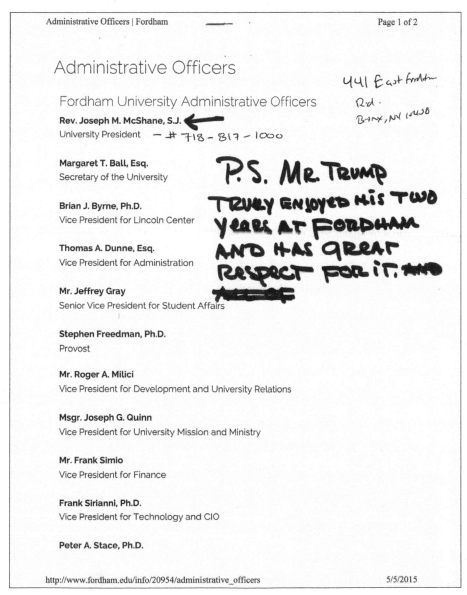

A note from Trump with the P.S. to add to my threat letter. © 2020 Michael Cohen

Before long, I started to believe my own lies, just like Trump, a measure of how deeply I was invested in creating the narrative. Trump was a self-made man, I told the press, a statement so ridiculous I can't believe I kept a straight face. I said that the other Republicans were right to be "afraid" of Trump, implying physical peril, as I inflated the achievements of the "mega-billionaire" celebrity, author, TV star, and business icon.

Paradoxically, I didn't officially join the campaign, in order to keep my title of Executive Vice President and Special Counsel to Donald Trump. I didn't talk about Trump the candidate, I talked about Trump the man, or the made-up version I touted. I wasn't a surrogate for Trump; I was speaking for myself as an extreme loyalist, as his dependable alter ego.

"Why do you give a shit about him?" my kids would ask.

"It's his deal, not yours," they'd say.

"I'm not going to talk about this anymore," I would reply. "It's repetitive."

So the subject would be dropped because my family didn't have the wherewithal to resist me—or to save me. It wasn't just as if I was an alcoholic or a drug addict refusing to get help. It was *exactly* that. I was an addict unable to stop myself from drinking or popping pills or shooting heroin into my veins. Worse, I brought my addiction home, constantly shouting on the phone to reporters and publishers when I should have been having a quiet breakfast with my children or a walk in the park. I never, ever, ever got through an entire meal in a restaurant with my wife without being interrupted by Trump. He'd call to ask a favor, or have me make a call on his behalf, or just to complain and rant.

My family hated it when I picked up his calls, as I always did, no matter the hour or the circumstances. I was always pressing his message, always pressing his message, always pressing his message. What I really needed was an intervention, but my wife and kids and parents and friends didn't know how to stage such a scene, or how I would react. "Badly," was the short answer, in hindsight, as it would likely have provoked me to go further and further into the madness, as I gradually and then rapidly took leave of my senses.

In the early days, I was running a one-man show for Trump, and that was no way to sustain a presidential campaign. I had my own freelance advisors I could lean on when the Drudge Report announced that it was going to conduct an online poll. I called my old pal John Gauger from Liberty University and got him to buy bots to cheat on the poll, just as we'd done with the CNBC poll the year before. This time we managed to land Trump in fifth place, with 24,000 votes, a spot that I thought of as the Goldilocks solution: not too high, not too low, just right.

But we needed a more formal and structured approach to have an effective team—or at least Trump's version of form and structure. What came next reminded me of the bar scene from *Star Wars*, with strange and unlikely characters from faraway galaxies turning up on the 26th floor in a seemingly endless stream over the next eighteen months. The first was the self-styled ultra-villain Roger Stone, back with his black sunglasses and flamboyant bad boy act, assless cowboy chaps at the ready. This time Stone was accompanied by his sidekick, Sam Nunberg. Sam was a talented and smart guy with substance-abuse issues and a propensity for getting in ridiculous feuds and sending idiotic tweets, no doubt while under the influence, including one using the N-word when referring to the Reverend Al Sharpton's daughter—the final straw that led Trump to fire Sam. But that wasn't entirely true, either, as Sam covertly continued to develop policy positions for Trump, conveyed via Stone—if something could be done secretly or dishonestly, that was always Stone's preferred way of operating, as if it proved he was dastardly and ruthless; the same was true for

Trump. I wound up having to call Reverend Sharpton to apologize on Sam's behalf and explain that his views weren't a reflection of the Trump campaign, which wasn't entirely true, and the Reverend was gracious in response, to my relief, as we'd known each other for years.

Hope Hicks was another early recruit, an aide taken from Ivanka's clothing company, and she proved to be extremely good at keeping track of Trump's calls and activities, which was no mean feat for a young women in her mid-twenties. I took a real shine to her as she reported to Trump and kept the trains running on time—or as close as possible.

Now we had to find a campaign manager. It soon became apparent that Trump wouldn't be able to engage any of the more experienced political handlers. The leading lights in the Republican party all wanted to be paid $200,000 a month, with the added requirement that they be paid up front for a full year. The reason was simple: they were convinced that Trump's candidacy was a publicity stunt and he'd withdraw after the initial rush of free press.

One thing I knew from long experience was that Trump didn't want to pay retail, and he would never agree to pay for services he might not actually require. This was even truer when it came to politics, I was learning, despite Trump's repeated brag that he would spend hundreds of millions of dollars to win the Presidency. In truth, he didn't want to spend a dime of his own money, if at all possible, and any and all expenditures had to be the absolute rock-bottom minimum.

Which was how a political operative and charmer named Corey Lewandowski walked into the Trump campaign and my life. He came recommended by David Bossie, the head of the right-leaning political group Citizens United, with Lewandowski boasting an inflated resume and an exaggerated sense of himself.

The real reason Trump went with Lewandowski was cost: he wanted ten percent of what the others commanded, and he didn't demand to be paid in advance. Like the cheap paint at Doral, Trump was going to get what he paid for—or didn't pay for. The reason Lewandowski came dirt-cheap should have been obvious with a simple Google check—but Trump didn't bother with such trivialities. Lewandowski was forty-one and worked as an executive at the Koch-funded group Americans for Prosperity, but he'd claimed to run the entire outfit when he was really only in charge of voter registration.

Within a day or two I didn't like the look of Lewandowski, walking around the office with a Red Bull in each hand bossing people around. As I quietly did my due diligence on him, I could see that Lewandowski's calling card was his propensity for absurd behavior and a long history of associating with unethical politicians. As an undergraduate, he'd run for the Massachusetts House of Representatives, receiving, at best, a grand total of seven votes, only to bounce around working for various lower-level state politicians and then wind up as an aide to Representative Bob Ney of Ohio, who'd become a surrogate father—before he was locked up for a wide range of fraudulent and corrupt behavior in the Jack Abramoff scandal of the 2000s.

Lewandowski liked to carry himself with an ex-cop swagger, but the reality was that he'd been a trainee officer at a marina in New Hampshire handing out lifejackets, and he was the kind of genius who carried a loaded handgun in a bag of dirty laundry into a federal building, only to be caught by the metal detector. To say that Corey and I didn't get along from the very start would be a massive understatement. I hated him, and he hated me. It was that simple, as we both contended for Trump's attention and praise.

Let Trump Be Trump was Lewandowski's motto, written on a

blackboard on the fifth floor of Trump Tower, where the campaign headquarters was established on the former set of *The Apprentice*, an apt setting for the reality TV show that was about to unfold. For the new campaign manager, that meant bending and scraping and praising Trump to an extent that embarrassed even me, and that's saying something, because I was one of the worst sycophants.

One thing that Lewandowski wanted to achieve was to keep me off TV and on the margins of the campaign, which pissed me off, and did nothing to stop me from regularly showing up on CNN and Fox to shill for the Boss. I was the only person Trump allowed to speak on TV without his prior notice and permission, and he refused to concede to Lewandowski on this front, to my delight.

"He's an asshole," I once said to Trump, with Lewandowski standing right there. "He treats everyone badly. He's a wannabe bully."

Funny, coming from me, right?

In the spring of 2015, I wanted Trump to launch the campaign as soon as possible, but the Boss wanted to delay for as long as possible, mostly because it postponed the day he would have to start spending real money. To Trump, the odds of winning the nomination were so long, he considered it almost certainly wasted money, so best to avoid expenses as long as he could.

Lewandowski was fine with moving slowly, likely not grasping the underlying rationale, but when he went away with his family for a long-planned vacation in Aruba, I pounced on the opportunity to corner Trump and get him to set a date. Lewandowski was on the phone day after day from his vacation trying to convince Trump to push the date back, in order to properly stage manage the event, while I urged the Boss to move quickly and get the campaign rolling at long last.

Finally, a summit meeting was called in Trump's office, with

Lewandowski, Hope Hicks, a lawyer named David Schwartz, and me convening to decide the timing and how to attract the greatest amount of attention and press. Everyone was in a great mood, joking around and throwing out ideas, but for me it was personal. I had been waiting for this day for five years and I wanted it to be even bigger and more sensational than Trump did, which would be no small feat.

The setting was going to be the lobby of Trump Tower, it was universally agreed. The atrium had grandeur and tying the campaign to the brand was the essential point of the entire campaign: running for president was going to be a long free informercial for the Trump Organization, and so the iconic pink marble womb in the mother ship of the brand had to be featured.

"Let's make it a proverbial circus," I told the group. "Hey, Boss, what about people on stilts, a few fire breathers, and some elephants?"

Trump looked at me quizzically, trying to decide if I was serious, as I laughed.

"Could you imagine if an elephant dropped a load on your marble floor?" I said.

Lewandowski hated the back and forth. He was a newcomer and an outsider and he resented the joking around.

"No elephants," he yelled. "No circus. This is a presidential campaign launch."

"Take it easy, tough guy," I told him. "It's a fucking joke. But if we do bring in elephants, and one takes a dump, it's your job to clean it up."

"C'mon, let's finish this," Trump interjected. "Let's do it as a regular event. Down in the atrium. That way people can line up around all the floors to get a view. I don't want balloons. We'll save those for when we win."

Trump smiled. He was joking, sort of, or was he? I couldn't tell for sure. But one thing was clear: Trump wanted a big crowd. He was focused on how the event was going to look. He wanted the lobby rocking when he emerged to make the announcement and it fell to the attorney David Schwartz and me to start working social media to attract as many people as possible. David and I had done events for Trump in the past, including a press conference we staged when the Boss had been trying to set up a catering hall at Jones Beach on Long Island in 2011. We'd gotten 500 people to attend that rally and you could see how thrilled Trump had been with the turnout. David had given a speech, or more like a screed—Trump called him "the Screamer"—and then the Boss had addressed the crowd. It was the first time he'd given a political speech to a large group of people and it was obvious that he'd absolutely loved it. It was that rally, in 2011, when I first glimpsed that element of the sheer talent he possessed—what the world was soon going to get to see for themselves.

To ensure there would be a great crowd, David hired a local acting agency for a few dozen extras at fifty bucks apiece to provide a guaranteed background of people wearing Trump-branded t-shirts. But the truth was that we didn't have to worry about attendance. When word circulated in the media and online that Trump was going to announce, people started signing up and the Trump t-shirt served as a form of a ticket to enter the lobby.

On the day of days, June 16, 2015, there was a crowd lined up along Fifth Avenue. I stepped outside to take a picture and then I went up to the 26th floor to show Trump. He was delighted.

"Wow," he said. "This is huge. I'm putting the finishing touches on my bullet points. This is going to be great."

"It sure is, Boss," I said. "I have Stephanopoulos with me, and a few other journalists. I'm going to head downstairs to do one last run-through to make sure everything is perfect. I'll schmooze the press so they write about the size and enthusiasm of the crowd."

On the ground floor, the atrium was now packed and getting tighter by the minute. We'd placed people at different points around the lobby to hand out Trump placards and Trump t-shirts and other promotional materials we'd cooked up. I could tell it was going to be a shit show, for sure, which was what the Boss wanted: something big and unpredictable and sensational, like him, I thought, as I double-checked the microphones and made sure the cameras were all in place for the announcement. David Schwartz was circulating, urging on the excitement, telling them it was only ten more minutes.

"Let's hear it when the elevator doors open," Schwartz implored the crowd.

Finally, I took another photo of the now thronging crowd and took the elevator up to see Trump one last time. I told him I'd made sure the mics were working and I showed him the photo. He grinned.

"It's show time," Trump said. "See you down there in ten minutes."

Downstairs, I made sure that the path from the elevator to the escalator was roped off and protected by security. We'd used the grand entrance down the escalator for press conferences in the past. The sight of Trump descending slowly, magisterially, like some kind of lord from on high, gave the scene the kind of dramatic flourish that he relished. Trump would look sternly forward, offering a thumbs up.

Then it happened: down the escalator came Trump and Melania, both tanning-booth bronzed, the Boss giving the crowd the thumbs up, the stereo cranking Neil Young's "Keep on Rockin' in the Free World," an admittedly unlikely use of the Canadian-born singer's ironic tribute to the excesses of capitalism—a nuance totally lost on Trump. I stood to one side with George Stephanopoulos, the former aide to President Clinton and an anchor at ABC News, in the VIP section outside the Trump Grill.

Trump stepped up on the makeshift stage we'd installed and he let rip in an hour-long tirade that was breathtaking in its lack of structure, compassion, or coherence. It was literally a rant, with frequent awkward silences in the press corps like they weren't entirely sure if this was a publicity stunt, or if Trump was perhaps joking, or out of his mind. Trump was spewing things that I found repulsive. Mexicans were rapists, he said, even though there was a very nice Mexican man working in Trump Ice Cream on the other side of the atrium no doubt listening in horror.

Stephanopoulos turned to me, a look of disbelief in his eyes as Trump's nativist and reactionary views spewed forth: Mexicans are bringing drugs and crime to America, the American Dream is over, promising to self-fund his campaign, boasting about his wealth of $8.7 billion, lying about the size of the crowd. Trump was pure id.

"Did he really just say that?" Stephanopoulos asked.

"Well, so much for this campaign," Stephanopoulos sighed a minute later.

"Did he ever really want to win?" he asked.

"Why would he say something like that?" Stephanopoulos finally said in disbelief.

For an hour I listened as I cringed, inwardly, but swelled outwardly at the sight of the crowd listening to Trump with real admiration, it seemed to me. That nascent political talent I'd witnessed at Jones Beach five years earlier—the way he could command a crowd, the way he reveled in the sound of his own voice, the way he seemed to naturally inhabit a permanent moving bully pulpit— was emerging. I didn't know the contours that would come forth in the months and years ahead, but I could see that he wasn't just a force to be reckoned with—he was a force of nature.

Once again, I had reached a fork in the road, and instead of trying to reconcile my moral compass with what I was enabling in Trump, I chose to look away and just keep rolling on, as if I wasn't actually making a choice. Trump was now a presidential candidate and I was in the middle of the action. I had a VIP section pass to the greatest political show of all time. Even if Trump didn't win, I'd won already, just by the association and the intoxicating rush of being inside a campaign for the highest office on the planet.

"Well, that was unusual," Stephanopoulos sighed as he departed and the exhausted crowd dissipated. "I'll speak to you later."

I went up to the 26th floor, to Trump's office, now filled with supplicants praising him as he ego surfed and wallowed in the fawning admiration—most of it faked, I figured, because it seemed like any sentient being who lived in New York City in 2015 would know that what he was saying was beyond the pale. But this was the onset of a phenomenon that continues to this day. No one ever tells Trump the truth about his behavior and beliefs, or the consequences of his conduct and ignorance and arrogance, in business or in his personal life and now in politics. Trump truly is the boy in the bubble, impervious to the thoughts and feelings or others, entirely and utterly focused on his own desires and ambitions.

Trump spotted me across the room.

"Michael!" he called. "What a crowd! What did you think?"

"Unbelievable," I said.

That was it: unbelievable. I didn't mean it the way he took it, as praise and astonishment at his performance. I meant it literally: it was unbelievable that any candidate would say the things that Trump said that day. But please take note of how truly, unbelievably cowardly and hypocritical my response was. If I told Trump what I really thought, if I critiqued even one element of the rant, I would be banished forever, I knew. Trump was beyond enthused:

he was ecstatic, like he had discovered a new drug, a new high, an entirely new thrill that he hadn't expected to feel as incredibly good as this did.

I could relate to Trump, as I was snorting from the same metaphorical mountain of cocaine, like Tony Montana in *Scarface*, stoned out of my mind on power.

When I got home, Samantha was furious. She knew I was friends with people from all walks of life, including different ethnicities and religions. She knew I knew better. She said that I was friends with lots of Muslims and Hispanics and there I was, cheering on a racist pig. How could I support Trump when he said such terrible things about Mexicans?

"This is going to be really bad," she said.

"Your grandmother was born in Buenos Aires, for God's sake," my son Jake said.

"It was taken out of context," I told them, as always, making excuses for Trump, excusing the inexcusable.

"He's not qualified to be president," Samantha said. "I'm a political science student and I know more about how the world works than he does. What does he know about the United Nations or NATO or nuclear weapons? Nothing is what he knows. I'm literally more qualified than him and I'm twenty-one-years old."

"I'm not going to discuss this again," I said, as our dispute escalated into a screaming argument that left us unable to talk to each other for two months. That was my mantra with Samantha and Jake when they begged me to stop working for Trump. They had made their views clear, but I needed to be able to do what I wanted without having to answer to my children. That's what I told myself. I wasn't going to be bossed around by anyone—except the Boss.

Imagine how it feels now to know my daughter and son weren't only right about Trump—they were right about me. I knew better, but I went along with the madness, thinking Trump was my ticket to the White House, or at least the best shot I'd ever have.

The news that night was relentlessly negative. Trump was condemned as a joke and a racist bully. But I knew that something else had been unleashed at that press conference. Trump was channeling the resentment of people labeled as racist during the Obama years: white folks, conservative and Christian men and women who were sick of political correctness and tolerating illegal immigration and having to pretend that they believed things they simply didn't believe. Trump was their champion. The undereducated, the reactionary, the people who believe abortion is murder—here was a blunt and fearless businessman calling bullshit on the American political order.

Globalization, climate change, gay marriage, the loss of American jobs to Third World countries, immigration, the central role of God—all of those with resentments and grievances had found their advocate.

Dangerous forces were let loose on the land that day, and I was there, not just complicit, but an active and cynical participant in the game of Russian roulette the United States of America was about to play.

* * *

THE DAYS FOLLOWING Trump's inglorious announcement were frantic inside the Trump Organization. I figured the Boss was going to stage the shortest political campaign in history, as he would inevitably be forced to withdraw and retract his rabid anti-Hispanic comments. The Trump kids were beside themselves with worry about the damage their father's tirade was doing to the brand and businesses. A significant part of the revenue of Trump's various golf clubs and resorts came from corporate events and large companies, all of which were cancelling events at an alarming rate. Univision, the Spanish-language broadcasting network, had its headquarters next to the Doral in Miami, and it simply ceased using that facility and then cancelled the contract to air the Miss USA and Miss Universe pageants.

"I'm going to have to sue Univision now," Trump said in reply. "They'll have to pay me a lot of money."

Like he was the victim. These were the early signs of the power dementia that would come to consume Trump during the campaign and then further as president. It was like he couldn't stop himself from going lower and lower, seeking to outrage more and more, the thrill of the spotlight bleaching out his few redeeming virtues. Like his attack on Univision's highly respected reporter Jorge Ramos, who stood up at a press conference and asked Trump to address his racist remarks about Hispanics. Trump ignored Ramos, then ordered him to sit down, then barked that he should "go back to Univision," then sicced his bodyguard Keith Schiller on him.

The older Trump kids were mortified, and horrified, but of course, as always, silent. Racist, reactionary, anti-Hispanic weren't exactly the terms that Ivanka Trump wanted associated with her clothing line. But she wasn't going to stand up to her father any more than her brothers were; fear radiated outward from Trump, but it also sent its radioactive waves inwardly into the family. Finally, in desperation, the three older kids came to my office on the 26th floor to ask me to talk to the Boss and convince him to drop out of the campaign before it totally destroyed the family's reputation, name, and brand. Their social position and legacy were being flushed down the drain, they knew, but there was nothing they could do to stop their father. Ivanka led the charge.

"MC, you've got to get Dad to stop the campaign," Ivanka said. "It's killing the company."

"If he keeps this up, you'll be named the CEO of the Rump

Organization," Don Jr. said to me, only half joking. "We're losing millions."

The concern was evident, but I knew I couldn't help. I truly felt for the kids, with their future lying in the balance. The stakes for me were much lower: I could just go work with Mark Cuban, or sell my taxi medallions and retire.

"This is your Dad's company," I said. "No one can change his mind on anything. I certainly don't like his position on Hispanics, either, but what can be done?"

Calls of protest from Univision executives began to flow in to myself and Larry Glick, who ran the golf operation. Hispanic executives were dismayed and disgusted by Trump's comments and his ongoing assaults on Jorge Ramos, which perfectly combined his disdain for the media and Spanish-speaking people. As it continued to get worse, I finally decided I really did need to talk to Trump and try to get him to ease up and not permanently and perhaps fatally harm his company over a candidacy that looked not just doomed but delusional.

"I don't care," Trump said, when I told him how concerned for the business his children were about all the cancellations. "Let them cancel the events. This is more important than all the events."

I was stunned. Something was more important than money? Since when? Maybe he really was ready to make a commitment to running for president, regardless of the consequences?

"Plus, I will never get the Hispanic vote," Trump said. "Like the blacks, they're too stupid to vote for Trump. They're not my people."

Trying to figure a way to moderate Trump, I leapt at a call from Javier Palomarez, the head of the United States Hispanic Chamber of Commerce, asking the Boss to attend a forthcoming town hall he was holding. I hoped that Javier would provide some cover for Trump as a way to disguise or at least muddy the waters

around the Boss's rampant anti-Hispanic and anti-immigrant language, as if it were a matter of public relations or a misunder-
standing of some sort—not substance. This was another form of
catch and twist I practiced, distorting Trump's distortions so that
common sense and basic perceptions like your eyes and ears
couldn't be trusted, a tactic that worked to a terrible extent, especially with those who enjoyed Trump's nativism and privately
agreed with his racism but needed a fig leaf to hide behind. It was
in that spirit that I told Palomarez that I would talk to Trump
about him attending a forum to discuss issues important to the
Hispanic community.

"It's a set up," Trump told me when I raised the idea. "They
will only attack me. Plus, no matter what I say, they'll never vote
for Trump."

"I agree," I toadied, if that's a word. "But before you reject the
forum, let me see if I can get Javier to come here to see you. One-
on-one. If you win him over, his organization and coalition could
be a big boost. He's got a ton of members and they're a huge voting bloc."

"OK," Trump huffed. "Do it and then we can decide."

After a lot of convincing, Palomarez agreed to come to Trump
Tower, but only if it was done privately, because his members were
furious at Trump and he didn't want to be seen as someone curry-
ing favor with the man engaged in an ongoing onslaught against
Hispanics, the very people he was supposed to represent. The
meeting would be strictly confidential, I reassured him, a sit down
with only Trump and I in attendance and the conversation entirely
off the record.

As soon as Palomarez walked into Trump's office with a couple
of colleagues, I could tell from the Boss's face that he didn't like
the look of him. Palomarez had slicked-back grey hair and a tai-
lored suit and he looked every bit the part of a talented and smooth

Trump with Palomarez, © 2020 Michael Cohen

salesman—a type Trump held in disdain. Rising from his desk and offering his hand, Trump disguised his disdain as he greeted Palomarez and the two other officials; I was the only other person present.

The meeting began with Trump's obligatory introductory lie. I'd told Trump a few small details about Palomarez and Hispanic Chamber of Commerce, but he'd done no preparation for the simple reason that he never prepares for anything, ever. Reading reports, taking briefings, seeking context and background for professional encounters—Trump does none of that, trusting that he can fake his way through life. More than that, he preferred to be ignorant, as it allowed him to rely on his gut instincts.

"So, Javier, tell me about your organization," Trump said. "I hear unbelievable things about what you've built."

Palomarez described his organization and all the town halls and rallies it staged, making it sound like a formidable political force with influence over millions of Hispanic voters. The endorsement of the Hispanic Chamber of Commerce would be invaluable for any politician, he said, and many had sought his support over the years. They were holding a town hall in the coming weeks, he said, and he would like Trump to attend.

"You know, Mr. Trump, our town hall is open to our members, who will be asking you some very difficult and direct questions,"

Palomarez said. "For example, are you anti-Hispanic, or anti-immigrant? Those are fair questions that need to be answered because of your campaign launch and the reports that there have been no legitimate answers from you."

"Javier, let me tell you, I am not anti-Hispanic or anti-immigrant," Trump said, adopting his best political mien, exactly as he'd done with the evangelicals back in 2011 when they laid hands on him—the spectacle that convinced me the Boss could become president because he was so adept at being deceptive and disingenuous. "In fact, both my parents were immigrants," he added, another gratuitous lie, because his father had been born in the United States. "Two of my three wives have been immigrants."

Back and forth they went, as Trump transformed himself into a thoughtful and compassionate businessman without a racist bone in his body, just as he'd pretended to be religious with the Falwells and the other Christian leaders. Like the evangelicals, Palomarez was eating it up, to my amazement. The sight of two grown men engaging in an elaborate charade was almost comical to behold. The meeting was going well, really well, largely because Trump was mouthing platitudes and Palomarez wasn't calling bullshit on the Boss's racist remarks by quoting them back.

"Mr. Trump, I am pleased by this meeting," Palomarez said as he departed. "I hope that we will continue to talk and that you will consider participating in my town hall."

"You and Michael stay in touch," Trump said. "I will speak to my team and try to set up a date for your event."

After Palomarez and the two others departed, Trump shook his head.

"What a phony bullshit artist," he said. "He and the whole Hispanic Chamber of Commerce thing is a fucking scam. Like Al Sharpton's bullshit group. Who knows, who cares. No matter what, I'm not doing his fucking town hall. And did you hear in the middle when I asked him how the organization supports itself? Through donations and dues and advertising, he said. He was looking for me to become one of his suckers. Fuck him. I don't regret what I said about Mexicans. What I said was fucking true."

When I returned to my desk, I received a call from security in the lobby that a press conference was being held. I knew immediately it was Javier, so I raced to the elevator and made it to the lobby in time to see him leaving the building with the press in tow. When I called his cell, he claimed his comments to the media had been neutral but when the stories hit the wire they were critical of Trump and I knew that would go down like a lead balloon with the Boss. I called Javier again, this time yelling and threatening to release a statement from Trump calling him a phony bullshit artist. How would he like that, I asked?

"Please," Javier said, trying to calm me down. "Let's put out a joint statement that can correct any issues you think exist and that is mutually beneficial."

The next morning, Trump was at his desk reading about his meeting with Palomarez, I saw nervously, waiting for him to go off on the fact that it was meant to be private and not in the press. But he wasn't pissed, for a change.

"Did you see the amount of press we got for meeting with the guy?" Trump said. "Not bad."

"I did, Boss," I replied. "They were mostly favorable. I know his people are going to call to ask about the town hall. What should I say?"

"That?" Trump said. "Not a chance."

* * *

As TRUMP STARTED to travel to early-primary states, like New Hampshire and Iowa, I remained in New York, working as his personal attorney and frequent surrogate on TV, with my ability to channel the Boss and his views with great impact. At least, that was how Trump and I saw my role. I'd do two or three shows in a row, with Fox inviting me to stay for the whole day doing hits every hour.

My regular appearances on TV outraged Lewandowski, mostly because he wanted to control everything, it seemed to me, and I wasn't going let him have any say-so about my media appearances. I didn't work for the campaign and he had no authority over my actions or words, which admittedly were often over the top or just plain crazy. Like the story about Trump allegedly raping his first wife, Ivana, based on her testimony from the nineties during their divorce proceedings. I first heard about this issue when Hope Hicks came to my office with a stricken look on her face. She had received an email from a young reporter named Tim Mak from *The Daily Beast* saying that he had information that Trump had raped Ivana during their marriage and he was running a story on the testimony from her deposition during their divorce—did Donald Trump's campaign have a comment? Hope was beside herself, not knowing what to do or say, but at least she had the presence of mind to come to my office, the correct destination for dirty work like this promised to be.

I walked to Trump's office and explained the situation with Mak and the *Daily Beast*. Trump didn't seem fazed at all. He called out to Rhona, who went to her trusty filing cabinet and pulled out one of the multitude of manila folders, handing it to me as I returned to Trump's office to read it while he sat silently watching me. I wasn't given the whole deposition, only the relevant pages, as if Trump had anticipated this subject coming up some day. The portrait in the testimony was of an aggrieved and scorned woman in a bitter fight with her soon-to-be ex-husband and using the occasion to cast any and all possible aspersions on Trump. Typical wealthy Manhattan divorce testimony, in other words, with Ivana Trump saying she didn't feel loved by her husband when they had sex in the aftermath of a failed hair replacement operation—the very surgery that prompted the Boss to design his intricate, three-step flip, flop, flap combover to hide the scars.

"Emotional rape" was the precise term Ivana had used to describe the encounter. But English was her third of four languages and her choice of words was obviously unsophisticated; a native of then-Czechoslovakia, she spoke English with a heavy accent and often didn't seem to know the implications or subtleties of what she was saying, Trump told me.

"This is bullshit, Boss," I said.

"I never raped anyone," Trump said.

He folded his arms, a scowl on his face. "Call Mak and set this straight."

Returning to my office, I started to think about the older Trump kids and how they'd lived through a messy and very public divorce as young children—one of the most notorious in decades in New York City. The private lives of their parents had played out on the front page of the tabloids as their father publicly betrayed their mother and put the children in an impossible situation. Don Jr. had often talked about how badly the kids had been scarred by the divorce and all the years when they'd not seen much of their father; for a period of time, Don Jr. had refused to speak to his father because of his fury and pain over how he'd treated his mother and siblings.

All that awful tabloid horror was now going to be relived in public? What about young Barron? My outrage was building as I reached for my phone to call Mak. Some two-bit reporter I'd never heard of—and I knew pretty much all the good journalists in New York—was going to hurt Trump's kids and make them go through all that pain again for a cheap-shot headline? What about the grandchildren? They were getting old enough to understand and read the news, and they would surely be inundated with sensational stories about their strange but loved grandfather raping their grandmother?

I was livid by the time I got Mak on the line and denied the Boss had done any such thing—and then added that it wasn't legally possible to rape your own wife. I knew this wasn't true, of course, but this was one of the ways that truth and I were starting to part ways.

Mak replied that he was in possession of the deposition and he was going to run the story, no matter what I said. Again and again, I demanded some basic human decency and consideration for the children and grandchildren, but he wasn't listening to me and his intransigence was making me insanely furious—not that I needed much provocation in those days.

I hissed at Mak that I was going to go after him personally, along with "everybody else you possibly know." I added, charmingly, "So I'm warning you, tread very fucking lightly, because what I'm going to do to you is going to be fucking disgusting. Do you understand me?"

Sound like someone in possession of their mind?

When Mak ran the story of the rape allegation, along with an extensive quote of my threats toward him, I immediately released a statement repenting my behavior. "As an attorney, husband, and father, there are many injustices that offend me, but none more than racism and rape," I said. "Rarely am I surprised by the press, but the gall of this particular reporter to make such a reprehensible and false allegation against Mr. Trump truly stunned me. In my moment of shock and anger I made an inarticulate comment—which I do not believe—and which I apologize for entirely."

There were calls for me to be fired, but Trump refused to let me go despite the demands of Lewandowski. But, of course, Trump went public to distance himself from me, saying he didn't agree that a husband couldn't rape his wife, and that I had been speaking for myself, not him, yet another foreshadowing that I didn't notice—or want to notice.

As I said in the introduction to this book, there was no excuse for my behavior, and no apology, no matter how sincere—and I am truly, sincerely sorry—erases my actions and or takes away my responsibility for my conduct. I offer this story by way of an explanation, to allow you to understand the nature and severity of the affliction that possessed me. In this way, I was like the millions of Americans who now line up for hours in the driving snow in some town in Wisconsin to hear Trump's hour-long stream-of-consciousness comedy act—because that's what he is, a stand-up comic, with a grotesque sense of humor.

But I get ahead of myself.

Sulking after my attack on Tim Mak of the *Daily Beast* came out, Lewandowski told me I was now in the "penalty box," his term for being out of his favor and not being allowed to play the game; he'd been a hockey player in high school, apparently, and imagined himself to be the referee of the Trump campaign, a notion I found insulting and ridiculous. I just ignored Lewandowski, safe in the knowledge that the Boss was pleased by my performances and that he privately approved of my hyper-aggressive and relentlessly attacking approach to advocating on his behalf.

But I wasn't the only one supposedly in Lewandowski's stupid penalty box. Sean Hannity and I were close. I'd met him in 2011, when the Boss was first thinking of running, and we hit it off as I appeared frequently on his show as a Trump promoter, providing good ratings by ranting and raving about the Boss. In the years since, we'd talked frequently, often on a daily basis, discussing the state of the world and the relative strengths of potential Republican candidates, including Trump. We'd also talked about business matters and our personal lives, as confidants and pals. Sean was making a boatload of money at Fox, somewhere around $30 million a year, and he wanted to learn about investing in real estate. He was building a portfolio of properties spread around the country as a way to ensure real and durable wealth for his family, and he frequently asked my opinion about particular deals and strategies and partnerships.

Sean never hired or paid me as his attorney, and now he claims I never represented him, and that was true, but it didn't stop him from talking to me as a counselor and confessor, roles that suited me. During this time, Sean said that his marriage was in serious trouble, with divorce looming in the air.

"You don't want to do that," I said. "What about your kids? You want to lose half your money?"

"You have a point there," Hannity said.

"Is there another woman involved?" I asked. "You been screwing around?"

Sean sighed. Like Trump, he knew how to say something without actually saying it, which is how men of power and wealth actually are, in my experience: they want to confess to their peers, by way of bragging, but they don't want to outright admit to cheating, finding a way both to express their virility and retain plausible deniability.

"There are so many women in the world," Hannity sighed. "There are just so many women out there."

In the summer of 2015, I knew that Hannity was doing what he could for the Trump campaign, but that he had to be careful. His viewership wasn't monolithically for Trump, yet, and there were more than a dozen candidates, some commanding large segments of the Republican Party. Jeb Bush, Ted Cruz, Marco Rubio, Ben Carson, and each of the other declared candidates had to be given time to make their case, meaning that Trump didn't absolutely dominate Hannity's highly rated show in the way that the Boss wanted—and that Lewandowski demanded.

Hannity's best efforts didn't stop Lewandowski from attacking him; like every reporter covering Trump, he was submitted to a brutal and frequently idiotic set of rules and expectations that required strict conformity to the Boss's campaign manager's idea of what the press should cover. Corey's way of punishing the allegedly wayward was to put them in the penalty box, just as he'd tried unsuccessfully to do to me. Reporters didn't take kindly to this treatment, of course, and neither did powerful opinion talk show hosts like Sean Hannity. This was especially true for a commentator who was on friendly terms with Trump's personal attorney and who was obviously trying to walk a fine line to maintain credibility with Fox's audience. Full-throated support of Trump wouldn't help ratings, I knew, and nor was there any indication that it would help the Boss's campaign.

"Why am I in the penalty box?" Hannity asked me one day. "We've got to stop this bullshit."

I rolled my eyes at the idiocy of the situation. I quickly discovered that Lewandowski was telling Trump that Hannity was secretly a Cruz supporter and that he was insidiously undermining the Boss by pretending to be neutral but subliminally messaging his viewers to vote for the Texas senator. Trump was always prone to listen to the last person who spoke to him, frequently the advisor floating the worst and most destructive idea, and in those days, Lewandowski was often that person. Appealing to Trump's paranoia and rage was a surefire way to get him to take rash action.

I made my way to Trump's office.

"We've got end this bullshit with Hannity," I said to Trump.

"Fuck him," Trump said. "The guy's a fucking traitor."

"A traitor in what way?" I asked.

"Corey told me he's backing Cruz," Trump said.

"Really, where did he get that information?" I asked. "How does he know this or anything at all on the matter?"

"You just hate Corey," Trump said. "No matter what he says, you always say the opposite."

"I acknowledge that I despise him," I said. "He's an alcoholic piece of shit. But what does that have to do with Hannity?"

I took a breath.

"Hannity is on your side," I said. "He just can't show it. He can't seem partial, otherwise he loses credibility, and so do you."

Trump tilted his head back and crinkled his nose and puckered his mouth in his distinctive fashion, like he'd sucked on a lemon or caught wind of a fart.

"Get him on the phone," he said.

I dialed Sean's digits and he picked up immediately, even though he was in the middle of performing his daily radio talk show, pausing to take a commercial break to field my call.

"What's up," he said. "I'm on air."

"I'm with the Boss," I said, my phone on speaker. "He's listening to us now. Feel free to tell Mr. Trump what you told me."

"Mr. Trump, Lewandowski's a piece of shit and a liar," Hannity said. "I can't come out publicly to endorse you at this time. It would destroy my credibility as it relates to you. But I want you to know that I am today and have always been behind you."

Trump was now listening intently, nodding at the ritualistic prostration of the Fox host explaining how his show really worked.

"I speak to Michael on a daily basis," Hannity said. "Anything he has asked me to do that benefits you, I have done."

"That's true, Boss," I said.

"Okay, fine, let's forget about it," Trump said.

Hannity was keen to do more supplication, it seemed. "Mr. Trump, I'd like to call you later."

"Okay," Trump said.

"Thank you, sir," Hannity said. "Thank you for believing in me, because I believe in you."

Thus ended the Hannity embargo, and thus it went in Trump's campaign with the internecine fighting always threatening to turn into outright warfare.

* * *

THE DEBATE OF August 6, 2015 was held in Cleveland, Ohio, and broadcast on Fox News and Facebook. It was the first debate and the most anticipated question that loomed was how Trump would perform. He'd never participated in a formal debate before, making him a neophyte up against practiced and supposedly ruthless opposition. The world had no idea what was coming, and neither did the deer-in-the-headlights Republicans who were helpless to counter the sheer aggressive force of Donald Trump.

I watched the debate from the house I'd rented in Bridgehampton, on Long Island, for the summer. With my personal wealth rising inexorably—I thought—I'd paid a quarter of a million dollars to rent a giant Italianate mansion with 15,000 square feet, a two-story pool house, tennis court, and more bedrooms than I could count. Padding around the palace with Laura and the kids and a constant stream of friends seeking an escape from Manhattan's oppressive summer heat, I had become more or less a spectator to the campaign. Trump and I talked most every day, and I was up to the minute on every development, but I also kept some distance in order to keep the peace.

The moderator was Fox News's Megyn Kelly, and she went after Trump in a far more aggressive manner than his opponents, questioning the way he'd treated women, including the crude insults he'd aimed at Rosie O'Donnell. I winced as Trump tried to push back, knowing that he'd be filled with rage afterwards. No one talked to Trump like that, I knew, and the O'Donnell feud had indeed been one of the lowest of his many Twitter lows. My knowledge was firsthand, because I had access to Trump's Twitter account and permission to post on his behalf, one of only two people with that privilege. I'd been part of the brain trust coming up with juvenile taunts to O'Donnell, and so I was acutely aware of the childish impulse behind the insults.

"You've called women you don't like fat pigs, dogs, slobs, and disgusting animals," Kelly said to Trump.

Sure enough, Trump went nuts, displaying the temperament that now passes for presidential. The next day he told the press, "There was blood coming out her eyes, blood coming out of her wherever," obviously referring to her supposedly menstruating, though how that was relevant was one of the many mysteries of what came out of Trump's mouth.

The usual shit show ensued, or, I should say, the unusual Trump shit show. So I discovered that weekend when my phone vibrated and I looked down to see a familiar name: Sean Hannity.

"What's up?" I asked, stepping outside to the mansion's basketball court for privacy.

"It's about Megyn Kelly," Hannity said. "She's in hiding."

"Okay," I said. "And how does that involve me?"

"Roger is going to call you," he said, referring to the head of Fox, Roger Ailes, I knew immediately.

"What does Roger have to do with this?" I asked.

"Roger wants to talk to you," Sean said.

"He has my number," I said. "What are you, his secretary now?"

"He called me to call you to make sure you know the basics for his call," Sean said.

"Just have him call me," I said. "I think the world of Roger Ailes."

"Roger tells me that the reason Megyn is in hiding is because of Mr. Trump," Hannity said. "She's with her family, hiding in a hotel. There are Trump supporters at the entrance to her apartment building. She's got little kids. The Trump supporters are threatening her."

"Have Roger call and I'll get Trump on the line and we'll figure this all out," I said.

"Thanks," Hannity said. "I really appreciate it."

A minute later, Roger Ailes's name appeared on my phone. Again, I picked up, and discussed for fifteen minutes the backstory to the so-called feud between Megyn Kelly and Trump, when really it was more like a beatdown. Kelly had asked Trump pointed questions that were justified by his decades-long mistreatment of women; the fact that Trump was a sexist pig was beyond dispute. But so was Roger Ailes, I thought, listening to his complaint that Trump had crossed a line by frightening his star and highest-rated host.

Trump had blown his temper, unsurprisingly, and he'd reacted the only way he knew how: destruction and total annihilation. What was I supposed to do about that, I asked?

"She's got small kids," Ailes said. "This has got to stop."

"I agree," I said. "Hold on."

I dialed Trump. He picked up first ring—because that's how we worked: if one of us called the other, we answered immediately, like the inhalation and exhalation of breathing together, or conspiring, as I've said. Partners in crime, you might say.

Joining up the calls, I oriented Trump.

"I've got Roger on the line," I told Trump, as greetings were exchanged.

"Donald, we've got a problem," Ailes said. "Megyn can't come to the studio to do the show. She can't go to her apartment. She's got little kids. We can't have this."

"She came after me," Trump replied. "If you come after me, I come after you ten times harder."

A moment of silence hung in the air. Trump had been told that he'd terrified a woman and forced her into hiding. She had young children. She was a famous news anchor who'd challenged him on national television in a political debate with questions that he didn't like, understandably, but that certainly fit well within the bounds of civil discourse. Roger Ailes was himself a sexual predator who'd harassed Megyn Kelly and countless other women, as would emerge when he met his own moment of disgrace and denouement.

The notion that Trump might apologize or recognize the boundaries of decency never even arose; Ailes didn't have the temerity or moral standing to glimpse that possibility. But the Fox head was able to perceive that there was something seriously wrong about terrorizing another person, let alone a woman and her vulnerable children. This was too much for Roger fucking Ailes, I thought, and Trump still can't conceive of the idea that he's going too far?

"We've got to figure out a way to work this out," Ailes said calmly, not wanting to rile the snarling pit bulls that were Trump and his attack-dog attorney in self-righteous, full Roy Cohn mode.

Another silence descended.

"We've got to have you come on Megyn's show," Ailes said awkwardly. "We'll make it go the way you want it to."

Now Trump could be magnanimous, I thought, or fake it, at least. Going on the highest-rated show on Fox would now be doing Ailes a favor that Trump would call in, in due course, and of course he'd be the beneficiary of craven, Soviet-style fawning coverage on Fox—a hint of what has come to be our national disaster. All because Trump had bullied a journalist and incited violence as a routine part of his way of practicing politics.

I had been pacing for more than an hour on the basketball court by now, getting sunburned in the searing August heat, but I was performing my loyal duty, as two old white male sexual predators decided how Megyn Kelly's life would play out, or not, which personified so much of what was fundamentally wrong about the campaign that I was cheering for so ardently.

Let me add this: there were three douchebags on that call, not two. I was enabling two fat, rich, old, disgusting creeps as surely as a drug dealer sliding a complimentary fix of heroin or Oxycodone across the bar to a drug addict would be. Complicity doesn't really convey my role because I wasn't passively observing events, I was shaping them.

"You can figure this out with Michael," Trump finally said, as always, leaving the dirty work to me, knowing that I'd know what he wanted without having to be told. "The show has to only ask the questions I want. It has to go the way I want."

"Of course," Ailes said. "We'll do whatever you want. We just have to work this out."

Trump hung up and I proceeded to negotiate a forthcoming appearance on Kelly's show. The questions would be pat and patently soft balls. Trump would have the forum to express his views on Mexicans and the wall and China, and in return Kelly would sit meekly in order to regain some personal security with Trump signaling to his rabid supporters that they can stand down—for the time being. But this feud was only beginning, I believed, and I knew Trump would be the one who eventually ended it, one way or another.

As I've been saying since the beginning, Trump was a mobster, plain and simple, and I had just participated in political and personal blackmail.

Chapter Twelve

Russia (Part One)

Felix Sater returned to the Trump Tower in the fall of 2015 to approach me about a project in Moscow—a subject that has attracted considerable attention in the years since. I knew Felix a little from my teenage years living on Long Island. Felix was a knock-around businessman who'd been involved in a pump-and-dump boiler-room stock market operation run by the mafia, I'd heard, and I knew that he had a criminal record dating back to a bar brawl in the early '90s. The way I heard the story, Sater got in an argument in a bar called El Rio Grande, about a girl or something like that, and he threatened to kill some stranger, saying he was going rip his head off—then Felix smashed his margarita glass on the bar and stabbed the guy in the face and neck. He was convicted of felony assault in that case.

A real charmer. Sater was well-known in the Trump Organization, mostly for bad reasons. He'd worked on the Trump Soho deal, nearly a decade earlier, as well as a development in Florida. But the kids really didn't like Sater and the negative publicity his felony assault conviction attracted, especially as it reflected on the Trump family associating with underworld figures. Ivanka and Don Jr. had been investigated for felony fraud over selling units in Trump Soho by, as alleged, falsely inflating the number of condos that had been purchased, so they were hardly as pure as the driven snow.

I know there's been speculation that Sater was somehow the Whitey Bulger of New York City, a mob figure who was an inform-ant for the FBI, giving him a free pass to continue committing crime. For all I know, that may be true. What I can say for sure is that Sater wasn't some criminal genius conspiring with Russian oligarchs to launder vast sums of money through the Trump Organization. The Felix I knew had connections, but not at the high level imagined by liberal conspiracy theorists. Sater was a wannabe, for the most part, a hanger-on and fantasist.

In other words, a perfect partner for Donald Trump. Which was how the Boss reacted when I took the deal to him. I explained that the idea was for a building of 120 stories in Red Square, the heart of Moscow. It would be by far the tallest building in Russia and one of the iconic developments in all of Eastern Europe or Asia. I'd tried to bring together other deals in Georgia and Kazakhstan, but this proposal was on another level altogether. The economics were incredible, at least superficially. Sater proposed that thirty floors would be for commercial office space. Another thirty would be dedicated to a five-star hotel, with an Ivanka Trump-branded spa and Trump restaurants. The top floors would consist of 250 high-end condominiums, aimed at the Russian rul-ing class. The residential condos would pay for the whole project, so in effect, it was like getting commercially leased office space and a luxury hotel for free and in perpetuity. The money was so favorable, according to Felix, we would be able to give the penthouse apartment to Russian President Vladimir Putin for free, partly as a marketing tool to attract other super-wealthy buyers and oligarchs, but also as a way to suck up to Putin. The genius part was that Trump wouldn't have to invest a dime; he was purely selling his name to the project to give it the sheen of luxury and quality that the Boss supposedly exuded.

Let me pause here to talk about Vladimir Putin. In the pages ahead, you will encounter overt and covert attempts to get Russia to interfere in the 2016 election, and I will elaborate on my insider knowledge about those efforts, but first, let me orient you on Donald Trump's views on the Russian leader. I'll start by saying that the answer is so simple and obvious that it still astounds me that no one has grasped the real attraction. Ask yourself this question: What does Trump most admire or worship? The answer is money. Now, ask yourself, who is the richest man in the world?

"Putin is the richest man in the world by a multiple," Trump often told me. "In fact, if you think about it, Putin controls twenty-five percent of the Russian economy, including every major business, like Gazprom. Imagine controlling twenty-five percent of the wealth of a country. Wouldn't that be fucking amazing?"

Trump held up a newspaper article about Gazprom, the giant Russian oil company. The photograph accompanying the story showed twenty-five trucks loaded with oil leaving a Gazprom facility. Twenty of the trucks were heading in one direction, while five were heading the opposite way.

"Those five trucks are for Putin," Trump said, with absolute certainty. "Putin isn't president of Russia. He's the ruler. He's the dictator. The tsar. He can do whatever he wants. He's going to be leader for the duration of his life."

Trump didn't say that disapprovingly, or with any emotion other than admiration bordering on awe. His impulses weren't democratic, in any sense of the word. Trump loved Putin because the Russian had the balls to take over an entire nation and run it like it was his personal company—like the Trump Organization, in fact. In Russia, no one questioned or doubted Putin, just as no one called out Trump on the 26th floor of Trump Tower. Putin's ability to bring the press to heel, the media's throat under his jackboot, was also an attraction to Trump, not a bad thing. The same was true for the banks and Russia's industrial complex; an entire society and civilization bent to the will of a single man was how Trump viewed the ideal historical form of government—with him as the man in charge, of course. Locking up your political enemies, criminalizing dissent, terrifying or bankrupting the free press through libel lawsuits—Trump's all-encompassing vision wasn't evident to me before he began to run for president. I honestly believe the most extreme ideas about power and its uses only really took shape as he began to seriously contemplate the implications of taking power and how he could leverage it to the absolute maximum level possible.

I should add here that this was generally true of Trump throughout the campaign and now during his Presidency. Trump didn't run for office with a coherent ideology, other than his Archie Bunker-like Queens reactionary worldview and a will to power, but as he got further and further into the process of becoming a politician, the implications began to emerge for him. One thing that was definitely true about Trump was that he was constantly calculating and assessing how to take maximum advantage of every situation. That was one of the reasons he and I got along so well: we both have a shark-like cunning that is constantly in motion and always looking for prey. Russia was the perfect example; Trump had been trying to get a project built in Moscow since the 1980s, just as he'd been contemplating running for president, but that was about prestige and spreading his name all over the world like a modern-day Pharaoh.

As the campaign went along, as Trump started to see ways to cheat and lie to win, he came to see that Russia could potentially be a great ally—not for the United States, but for him personally, a distinction that was starting to blur. The equation was as simple as it was treasonous: Hillary Clinton had criticized Russia's parliamentary elections in 2011, enraging Putin, the onset of a downward-spiraling relationship that hardened into hatred. That was an emotion Trump was a master at manipulating and encouraging, especially when it was useful to his purposes. If Trump could successfully encourage Putin's hatred of Clinton, the dictator might be inclined to come to the assistance of her opponent, on the theory of the ancient proverb that the enemy of your enemy is your friend.

That was the true nature of Trump's collusion with Putin, despite all the hype and speculation. The Trump campaign wasn't organized enough to have secure back channels to the Kremlin, and people like Corey Lewandowski wouldn't have a clue how to pull off such an operation. Steven Bannon loved to portray himself as an evil genius—and he truly was an evil, racist human being, like the character Al Pacino played in *The Devil's Advocate* who was actually the antichrist—but he wasn't going to try something as fraught and potentially destructive as contacting the Russians. What appeared to be collusion was really a confluence of shared interests in harming Hillary Clinton in any way possible, up to and including interfering in the American election—a subject that caused Trump precisely zero unease.

Always open to moral equivalence when defining good behavior, Trump told me that America intervenes in other country's elections all the time, even overthrowing regimes in places like Afghanistan and Iraq, so what was wrong with the Russians trying to influence the American election? That was Trump's rationale, so long as the cheating was done in his favor. If it had gone the other way, he would have screamed murder and threatened war with Russia, I'm sure. That was the nature and extent of Trump's patriotism as he came to see what he could potentially harness.

All of that mostly seemed moot at the time. Because we all expected Trump to lose, including the Boss himself, a large part of the posturing and praising of Putin was a way to keep the Trump Organization's options open with the Russian leader. American banks had long since given up on lending to Trump, and the German Deutsche Bank was also shrinking the level of financing they were willing to provide to him, making liquidity a serious problem. When Trump lost the election, he would have many options, including starting a TV network to rival Fox, but he wanted to do all he could to enable him to be able to borrow money from people in Putin's circle, and that meant sucking up to the Russians. Calling Putin smart and successful and all the other sycophantic things Trump said wasn't collusion so much as business as usual. Trump didn't care about American national security, or the plight of Ukraine fighting a hot war with an invading power, or that Putin and the Russian oligarchs were mobsters stealing their nation's wealth blind. Criminally robbing Russia made them smart, to Trump's way of thinking, and he was more than happy to take their money.

Trump had long experience benefitting from ill-gotten Russian largesse, selling luxury condos to many oligarchs and their minions. A decade earlier, Trump had bought a Palm Beach monstrosity called the Maison de l'Amitie, a 66,000-square-foot architectural nightmare built by a terrible-taste tycoon who moved to Florida from Massachusetts to become a philanthropist and socialite only to declare bankruptcy. The mansion was gaudy, over the top, a sprawl of rambling and disconnected styles and an eye sore. Right up Trump's alley, in other words, with the added benefit of the deal offering him the chance to prey on the remains of the formerly super-rich estate.

Trump paid just over $40 million, put a few licks of paint on the mansion—no doubt third-rate Super Hide from Benjamin Moore, like at Doral—and then listed it for $125 million. It was the jet-set version of *Flip This House*.

The house sat on the market for more than a year until a Russian oligarch named Dmitry Rybolovlev came along and Trump knew he had a live one on the hook. Rybolovlev was known as the "fertilizer king" of Russia, worth $10 billion, and he and his daughter bought the world's most expensive real estate the way others might splurge on a pair of shoes. Rybolovlev's tastes and appetites matched the Boss in their shameless conspicuous consumption; there was no question that the Russian's wealth had been obtained in dubious ways, if not outright theft. Collapsing mines, murder plots, polluted Russian rivers, embezzlement scandals—Rybolovlev and his daughter Ekaterina were what Trump would call "real beauties."

The Russians bought the house from Trump for $95 million in 2008, an inflated price paid on the eve of the real estate collapse and global financial crisis, at the time the largest price ever paid for a private residence in the United States. Trump told me that the price hadn't really been an issue. He explained that the Russians weren't really spending their own money when they made their excessive purchases of European soccer teams and super yachts and Central Park South penthouses. The oligarchs could enjoy the assets, but always and forever at the pleasure of Vladimir Putin, the new tsar, and displeasing him meant risking their fortunes but also their lives.

"The oligarchs are just fronts for Putin," Trump told me. "He puts them into wealth to invest his money. That's all they are doing—investing Putin's money."

Trump was convinced the real buyer of Maison de l'Amitie was Vladimir Putin.

"There's a bank in Switzerland that's got one and only one customer," Trump told me.

"There are rumors about that," I replied.

"I know it for a fact," Trump replied. "Putin is worth more than a trillion dollars."

As the election wore on, I began to believe that Trump secretly wanted Putin's kind of power for himself, which is part of why I'm convinced he won't leave office voluntarily—but I will get to that subject in due course. To Trump, Putin was like the Saudi royal family, or Kim Jong-un in North Korea: the incarnation of dynastic wealth and the real ruling class of the planet. Everyone other than the ruling class on the earth was like an ant, to his way of thinking, their lives meaningless and always subject to the whims of the true rulers of the world. Murdering an American green-card-holding journalist of Saudi dissent writing for the *Washington Post* by luring him to an embassy in Turkey and butchering his body—that was just fine by Trump, as the world saw in the brutal killing of Jamal Khashoggi, a crime that has had precisely zero impact on American foreign policy with the Saudis. Here was what Trump would say when informed of the killing of a journalist: "What the fuck do I care? He shouldn't have written what he did. He should have shut the fuck up."

The cosmic joke was that Trump convinced a vast swathe of working-class white folks in the Midwest that he cared about their well-being. The truth was that he couldn't care less. I don't mean that as speculation or an opinion. That was a stone-cold fact during the 2016 campaign and throughout Trump's presidency to this very day. To Trump, his voters are his audience, his chumps, his patsies, his base. Guns, criminalizing abortion—Trump took up those conservative positions not because he believed in them but because they were his path to power. That was what I meant when I told Congress that Trump is a con man.

Speaking of which, let me address my own credibility for a moment before I dive into the Russian idiocy. Because I'm so often portrayed as a serial liar and an unreliable narrator, please allow me to quote from the Mueller Report. The section I will cite only appeared in a footnote, which was the ultimate example of how an accusation always gets the front-page headline and the correction ends up in small print long after the damage has been done. Here is what Mueller and his team said about my cooperation after I agreed to proffer evidence to them, in particular regarding the Trump-Russia nexus and the Moscow Tower, buried in footnote 909 in Volume Two of the report—not exactly the front page of *The New York Times.*

"The Office found Cohen's testimony in these subsequent proffer sessions to be consistent with and corroborated by other information obtained in the course of the Office's investigation. The Office sentencing submission in Cohen's criminal case stated: 'Starting with his second meeting with [the Special Counsel's Office] in September, 2018, the defendant accepted responsibility not only for his false statements concerning the [Trump Tower] Moscow Project, but also in his broader efforts through false statement and testimony before Congress to minimize his role and what he knew about contacts between the [Trump Organization] and Russian interests during the course of the campaign . . . The defendant, without prompting by the [Special Counsel's Office], also corrected other false and misleading statements that he had made concerning his outreach in and contacts with Russian officials during the course of the campaign."

Compare and contrast that with Trump's insistent refrain that collusion with Russia was a "hoax" and he had "no business in Russia." Who do you think you should believe? Remember, I was talking to Mueller's lawyers under oath and on pain of perjury, perhaps an ironic statement given my present circumstances, but I can assure you that I was not going to lie or shade the truth when I cooperated with the authorities—and I won't here, either. This is the straight-up truth, no ice, no mixer, just a shot of reality.

To that end, let me clarify once and for all questions about my travels to Europe during the 2016 campaign, and in the years before. First, I have never been to Prague. Never, ever, not once. In 2002, I traveled to Ukraine with my brother to help him with a business opportunity he was pursuing with his father-in-law, but I was really there as support and comfort for him, not as a business principal, and I met precisely zero people involved in politics in any capacity. I also traveled to Zurich around the same time in 2002, as I told a *New York Times* journalist, Meghan Twohey, when the Russia story blew up and Christopher Steele's dossier was published in the weeks after the election. Despite protestations to the Editor-in-Chief, the story was wrongly reported as an admission that I went to Prague—but again, I don't want to rush ahead.

The reason Felix Sater approached me in September was easy to understand: the Trump kids hated him, and he knew it. He'd brought terrible publicity to the Trump family through the Trump Soho project from the very start in 2007, when his criminal history was revealed in *The New York Times*, mortifying the supposedly aristocratic Trump children, who were in charge of the sales and marketing effort for the building. The kids had proceeded to pump sales of the condos in Trump Soho, after the global crash of 2008 blindsided the Trump Organization, by telling potential buyers that "more than half" of the units had been sold, when the truth was that fewer than twenty percent had been purchased—potentially committing fraud in the process.

To say that Felix had an unusual resume would be an understatement. His attorney provided me with a five-page letter describing his accomplishments as a cooperating witness for the federal government and an international man of mystery. He'd thwarted an assassination attempt on former Secretary of State Colin Powell, and he'd testified to Congress during Condoleeza Rice's confirmation hearings, but the most incredible was the claim that he'd located Osama bin Laden after the 9/11 attack hiding in a cave in the mountains of Tora Bora. That's correct, as crazy as it sounds, but that was Felix, a kind of global grifter trying to convince billionaires to do deals with him, for a commission.

The Trump kids wouldn't deal with Sater, but the Boss had no compunction about working with a man with a felony assault conviction and extremely dubious track record, back channeling to shady Russian oligarchs, in the middle of a presidential campaign, no less. Trump just wanted to know the terms of the deal and how much money he could make, risk free. The answer was a lot. The Russian deal started with a Letter of Intent, signed in September of 2015, which laid out the benefits for Trump, no money down. LOIs, as Letters of Intent are known, really amounted to a statement of hope, rather than a binding legal agreement. Trump was to receive a payment of $4 million up front under the LOI, and, in addition, a cut of the revenues worth hundreds of millions of dollars. More importantly, Trump would finally achieve his dream of a branded skyscraper in the capital city of the former Soviet Union.

"Just make sure his name doesn't show up anywhere in the documents," Trump told me regarding Sater.

I went down to the 25th floor to discuss the proposed deal with Don Jr. The three children had identical offices in a row, ranked by seniority of age, with Don Jr. first, Ivanka in the middle, and Eric at the end of the line. The offices were furnished identically, with modern minimalist design and views of Fifth Avenue.

"Felix Sater brought me the deal," I told Don Jr. "I've already spoken with your Dad and he says it's okay as long as Sater's name doesn't show up anywhere."

"Okay," Don Jr. said. "I don't have a problem with Felix but I agree his name shouldn't be anywhere."

"We're going to go over to Russia," I said. "Think about how great it's going to be running off to Moscow on a multi-year deal."

"I love it," Don Jr. said. "Keep me in the loop."

Don Jr. said he'd let Ivanka and Eric know about the Moscow Tower at their next weekly meeting. I made five copies of the LOI, one on the Trump letterhead for execution, and walked the documents to each of the Trump family principals. Ivanka was the least positive about the potential deal, with nothing good to say about doing business with Sater.

"I don't like him," she told me. "I don't trust him. He's just a bad guy."

"The economics of the deal are very favorable," I said. "The LOI is non-binding and we have full termination rights at any time. I'll keep you updated on the location of the proposed site."

"As long as it's non-binding," Ivanka said. "I want this terminated at the first inkling of trouble."

Ivanka kept a hands-off policy at first, until she found out there was a plan to include a 20,000-square-foot health-and-wellness center called the Ivanka Spa. She started to want to work on the design, not just for the spa but for the whole building, rejecting the drawings I'd had a New York City architect work up for a tower that looked like the Washington Monument obelisk, only in dark glass. Ivanka wanted to hire Zaha Hadid, the British starchitect famous for her curved structures, and Trump's elder daughter was soon working on the interior design following a spare modern look. Trump hated modern architecture, preferring his gilded aesthetic. With the Trump Organization being paid an escalating commission based on the costs of the project, and always with an eye trained on making more money, Ivanka was soon adding expensive details like high-end glass finishes.

I liked Ivanka, but she has always been very cautious and protective of her image and appearance, and even more so in recent years. Before Ivanka married Jared Kushner, she'd been a much more approachable and down-to-earth person and we'd had a good relationship. I was MC to her, my initials her shorthand way of addressing me a method of expressing affection, and the feeling was mutual. I

A mockup of Trump Tower Moscow.
© 2020 Michael Cohen

remember being in a Trump corporate helicopter with Ivanka one day, flying over Manhattan after she'd broken up with Kushner, or I should say he'd broken up with her, or more correctly, he'd ended the relationship because his mother wanted him to marry an Orthodox Jewish woman. She was sitting quietly in the helicopter with a real sadness in her manner, like she was in mourning.

"Are you okay?" I asked.

"Jared and I broke up, MC," she said. "His mother wants him to marry an Orthodox girl."

There were now tears in her eyes.

"He's a fool to lose you," I said. "I'll bet you ten bucks he'll be back."

Ivanka laughed through her tears.

"I hope you're right, MC," she said. "I really do love him."

I tell you that story because here's the thing about the Trump kids: they're human beings. The truth was that they loved and hurt and yearned just like everyone else, at least in those days, before the kids entirely vanished into their father's hellish nightmare vision of life. Don Jr. aspired to be a better father than the Boss, even if he didn't deliver by staying in his marriage to Vanessa. The truth was that all three kids were starved for their father's love. They'd received no love from their father as children, abandoned by their egomaniacal Dad and humiliated when he openly cheated on their mother, and now all three are forever trapped in a cycle of seeking his approval. The impact can be seen in how the children remained quiet when their father acted out in racist or bigoted or bullying ways, behavior they used to know was wrong, and it can be seen in how Don Jr. more and more resembles his father. The same was true for Trump's lies: the kids knew he was lying, but they went along out of fear and misplaced loyalty, though I do wonder now if they still understand the harm they're perpetuating on society, especially children, by slavishly enabling their father, or if they've stopped caring and are intent only on accumulating as much power and wealth as possible while they can.

Trump Moscow wasn't Ivanka's deal per se, but she was kept aware of all the details and specifications, as were Don Jr. and the Boss. In a way, the Moscow project was like the Doral deal a few years earlier, with Ivanka granting herself control over the fun aspects of the deal while I was left with the miserable work of trying to get Felix Sater to deliver. I had to listen to Sater boast about getting Ivanka into Vladimir Putin's office to sit in his chair during a trip to Moscow and read his rah-rah emails as he tried to inveigle his way into the campaign. "Buddy our boy can become President of the USA and we can engineer it," he wrote to me in an email on November 3rd. "I will get all of Putin's team to buy in on this. I will manage the process . . . Michael, Putin gets on a stage with

Donald for a ribbon cutting for Trump Moscow, and Donald owns the nomination. And possibly beats Hillary and our boy is in."

I liked Sater's enthusiasm, and I really hoped to pull off a deal Trump had been chasing for decades. But I was skeptical. Felix kept trying to convince me to travel to Russia, to meet with his connections there. He asked for a copy of my passport, and he pushed for a copy of Trump's passport as well. I kept playing for time, demanding that Sater first accomplish three things: one, obtain proof of ownership or control of the site for the property; two, display the ability to get the necessary licensing and zoning permissions; and three, provide proof that he had the financing in place. Until then, I turned down the free first-class trips to Moscow.

We all knew that a project on the scale proposed would have to be approved by Putin. I knew that was partly why Trump was praising the Russian president to the heavens—as a way of insinuating himself with the strongman. That was the true nature of the "collusion" with Russia. By ingratiating himself with Putin, and hinting at changes in American sanctions policy against the country under a Trump Presidency, the Boss was trying to nudge the Moscow Trump Tower project along. The campaign was far too chaotic and incompetent to actually conspire with the Russian government. The reality was that Trump saw politics as an opportunity to make money, and he had no hesitation in bending American foreign policy to his personal financial benefit. Worse, he didn't do it openly, but in his perverse combination of working in broad daylight—praising Putin—while his real motivations and alliances were hidden from the public. In this way, the whole idea of patriotism and treason became irrelevant, in his mind. Trump was using the campaign to make money for himself: of course he was.

On December 10th, a story appeared on ABC's website that sunk Felix Sater's chances of dealing with the Trump Organization.

The article was just awful for Felix. The headline said, "Memory Lapse? Trump Seeks Distance from 'Advisor' With Past Ties to Mafia." Citing an unnamed source, the journalist Matt Mosk described Trump likely committing perjury during sworn testimony when he had been asked under oath if he knew Sater. Trump testified that he wouldn't recognize Sater if he saw him—a ridiculous lie. There was an image of Sater's Trump Organization business card, identifying him as a "Senior Advisor to Donald Trump," and reference to boasts on Felix's company's website about Trump Soho being his "most prized project."

Trump denied any connection to Sater, but that didn't stop Felix from trying to convince me to work with him. We discussed how we could get the Kremlin to approve the deal, and the Russian billionaires Sater could get to finance the building, and, as I've said before, he suggested we include a free condo worth $50 million to Putin personally as a sweetener. Sater wanted to arrange for Trump to travel to Moscow in the middle of the presidential campaign, and the idea was floated with Lewandowski and Trump, with the Boss agreeing to go sometime in the future if it would get the deal done. But no dates were ever agreed upon. Nevertheless, there were signs that Trump's efforts to flatter Putin into supporting the Moscow Tower were working, as the Russian dictator was quoted in the press calling the Boss "talented" and "colorful," a story I forwarded to Sater.

Two weeks later, another story appeared that outraged Trump. This time Don Jr. was the subject of his fury. I knew the kids were always walking a tightrope with their father, fearing his temper and rage. I witnessed this at close quarters when photographs of the Trump sons Don Jr. and Eric turned up on social media in late December of 2015. The photos had been taken years earlier, appearing in an article with the headline "Donald Trump's Sons

Awesome at Killing Elephants and Other Wildlife." The images were brutal. In one, Don Jr. was holding a knife and a dead elephant's tail; in another, Eric held the limp body of a lioness as the pair grinned for the camera, looking for all the world like a couple of soulless morons. A dead crocodile in a noose, civet cat, kudu, waterbuck . . . the pair had been a two-man murder squad on their visit to Zimbabwe, but it was worse than that. Social media exploded with Don Jr.'s old tweets that bragged about how he loved to "HUNT & EAT" wild game because "I AM A HUNTER," as a way to troll the organization People for the Ethical Treatment of Animals.

Looking at the photos and press reports on his sons gleefully celebrating killing endangered animals, I could see Trump's rage beginning to boil over. Trump routinely lamented his eldest son's lack of judgment, in saltier language, but this was a new low. Bad press enraged Trump, especially at a time when he was suffering in the polls and failing to get endorsements or party support. When Trump was flailing and failing, it was always a dangerous time to be in his presence, but Trump's reaction to Don Jr. shocked even me, and I'd seen it all, or so I thought.

"What the fuck is wrong with you?" Trump screamed at his namesake. "You think you're a big man with a ten-thousand-dollar gun sitting on the rocks and then boom! You kill some fucking animal? Then you drag your brother into this bullshit? Why the fuck would you post photos like that? You think you're a fucking big man? Get the fuck out of my office."

Don Jr. left without saying a word, head downcast. An awkward silence followed. Trump and I were alone, and he wanted affirmation that his fury was justified, so he screamed the same complaints in my direction about his sons being idiots and fools. But I wasn't going to give Trump the satisfaction of agreeing with him after he'd humiliated and verbally abused his own child.

"He fed a village for half a year," I said. "None of those animals went to waste."

"Fuck that," Trump replied.

Chapter Thirteen

Russia, If You're Listening (Part Two)

By the summer of 2016, I rarely went down to the 5th floor headquarters of the campaign, except to graze the excellent snack selection and catch up on gossip. It was in this way that I came across the rumors that Corey Lewandowski was having an affair with Hope Hicks, Trump's young and pretty assistant. I was very fond of Hope and thought she was making a terrible mistake getting involved with a married man with five children and a wife at home, even in the hothouse atmosphere of the campaign, when improbable bonds can be formed. When I confronted Hope, she denied the liaison, initially, but Lewandowski was barely disguising his connection with a woman many years his junior. When I returned to talk to Hope again, she relented and said she'd end it with Lewandowski, and she did, eventually.

This was part of Lewandowski's course of conduct that infuriated me. Assaulting a reporter and manhandling a protestor were just two of the many bone-headed mistakes he made. One night,

Trump's campaign manager was drinking so heavily that I took him out for dinner. He could barely walk and he passed out in a pool of drool in the restaurant as I ordered food for him. I told all of this to Trump, but the Boss dismissed my objections, saying I was acting out of spite, which was true, I admit. But I was also telling him the truth.

Around the office, Lewandowski was known as "the leaker." When Trump brought veteran GOP operative Paul Manafort on to his campaign, Lewandowski began to snipe and complain about the competition for the Boss's attention. Trump's ongoing lawsuit over Trump University made headlines when the Boss said that the judge in the case couldn't be fair because he was "Mexican," when he'd been born in Indiana, which was blamed on Lewandowski, and when Trump lost the Wisconsin primary, Manafort blamed it on the campaign manager. The newcomer Manafort now had the ears of Ivanka and Jared, and that was a very dangerous specter for Lewandowski if he didn't handle himself well, as I knew he wouldn't. Bickering about control of the digital campaign with Kushner was also a major misstep. As events have shown, for the Trumps, family ultimately always prevails, and Lewandowski wasn't even close to family.

The straw that broke the camel's back came in June of 2016, when a reporter called to tell me that Lewandowski was shopping a nasty story about Ivanka and Jared. The reporter was in Lewandowski's penalty box, apparently, and the offer was for Lewandowski to provide an interview with Trump as an exclusive. That was a coup for any reporter at the time, but in return the reporter told me he would have to run a hit piece on Ivanka and Jared. And not just any hit piece—Lewandowski was pushing a story that their marriage was in deep trouble. Worse, Lewandowski said that Jared was gay and that Ivanka was having an affair. Imagine the stupidity of spreading that kind of ridiculous and scurrilous nonsense and not expecting it to come back to bite you in the ass. But that was Lewandowski: idiotic to the last drop.

I went to Ivanka's office on the 25th floor, her sleek all-glass executive suite, like an exotic bird in a gilded cage. She was on the phone, so I waited for her to hang up.

Corey R. Lewandowski

From:	Robert Draper <robertldraper@█████████
Sent:	Thursday, May 12, 2016 12:35 AM
To:	Corey R. Lewandowski
Subject:	on the Christie thing

You're not named as a source--no one is. It's written in a way that would lead readers to think the source is likeliest a Christie person. OK?

Lewandowski wanted the story to appear to be from a supporter of Chris Christie, whom Jared Kushner hated. © 2020 Michael Cohen

"What's up, MC?" she asked as she ended her call.

"I just received a call from a journalist friend," I said. "Corey is trying to place a story about you and Jared."

"What?" she said. "Are you sure?"

I explained how Lewandowski was trying to get a reputable national publication to question her husband's sexual orientation and her own fidelity.

"He offered to let the journalist out of the penalty box and get an interview with your Dad, if he runs the story," I replied.

"I hate him," Ivanka said.

She picked up the phone and dialed Jared, who picked up on the first ring. Ivanka asked me to tell Jared what I'd just told her, and so I obliged. Jared was calm and measured.

"Is your friend going to run the story?" he asked.

"No," I said.

"Lewandowski's a lowlife," Jared said. "You two know what to do. I'll see you later."

Ivanka had rage in her eyes as she hung up.

"MC, you need to go upstairs and tell Dad about this," she said. "Jared and I will back you."

"Ivanka," I said. "I was hoping you'd talk to him."

"No, MC, it has to be you," she said. "Please."

"Fine," I replied. "I'll do it now."

Up on the 26th floor, the Boss waved me into his office as he spoke on a call, and I listened as he regaled whoever he was talking to about the latest polling results and what a nasty woman Hillary Clinton was. Because here was the thing about Trump and the Clintons—it really was personal for Trump. Bill and Hillary had attended his wedding, but only because they had to, because he'd made a substantial donation to the Clinton Foundation, in his opinion. He despised Hillary in a way that went beyond the personal animosity towards anyone opposed to Trump. He told me that he believed the Clintons were using the billion dollars they'd raised for their foundation as their personal piggy bank, while offering no proof other than the terms of the charity, which he claimed allowed them to direct how ninety percent of the money was spent and pay their daughter Chelsea an exorbitant salary. That was what enraged Trump, as he told me repeatedly: they were fucking cheaters. His tirade over, Trump hung up and grinned at me.

"What's up?" Trump asked.

"Boss, I just came from Ivanka's office," I replied. "I shared with her a call I received earlier from a journalist friend regarding a hit piece on Ivanka and Jared."

I laid out the allegation that Jared was gay and that Ivanka was unfaithful. Trump nodded, listening, but I could tell he was skeptical.

"The journalist is a friend of yours?" Trump asked.

"Yes," I said.

"So take care of it," Trump said.

"I have," I replied. "But that's not the issue. Boss, the story is

Lewandowski, drunk. © 2020 Michael Cohen

being shopped by Corey. He's been leaking a ton of shit to a multitude of reporters."

"Bullshit," Trump said. "No fucking way."

Trump hollered for his assistant Rhona to get Ivanka on the phone.

"You all hate Corey," Trump said. "This is bullshit."

"No it isn't," I said, now getting angry. "That is not the response I was expecting from you. He's fucking sick. He's a fucking drunk. I grabbed him on the street the other day, drunk, and took him to get some food in his stomach and the asshole fell asleep at the table with a slice of pizza in his hand."

Ivanka was patched through, talking on the speakerphone in Trump's office. She agreed with me that Lewandowski had to go, that he was a menace to the campaign, spreading malicious and untrue rumors about her marriage and husband as a way to grab more power for himself by marginalizing others.

"Listen, honey," Trump said. "You all hate Corey. But he's doing a great job, and you want me to fire him?"

"He's not, Daddy," Ivanka said. "If MC didn't know the reporter we would never—"

Trump interrupted. "Bullshit, I don't believe you, Michael," he said.

Now I exploded, an extremely rare occurrence in front of Trump, but a confrontation that Ivanka knew I would risk—it was why she'd said it had to be me who went to her father, because I wouldn't cave on Lewandowski. I truly loathed Lewandowski and knew he needed to be fired, urgently, but now the Boss was doubting my loyalty?

"What?" I yelled. "Have I ever lied to you?"

With that, I stood up and stormed out of Trump's office without another word. I wasn't going to be called a liar, especially when I was actually acting in the interests of the Boss and his family. I was beyond angry, as I pulled on my coat and told the secretarial pool to hold all my calls. I walked out of the atrium of the Trump Tower, ignoring the repeated calls that came into my two cell phones from a number from the Manhattan area code of 212, because that was how landline calls from the Trump Organization appeared. I had once been thrilled to be an initiate to the intrigues of Donald J. Trump, but now I was disgusted by the experience. Trump had called me a liar to my face, and worse, he was showing me that his loyalties lay with some jerkoff spreading false rumors about his daughter and son-in-law in an attempt to plot against the family. That was what a decade of abject sycophancy to Donald Trump got me: absolutely nothing.

I called Laura and told her what had just happened.

"Good," she said. "Maybe now you can see his true colors. It's time for you to quit. He appreciates no one. He's the most disloyal person."

"I'll be home in an hour," I said.

After going for a walk to calm down, I received a call from Ivanka and Don Jr. When I relented and picked up, they said they were concerned about me.

"MC, I called your office and they said you'd left," Ivanka said. "Are you okay?"

"No," I said.

"Corey has got to go," Don Jr. said, jumping into the call. "Tomorrow morning, let's meet in Ivanka's office. I despise him.

He's a total piece of shit. Ivanka, Eric and I are going to speak to Dad and get his authority to fire him."

"Okay," I said. "Let me know tomorrow when you want me to come down for the meeting."

"Thanks, MC," Ivanka said.

"We got you, Mike," Don Jr. said. "See you tomorrow."

At ten the next morning, I was summoned to Trump's office, where I found he was talking with Don Jr., Ivanka, and Eric, all three children united in their stance against Lewandowski. Trump looked over as I entered his office.

"You okay?" he asked.

"Yes, Boss," I said. "So, what are we doing with this mutt?"

"He has to go—if all four of you believe it so strongly, then he has to go," Trump said. "Who's going to fire him?"

This was a display of a fact that was very little known at the time: Trump actually hated firing people and facing personal confrontation, despite his fame for barking "you're fired" on *The Apprentice*. He had others do his dirty work for him, often delighting in the details about how humiliated or badly treated the victim of his firings were. But he didn't have the guts to do it himself. Nor did Eric, it seemed, who said he had to go to a meeting. Nor did Ivanka, who likewise suddenly found her calendar extremely busy.

But I wasn't going to let this vindication and victory go without my personal attention. I had put up with too many of Lewandowski's petty put downs and too much of his disrespectful and dishonest double dealing not to want to be there to see the expression on his face as the realization that the game was well and truly over dawned on him. Lewandowski had schemed and connived his way out of a job running a national campaign and now he was going to be humiliated in front of the world. Couldn't happen to a nicer guy, was my thought, smiling as I imagined the scene.

"I'll do it," I said.

"I will too," Don Jr. said.

Trump wanted us to take his COO, Matt Calamari, with us, as he was familiar with the protocols of summarily firing someone and then escorting them out of the building. Frog marching, more like. Don Jr. called Lewandowski and instructed him to come to the conference room on the 25th floor for a meeting in fifteen minutes.

Lewandowski entered with his usual cocky strut, a Red Bull in hand, as if he was jacked for whatever was coming his way. But the smirk on his face didn't last long, as we all sat at the long conference table and a moment of silence followed. Lewandowski knew I hated him, so my presence couldn't be a good sign, he had to know, and what was Trump's COO doing in the meeting?

"You're through, Corey," Don Jr. said. "You're fired."

"What?" Lewandowski yelped, rising to his feet.

"Do you speak English?" I asked. "Fired as in you're out of here. And if you ever try to plant another story about Trump or any of the kids I will ruin you."

I turned to Calamari with a gesture.

"Matt, please escort Corey to his office, confiscate all the computers, take his credentials, and walk him out of the building," I said.

"I want to hear Mr. Trump tell me directly," Lewandowski said, remonstrating as his voice rose in anger, but his eyes telling another story. He looked like a kid who had been caught cheating and it was suddenly dawning on him that he was going to face a serious consequence; he thought he was getting away with his backstabbing of the Trump kids, but he had been busted.

"Not going to happen," Don Jr. said to him.

Calamari indicated that the meeting was over, in his thick Brooklyn accent, and thus ended the time of Corey Lewandowski as Trump's campaign manager. His replacement, Paul Manafort, released a press notice before Lewandowski had left the building, turning him into the lead story for the day, his firing seen as yet another sign of Trump's chaotic and disorganized campaign, which it really actually was; the in-fighting and backstabbing and leaking that were endemic revealed a candidate who didn't have the first clue about how to run a disciplined presidential campaign, let alone a nation.

I felt great, protecting the kids and getting rid of a major risk for the Trumps. But I have to hand it to Lewandowski: even after he was unceremoniously dumped in the most public way imaginable, he never stopped going in front of cameras and playing Trump perfectly. I knew what Lewandowski was doing, because I was doing the same thing, in essence, as do countless Trump courtiers and sycophants to this day: talking to an audience of one. Lewandowski continued to talk about Trump's ten billion dollars, his intelligence, Wharton degree, superior understanding of the media, and his appeal to the vast majority of voters who were craving change and an outsider to fix the country—the Boss's litany recited with religious fervor. Behind Trump's back, Lewandowski called him a moron. This innate talent for being two-faced connected him to Trump, like they were two birds of a feather, two political animals. Because that is a central insight into Trump, as well as his children and Jared Kushner: they are all intensely political. Not in the sense of ideology or policy or any sense of the common good or a desire to improve society; they are political in the personal sense: they want to win, no matter what the cost, and they will do anything to achieve that end. Like Kushner and the kids plotting against Lewandowski—they'd ousted their enemy but they had no idea what to do next; they'd won the knife fight but what came next was even worse, if that's imaginable, in the persona of the criminal train wreck named Paul Manafort and his ruinous Russian-related conspiracies.

* * *

IN THOSE HECTIC days, I had a hundred things to deal with on Trump's behalf, and I was a fixture in his office. I would meet with him to discuss an invoice, and how to stiff a random vendor, or an allegation of sexually inappropriate behavior, or the unfolding scandals surrounding Trump University or the Trump Network. But one major subject of conversation was the Moscow Trump Tower I was trying to get off the ground, without the assistance of Felix Sater.

A few months earlier, I'd written to the Kremlin's press secretary asking to be able to speak to Putin's chief of staff, Sergei Ivanov, but I misspelled the email address, so I had to follow up a few days later. I explained that the Trump Moscow project was stalled, and I asked for his assistance, but I didn't hear back. When I followed up a couple of weeks later, I got through to an assistant of the press secretary and we chatted for twenty minutes, but again, nothing came of it.

By June, I told the Boss and Ivanka and Don Jr. that I'd given up on the Moscow project. I just wasn't making any progress and it wasn't a good use of my time and energy.

It wasn't long after Paul Manafort became the true campaign manager that I was sitting in the Boss's office one afternoon. I can't recall what Trump and I were discussing, but Don Jr. came into the office and walked over to his father's desk. This was very unusual, as Trump treated the territory behind his desk as his personal space and very rarely invited anyone into that part of his sanctuary. I'd only ever gone to the far side of his desk when he was showing me golf clips on his laptop. But this time Don Jr. walked over to his father's side of the desk and leaned over and spoke quietly.

"The meeting is all set," Don Jr. said.

"Okay, good, let me know," Trump replied.

I didn't think much of this exchange at the time.

As the world found out after the election, at the time, a Russian lawyer was offering "dirt" on Hillary Clinton to Jared, Don Jr., and the genius Paul Manafort, all courtesy of Trump's golden shower nightclub buddy from Las Vegas and Moscow, Russian pop star and oligarch Emin Agalarov.

Chapter Fourteen

Hurricane Stormy (Part Two)

The late great crime writer Elmore Leonard, a personal favorite of mine, once advised aspiring writers to leave out the parts of a book that people tend to skip, so in that spirit I'm not going to recite each and every ridiculous story and headline that occurred during the 2016 cycle. I'll spare you the grim details of all the people I screamed at, threatened, and lied to, but suffice it to say that I went on a tear during the election.

One of my central tasks was raising money for the campaign, and I was constantly working the phones on Trump's behalf, raising millions upon millions. Another initiative I came up with was outreach to minority voters. Watching commentators on CNN casually call Trump a racist and a bigot and an Islamophobe wore out my last nerve, as I figured this political attack needed to be resisted. Trump was being pilloried in the press for his racist remarks about Hispanic people, and for good reason, but I knew that his message would resonate with voters who weren't only white. The problem was figuring out how to go about the business of forming an organization. So I called my friend, the pastor Darrell Scott, a leading African American religious figure from Cleveland, Ohio I'd come to know, and explained that I wanted to create a coalition of minorities who support Trump, with Pastor Scott as the founder.

"Let me pray on it tonight," Darrell said. "I'll get back to you tomorrow."

The next day I was at a baseball training facility in New York City, watching my son working with his hitting and pitching coach, when my phone rang. It was Darrell. He said he'd work with me to form a group dedicated to issues related to race and culture focused on Trump and the Republican Party, but he had one condition: the group had to be called the National Diversity Coalition, dropping the word minority.

"Why?" I asked.

"Because if I'm doing it, I want you with me," he replied. "You're white. You don't fit under the definition of a minority."

"I'm a minority," I said. "I'm Jewish."

"That's not going to work," Darrell said. "If you're in, I'm in."

I was all in for Trump, and I eagerly set about proving the case that he wasn't racist by finding folks from different racial and ethnic and religious groups to speak in his defense. This was the kind of soft power that I could wield for the Boss. As with evangelicals, the essence of the operation was to invert reality, to take an impious and vulgar man and make him appear god-fearing, and in turn magically transform Trump's white nationalist impulses into the illusion of an open-minded and inclusive leader—putting lipstick on a racist, chauvinist pig would be another way to put it. The task wasn't made easier by Trump's incessant, impulsive, self-destructive habit of picking fights with folks like the parents of a Gold Star family whose deceased son happened to have been

Muslim, enraging his mourning parents. It was a low that I figured had to be the nadir of the Boss's rhetoric—but, of course, it wasn't.

Sure enough, Hispanics, Muslims, African Americans, the calls started to come in from all corners of the country as Trump campaigned and his rallies grew in size and intensity—always with a few token minorities in the background as he spoke to avoid the KKK appearance lurking just below the surface. In this way, I turned obscure bloggers and social media posters into celebrities, as with the online sensations Diamond and Silk. That connection began when I put out my statement of apology to the *Daily Beast* reporter Tim Mak about my over the top Trump-like reaction to the Ivana rape story. Two black women had posted a video on YouTube defending me in the kindest possible way, I was told, and

it was going viral. When I watched what they'd said, I immediately reached out and we had a long conversation about the Diversity Coalition. They sent me t-shirts with their faces on them, so I sent them a bunch of red MAGA hats, supposedly signed by Trump (his secretaries signed the vast majority on his behalf). I was soon helping them get booked on shows on Fox, which caught Trump's attention when he saw them one evening.

"Holy shit, who are those two?" Trump asked me, so I told him the story.

Me with Diamond and Silk. © 2020 Michael Cohen

Me and Trump at the New Spirit Revival Center Gathering.© 2020 *Michael Cohen*

In the *Alice in Wonderland* upside-down world I was helping create, to my eternal shame, I once addressed a gathering at Darrell Scott's New Spirit Revival Center in Cleveland, Ohio, in a way that captured how lost I had become in the will to power that went from a frenzy to outright insanity. "I've long lost track of how many times the disgusting liberal mainstream media have attempted to label Mr. Donald Trump as a racist, a xenophobe, and a bigot," I told the congregation. "And let's not forget sexist, narcissist, Islamophobic, anti-Hispanic, anti-Semitic, a demagogue, and countless others. It's disgraceful."

An ad for Trump's appearance at the New Spirit Revival Center. © 2020 *Michael Cohen*

The mostly African American crowd laughed in delight. At that moment, Trump was sitting on the dais behind me with more than a dozen pastors and political supporters, including Mike Pence and Michael Flynn, nodding his head and smirking and mouthing to others the words "he's right, he's right." The Boss loved it when

I got on my high horse on his behalf. The crowd was murmuring in delight and agreement, and I reveled in Trump's approval as I gave sycophancy a new definition.

"As the son of a Holocaust survivor, it's morally wrong to sit back and do nothing when someone you know, someone you hold in great esteem, and truly care about, is being so viciously attacked day in and day out. Not only is Donald Trump not a racist, he believes that all people are part of one race—the human race."

Pass the Kool-Aid, right. But here's the thing that I never hear mentioned, but is fundamental to understanding the cult thinking that envelopes Trump's world: Jim Jones drank the Kool-Aid in Guyana too. Jones believed his own apocalyptic bullshit, just as Trump nodded in agreement and looked around for approval as I spoke that day in church; the reason cults exist is because the cult leader has manifested his own crazy way of seeing the world.

Jared Kushner personifies this illness. As the grandson of a Holocaust survivor who was forced to hide in the woods in the family's village in Poland from the Nazis during the Second World War, he now stood silently to the side while Trump demeaned and dehumanized immigrants.

Remember when I said in the foreword that you're not going to like me, or the things I did? Well, this is an example. I praised Trump in ways that I knew were not only untrue but downright dishonest, stooping so low as to invoke the plight of my own ancestors in Eastern Europe during the Second World War. Hard to think of a way I could have topped that particular load of horse-shit, except to say that I actually believed myself at the time, at least on some level, as I willfully turned a blind eye to all the red-alert signals I had witnessed.

At the end of this event, there was the laying on of hands, wherein religious leaders surrounded Trump, closed their eyes and prayed for his victory, as they do so often these days. I participated in this charade, laying my hands on Trump as if he were some deity or demigod.

Bullshit, as Trump himself would say, but please understand that I was totally out of my mind and unable to have any perspective on what I was doing.

* * *

By the spring of 2016, the GOP campaign narrowed to Trump and Ted Cruz as the last candidates standing. It was then that I took yet another master lesson at the Trump University of sleaze and deception and participated in manufacturing what really amounted to actual fake news. Whatever else the *National Enquirer* was, it most definitely wasn't a legitimate media outlet, as Trump well knew, despite his repeated claim that it should win the Pulitzer Prize for exposing the sexual escapades of then-candidate for president John Edwards in 2008. To call this hypocrisy doesn't begin to describe how dishonest and disingenuous Trump's statements really were. David Pecker wasn't just a friend and supporter of Trump— he was a sycophant and supplicant and propagandist. Trump's opponents have long obsessed about Russian interference in the 2016 election, while overlooking the incredible disinformation campaign run by Americans like Pecker, by far the more insidious and dangerous development of the last cycle—and the most threatening for 2020.

Consider the story about Ted Cruz's father's alleged involvement in the assassination of President John F. Kennedy in 1963. I know exactly how this story developed because I was present at the birth of the slander. The story begins with an email and call from Pecker in April of 2016. We were winning primary after primary by this time, and the last real threat to the Boss was the Texas Senator and his evangelical base. We needed a scandal of some sort to harm Cruz and help our candidate, and there was no question of scruples or truth or political norms when it came to the Trump campaign. In this, we truly did resemble the worst political extremists of the twentieth century; Trump warped reality to fit his needs with no remorse or conscience. That was the atmosphere at Trump headquarters the day I picked up the call from Pecker.

"We have a picture of Ted Cruz's father with Lee Harvey Oswald," Pecker said, with glee.

"What are you talking about?"

"Someone is trying to sell us a picture of Rafael Cruz in Dallas, Texas, on the day Kennedy was assassinated. He's with Oswald."

"Get the fuck out of here!" I exclaimed.

"Check your email," Pecker said.

I opened my email and clicked on the attached PDF from Pecker, revealing a grainy photograph of two men. One was clearly Oswald, I could see, but the other face was less easy to identify.

"Do you know that's Cruz's father?" I asked.

"Does it matter?" Pecker said. "All we have to do is allege that it is."

I shook my head in amazement, whistling as the possibilities and implications cascaded through my mind. This was like a neutron bomb, I thought, a thermonuclear explosion that would send wave after wave of toxic radiation into the primary season. How could the Cruz campaign counter such an allegation and dignify it with a response? Just engaging with the idea that his Cuban-born father was acquainted with Oswald was in itself very bad; the idea that he might have been a co-conspirator in the murder of one of America's most beloved presidents was a blood libel of mindboggling audacity.

"Give me half an hour," Pecker said. "I'll do a mock-up of the story—how it will look."

"Sounds good," I said. "Let's see what it looks like."

The story was ridiculous, of course. But I knew the Boss would love it. The tale was right up his alley, the kind of scurrilous and unanswerable lie that would cast doubt on Cruz by association with his father, a Cuban who had been involved in fighting Fidel Castro's revolution in the early '60s. Just putting the words assassination and Cruz and Oswald and President Kennedy in the same sentence would cast doubt on the Texan's family history. To say it would be a low blow would be an insult to low blows; can you think of another American politician, ever, who would stoop this low?

During the campaign, the *Enquirer* had tied hit pieces on Trump's opponents to the polls, slamming every candidate that appeared to be rising and threatening the Boss. There was the "bungling surgeon" Ben Carson leaving a sponge inside the brain of a patient he'd operated on, or Marco Rubio's "Cocaine Connection," or Carly Fiorina's "druggie daughter," each article published to counter their momentum and suppress their poll numbers, with the so-called media outlet operating as an unpaid propaganda wing for Trump.

And here's the thing: it worked. It really, really worked. The journalists at the *Enquirer* delighted in taking the worst rumors or bullshit conspiracy theories circulating online and turning them into ridiculous headlines sitting at the cash register of almost every grocery store in the country and seen by 100 million Americans—a formidable form of attack advertising for us. For free, of course, because that was what the free press was to Trump. The mainstream media would then write disapproving articles about the made-up story, but they'd always repeated the slander, providing yet more free press as the news cycle started to best resemble the eddy of a flushed toilet.

The most talented character assassin was a young Australian named Dylan Howard, and he and I talked regularly. Dylan would come up with crazy story lines, pulled directly out of his backside,

MARCO RUBIO

ENQ
12/28/2015
Marco Rubio's Love Child
- New book, "The Wilderness", claims a woman "had supposedly been impregnated by Rubio, and then went on to have an abortion.
- Book also claims Marco has been hiding a secret second family

GLOBE
01/04/2016
Rubio's Cocaine Connection
- Rubio's brother-in-law was a key player in the so-called "Cocaine Cowboys"

ENQ
02/01/2016
Woman (Mistress) Who Could Ruin Rubio
- According to a book, Rubio authorized a $40K probe into whether his rivals had dug up evidence of an affair

ENQ
02/29/2016
Secret Gay Past
- Marco was busted at a notorious "cruising" spot for gay guys on the prowl for casual sex
- Photos of Marco at a man-fest "foam party" in a skimpy bathing suit
- Photo of Marco performing a hunky gay dance after stripping

ENQ
03/14/2016
Sex & Drug Secrets
- Marco's wife Jeanette, who flaunts her family values, was a Miami Dolphins cheerleader
- Jeanette has racked up 13 traffic citations in Florida since 1997
- The two met at a foam party, where partygoers are encouraged to strip. According to an insider, the events are "an excuse to get f----- in public."

The *Enquirer's* "Rubio takedown plan" document. © *2020 Michael Cohen* so I figured he had a hand in this latest Cruz attack. He'd already been behind stories about Cruz's alleged marital infidelity, with no proof whatsoever, and that seemed true for this new JFK gambit. In recent weeks, I learned, a website trafficking in conspiracy theories had floated the Cruz-Oswald connection, along with two blurry photographs, but it had largely gone unnoticed; Pecker, Howard, the *Enquirer*, Trump, and I were going to change that.

Within minutes another email hit my inbox and I clicked on the PDF attached and gasped in horror and delight. Pecker called as I stared at the mocked-up story, the layout, and the banner headline: Ted Cruz's Dad Tied to JFK Murder Plot! There were quotes from a "court certified witness," whatever that meant, and references to "secret US government files," and the bald factual assertion that Cruz's father had indeed been involved with Oswald at the time of the murder.

"This is amazing," I said, as Pecker chuckled. "I've got to show the Boss. I'll call you from his office in a minute."

I printed a copy of the article and took it to Trump. He was on the phone with a reporter, so I listened quietly as he bad-mouthed Cruz and his wife, especially taking delight in comparing Cruz's wife's looks to Melania. Predictably, this form of juvenile competition caused a stir, with Trump haters aghast at yet another indication of his inability to behave in a way that was remotely presidential, while his supporters reveled in precisely that quality. Cruz was left sputtering in outrage, but the damage was done.

Trump was truly shameless in his verbal attacks on Cruz, alleging an impending divorce, along with substance abuse and financial wrongdoing. Whatever somebody thought of the unctuous Cruz, in Trump's telling, he was an awful human being, and all good Christians should run a million miles away from him— which, of course, was Trump projecting his worst qualities onto Cruz, as he now does onto the world.

In recent weeks, Cruz's Protestant preacher father had been getting under Trump's skin in a way that was very effective, I thought, using his pulpit to exhort Christians to vote according to the word of God—and support his evangelical son.

"The alternative could be the destruction of America," Pastor Cruz claimed, enraging Trump.

"I think it's horrible," Trump told the press in response. "I think it's absolutely horrible that a man can go and do that, what he's saying there."

Walking into Trump's office with my *Enquirer* mock up, I knew I was bearing Trump's best chance for revenge, handing him the document and explaining that Pecker had just sent it to me.

"Jesus Christ, what is this?" Trump asked, looking at the blaring headline and blurred photograph.

"It's Ted Cruz's father with Lee Harvey Oswald," I said.

"No shit?" Trump asked.

"On the day Kennedy was shot," I said. "Having lunch."

"You've got to be fucking kidding me," Trump said. "It's not real, right?"

I shrugged, grinning. "Looks real to me," I said.

"Holy fuck," Trump said, bursting out laughing. "Is David going to run this story? I've got to call him."

"Of course he is," I said.

"Story like this, it has to be the front page," Trump said. "Holy fuck."

Trump hollered to Rhona to get Pecker on the line and soon the three of us were laughing and joking about what a great story it was going to be. The Indiana primary was coming up in a couple of weeks for Cruz and we were excited to see how this latest piece of agitprop would play.

Then something strange happened. The story ran on the front page of the *Enquirer*, but no one picked it up. The tale was just too preposterous, it seemed, and maybe the mainstream media was wising up to the racket Trump was running with the connivance of Pecker (and me). We waited and waited. The Indiana primary was looming and the polls showed Cruz surging, a trend that unnerved Trump, as the Republican Party appeared to be reconsidering the headlong rush to nominate the Boss. Our strategy was coming from the same playbook as birtherism, only this time, it appeared not to be working; that would be good news for political discourse and the future of the country, but bad news for Trump, and I was keenly aware of which was more important for us.

Finally, fed up, Trump took to one of his other trusty lackey propaganda outlets, *Fox and Friends*. Appearing on the morning of May 3, the day of the vote in Indiana, Trump complained that the story about Cruz's father wasn't getting enough attention in the press. He said it was horrible that Cruz's father had been with Oswald right before Kennedy's death and he insisted that the fake news media should be covering what was actually fake news— how's that for deception?

And it worked, like a charm, or a curse, with the story going viral, like a deadly poison injected into the body politic.

Cruz lost in Indiana, 53-37.

If that's not gangster, I don't know what is.

In the aftermath, Trump praised the excellent reporting by the *Enquirer*, as if it had actually engaged in journalism instead of conspiring to deceive the American people. But Trump couldn't let things stand at that: he had to rub it in, and mock the real news and even reality. "I mean, if it was in *The New York Times*, they would have gotten Pulitzer Prizes for their reporting," Trump said.

Apart from efforts like the Cruz lie, my role in the campaign was limited, and deliberately so; I was more useful to Trump as a resource he could use quietly, without having to tell the campaign staff. I'd see Trump around the office and we'd talk politics. I did television hits often, as I loved the whole process. My contributions were intermittent but occasionally I offered my assistance or opinion. I'll never know the full truth on this matter, but I know that I was watching one of Trump's rallies on television one night during the spring when it struck me that every single person in the stands in the background was white. All the grinning rednecks in red MAGA hats, the Moms in MAGA t-shirts, the gap-tooth kids waving to the camera—the Trump-heads were all lily white. I told Trump about this observation.

"Your rallies look like fucking Ku Klux Klan meetings," I said. "All of your supporters are white. Instead of hoods, they are all wearing MAGA hats. You need some diversity in your audience. The optics are terrible."

"You're right," Trump agreed. He didn't care about racial justice, needless to say, and his only real goal with black voters was suppression, especially aiming his efforts at African American women in swing states like Michigan and Wisconsin and Ohio, trying to convince them that Hillary Clinton was so awful that they shouldn't bother to turn out. "What do you have to lose by supporting Trump?" he asked, but the real question he posed was why they should support the Clintons and their criminal justice and welfare reforms, which proved so catastrophic for minorities.

From the time I mentioned the racial component of his rallies, I noticed there were always at least one or two black or brown men or women positioned directly behind Trump's head when he spoke, minorities I'm sure were identified and recruited by the campaign team and carefully placed to appear directly in the middle of the cable news shots. The gesture wasn't aimed at minority voters so much as his base. It was a form of subliminal communication that it wasn't racist to support a politician employing transparently racist rhetoric, the kind of reassurance that appealed to white suburban moms turned off by Trump but willing to hold their noses and vote for him, partly out of dislike for Clinton's sense of entitlement but also because of the promise of Supreme Court justices who would make abortion illegal.

Throughout the campaign, rumors of Trump's past sexual encounters circulated from time to time, but the real impetus for the oncoming tsunami was Trump's trouncing of Cruz. The Boss was no longer the frontrunner, nor was he the presumptive nominee; he was the candidate.

I had been at Trump headquarters the night he beat Cruz as the Boss strutted up to the podium in front of a sea of reporters and cameras and entered an entirely new dimension of the race for the Presidency. We had all been delirious, feeling vindicated but also amazed; what had started as a lark and a PR stunt had turned into a triumph.

"I won with women," Trump said. "I love winning with women."

I laughed and so did everyone in attendance, including the press. Trump had the world eating out of his hands—and, even better, his enemies were howling in outrage.

But Trump was taunting the gods, or fate, or kismet, when he bragged about his success with women, because of course it would be women who would come to define the 2016 campaign, in a myriad of ways. I knew the risks Trump was running by gloating over his appeal to women, and the threat of a sexual scandal was real, for sure. As Trump's political fortunes rose, stories about women claiming to have had sexual relationships with him while he was married to Melania were circulating. This was my territory: the filth and muck of politics, the assignment the Boss gave to his most trusted lawyer and consigliore and fall guy.

In June of 2016, Dylan Howard from the *Enquirer* called to tell me about a former *Playboy* centerfold named Karen McDougal who was alleging that she'd been in an intimate and ongoing sexual relationship with Trump for nine months in 2006 and 2007. This overlapped with the Stormy Daniels affair from years earlier, I knew, and it was a particularly sensitive timeframe because Mrs. Trump had just given birth to their son Barron at the time. I'm not a woman, of course, but I'm smart enough to know that cheating on your wife while she's breastfeeding your newborn son was not going to please your wife.

Listening to Howard's account of the *Playboy* centerfold, I didn't know if McDougal was telling the truth—but I did know the truth didn't matter. Howard told me he'd flown to LA to meet with McDougal, a beautiful brunette who'd been one of the most popular *Playboy* centerfolds of all time. In other words, exactly Trump's type: a conquest that he no doubt viewed as extra prestigious because of her sex-symbol status, like sleeping with a porn star. Dylan said McDougal was believable, but that he'd managed to get her lawyer to agree to twelve-hour period of silence when they wouldn't talk to other media outlets. Keith Davidson was back in the frame, Howard told me; the attorney who'd represented Stormy Daniels in 2011 was once again trying to get American Media to buy off his client in return for her story—and silence.

I went to Trump's office on June 27 to tell him about McDougal's claim. He immediately called Pecker, as I knew he would. . . .

By late July, Davidson was pitting ABC News and American Media against each other. McDougal was trying to parlay her affair with Trump into a way to revive her career, or what tiny bit of it might be left, an understandable ambition, but the last thing on anyone else's mind. When I heard about the ABC initiative, I knew it was time to act.

On August 6th, McDougal signed the contract. The deal included $150,000, with $25,000 allocated for payment for her appearance on the cover of two magazines owned by American Media. That meant Trump was on the hook for $125,000 to be repaid to Pecker's company. How this was all going to work wasn't clear to me. Trump and his CFO Allen Weisselberg were past masters at allocating expenses that related to non-business matters and finding a way to categorize them so they weren't taxed. The plane rides, the lavish dinners, even purchasing clothes—Trump's entire life was one giant, or huuuuggggeeee tax deduction, I knew.

Pecker also needed to find another, non-obvious way to pay McDougal. To that end, Pecker reached out to a trusted former employee named Daniel Rotstein and got him to use his consulting company in Florida as the front for the transaction; Rotstein's company would execute the agreement and send the money to Davidson's trust account to be held on behalf of McDougal. All the details seemed to have been satisfactorily resolved.

But I was still antsy and uneasy. Trump's poll numbers were rising during the summer. He was reckless. He had long accused others of doing the very things he did; that was a central element of his *modus operandi*. If Trump claimed you cheated or lied or stole, you could be sure that he'd done those things himself; it was almost as if he had a compulsion to confess to his terrible actions by way of accusation. My biggest and growing fear was what would happen if all this conniving ever emerged. For months, it had amazed me that the national press investigated every accusation made against Hillary Clinton, as if she were the most devious and corrupt politician in history, while Trump's long history of bankruptcies and infidelities and dubious business practices received relatively little scrutiny. I knew it was because no one really believed he would win, so the presumptive president deserved more attention, but giving Trump that kind of leeway seemed like lazy journalism.

By early September, I was starting to feel hinky about the entire McDougal affair. Pecker paid the $150,000 and repeatedly asked me about the repayment. Would Trump really stiff him? What if the deal leaked to the press? I decided I needed to record a conversation with Trump about the payment for two reasons. First, to show Pecker that I was asking Trump to repay the obligation, and second, to have a record of his participation if the conspiracy ever came out. I was certain that Trump would throw me under the bus in that event, claiming ignorance and laying all the blame on a rogue lawyer, namely me. I had no idea how prescient I was, but at the time, I could sense the stakes were getting higher and higher as I explained the details of the transaction with McDougal to Trump. As a precaution, my iPhone was digitally memorializing our exchange.

"I need to open up a company for the transfer of all that info regarding our friend, David, you know, so that—I'm going to do that right away," I said.

That was how we talked: euphemistically, circling a subject carefully, choosing words that might allow for some ambiguity.

"So what do we got to pay for this?" Trump asked. "One-fifty?"

I told Trump that the amount we're paying should include all the "stuff" that Pecker had on him. By "stuff" I meant any and all other salacious Trump stories we believed he possessed.

"Yeah, I was thinking about that," Trump said.

"All the stuff," I said. "Because—here, you never know where that company—you never know what he's—"

"Maybe he gets hit by a truck," Trump said, addressing the point I was making.

"Correct," I said. "So I'm all over that."

Trump was surrounded by newly famous political advisors writing speeches and running get out the vote operations, not to mention disinformation campaigns on social media, but I was dealing with the personal and extremely confidential matters that could make or break the Boss. I may not have looked like I had a lot of power in Trump's world, but I knew my place and role and how central I was to Trump's life, in politics and business.

To facilitate the payment, I incorporated an LLC in Delaware. I called the company Resolutions Consultants, but changed it to Essential Consultants soon after. Delaware had strict secrecy laws, and it was the jurisdiction long used by wealthy men to hide their assets during messy divorces, so I felt confident that all of this would remain secret and that I had a reliable conduit for Trump's covert payments.

There was only one problem: Trump was having another "cheap attack." This was like faking the CNBC poll, or any of the other countless times he welched on his obligations. But this situation was more complicated, I knew, because the money was one thing—the risk of the transaction becoming public was another. If Trump could avoid payment, especially if it would look bad if he was directly connected to an underhanded financial transaction, he would try to do it. It was a shortsighted way of conducting himself, as we would all come to learn, but it was an example of how Trump truly and sincerely didn't believe the rules or law applied to him.

Gradually, by way of evasion and obfuscation, it became clear that Trump wasn't going to reimburse Pecker and the *Enquirer* for the payment to McDougal. When Pecker figured out that Trump wasn't going to keep his word, he blamed me. When I explained that it was out my hands, he called and insisted that we meet for lunch to discuss, specifying we meet at a place called Il Postino, an upscale midtown Italian restaurant he frequented. American Media had taken significant investment from a hedge fund called Chatham Asset Management, which was run by a hard-charging trader named Anthony Melchiorre, effectively making him Pecker's boss. Pecker told me he was hoping to move up the management chain with Chatham, and that meant keeping in the good graces of

Melchiorre, so it followed that if word got out that the *Enquirer* had spent $150,000 to silence a former Playboy centerfold on behalf of Donald Trump, Pecker's boss would go berserk. Pecker could hide a small amount of money on his books, around $10,000, say, but a hundred and fifty thousand dollars was just too big to disguise or explain away. I sympathized, but told him that my hands were tied, and that was where the matter sat, a festering wound waiting to become infected.

In early October, I flew to London with Laura and two other couples who were also visiting their college kids studying abroad for a semester; Samantha had left the University of Pennsylvania to study at Queen Mary College. This was a real treat for our family, a chance to see Samantha thriving in a foreign country and to catch up with some folks we knew who lived in the United Kingdom, including former PM Tony Blair. Everything was going well, and I was relaxing and taking a break from the constant chaos of Trump's campaign and business, when my phone rang in the middle of dinner, as it so often did.

It was Saturday night in London and I was in a noisy bistro with friends. I excused myself to find a quiet place to talk, retreating to a corner by the washrooms. Hope Hicks was on the line from New York and she gave me a download on the *Access Hollywood* tape and Trump being recorded boasting about grabbing women by the pussy and kissing them without their consent, advocating sexual assault as the entitled right of celebrities.

I could hear the panic in Hope's voice. She was a nice kid, and a quick study, and she'd been an important part of the campaign, but that was what she was: a kid. Her low self-esteem had led her into an extramarital affair with Corey Lewandowski, of all losers, and she had a very poor appreciation of how to take the measure of people, especially men. In other words, she was way, way, way over her head in dealing with a scandal like this.

Me with Tony Blair. © 2020 Michael Cohen

My dinner party was now officially over and I had to dedicate myself to figuring out how to play this latest sex scandal, which had the appearance of killing Trump's campaign as the Speaker of the House Paul Ryan denounced the Boss and the Republican mice started to run for the life boats on the rapidly sinking USS Trump.

The *Access Hollywood* tape had another ripple effect, suddenly potentially putting Stormy Daniels and her porn star story back in play. With Trump's campaign teetering, the Stormy story became far more marketable, but also far more dangerous politically, or at least that was the calculation Daniels and her advisors apparently made. I discovered this as soon as I returned from London and I received another call from Pecker; it was like he and I were engaged in a parallel campaign, with the outcome of the 2016 election being decided in secret. That was really how it felt, on the inside: everything that I knew had to remain far from the public's knowledge or Trump would lose in a landslide. This knowledge was a burden, in many ways, and I knew that the deceptions I was engaging in were designed to hide the true nature of Trump's character, and some deeply buried part of my psyche had to be able to understand that I was doing truly undemocratic and dangerous and dirty deeds—but all I was focused on was accomplishing my goal: helping Trump to win the Presidency.

"We have a real problem," Pecker said. "Stormy is back and with her manager Gina Rodriguez. She's out shopping the story."

"What story?" I asked.

"C'mon," Pecker said. "The sexual encounter in Utah."

"But I thought that was already dealt with," I said. "I have a statement in my files with her denying the allegation."

"This is me you're talking to," Pecker said. "Knowing you have this denial, she took a polygraph and guess what—the test said she's telling the truth."

Pecker told me he was sending Dylan Howard to LA that day

to review the polygraph and begin talks with Daniels's representatives.

"Of course she will bring this up now," I said. "Its value only exists until the election because there's no way the Boss beats the Clinton machine."

Pecker agreed, I knew, and so did Trump.

"Remind me of the name of the Los Angeles lawyer again," I said. "Keith?"

"Davidson. You should call him right away."

I hunted in my Outlook Express for his contact information while we were speaking. I told Pecker I'd call him back as soon as I spoke to Davidson, dialing as I hung up, and getting an answer right away; like any good fixer dealing in the world as he and I did, Keith was very attentive to his cell phone.

"Keith, it's Michael Cohen from Trump," I said. "I hear your client and her manager are out shopping the 2011 story. Are you aware of this?"

"I am," Davidson said. "Look, she needs the money and Gina convinced her that the story is worth some money. To prove her case, she took a lie-detector test. That's part of what she's selling. ABC TV is interested."

I was trying to calculate my next move when Davidson offered a suggestion.

"What I think you should do is buy the story," he said. "We can write up an NDA together and stop the story again."

"How much is she looking for?" I asked. "I will need to discuss this with Mr. Trump before agreeing to anything."

"Let me go speak to her and get back to you with a number," Davidson said. "I'm sorry, Michael, I thought this matter was killed."

"But obviously since he's the nominee, the story can be exploited," I said.

As soon as we hung up, I raced to Trump's office, a pit forming in my stomach. The room was filled with political operatives, along with executives from the business side of Trump Org, the atmosphere like a bazaar, with people shoving and pushing to get the Boss's attention.

Trump saw me peering in through the crowd, and he called out. "Hey, Michael, what's up?"

"Need to talk to you, sir," I replied. "But privately."

"Is thirty minutes from now okay?" he asked.

"Yes, of course. I need five minutes, max."

Hope Hicks consulted Trump's schedule, reminding him of interview commitments, and the chaos rose back to a roar, so I departed to tell his assistant Rhona Graff that I needed five minutes of Trump's time. She sighed and said she'd long since lost control of his schedule; it was like Grand Central Station at rush hour in his office. She suggested I just come back in half an hour and kick everyone out of Trump's office, as I'd done in the past.

"That's a good idea," I said. "This is too important."

Back in my office, pacing frantically, I rehearsed what I would say and how Trump would respond. He'd be pissed, I knew, and he'd blame me for the issue coming up again. That was part of the way Trump thought: blame came first, and then the facts, although that's not really accurate, because the facts were always so distorted that it was impossible to communicate reality to him. Like the fact that he'd actually slept with Daniels: did he even know? Or the fact that it was the result of his behavior in the first place, not that of his personal attorney, and that the best way to avoid this kind of trouble was not to sleep with a porn star who was, by definition, an expert at exchanging sex for money.

The *Access Hollywood* storm would pass, I figured, and Trump was still packing rallies. His poll numbers dipped, at least temporarily, and a Clinton victory seemed inevitable, but the hurricane of a Stormy Daniels scandal would be ruinous. Needing someone to confide in, I called Pecker.

"I just finished with Keith," I said. "She wants money in exchange for an NDA. Trump is going to lose it and I will need your help. In half an hour I'll be in his office, just the two of us, and I'll suggest we call you."

"Good idea," Pecker said. "I hear that ABC is offering Stormy $150,000 for the story."

"Wait," I said, incredulous. "What? A hundred and fifty grand? That's what she's asking? You have to be kidding. If I was a porn star going to extort a billionaire, I wouldn't be asking for $150,000. She's either incredibly desperate, or incredibly stupid."

Pecker laughed. "You have to think like her," he said. "That translates into 75,000 lap dances, at two minutes a pop, so she's saving herself 150,000 minutes shaking her ass."

"Good point," I said. "I'm going to call you shortly, so please keep your line green for me."

Knowing the ballpark figure, I called Keith Davidson again.

"Did you speak with your client and what's the number?" I asked. "I have a meeting with Mr. Trump in a few minutes and he's beyond busy, so I need to be quick with giving him the scenario and his options and getting a plan agreed."

"Yes, I did," Davidson said. "She wants $250,000 for the NDA."

"I know that ABC is offering $150,000," I said. "Why in the world would anyone pay more than that?"

I explained to Davidson that I had her denial, along with press reports of her expressly saying the story was "bullshit." I had no idea about the veracity of her so-called polygraph; it could be fake, for all I know, I said. Her negotiating position wasn't strong, I said, so I suggested a nuisance fee of $50,000 to make the whole thing go away once and for all time.

Davidson was getting angry, I could tell, a sign of a hardening of his position, but also an admission that he was trapped and didn't have any strong cards to play. This kind of anger was very familiar to me: it was frequently my only resort when Trump was trying to screw someone over.

"She'll never accept that," he said. "How about $200,000?"

"How about no," I said, but being careful not to be too declarative. "Whatever number we agree to, it's ultimately Trump's decision. However, I would like to go to him with a number, and I've got a few minutes to figure this out. I need a number and a solution for him."

I paused.

"How about $100,000?" I said. "I just doubled my offer."

Davidson said he'd call me back, after talking to Daniels. He called back in a couple of minutes saying he'd spoken to his client. She wanted to clear $100,000 from the deal, so with Davidson's fee and the cut for her representative, Gina Rodriguez, that meant a total of $130,000. I had my number, at least and at last, a sum that seemed almost laughably low. Daniels had a presidential candidate with a gun to his head days before the election, so to speak, and that was all she wanted? It reminded me of the movie *Austin Powers*, where the archvillain Dr. Evil is blackmailing the world and he puts his pinkie to mouth, in imitation of *Saturday Night Live's* Lorne Michaels, and names his number for not destroying the planet: "One million dollars."

Trump's office was just as chaotic as before, but this time he ordered everyone to leave. I closed the door ceremoniously, something that almost never happened at Trump Org or, later, in the White House. The Boss's version of an open-office plan was to keep his office door always open. The Secret Service agents assigned to provide his security didn't like the idea, but grudgingly agreed to wait in the hallway while Trump and I conducted our business.

Alone together, I told Trump that Stormy Daniels was back,

demanding payment in return for her silence. He didn't explode as I expected, perhaps slightly chastened by the *Access Hollywood* episode and his vulnerable position in the campaign. Another sex scandal would be brutal, it went without saying, so I suggested we call Pecker and get his thoughts. Before we called, I told Trump that I'd tried to convince Pecker to pay Daniels off, as he'd done with McDougal, but that he'd decided that American Media couldn't justify another outlay in defense of Trump. I didn't mention that refusing to repay the money for McDougal, as agreed, was hardly the way to endear himself to Pecker, nor did I mention the reputational risk American Media would take if its efforts to suppress Daniels's story ever emerged. The truth was that Trump was now the author of this further complication in the plot—stiffing American Media meant they weren't going to come to his financial assistance again.

"It's not a lot of money for a mega-billionaire," Pecker told Trump, using flattery as a way of persuasion—a tactic I recognized with a smile. In Trump's world, flattery gets you everywhere.

"How bad do you think this could hurt me with the campaign?" Trump asked.

"Look, I don't know the answer, but it can't be good," Pecker said.

"Let's not forget about upstairs," Trump joked, referring to his Slovenian-born wife, who was, despite all the various hopes and disappointments projected onto her, actually a human being, a wife, and a mother, with all that includes.

"I just don't pay these kinds of things," Trump said. "Let me think about it and I'll let you know what I want to do tomorrow."

The next morning, I was summoned to the Boss's office first thing, well before eight and the arrival of the rest of the staff. We were both homebodies and early-to-bed types who preferred a TV remote to the seductions of Manhattan's boozy nightlife. The fact that I'd never consumed alcohol in my life endeared me to Trump in an unspoken way; he'd watched his older brother drink himself to death at an early age and held drunks in contempt—avoiding alcohol was a major element of his way of life. First thing in the morning was also the only time I could reliably count on his undivided attention and the freedom from prying eyes and ears.

Trump explained to me that he'd been canvassing his friends about what he should do about the Stormy Daniels situation. He was still torn, I could see, but he wanted a resolution of some kind.

"What do you think I should do with this Stormy bullshit?" Trump asked.

He knew that I knew that the Stormy Daniels story wasn't bullshit, but, like the very first lie he told me the first time we talked—that I'd somehow gotten a great deal on my place at Trump Park Avenue when I'd paid retail like everyone else—I went along with the game. I wasn't going to call him on this latest clusterfuck, he knew, so he could indulge in a little self-righteous indignation—one of his favorite dishes when he's forced to confront his own bad behavior or mistakes.

By now, I had an answer ready for Trump. I'd given the matter real thought and realized that there had to be a way to convince Trump to make the payment, without having to admit to himself that he was paying to hide the truth. To counter his illogical proposition, I needed an illogical proposition of my own, one with some truth to it but that fundamentally altered the thinking to paint Trump as the victim, forced to pay off a lowlife porn star to protect his presidential campaign and good name. The reality was that another scandal, after Pussygrabgate, or whatever you called the *Access Hollywood* tape scandal, would likely kill Trump. I knew it. He knew it. He was already very likely to lose in a landslide, as he knew perfectly well, but another scandal could turn a loss into a historical embarrassment he would carry for the rest of his life; one more sex revelation and the evangelicals and suburban women he needed to have any chance would completely abandon him, we figured; sleeping with the blonde bombshell porn star of the films *Revenge of the Dildos* and *Big Boob Bonanza* wouldn't help in the swing states.

To guide Trump to a good decision, I trotted out the syllogism I'd cooked up and would rely on in dealing with questions from the press about Stormy Daniels in the months and years ahead. I thought it had a certain charm to it, mostly in its simplicity, but also in the way it inverted the truth and made Trump's proposed payment not only sensible, but really the only possible response to blackmail—even though her allegations were true. I also knew Trump could use this line on his wife and it would provide her with just enough justification to allow her to turn a blind eye; it was plausible and it was a denial, and I felt sure it would appeal to Trump's rat-like survival instinct.

"Mr. Trump," I said, measuring my words carefully, "just because something isn't true doesn't mean it can't hurt you."

There it was: my years learning at the foot of Donald J. Trump distilled to their essence. The Boss pouted and nodded. I was doing what everyone at Trump Organization was always supposed to do: stick with the narrative. Deny, deny, deny. Accuse, accuse, accuse. Never, ever, ever concede defeat or admit weakness. But with a twist. To get Trump to settle, despite his protestations that he didn't settle, I'd come up with a way to explain his capitulation in a way that made him look like he was wise, measured, and only doing what was necessary.

"It's only $130,000," he sighed finally. "Fuck it, Michael. Go talk to Allen and figure it all out."

"Sure, Boss," I said.

Allen Weisselberg's office was just down the hall, and within a minute we were discussing how to pay Daniels the money in the most discreet and untraceable way possible. It was obvious that he'd been briefed on the matter, so there was no need to explain that background. But there was another matter that loomed over our conversation without being mentioned. In the past, we'd relied on David Pecker and American Media to partner in catch and kill operations, the media mogul providing a very handy way to distance the payment from Trump, as the world now knows. But Trump had cheated Pecker out of the $150,000 paid to Karen McDougal, partly to avoid the possibility of being linked to the payment (which failed) but also out of his personal cheapness. If Trump could screw a law firm, or a paint vendor, or a salesperson, he'd do it almost as a matter of principle. It was like paying taxes: that was only for the little people.

"We need to create a corporation to pay the money to Keith Davidson," I said. "Also, we need to figure out which Trump entity to use to make the payment."

"Did the Boss approve payment?" Weisselberg asked.

"Yes, I just left his office," I replied. "You know what, time is of the essence here, so let's go speak to him together."

Back in Trump's office, we sat quietly, listening to his booming voice on a call on the speaker box. Despite all the promises made to the public that he would recuse himself from running his companies, he never gave an inch of control to his kids. Trump knew he wasn't going to win, so why take any risk with his businesses in the meantime?

Trump hung up and Allen jumped in, asking him if he'd approved the number of $130,000.

"It's a lot of money for nothing," Trump said, continuing the charade. "It never pays to settle these things. But many, many friends have advised me to pay."

He fell into meditative silence for a beat, a rare occasion for Trump.

"A hundred and thirty thousand is a lot less than I would have to pay Melania," he said. "If it comes out, I'm not sure how it would play with my supporters. But I'd bet they think it's cool that I slept with a porn star."

Finally, he shrugged. "Allen, I approved Michael to do the deal," he said. "You two figure this out and let me know."

After I confirmed with Keith Davidson that the number was still on the table, I went to Allen's office to resolve the details of executing a money transfer. Setting up a company for this purpose would be simple, but this was when I began to see that the deal was going to be more complicated than I'd anticipated.

"Michael, how are we going to make the payment?" Allen asked. "It is possible to run the invoice through one of the golf courses, like Palos Verde, for example. What about selling a Mar-a-Lago membership to someone you know? Or maybe you know someone who's having an affair that will be willing to pay the sum?"

I swallowed that thought for a moment. Allen was twenty years older than me, and we weren't particularly close; our relationship was correct and business-like; and he wasn't part of the banter and joking on the 26th floor. I could see that Alan had never dealt with this kind of sensitive matter personally, as he'd always had Pecker to clean up Trump's messes. But was he serious, I wondered, prefacing the thought with the f-word in my head, trying to keep my patience.

"Allen, I don't know anyone who is having an affair at a Trump property, or is interested in purchasing a membership," I said.

"We definitely don't want any paper trail leading back to the Boss," Allen said. "If the Boss pays it and signs the check, it's like disclosing it to the world. It's the same if it's a wire from one of his accounts. It needs to come from a third-party to ensure secrecy."

"I see your point," I said.

"Let's think about this and discuss it in the morning," Allen said.

Meanwhile, Davidson wasn't patiently awaiting the payment. He was convinced, correctly, that we were dragging our feet because the election was only a matter of weeks away. If we could play for time, Keith told me, and Trump lost, as the entire universe now agreed was going to happen, including the candidate himself, then the value of Ms. Daniels's salacious story would go to zero. Texting and calling my cell, Keith was pressing for the deal to close, and I sympathized with his position, but I couldn't think of a way to resolve the matter and I didn't want to bother Trump with the issue. He was campaigning furiously, flying to three or four states a day to hold his massive rallies in arenas and stadiums and airplane hangars, the red MAGA hats proliferating in a way that exceeded even my wildest dreams. Trump was going to lose, I figured, but he was going to go down in a blaze of glory.

Davidson emailed a draft of the agreement between David Dennison and Peggy Peterson, two pseudonyms he'd concocted to substitute for Trump and Daniels, another layer of deniability, albeit a flimsy one. I racked my brain trying to think of someone to wire the money for Trump, ruling out the usual suspects like Stewie Rah Rah because of the intense political scrutiny the Boss was under; the stakes were too high to involve an outsider. In truth, Trump lacked intimates and true friends, so he had nowhere to turn in his hour of need, a reality I now see playing out on the nightly news as he gets more and more isolated as president.

To stall, I reviewed and edited the terms of Davidson's fairly standard Non-Disclosure Agreement, buying another day, then I signed the contract on behalf of the Delaware LLC I'd set up to make the payment, leaving Trump/Dennison's signature line blank. I insisted on keeping the only copy of the side letter agreement that identified Trump and Daniels as the real people behind the fake names in the NDA, but there was still no money, so I had to slow-walk the deal. I came up with a litany of excuses: first it was travel, then it was Yom Kippur, then I said Trump was impossible to reach in the crush of the campaign, as one deadline passed and then another, but it became clear that there was really no way to buy time anymore when Davidson sent me an email saying that the deal was now off.

Pecker and the *National Enquirer* weren't going to catch and kill the story, but the young Australian journalist Dylan Howard continued to try to broker the deal, acting as a go-between for Davidson and me. Howard trafficked in celebrity gossip, often of the most vicious and destructive variety, but he'd clearly been instructed by his boss Pecker to do his best to protect the Boss. Texts and emails and calls and encrypted conversations were heating up as the election in November loomed, but there was nothing I could do to mollify Howard when he pleaded that it would be a disaster for the *National Enquirer* if their participation in the effort to silence Daniels was revealed. Pecker had an interest in silence, I realized, but that didn't solve the problem.

With Daniels by now again talking to reporters to sell her story, I felt sure, I realized the walls were closing in: the story could break at any moment. I finally made my way to Allen's office.

"What about you?" I asked.

"What about me?" Weisselberg asked.

"Why don't you advance the payment on behalf of the Boss?" I said.

Weisselberg went as white as a sheet—like he'd seen a ghost. Or been asked to really put his neck on the line for the man he'd supposedly served so loyally.

"I can't," he said. "I can't," he said again. "You know that I pay for my two grandchildren at Columbia Grammar. That's one hundred thousand a year. I don't have the money to pay it."

This was rich, I knew. He was making an excellent salary with Trump and he'd been working for the company for decades, but when push came to shove he immediately became a spineless wonder. What an asshole, I remember thinking, you're a millionaire many times over and you can't come up with a lousy $130,000 for the Boss? Pathetic. But I also knew that there was another factor at work. The mouse wheel in Allen's head was spinning at a hundred miles an hour. He figured he'd never see the money again—like the Boss stiffing Pecker by welching on the $150,000 for Karen McDougal, Trump would conveniently find a way to ignore the debt and the accountant would have to quietly eat the loss to pay off a porn star, not exactly a story that he'd want his grandchildren to hear as he sat on a rocking chair.

I could see Allen's deviousness at work and I knew where things were heading: he was calculating how to put the onus on me. I was like the kid, Little Mikey, in the 1970s commercial for Life cereal. I was the one that inevitably got the shit sandwich placed in front of him to consume, like Mikey eating the new cereal. I was the cliché: Mikey Will Eat Anything. This was the nadir of my time with Trump, at least up to that point, with the Presidency fading away and me stuck with the tab for Trump's sex romp in a hotel room in Utah a decade ago; I could foretell Trump stiffing me on the money, too, a further indignity and outrage.

This was the job I loved? He was my hero? Was I out of my mind?

Yes.

"Michael," Allen said, pretending to be an earnest colleague trying to solve an urgent problem in the fairest way possible. "You have money. You're the richest guy in the office. What about you?"

"Allen," I replied, reciting his name as a way to keep myself calm and not start screaming at him. "Laura does all the banking in our house. She's the CEO of the household. When she sees a withdrawal of $130,000 from our account she will no doubt ask me about it. I can't tell her, obviously."

Our conversation was going nowhere, I could see, and a solution had to be found. I knew of one way I could find that amount of money and stay under the radar with my wife: we had a home equity line of credit for $500,000 for our apartment at Trump Park Avenue. We owned the property almost outright, and we had no real need for the line of credit, but it made sense to have access to a good amount of cash in the event of an emergency; especially at a ridiculously low interest rate. Trump's roving eye wasn't my emergency, of course, but under the pressure of the moment I felt obligated to fix the problem; a fixer fixes things, I reasoned, and a lawyer like me is needed when things are broken.

There was nothing inherently wrong about using the home equity line in this manner, apart from the stupidity and dubious morality of the situation. I had $2.5M in cash in the same bank, and I'd never, ever been behind on any payments or transactions. In the end, as you'll discover, I was forced to plead guilty to a count of lying to the bank about what I was going to do with this money, but that was a fantasy of the federal prosecutors from the Southern District of New York. I didn't lie for the simplest reason: the bank never asked what I wanted the money for. I'd fill in a form and wire the money to the account of the Delaware company I'd set up for the payment and that would be the end of it. With a heavy heart, I made the suggestion to the weasel, Weisselberg.

"I'll do it," I said. "But I can only do it from my equity line. The interest on a hundred thirty K will be $500 a month. Let's say we figure out how I get repaid the money in the next two months."

"One hundred percent the Boss will pay you back," Allen said, relieved. "I give you my word on it."

"Please make sure," I said.

"Don't worry," he replied.

Weisselberg and I went to Trump's office to report our solution. I told the Boss that I would make the payment personally and we'd figure out the repayment in a couple of months—after you've lost the election, I could have said.

"Wow, Michael," Trump said. "That's great. Perfect. Right after the election, when things calm down, we'll figure this all out."

So there is your answer: Did Donald J. Trump know that I paid off Stormy Daniels to catch and kill her story?

Of course he did.

On October 27, I wired $130,000 to the trust account of Keith Davidson, and in return I received a signed NDA the following day. I called Trump to confirm that the transaction was completed, and the documentation all in place, but he didn't take my call—obviously a very bad sign, in hindsight. Instead, my old pal Kellyanne Conway, from the Trump World Tower board dispute, when I'd first met Trump, called and said she'd pass along the good news.

Paying off the porn star was an open secret in the Trump campaign, one of countless lies and deceptions that his acolytes agreed to hide, always in service of the greater good. That was how cheating and lying were perceived by otherwise reasonably honorable and sensible people, without pausing to consider the context or the consequences of enabling Trump: the greater good and beating Clinton and MAGA were all-consuming obsessions.

The only person who seemed to have some perspective was Trump, despite his public performances and seemingly endless store of energy for insult and bombast and fury. The election was now one week away, but he knew how it was going to go. Trump telling me that we'd sort out the money when things would "calm down" after the election sounded to me like a confession that he knew he was going to lose. All of this would have blown over then, no doubt, in that eventuality. But the Gods and James Comey had another outcome in mind, as we all know.

Chapter Fifteen

Election Night

I had waited five years for election day, and I had long pictured how the night would go: Laura, Samantha, Jake, and I would all go together to watch Trump win, and the world—and my family's world—would be transformed forever. But reality wasn't going to match my imagination on November 4th of that year. Laura had no interest in going, for a start, and Jake had a school assignment to complete, so he was out, as well. That left Samantha and me, a situation that wasn't that unusual, as she often came with me to campaign cocktail parties and fundraisers. Sami, as we call her, is a pistol, a dynamic and funny and socially adept young woman who is at ease mingling with older, sophisticated wealthy people. In the way she makes and keeps friends, and adapts to any environment quickly, she resembles me, I thought, and the two of us are very close.

The only thing that really separated us was Trump. The reason Samantha was coming, she made clear, was to watch Trump lose and suffer the indignity of being humiliated in front of the world. She had watched the campaign with a combination of dread and disgust, like many Americans, constantly barraging me with complaints about Trump's racism and nativism, as I offered excuses and justifications and evasions. But she agreed to come on election night and dressed to the nines, in a black dress, with her hair and makeup done like she was going to the Oscars. I wore a black suit and pink tie, a classic Trump signifier, putting a triangular pink pin on my lapel that the Secret Service had given me to indicate I was a senior staffer. Whatever happened, we both figured it was going to be a once-in-a-lifetime experience.

On the West Side of Manhattan, the Clinton campaign had taken over the entire half-a-million-square-foot Javits Center, a project that Trump had been involved in developing in the 1980s and tried to have named after his father, Fred. The Clinton people had spared no expense, with a giant stage shaped like a map of the United States and tons of green confetti ready to be unloaded to look like a shattered glass ceiling—but the shattering wasn't going to be in a ceiling that night.

In sharp contrast, Trump had hired a drab ballroom at the Marriot, in recognition of the fact he expected to lose, but also a reflection of his congenital stinginess. Walking into the party that evening was when I got the first inkling that my status in Trump's inner circle might be changing. It came in small signs, but they were the kind of unmistakable and miniscule symbols and snubs that indicated you were being downgraded by Trump, for whatever reason. Like a mobster being hugged too hard by the boss, or not being hugged at all, sensing that he was going to get whacked, I was a wise guy wise to the ways of Trump as I received an envelope with my name on it and a VIP placard inside. The real action was upstairs, I knew, with the true insiders, watching the results in suites near Trump and his wife.

We went to the VIP room as the crowd filed in, the names and faces of folks who'd worked on the campaign familiar by now. There were two giant TVs on, one tuned to CNN, the other to Fox. The early results weren't good for Trump, as the commentators speculated on a big Clinton win. Still, the atmosphere in the VIP room was positive, if resigned, with remarks exchanged in amazement that Trump had gotten as far as he had. He was now a political force to be reckoned with, all agreed, and he would remain one for years to come. Speculation was widespread about what he'd do next, from starting a Trump TV station to rival Fox, to a life as a power broker and kingmaker. Whatever happened, I'd already had the ride of a lifetime and I'd been at the white-hot center of an unprecedented national campaign, so everything from here on was gravy to me.

Watching the dueling TV coverage, the disparity between the two cable stations was incredible to see. John King was on CNN working his "magic board" and predicting that Clinton would win, with the early contested states seeming to go her way. As an insider, I knew that the numbers were closer than the pundits were saying, as the internal polls showed the race tightening at a rapid rate after James Comey announced his renewed investigation into Hillary Clinton, looking for all the world like he was deliberately throwing the election for Trump. That was how it looked inside the campaign.

I tweeted out a split-screen shot with my observation: "Is this the same election?"

After many hours of watching the screens, I received a phone call from a friend who was a *New York Times* analytics expert. He expressed to me that he'd run an analysis and that they'd call Trump's win in Florida within fifteen minutes. I replied to him, "Are you kidding? If that's true, Trump just won the election."

He responded, "I'm one hundred percent certain."

And, as we all know, Trump won, becoming the 45th President of the United States.

I didn't know where the real celebration party was happening. I wasn't summoned to the rooms upstairs in the hotel, to hug the president-elect and share our amazement at this incredible journey we had started together, just the two of us. Sami and I didn't discuss what was transpiring, but I could tell she felt it too, and that she felt for me.

In the weeks that followed, I watched in amazement as the chaos of the campaign morphed into the exponentially larger chaos of the so-called transition. There was absolutely no plan, as countries and corporations connived to find a way to get a message through to Trump. Russia, Canada, Britain, IBM, Microsoft, Ford, every lobbyist and diplomat was trying to solve the Rubik's Cube of Trump, and in record time. . . .

I had tried to get Trump to think about the possibility of having to lead a transition team in the weeks before the vote. I took a copy of the contingency plans drawn up by the Mitt Romney campaign in 2012 from the office of Anthony Scaramucci and brought it to the Boss's office. I begged him to look at the book, to at least open the effing thing, but Trump refused. He wouldn't even touch it. There were a few reasons for this unwillingness to prepare for victory in the way any sane politician would when faced with the prospect of becoming the leader of the free world in a matter of days. The biggest was that he thought he was going to lose. Next, Trump never, ever prepared or studied or planned, instead trusting his instincts, a practice that seemed certifiably insane to me. He considered that kind of effort a waste of time and beneath his stature. The last reason, improbably, was that Trump thought it would be a jinx to actually anticipate a victory, preferring not to tempt fate in a way that was beyond reckless.

"Get out of my office," Trump said. "That's bad luck."

Kushner was suddenly the global dauphin, an inexperienced and totally unqualified figure acting as the gatekeeper to the president-elect, who was equally inexperienced and unqualified. The voters had decided to blow up the establishment—or drain the swamp, if you prefer—and suddenly Kushner, an aristocratic man-child possessed of supreme arrogance and a completely amoral will to power, like his father-in-law and wife, was going to simultaneously bring peace to the Middle East and somehow navigate a looming global trade war? The cliché about sending a boy on a man's errand had never been truer than in Trump Tower in the days after the election, as Prime Ministers and CEOs and diplomats tried to insinuate themselves with the simpering boy with the voice of Alvin Chipmunk.

I thought about a big job in DC, like anyone would. Chief of Staff? Hell yeah, I'd take that job. How about White House Counsel? A graduate of the Thomas M. Cooley School of Law in that position was beyond preposterous, I knew, but who wouldn't let their imagination run wild at the possibilities? The idea that I was begging for a position, as has been claimed repeatedly, was silly and unfounded. I was a sycophant to Trump, like so many then and now, but that doesn't mean that every dumb rumor or piece of revenge gossip was true. I have precisely no reason to try to hide any effort to land some top job. I knew that there was really only one job that was appropriate for me, and I knew it was to be the Personal Attorney to President Donald J. Trump.

I really discovered where I stood with Trump when I received my 2016 annual Christmas card from his assistant, Rhona Graff. She did this every year, giving out the season greetings, the envelopes containing the staff's annual bonus. I figured that Trump would use this check to reimburse me for the Daniels payment, so I was anticipating a number around $500,000, with my bonus $150,000 from the prior year increased because of my loyalty and secrecy and sacrifice. But I should have known better when I saw Trump take off for Mar-a-Lago before the checks were distributed.

To say I was surprised and dismayed by the number on the check would be an understatement. I was astounded. My bonus was $50,000? I thought there must be a typo for a second, as I confirmed the number and muttered in disbelief. My bonus was cut by two-thirds? I was outraged, as I marched over to Allen Weisselberg's office.

"What the fuck?" I asked the CFO.

Allen pretended to be surprised, but of course he knew exactly what was going on. With the election as a huge distraction, the company'd had a bad year.

"Sit down," he said, trying to reassure me. "You know better than anyone that the company lost a lot of money over the past year and Trump spent a lot of his own money on the campaign."

"What the fuck, Allen?" I replied. "The man is a billionaire who is now the president-elect. What does any of the money lost have to do with me? I worked my ass off for him, both corporate and campaign shit. I laid out $130,000 of my own money for him to get laid. The Boss knew exactly what he was doing. That's why he got out of town."

Weisselberg was searching for weasel words, I could see, some way to justify Trump's disrespect, or to mollify my justified anger.

"You know the Boss loves you," he said. "He will make it right when we all come back in January. You know this is the game he plays. He does this every year, and then he makes it right. Let me speak with the Boss or maybe Don or Eric and see where we come out on the bonus. Don't worry. You know how much he values you. Now, go and enjoy your vacation. This will be sorted out when you return."

"It better be," I said to Allen, my anger self-evident.

Something in me was broken by this disrespect and presumption at the whim of now President-Elect Trump. I was going to eat the $130,000, just like Pecker had eaten the $150,000, as a way to provide deniability to Trump, adding insult to injury? I had seen firsthand how Trump justified screwing people and the terrible consequences it provoked. The reason I'd had to pay Daniels in the first place was solely because he'd screwed David Pecker out of the $150,000 paid to silence Karen McDougal. Consider that fact. My payment, and all the hellfire and damnation that ensued, up to and including my circumstances as inmate number 86067-054 in Otisville federal prison, stemmed from that ingratitude and dishonesty. If Trump had repaid Pecker, chances are high none of the nonsense and idiocy that ensued would have happened. As with so much, in business and in politics, Trump was the author of his own troubles, though of course this reality was completely lost on him—a side effect of the shallow and childish world he inhabits.

There was no way I was going to tolerate Trump fucking me like this, I thought. No fucking way. As I walked back to my office in a fury, I was calculating what I could get for selling the Daniels story to the press, though not the *National Enquirer,* of course. I was the owner of her rights, after all, through my Delaware company Essential Consulting LLC, so the story of the newly elected President cheating on his wife with a porn star only weeks after she'd given birth to Barron was sure to fetch a pretty penny. Millions, I figured, maybe multiple millions, as I cursed inwardly and swore I wouldn't allow myself to be treated in such a shabby way. Two can play this game, I thought, as I imagined the headlines that would turn the nightmare that constituted his transition to the White House into a biblical-level sex scandal.

The next day, my phone rang. It was Trump, talking as if nothing had happened and all was fine between us. I figured that Allen

Weisselberg must have told him how pissed I was, and he was trying to put out my flaming temper before it turned into a wildfire.

"Michael, my man," he began as usual. "Don't worry about
that thing. We will fix it when I get back."

I wanted to shout at him for treating me with such slimy contempt, after all I'd done for him, not just with the Daniels deal, but
over the years stretching back a decade. I'd disappointed my wife
and children. I'd lied, cheated, and bullied on his behalf, over and
over again, behaving like a heartless jerk in the service of the great
and mighty Donald J. Trump. My wife and kids had wanted me to
quit, this time for real, and reminded me that I'd had the opportunity to partner with Mark Cuban, the billionaire owner of the
Dallas Mavericks, who'd become a friend of mine and whom my
family respected enormously. I'd stayed loyal to Trump and that
drove them crazy, mostly because he drove me crazy—and treated
me terribly.

But I didn't, of course. I knew that he'd see that I was fully
repaid. A simple phone call was all it took.

"Thanks, Boss," I sighed. "I appreciate it."

I took my family to St. Barts for the Christmas and New Year
break, a needed respite from the election and its aftermath. But, of
course, it wasn't a real holiday, with Trump calling me anytime
something related to my duties crossed his mind. On several occasions, Trump suggested that I take a job as Assistant White House
General Counsel, to work closely with Don McGahn. As often as
he asked, this was not a job I had any interest in.

Every time Trump called, my wife and kids would moan and
complain, saying that all he ever did was hand his problems over
for me to fix, ruining our vacation and imposing on our family
time, and it was true. I was also constantly dealing with Felix Sater
on the Trump Tower Moscow Deal at the time.

"You need to recharge," my wife Laura said, finally. "This is your time. Come on, let's go for a walk on the beach."

The truth was that I didn't like beaches much, a view that my time behind bars has given me the time to reflect on. Work was never a burden for me. I loved the action and taking calls from the president-elect was hardly an imposition, at least not for me, no matter how intrusive and annoying to my family. I was a worka-holic, like Trump, constantly in motion and always working my two cell phones, looking for deals and ways to make money or exert power. But I took the walk with Laura, quietly tucking a cell phone into the back pocket of my shorts, even though I don't like the feel of sand on my feet.

The morning I returned to work back in New York, an early bird as always, Allen Weisselberg appeared at my door the moment I flicked on the lights. "Come to my office, please," Allen said, as he was very eager to talk, and so was I. When we sat down, he started to explain how Trump was going to make me "whole" on the Daniels payment. First, the $130,000 would be doubled, grossed up as he described it, to make up for the taxes I would have to pay on that money, meaning the starting sum would be $260,000.

"And, how much was the RedFinch deal?" he asked.

"Fifty thousand," I lied. I'd only paid $13,000 for the digital work done by my friend on behalf of Trump, but I figured I was going to get screwed by Trump on my bonus, just as I'd screwed so many others on his behalf, so I was going to do some counter screwing myself.

"Okay," Allen said. "That's $100,000."

He punched in the numbers on his calculator, looking up.

"You know the Boss really appreciates what you did," he said, referring to the Daniels payment without saying so—in the tradi-tion of criminal enterprises since time immemorial.

"Not with that bonus," I said.

"I know," Allen replied. "The Boss wants to settle up on everything so he can talk to you about other things. Like the position you've been talking to him about."

There it was: what I really wanted. I wanted to be Personal Attorney to the President of the United States. I was beyond elated. It felt like the day he'd first asked me to come to work for him, like I'd been selected to join a tiny, elite, and special cadre. In the weeks since the election, the gossip and rumor mongering had been out of control, with everyone Trump had ever met seeming to want a job of some sort—ambassador, secretary of a federal department, a judgeship, the head of a regulatory agency. Trump was suddenly in charge of the largest favor factory in the history of the world and I was the person charged with keeping track of exactly who was owed what and why.

I knew that people were saying I was begging Trump for a job as his Chief of Staff, even though I had never discussed the matter with him. Of course I'd take that job—I'd kill for it—but I knew it wasn't a great idea, given all that I'd said and done on behalf of Trump.

But first, it was back to business and Trump squeezing every lousy penny he could without risking alienating me. I'd been thrown a big bone, in my position as the personal lawyer for Trump, and now I was going to have to eat crow.

"So that's two-sixty, plus the hundred, and the Boss wants to do another sixty, to make the total four-twenty," Allen said.

"You know that bonus is a fraction of what I got last year," I said.

"I know," Allen said. "He reduced everyone's bonus this year."

I said nothing. I'd been one step ahead of Trump, thinking through what he'd do, so I'd loaded up on the RedFinch payment, sneakily upping my bonus. Classic Trump move, I thought. Score one for me, and I'm getting the position I most wanted. I knew the opportunities would be immense, as I'll explain momentarily. I figured I was going to be the new Bob Bauer, Obama's horse-whisperer attorney, the innermost of the President's innermost advisors. I wasn't knighted by Harvard, but it was exactly as I'd anticipated in law school. Graduate and pass the bar exam and my title would be like every other attorney—Counselor—only with the lucrative and undeniably astoundingly powerful addition of "to the President of the United States."

Huuuggeee, I was thinking: I'm going to be huuugggeeeee. Effing huuuuggggeeee.

An hour later Allen and I were summoned to Trump's office, now bristling with even more Secret Service agents. The Boss motioned for us to sit as he basked in yet another supporter praising him to the heavens on the speakerphone so I'd have the honor of sharing the offer of fealty to Trump. There was no amount of this that was too much for him, never a time when he recognized he was being stroked and flattered for transparently self-serving reasons; he never rolled his eyes, or yawned, no matter how preposterous or sycophantic the supplicant.

"So, you and Allen worked out the numbers?" Trump asked me, hanging up.

I knew he could see in my facial expression that I was more than fine with the arrangements. Besides, it wasn't really a question. I wasn't expected to answer, or better yet, I was not permitted to reply. It was a statement of fact, a confirmation that he didn't have to bother with any outstanding issues and he could move on, and so he did.

"Are you sure you don't want a job in DC?" he asked. "Maybe with Don McGahn as an assistant White House Counsel?"

"Boss," I said. "If I take that position I don't work for you. I work for the government. There is no attorney-client privilege. We went over this. There are still open matters that need to be handled. I can be in Washington as often as you like or need me to be. I'll come down even if it's just to keep you company. Shit, I'll park my ass on the Oval Office couch, if that's what you want."

"Okay, Michael," Trump said. "Congratulations. You have the job."

I tried to disguise my glee, probably unsuccessfully.

"So here's what we'll do," he said. "We'll use the number Allen came up with. What's the number again?"

"Four hundred and twenty thousand," I said.

"Wow, that's a lot," he said. "We can use this as a retainer for the work you will be doing for me privately. Allen, you can pay Michael $35,000 for each month of the year. Michael, you will send Allen an invoice each month. This is okay with you, right?"

"Sure, Boss," I said. "I'm really honored."

One of my $35,000 checks from Trump. © 2020 Michael Cohen

"Okay, good, I'll see you in DC for the Inauguration," Trump said. "Man, can you believe this shit? You called it from the beginning, Michael."

"Yes, Boss, I did," I said. "I'm really looking forward."

Allen and I departed, but I was no longer walking—I was floating on cloud nine. Trump's maneuver was classic, gangster, the kind of deception that I had to say I appreciated in all its dimensions. Trump was going to pay me for my services with my own money. He'd get the tax deduction for legal fees, almost certainly a criminal offense if any mortal lied on their tax returns about a business expense of nearly half a million dollars, a reality that I would come to understand in time. The payments would be spread out over twelve months and look like a perfectly ordinary arrangement for a sitting president devolving the management of his business interests to his two sons, but still in need of an experienced lawyer who knows his affairs—pardon the pun—and who could advise him confidentially.

As I thought about the arrangement, Trump was actually *making* money on the deal, by way of his tax cheat, and he had my legal services free for the year.

But Trump's supposed genius didn't account for who the real fool was, and who was really sailing in a ship of fools, as time and history would tell. Trump had been too clever by half, the kind of dishonest, cunning, conspiratorial and short-term thinking that constituted the worst-possible mindset for the democratically elected leader of the United States. But I didn't care about those details. My life had taken the most amazing, exciting, even delirious turn, and even though my wife and kids would never really understand my elation—or the moral decisions I made to get to this place—I wasn't just vindicated; I was validated.

Michael D. Cohen, Esq., Personal Attorney to President Donald J. Trump!

I'd always loved my Trump Organization business card and the cachet it brought to me by association, but this wasn't next level—it was out of this world, as I imagined the financial implications and possibilities. I wasn't a kid in a candy store, I was the kid with a ticket to Willy Wonka's Chocolate Factory.

* * *

RUMORS ABOUT THE shady Russians having videotape of Donald Trump with hookers performing a golden shower during the Miss Universe pageant in 2013 in Moscow had circulated for years. The tape was supposedly taken in the presidential suite of a Moscow hotel where Barack Obama and his wife Michelle had stayed, as a way to ritualistically taunt them, if peeing on a bed can be said to constitute a ritual. I know those sentences sound preposterous, but knowing the Boss, anything was possible. I didn't believe it and have said so publicly, but I also could not definitely rule out the possibility it was true, nor did I particularly care—unless someone could prove it.

During the summer of 2016, around the time of the Republican convention in mid-July, the landline in my office rang, with the caller ID blocked. I picked up to discover a man on the line claiming he had a personal matter related to Trump, which was why he'd been patched through to me; in the Trump Organization, I was known to handle all matters that were personal for the Boss and the family. The particular gentleman refused to identify himself, but he said he was in possession of a tape showing Trump with a group of prostitutes in Moscow and that the women were peeing on a bed with the Boss visibly watching them.

I calmly told the man that he would need to prove that he actually had the pee tape, as I called it. I demanded that he provide me with a clip from the tape. Not the entire thing, just three or four seconds so I could discern with my own eyes if it was real.

"I need to see the tape, so I know, and then we can discuss a price," I said.

"I can't do that," the anonymous caller said.

"How can I verify that it exists?" I asked.

"It exists," he said. "I've seen it."

"Send it on a flash drive," I said. "Send it anonymously, so that I can verify the contents."

"I can verify that it's real," the man said.

"How much do you want?" I asked.

"Twenty million," the man said.

"So what's your name?" I asked. "What's your bank account number? Give me the name of your lawyer and I can put the money in escrow until I have assurances that it's the only copy of the tape. It is the only copy, right?"

Click. The man hung up.

I had no intention of putting any money in escrow, of course, but that was my way of forcing the issue. If he was serious, he was going to have to take next steps. If the caller really had the tape, and had really thought through what would happen next, then he would be prepared with concrete plans on how to actually receive the money. The chances that he was a crank, or an idiot, were extremely high, but nonetheless, the call was concerning.

I immediately called David Pecker to tell him what had just transpired. Pecker and I traded information like this all the time, with wild rumors and wilder accusations always circulating about Trump, so that we could coordinate our actions and ensure both of us were fully informed at all times. Pecker's journalists reported all the scurrilous rumors they heard, not to the public but to their boss, who routinely passed along these tales to me, so I could be prepared if any of them threatened to go public. This was another aspect of catch and kill, in this case, really keeping track of potential threats rather than taking action.

Pecker told me that there was a lot of chatter in the air about the possible existence of the Moscow tape, but he hadn't heard of anyone in actual possession of the tape. Hanging up, I decided this was a rare, rare case where the truth actually did matter. If there really was a tape circulating showing the Republican presidential candidate engaged in such a crude and frankly disgusting, not to mention juvenile, act with hookers in Moscow—well, that would be mind boggling. I had to get to the bottom of this particular cesspool, I decided, as I walked to Trump's office, knocked, entered, and sat in the middle Egg, explaining the anonymous call I'd just received.

"Boss, does this tape exist?" I asked. "I need to know if it's true or false. Is there any truth to this?"

"Absolutely not," Trump said.

"You're sure?" I said. "Because there's a lot of chatter. The guy who just called me wanted $20 million."

"It's bullshit," Trump said. "It never happened. Do you know who the guy was?"

"No," I replied. "The call came in anonymous. I asked for his lawyer to put the money in escrow and he hung up on me."

"It's bullshit," Trump said.

"Excellent."

But Trump's word wasn't enough, needless to say. I'd seen Trump at The Act in Las Vegas with the Agalarovs, father and son, so I knew that Russian tastes in entertainment were risqué, to put it mildly. The atmosphere at beauty pageants like Miss Universe was heavy on the testosterone for the men in attendance, especially for older men like Trump, surrounded by young, beautiful women enthralled by the American celebrity. More, the Boss was away from his wife, in a distant country and different time zone, so he had latitude to let loose. It didn't strike me as improbable that the Agalarovs would want to impress Trump by presenting him with a sampling of their finest prostitutes, famously the most beautiful in the world, at least according to Vladimir Putin.

All I now knew was that Trump had denied that there could be the possibility of such a tape existing, but that still left open the possibility that it would emerge, and I needed to be prepared for all contingencies, for the Boss's own good. It was entirely plausible that Trump had been involved in such a tape and he'd wished away the memory, but the more likely contingency was that Trump had been surreptitiously videotaped, so he wouldn't know about the tape—and figured no one had seen him. I knew that during the Cold War, the KGB had conducted all kinds of secret surveillance on diplomats stationed in Moscow, as well as visiting dignitaries, in order to develop compromising information. There was a Russian word for it: *Kompromat.*

The first question, I realized, had to be whether the Boss had been with prostitutes in Russia at all, and the best way to get an answer to that was to ask his security guard, Keith Schiller. An ex-cop fiercely loyal to Trump, Keith was with Trump during all his waking hours when he traveled, and I knew he'd been glued to the Boss's side during the Russia trip, with so many security risks involved.

I told Keith about the anonymous call and the demand for $20 million, as well as Trump's denial.

"Does this tape exist?" I asked. "Because if it does, I'll figure out a way to get it and buy it."

"It never happened," Schiller said. "I never saw anything like this, and I was with the Boss throughout the whole trip. I took him back to the hotel and I stood outside his room for half an hour after he went to bed. I checked and the door was locked until I went to see the Boss in the morning."

Keith I could trust, and so the matter lay there until days before the election, when I got a call from a friend named Georgi Rtskhiladze, a Georgian-born businessman I'd met socially and whom I'd worked with on the potential Trump-branded hotels in Tbilisi and Batumi. Georgi and I bonded over tennis and real estate, and we talked from time to time about politics and Trump's candidacy. But this call was different. I knew he'd lived in Moscow and remained connected there, so I wasn't shocked when he told me he'd heard rumors about Trump through the grapevine. But when he specified it was the "pee tape" report that was making the rounds, my heart sank. I'd just dealt with Stormy Daniels, and before that Karen McDougal, and now Trump was threatened with a videotape of him gloating over golden showers in a Moscow hotel to taunt President Obama, and this man was going to be the 45th President?

Giorgi was offering me the use of his network of business and government contacts in Moscow, as a favor, and I appreciated the kindness. We exchanged texts, and Giorgi told me he'd "stopped flow of some tapes from Russia," but I doubted he'd been able to actually do that—if the tapes even existed at all. When the Mueller Report came out, as I will discuss later, a small example of their maximally antagonistic approach to interpreting events was how the footnote that dealt with my conversation with Georgi left out the word "some," trying to imply somehow that he knew about the contents of the alleged recordings, when he didn't. Georgi told me he'd just heard stupid rumors and there were plenty of those in the final days of the 2016 campaign.

Which was why my jaw dropped when I heard about the so-called Steele Dossier. I was in Florida, watching my son Jake pitch against the IMG Academy baseball team, likely the finest high-school outfit in the country, when my phone rang and it was a *Wall Street Journal* reporter who started asking me questions about the dossier. I didn't know what she was talking about, so I asked her to email the story in *Buzzfeed* that published the dossier to my phone. As I scanned the pages, I was astounded to see my name repeated again and again, as if I were some demented, evil mastermind secretly and mostly single-handedly brokering the worst case of treason in the history of the United States. I had supposedly clandestinely traveled to Prague to meet with Russian officials aiming to intervene in the 2016 election on behalf of Trump, a story so ridiculous I couldn't believe what I was seeing with my own two eyes—and remember, I not only had seen news I knew to be fake, I'd also manufactured it.

Because here's the thing: I've never been to Prague. Never, ever. But that didn't stop the *Wall Street Journal* reporter from haranguing me about my fictional voyage to the capital of the Czech Republic or demanding answers about my connections to Paul Manafort and my father-in-law's nonexistent best-friend relationship with Putin. On and on the reporter went, like I actually did own a dacha in Sochi, in Krasnodar Krai province. I thought it was a joke. It had to be a joke—the karmic reply to the bullshit about Ted Cruz's father being involved in the assassination of JFK. I was mentioned more than ten times, and each allegation was crazier than the last. But still they came: did I pay hackers? My father-in-law was supposedly a tycoon in Russia, but the problem was, he was Ukrainian, and he'd only been in the Russian capital once, as a teenager in the military of the Soviet Union.

I was pacing up and down behind the dugout, yelling on my phone, getting angrier and angrier, and my son was on the mound pitching against some of the top baseball prospects in the world, and he was severely distracted by the sight of his father going ballistic. Of course, he got hit up that day as I completely threw him off his game.

Thousands upon thousands of articles appeared in the press all over the planet that day, as I went from a loud and brash advocate for Donald Trump on cable television, to Public Enemy Number One because of the horseshit report of some washed-up former MI-6 intelligence operative in England who I knew for a fact didn't have his facts straight. Not a single one! This was not the kind of celebrity anyone would want, with half the nation seeing me as a traitor, and the other half eagerly awaiting the Inauguration. One thing I knew for sure: the Boss wouldn't like all the attention I was getting, not because I was dominating news cycles, but because it was distracting from his pending presidency.

Sure enough, as soon as I got back to New York, my phone rang. It was the president-elect.

"What the fuck?" Trump said. "What's this about?"

"What?" I replied.

"You going to Prague," Trump said. "This is very bad. It's blowing up on the Internet."

"Hold on a second, Mr. Trump," I said. "It's complete bullshit. I have no idea where it's coming from. I've never been to Prague. I never worked with Russian *kompromats*. Would you like to see my passport?"

Trump yelled out to the people in the room and they all agreed that they wanted to see my passport in person. Trump ordered me to come to the office, so I took the five-minute walk west across midtown Manhattan to the 26th floor of Trump Tower. There were a bunch of people in Trump's office: Jared Kushner, Steven Bannon, Reince Priebus, Hope Hicks.

I handed Trump my passport and he started to flick through the pages.

"I'm really disappointed you don't believe me," I said. "I believe everything you tell me."

Which wasn't true, of course, but I was trying to make a point. Trump continued to silently page through my passport, which was filled with stamps, mainly from island nations in the Caribbean. Trump handed the passport to Bannon, who looked through it, and they passed it all around the room. There was no mark from the Czech Republic, of course, as they all acknowledged with nods.

"I told you so," I said to Trump.

"Do you have any other passports?" Priebus asked.

"Nope," I said. "Only this one."

"I believe you," Trump said finally.

"We should take a picture of his passport and post it and tweet it out, to show he's never been to Prague," Priebus said to Trump.

"Great idea," said Trump.

Thus was born a meme and a million conspiracy theories and wrongly reported articles and news reports. I'd been to many countries, including Britain and Italy during a vacation to the island of Capri, but the lack of a Czech stamp only made reporters speculate on possible explanations. Italy was in the Schengen Area, for example, the twenty-six nations of continental Europe where visas and passport stamps aren't needed once an entry into any member country has been stamped. Or there was the possibility that I had another passport I was hiding, but I reassured reporters that I only had the one—and I can reassure you that was all I have ever had.

To this day, there are reporters who insist that I went to Prague, despite the denial from the FBI and a complete absence of any evidence. Nevertheless, people like Christopher Steele continue this charade and insist that I'm hiding some nefarious plot hatched in the Czech city.

What's behind this insistence? Or madness? The fact of the matter was that the FBI investigated this allegation and called it garbage. But this nonexistent element of the Steele Dossier was only part of the larger narrative that Trump had used me as his covert connection to Putin and the Kremlin, like the plot of a third-rate thriller. But if my highly believable explanation was accepted, then the entire logic of the Russia-Trump conspiracy theory fell apart. The Russia connection had to be true because it had to be true, circular thinking that in its way provided the perfect counter-point to the idol worship of Trump dead enders willing to justify, or ignore, or rationalize, or simply lie about the worst excesses of Donald Trump.

In this way, I became the personification of all that was wrong and terrible about Donald Trump's victory. Russian interference, the nonstop lying and racism and nativism, the outrageous, over-the-top gloating, the *schadenfreude*, the Electoral College, the tax cuts for the rich, the Supreme Court justices, the constant, unceasing bullying, all the outrages.

I became the lightning rod.

In the summer before the election, I told a reporter for *Vanity Fair*, Emily Jane Fox, that I'd take a bullet for Trump, and I meant it.

But not if Donald Trump pulled the trigger.

In time, this fact would turn me into the lightning rod for the other half of America, as I discovered soon enough.

In early February, I went to DC to meet with the President on some legal matters. I can't remember the details—another of the law suits from women he'd allegedly tried to force himself on, no doubt—but I do remember the trip very well. I stayed at the Trump International Hotel, in the old Post Office, and took a limo to the White House. It was like the first day I went to see the Boss in Trump Tower, with my name left at security as confirmation that I really wasn't dreaming. Only now it was the freaking White House. I was shown into the West Wing, walking along a corridor and saying a polite hello to Jared Kushner, who had a small office down the hall from the Oval.

Trump was expecting me and he saw me in the ante-room, hollering to me.

"Get in here!"

Trump cleared out the Oval.

"I need Michael alone," he said, as the aides filed out.

He turned to me. "Is this place unbelievable or what?"

He swept his arms to show off the majesty of the space, as if he were displaying his booty of gold pieces of eight from a pirate's raid, giddy at the sight of his treasure. He showed me the oil painting of George Washington, with a wide grin.

"Can you believe this?" Trump said. "From 2011 to today. The history. The desk. Everything."

For the next fifteen minutes, he gave me a tour of his space, with the Resolute Desk and the Winston Churchill bust on display. Trump showed me the gold drapes he'd installed, along with the portrait of Andrew "Old Hickory" Jackson, the charismatic 1830s president that Steve Bannon had convinced the historically ignorant Trump he most resembled for his populism and bluster.

"What did you think about the travel ban?" Trump asked.

"No, you mean the Muslim ban," I replied. "I hate it. It's disgraceful. I thought your first policy roll out was going to be infrastructure."

"That was Bannon and [Stephen] Miller," Trump said. "They'll fix it the next time around."

Chapter Sixteen

Typhoon Stormy (Part Three)

The *Wall Street Journal* story in early January of 2018 caused a shitstorm of biblical proportions, even by the Trump Presidency standards. It was reported that I had paid Stormy Daniels $130,000 through a Delaware company called Essential Consulting, LLC, in the days before the 2016 election. That was perfectly true, as the world now knows, but at the time I was fully dedicated to enforcing the NDA with Daniels and making sure she was silenced in order to protect Trump.

I will spare you, gentle reader, all the tawdry details of the ensuing weeks, as I started legal proceedings against Daniels and her attorney, a charmer named Michael Avenatti, who rolled out their campaign to make money from the porn star's encounter with Trump more than a decade earlier. As the cable news talking heads exploded, and I went from being Trump's personal attorney to a household name, events started to move incredibly quickly. Stormy Daniels went from being a small-time porn impresario to the most

famous adult actress in history, thanks to a coordinated and
sophisticated media campaign with her teasing the nation on *60
Minutes* and slyly hinting about her knowledge of the President's
genitals, a swirl of news that remains hard to believe actually happened in the real world, but remember, this was the real real—
Trump's reality.

The simultaneous nature of the ensuing chaos can be shown
best by way of example. Around the same time, the book *Fire and
Fury* was published, and immediately it went to number one on
the bestseller lists, triggering a series of events that upended the
nation's politics and resulted in yours truly writing this account
from the sewage treatment plant in a federal prison camp. I read
the book and was unimpressed. The author captured some of the
chaos around Trump, I could see, but he was barely even an outsider. Some schlub reporter sitting on a couch in the hallway of the
White House was suddenly the author with the best access to
Donald Trump? The whole idea seemed preposterous to me, giving me the inspiration to write my own book about me and the
Boss—one that would be far more intimate. The idea was to portray Trump's real estate deals, and the genius he'd displayed, as a
companion to *The Art of the Deal*.

The story about Trump's acquisition of 40 Wall Street in the
1990s showed how incredibly smart he could be in real estate,
despite his many failings and weaknesses in other areas of life. For
years, Trump claimed to have purchased the landmark downtown
skyscraper for $1M, boasting repeatedly on *The Apprentice* that it
was worth hundreds of millions. Whatever the truth of the purchase price, it was indisputable that he'd cleaned up on the deal by
buying the seventy story neo-gothic 1920s skyscraper in a real
estate slump for pennies on the dollar. The Kluge estate, Doral,
Mar-a-Lago, the Grand Hyatt in the 80s—for all the frantic and

nonstop news that always surrounded Trump, it was clear that when it came to real estate, his father had taught him well.

"There truly is a method to his madness," I wrote in the book proposal, "and people who think otherwise can quickly get buried."

Trump Revolution: From the Tower to the White House, Understanding Donald J. Trump was the title I was thinking about. I had a ghostwriter and fancy agent to represent the project, and we drew up a proposal that outlined the basic approach. Unlike others writing about Trump, I wrote, I really had known the man for a decade. I promised to write about the Russia investigation and my role, continuing to lie about the Moscow Tower deal, of course, and I was going to seek revenge on reporters I thought had dealt unfairly with the Boss and me.

But I couldn't leave sleeping dogs alone, of course, so I also promised to clear up the "unfortunate saga" of Stormy Daniels and the $130,000 I had paid her in the week before the 2016 election. I wasn't going to reveal the fact that I had been repaid the money by Trump, in the form of fake legal fees, or that I had done everything at the direction of the President of the United States, needless to say. The proposal was twenty pages long and really didn't amount to much, at least to my thinking. The White House let it be known that the President preferred that I didn't write a book, without saying why; I figured it was because of my role as his longtime attorney and the Stormy Daniels story and the risk of further fanning those flames.

To sell the book, I did a road show with my agent, meeting with the top editors for the five largest publishing houses in New York, and the feedback was very good. There was a lot of interest in a book that portrayed Trump in a new way, even if I was going to pull many, many, many punches. I was going to be truthful, but

I also had good reason to be economical with the truth. Because here is the thing: I care for Donald Trump, even to this day, and I had and still have a lot of affection for him.

In any event, there was a handshake deal with the publisher Hachette, as I hit pause to think through the reaction of the White House and to decide if, given the complexities, I really wanted to go through with a book, even a limited portrait that didn't show Trump screwing vendors or taking advantage of old friends in a cutthroat way.

Then the book proposal leaked to the *Daily Beast* and all hell broke loose. I don't know exactly who leaked the proposal, but I have a pretty good idea that it was one of the publishing houses that didn't acquire the title, a petty act of petulance that had mind-bending consequences. The root of all that followed lay in the simple fact that Stormy Daniels wanted to sell her story, and she didn't want me to beat her to the payday. At least, that's my best guess, because her reaction came as soon as the story ran and the media madness began to show the first signs of emerging. The true genesis of all that ensued lay in the revelation of the amount of money that I would receive as an advance for the book: $500,000.

In the days that followed, I screamed and bullied and misled reporters I'd known for years, all in the service of trying to stop the truth from emerging. The long and the short of it all was that Daniels wanted to cash in, and after she fired Keith Davidson and took up with the charming—I'm being sarcastic, of course—Michael Avenatti, the outcome was inevitable, at least in hindsight. There was never going to be any Trump book, of course, and the only thing I was going to author was catastrophe.

Statements of denial were issued, legal proceedings were brought to get a restraining order, but Daniels was clearly going to talk at some point. The Karen McDougal story also surfaced, to the fury of David Pecker, but that story didn't excite and titillate the imagination of the nation in quite the same way as the Daniels story. In the end, there was no way to stop the "sources" leaking to the major newspapers and networks about the payment to Daniels, and once I was forced to admit to it, I issued a statement to *The New York Times*. The headline appeared on page twelve of the *Times* on the morning of February 14, 2018. It succinctly summarized my role in the latest twist in the tawdry tale of Donald Trump and Stormy Daniels: "Trump's Longtime Lawyer Says He Paid Actress Out of His Own Pocket."

"Neither the Trump Organization nor the Trump campaign was party to the transaction with Ms. Clifford, and neither reimbursed me for the payment, either directly or indirectly," my statement said. "The payment to Ms. Clifford was lawful, and was not a campaign contribution or a campaign expenditure by anyone."

I added the bromide I'd used to convince Trump to make the payment in the first place: "Just because something isn't true doesn't mean that it can't cause you harm or damage."

Of course, as you know, I was lying. I had been reimbursed for the payments, plus money for income tax on the sum, plus a bonus, but that was no one's business, as far as I was concerned. The *Times* reporter was Maggie Haberman. As I've mentioned, Maggie and I often exchanged information and gossip and tips, but this latest conversation verged on the absurd. Was I really expecting the world to believe I'd spent $130,000 of my own money to hide the sexual past of Donald Trump? After issuing the statement, I refused to answer follow-up questions, apart from saying it was a "private transaction" and that Trump had no knowledge of the payment. Maggie noted in her piece that I had relied on the same seemingly true aphorism during the campaign to explain why I'd supposedly made the payment to Daniels: even false information about Trump could cause him harm if it were published.

But the premise of my explanation left obvious questions: why would a lawyer, any lawyer, pay a client's expenses, without their knowledge? Was that legal? Ethical? Rational? Cable television lit up in response, as usual, with liberal TV attorneys shaking their heads in disbelief, and conservatives claiming yet again that Trump had been exonerated, willfully ignoring the vast holes in my story. This was the pattern that I had grown accustomed to, not just since Trump entered politics, but in all the years I had represented the Boss. If you're caught in a lie, double and triple down. It was the opposite of Occam's Razor: instead of the simplest explanation being the likeliest, this strategy involved complicating the narrative, throwing sand in the eyes of the onlooker, claiming that transparently implausible stories were true unless proven otherwise, and even then denying the obvious truth. It was a variation of the old joke: Are you going to believe me or your lying eyes? It was surprisingly effective over time, if you're willing to be brazen and relentless. It helped if you never truly thought about the past, or the consequences of lying, and if you always lived in the present tense, like a shark swimming through water, only able to survive through constant motion.

Underneath my defiant stance lay the bedrock of what I had learned at the foot of Donald Trump when trouble arose: Just say . . . fuck you!

That cold February morning, I was waiting outside my place at the Trump Park Avenue to meet a wealthy businessman friend to fly to Nevada. My friend was going to Las Vegas to appraise a commercial property for sale, with a price in excess of $1 billion, and at the last moment he'd invited me to join him to solicit my opinion on the deal—and to give me a respite from the incessant swirl of scandal that had come to define my life. I had long inhabited the world of private jets, but as I sat in his SUV and looked over the prospectus for the property, my friend regaled me excitedly about features of his ultra-lush G550 Gulfstream.

Driving through light Saturday morning midtown traffic, we emerged from the Lincoln Tunnel en route to Teterboro Airport, in New Jersey, when my cell phone rang. It was President Trump. I wasn't surprised. He was the President, but we still spoke often, particularly lately, with the headlines crowded with salacious details about the President's alleged affair with the porn star and my role in paying Daniels hush money. For more than a decade, I had been Trump's fixer, through thick and thin, but this latest scandal was perhaps the hardest one I'd ever confronted, as it involved Trump as the leader of the United States government and all of the complications and jeopardies that included.

Over the years, I had become fluent in the language Trump used to communicate his desires and demands. He used inferences, nods, silences, euphemisms, signals. It was similar to how Trump never used email, for the simple reason that it created a digital fingerprint that would permanently record his words—and thus potentially ensnare him. Like a crime boss, Trump wanted no evidence that could connect him to any of his deeds, or deeds that he indirectly or directly ordered others to do. The same applied with conversations. If the President explicitly said what he wanted, or needed, it could potentially be used against him. Better to say nothing that could be held against you, but surround yourself with people who can translate your intentions. Trump's mind was so permeated with deception and delusion—of others, but also of himself—that I had to be prepared to literally depart from reality and enter a kind of fantasyland when I spoke with the President.

"Michael, my man, how are you?" Trump asked.

"I'm well, Mr. President," I replied, waiting to get the signals I was sure were coming. "How are things in DC?"

"Good, all good," Trump said. "Listen, I have Melania on the line with us."

"Hi Michael," the First Lady said.

Melania Trump didn't sound pleased to be on the phone. I knew Mrs. Trump well, and I could tell instantly from her tone of voice that she had been compelled to participate in the call. The reasons for her reluctance were understandable. In the press, I had claimed that I had paid Daniels from my own funds, as a way to protect Donald Trump—as a kind of selfless act meant to protect the then-candidate from a scurrilous and false accusation of sexual infidelity in the hothouse days before the election. My claim was risible on its face, but that was how the game was played, I knew: lies followed lies followed lies, a spiral of logic that inevitably sullied me and everyone else involved. But I sensed that the degrading process was about to hit yet another new low, and I was desperate to spare the First Lady from the humiliating charade that I could see was about to be played out.

To me, Melania was the epitome of class. Her life was dedicated to being a mother to Barron, and she was never shy about letting everyone know that, including DJT. That's part of what made lying to her so difficult. Over the years, Mr. Trump would repeatedly have me call Melania to reaffirm his innocence when he was accused of cheating on her.

At the urging of the President, I started to recite the same story I'd told *The New York Times*. It was sickening that I was lying to another man's wife about that man's infidelity, crossing so many boundaries of basic decency it boggled the mind. The lies kept compounding, because I had been forced to lie to *my* wife about the funds, taking money out of our home equity line of credit on our Park Avenue apartment to disguise the use of the money; as I've said, Laura ran our family's finances, and she wasn't going to agree to spend a large amount of our money to cover up Donald Trump's sexual escapades, whether I was going to be reimbursed or not, as I well knew.

As I talked, it seemed to me that it was almost like Trump

believed the lies himself—as if he might actually believe that he hadn't had sex with Stormy Daniels in 2006 and that he hadn't repaid me the hush money. At the very least Trump didn't care about the truth. If facts didn't suit him, he denied them, changed them, invented them, and then seemingly believed them—to hell with reality—and I willingly played along. But that was only part of this strange marital dance. Like many wealthy women with unfaithful husbands, it appeared to me that Mrs. Trump preferred not to know what her partner really was up to, or to be forced to think about the implications of his behavior for their marriage and their son and her sense of dignity.

As I duly recited the lines about paying Daniels myself, at Trump's prompting, speaking in the tone of a highly responsible attorney who had selflessly protected his client from the slings and arrows of vicious liars and scammers and their sleazy attorneys, Trump interrupted.

"Wait, are you telling me that you paid $130,000 from your own pocket?" he said to me, incredulously.

I again knew precisely what to say. "I did, sir," I said, repeating again the lines about my sacrifice to protect the Trump campaign and my mentor's reputation and marriage and good name.

Leading me on, Trump then asked a specific question about the Daniels accusations. Trump and I had been talking about the alleged affair since October of 2011, when the story about Daniels first surfaced in a blog called thedirty.com and a magazine called *Life & Style*. Now Trump asked about my first interactions with the attorney Keith Davidson, who then represented Ms. Daniels, so I dutifully recited how I had made the blog take down the report about Trump and the porn star years earlier, with signed denials from both parties. I explained how I had fought on Trump's behalf to silence such a libelous and predatory fake story, feeling badly about baldly lying to Mrs. Trump, but also sure I had no choice.

As I droned on about the Daniels affair, I was interrupted by the First Lady.

"I know all of this," she said curtly.

I stopped talking, shaking my head. It was evident to me that she didn't believe the story, or want anything further to do with the transparent lies the President was childishly attempting to tell her via me. As usual with the Trumps when this kind of subject came up, in my experience, the First Lady changed the subject, this time to her son Barron and his new school in Washington. I was on the board of Barron's school in Manhattan and I'd played an active role in making sure the youngest Trump had an excellent experience there, so the subject of education was safe territory for us. Mrs. Trump said that Barron loved his new school in DC, and I said how happy I was to hear that.

"I hope to see you the next time you're at the White House," Mrs. Trump said.

And with that she hung up, with the President remaining on the line. The President and I could have commiserated about how the attempt to fool the First Lady hadn't worked, like a couple of frat bros lamenting the demands of women. We could have strategized about next steps in deceiving the nation about the true nature of the Daniels transaction. At the very least, we could have acknowledged the reality that two grown men—one the most powerful on the planet—had engaged in an inane and hopelessly inept attempt to lie. But that wasn't how Trump operated. That would have required some self-awareness. He would have to say out loud that we both knew we were lying. Instead, as always, Trump insisted we keep up the charade, as if life itself was a vast, ongoing, never-ending game of deception.

"You're the best, Michael," Trump said. "Keep fighting this fight and I will be seeing you soon."

"Thank you for the call, Mr. President," I said.

Hanging up, my friend turned to me. He had only heard one side of the conversation, but even to him it was obvious what had transpired.

"Do you think she believed you?" my friend asked.

"Not a chance," I said. "Not a chance."

* * *

HERE'S AN IDEA: why don't I spare you all the nonsense involving Michael Avenatti and me? I hope the reviewers will take note of this tender mercy.

While Avenatti was taunting me on television and calling me an idiot, all leading to his own seemingly inevitable downfall, I was getting the best form of revenge possible: I was living well. After the election, I'd set myself up in the New York office of Squire Patton Boggs, a top-tier law firm located at Rockefeller Plaza, as a strategic alliance, which really meant the partners could brag to their clients that the personal attorney to the President of the United States was part of their outfit. I was also using my company, Essential Consultants, to take on clients like AT&T, Novartis, Columbus Nova, and BTA Bank—high-level companies desperate for insights and connections to the President and willing to pay for my assistance.

Was I cashing in on my relationship with Trump? Of course I was. What would you do? By March of 2018, to give but one example, I was brokering deals at the level of global, multi-billion-dollar transactions. Take the private dinner I had at Mar-a-Lago at the time, flying down to Florida in the private jet of Ben Ashkenazy, a real estate investor who runs a multi-billion-dollar fund with interests in the Plaza Hotel, Union Station in Washington, DC, and Faneuil Hall in Boston; he was the kind of dude who had Drake sing at his daughter's bat mitzvah. Down in Palm Springs, I met with Franklin Haney, a Memphis businessman who'd long been a

Democrat but who gave $1M to Trump's inaugural committee and hired me to help finance a proposed nuclear power plant in Alabama. Haney also needed a ton of federal approvals to complete the project, which was where I came in to help and guide his attorneys greasing the wheels of commerce and government.

These were super-yacht types of people, and that constituted my reality under President Trump, so all the cable TV yapping from Avenatti and the tut-tuts on liberal cable networks were like water off a duck's back. The real reason I'd come to Florida was to meet with Hamad bin Jassim, who had been the Prime Minister of Qatar from 2007 to 2013, the Foreign Minister from 1992 to 2013, and the CEO of the Qatar Investment Authority, or QIA, from 2005 to 2013. But those titles didn't remotely describe his real authority, as the single person responsible for the disposition of the QIA's $320 billion fund. That made him perhaps the only human being on the planet with power comparable to Vladimir Putin when it came to money and decision-making.

At the time, Qatar was being isolated by the Saudi Kingdom, and I was trying to put Hamad in the good graces of the President of the United States as a way for the tiny, mega-rich emirate to hedge their geopolitical risk. I knew Hamad from years earlier, when the Qataris had considering investing in a building in New York and I'd tried to broker the deal, but now I was treated entirely differently by the Emir and others as the lawyer for Donald Trump. Hamad was deferential and highly respectful of my role. When Hamad asked for a one-on-one sit down with Trump, I reached out to Jay Sekulow, a lawyer who'd represented Sean Hannity and whom I introduced to Trump, and had become his day-to-day point man for me in the White House.

There I was, going into Mar-a-Lago as the power broker who'd set up a meal between one of the richest men in the world and the President of the United States, and I'd done it with incredible ease.

That was what I was talking about when I wrote about the mesmerizing effect of being around Trump: for all the bullshit and bluster, he really was running the world, and I really was an incredible, unbelievably, insanely powerful attorney and fixer, on an intergalactic plane of existence.

The dining room was packed with billionaires, like Nelson Peltz and Ike Perlmutter, but in that crowd, Trump was a God amongst Gods. In the middle of the room there was a single table, surrounded by red velvet rope to isolate it from the others, and there were three places set at the table—one for the President, one for Hamad, and one for me. The most powerful, the richest, and yours truly, a reality that I still can't quite fathom to this day. Trump was likewise in a fantasyland, I could tell; he always had rich people floating around him, but now he was literally the center of attention, as he'd always wanted to be. The truth was that I felt like a billion dollars. I was unstoppable, I figured; all I had to do was ask, and there I was with one of the richest men in the world, deferentially awaiting the leader of the free world.

"Ladies and gentlemen, the President of the United States," one of the staff members announced, and in came Trump to a standing ovation. The only thing I can compare the rapturous reception to was the way North Koreans bow and scrape at the sight of Kim Jong-un.

"Hamad, you are one of the richest men in the world," Trump said by way of introduction as he reached the table, "and you know my lawyer, Michael."

The acknowledgement made me feel special, for sure. The conversation ranged from Middle East geopolitics to the economy, a level of abstraction about the world's most important questions I'd only ever witnessed when I met Henry Kissinger. Hamad bin Jassim had deep knowledge about the needs of the region and the underlying reasons for the Sunni-Shiite division and the war in Yemen.

The Emir talked about ISIS and Hezbollah and Iran and the justness of the cause of the Houthi insurgents in Yemen. Jared Kushner was working on a plan for an overall peace in the Middle East, at least in theory, but here the Emir was going directly to Trump to ensure that his views on the most pressing existential questions facing his nation were heard. He had good reason to want the meeting. Trump was close with the young Saudi leader Mohammed bin Salman, or MBS, and the Saudis hated the Qataris, so Hamad meeting with Trump was an opportunity of infinite value.

Trump with Hamad bin Jassim. © 2020 Michael Cohen

Shrimp cocktail, steak, grilled salmon—the food was always excellent at Trump's properties, and the dinner went on for a couple of hours, with my opinion sought on various questions by the President and Hamad. I could feel everyone in the room staring at the three of us at the table reverentially. So you think Avenatti and the porn star were on my mind? You think that nitwit calling me an idiot had any impact? I mean, who was the real idiot? I felt like I was staring at a Power Ball ticket and I had all the correct numbers and the jackpot was $700M. I was sure that Donald Trump had my back and in the end the whole Stormy Daniels mess would be a storm in a teacup. Nothing would happen to me, I was sure, no matter what.

As Trump, Hamad, and I made our way through the room after eating, I made sure to introduce him to Franklin Haney, the developer who was going to pay me a broker fee of $10M, plus a sizable fifteen percent interest in the company, if I assisted him in getting money for his nuclear plant. Hamad bin Jassim had just undertaken to invest up to $45 billion in the United States, so a simple $2 billion in Haney's project seemed not only reasonable but highly likely.

A few days later, I was back in Manhattan, at the hotel rooms I'd taken for the family while we fixed up our apartment in Trump Park Avenue after a broken pipe in a neighbor's place had burst. I wasn't on the lam, as some have suggested, and my wife and I weren't estranged, when I woke early on the morning of April 9, 2018, and roused my son Jake at six a.m. with a mixture of a kiss and WWE wrestling moves. I made coffee and oatmeal and turned on the TV and started to flip through *The New York Times*. By seven, Jake had gone to school, and I was walking around in Nike shorts and Laura was in her dressing gown when there was a knock on the door. I looked through the peep-hole and saw a crowd of men in the hallway holding up badges.

"FBI, Mr. Cohen," one of them said. "Please open the door."

Stepping inside as I obliged, two of the men grabbed me at my waist, to immobilize me.

"It's okay," the lead agent said. "Everything is fine."

The lead agent explained that they had a warrant for the three hotel rooms my family occupied, along with my cell phones, office, safe deposit box, law office, and apartment.

"We know you have firearms," the lead agent said to me. "How many?"

"Two," I said.

"Loaded?"

"Yes," I replied. "But not chambered."

I showed them to the nightstand, where I kept both Glocks, the .40 caliber and 9mm.

To say I was in shock would be a huge understatement. I had no clue I was the target of an investigation, or that the Mueller Special Counsel had taken an interest in me. I was still in regular contact with President Trump, and in his good graces, and the attorney we had retained for our joint defense in case an issue came up had assured me that I wasn't on the agenda for the prosecutions then being conducted in secret. The Avenatti nonsense was going full throttle, I knew, but it was all white noise to me. I'd just had dinner at Mar-a-Lago with the President and one of the richest men in the world; I was bulletproof, I thought.

There were now dozens of agents swarming the hotel and pulling all my books and records off the shelves, downloading my computers, going through my drawers shooting photographs and taking personal items. My first thought as I watched in disbelief was simple: What the fuck, am I El Chapo all of a sudden, some narcotrafficker outlaw on the Most Wanted List? Laura and I just sat on the bed and watched the news on TV, where talking heads were holding forth on Stormy Daniels and me—oblivious to the raid and what was about to become the single biggest story in the world.

"You don't have to stay here," the lead agent. "You're not under arrest."

"Do you guys want coffee?" I asked. "How long does this last?"

"It will be as quick and painless as possible," the lead agent said. "Thanks for the offer, but we're okay."

"Thank you for waiting until my son went to school," I said.

I was now on the other side of the power dynamic I had exploited so often on behalf of Donald Trump. I was effectively in the position of E.J. Ridings at Trump Mortgage all those years ago, having my reality dictated to me in real time. It was mind-boggling. I'd had one speeding ticket in my life, in the 1980s, along with a handful of parking tickets, but that was the sum total of all of my brushes with the law. I'd never been in any kind of trouble, and now there were FBI agents going through my couches and searching the drapes.

"What the hell are they looking for?" Laura asked.

"I have no clue," I said. "Let them look all they want."

My second thought was that I had to get word to Mr. Trump. I asked for my phone back, to make calls, but they refused. I said I just wanted to retrieve the private number of the President of the United States but they said I couldn't touch the phone. I asked them to at least let me retrieve the number, so I instructed them how to find the number and they read it to me. I was worried that the President would hear about the raid from a third party and go insane. Two hours passed and then my daughter Samantha walked through the door, to our great surprise, asking what the hell was going on.

After five hours, the FBI left, carrying boxes loaded with my possessions. I went directly to the AT&T store on Lexington Avenue and bought a new phone, using my old number, and I called Madeline Westerhout at the White House.

"Tell the President that my hotel and apartment and law office and safe deposit box have been raided by the FBI," I said.

"The President will be notified immediately," she said.

Minutes later, my phone rang. It was the President.

"Michael, are you and the family okay?" he asked.

"Yes, Mr. President," I replied. "I have no idea where this is coming from. I have no idea why this has happened."

"They're coming after all of us," Trump said. "This is all part of the witch hunt. Stay strong. I have your back. You're going to be fine."

"Thank you for your call and concern," I said.

The President of the United States hung up, the words "I have your back," ringing in my ears. That was Trump's mantra and exhortation: the President had my back. If I stayed loyal to Trump, he would stay loyal to me. I had to stay the course. Always stay the course. Be loyal. I was going to be fine.

But in the back of my mind, I knew trouble was coming. That afternoon, I'd watched the President sitting at a long table in the White House talking to the press. Trump spoke about the FBI raid on my office and apartment. What worried me, knowing how he speaks and acts and thinks, was that Trump had described me as "one of my personal attorneys." All of a sudden I didn't have a name? All of a sudden I'm only one of his attorneys? This was how Trump distanced himself from people. I was still blind to the implications, unable to actually acknowledge and confront what I knew in my heart, but a sense of dread began to shroud my thoughts.

That was the last time I ever spoke to Donald Trump.

Chapter Seventeen

The Conviction Machine

Over the course of the next several weeks, Trump continued to make statements putting more and more distance between us, including the most hurtful, to me, that I really wasn't an attorney—I was just a low-level PR guy. Hindsight being 20-20, what I realized sitting in prison is that there is no way in the world that Trump wasn't notified in advance by the Department of Justice that the raid was going to take place. He was the chief law enforcement officer in the country, so it's unimaginable that he didn't know—and that he didn't have a plan.

After the raid, I had no choice but to continue to stay the course as we entered into a joint defense agreement. Trump, Jared, Ivanka, and I all collaborated using my attorney, Stephen Ryan, as the lead attorney. I never expected that Trump was going to do to me what I'd done to so many others over the years on his behalf: stiff me on the legal fees I owed to lawyers.

Staying on message meant calling the investigation a witch hunt, no Russian connections, all of the various ways to delegitimize the investigation. I'd already testified to Congress, for the first time, and I'd lied and lied and lied. I was stuck with that reality. I'd lied because that was what they wanted me to do, and also because I thought the lies were immaterial. What's the difference between three conversations with Trump about a failed Russian real estate deal, or ten conversations? I saw no danger in that statement. I was thinking straight. All I wanted to do was get rid of the problem, believing that the most powerful person on the planet was going to make sure that this headache would go away.

I knew I was in deep, deep trouble when Trump stopped paying my lawyer, who was lead counsel to the entire joint defense agreement, causing a rift between me and the law firm at a time when I was completely overwhelmed with anxiety. I'd never had to deal with law enforcement in my life; I'd never imagined I'd experience what had become a waking nightmare. The outstanding legal fees were more than $1 million. I was supposed to be concentrating on the substance of the case, but I was sidetracked and my mind was racing with fear. There were millions of documents to review to ensure that nothing damaging to Trump and his family was revealed, so I kept going and kept going, still believing that he would stay loyal to me and at least pay the legal bill.

Reporters were outside my apartment all the time, adding another level of tension. Ultimately, the review was completed and the judge identified a relatively small number of documents that would be considered privileged. My counsel said he couldn't represent me going forward if I was criminally charged. He recommended I find a criminal attorney in New York City, who would know how to deal with the Southern District's federal prosecutors. I wound up engaging Guy Petrillo. He was a former head of the criminal division of the Southern District, so I figured he'd know

what to do and have the best relationships. Despite Petrillo's continuous requests with the SDNY prosecutors for a sit-down meeting with me, they refused.

Queen for the Day is the term used for a meeting with prosecutors to tell law enforcement the truth about any and all criminal
activity, without prejudice, in order to negotiate a plea-bargain
agreement. The SDNY response was always the same: we're not
ready yet. Four months passed. I was sitting in my apartment with
Laura and the kids and dealing with legal issues as they arose, but
mostly I was spinning my wheels and waiting, the dread and anxiety growing and growing and growing. Petrillo told me that the
longer things went on, the better, because it likely meant that they
didn't have a case.

On Thursday, August 16, 2018, fed up with sitting idle, and
unable to do anything, I demanded that Petrillo send to the acting Assistant United States attorney handling the case a letter
saying that we needed to meet, outlining our continuous requests
and how I was being strung along. That night, Petrillo received a
call from the Southern District stating that he had until tomorrow to meet with them. Petrillo said he'd have to call me to
ensure I was available, but they said I couldn't participate in a
meeting—it was lawyers only.

I was just thankful that someone finally responded. On Friday,
Petrillo took the meeting and late that afternoon he called my cell.
I was at a friend's place, with my wife, so I placed the call on
speaker so Laura could hear it. The three of us were horrified when
Petrillo advised Laura and me that it didn't go well and we'd have
to come to his office first thing Saturday morning.

"What the fuck is going on?" I said.

"They want you to plead guilty to tax evasion, lying to
Congress, and misrepresentation to a bank," Petrillo said. "On
Monday."

He paused, to let that sink in.

"If you refuse, on Monday they are going to file an eighty-five-page indictment," Petrillo said. "They are going to drag you out of your apartment on national television. They are also going to indict Laura."

So there it was: the government was going after my wife? It was like getting sucker punched in the gut.

"Tax evasion," I yelled. "Where does that even fucking come from?"

Petrillo fell silent as I continued to rant and rave about how I'd never filed a late tax return in my life. I'd never been audited. I'd never received a single letter from the IRS.

"I know," Petrillo said. "I know, I know."

Early the next morning, Laura and I met Petrillo and his co-counsel. He said I was definitely going to be indicted unless I was prepared to plead guilty. I kept asking, over and over, why I was facing these charges when I was always a legitimate local business-man who followed the letter of the law and only dealt with respectable banks and financial institutions. The government was saying I had evaded taxes, and I was sure I hadn't. There was no explanation about the allegation. All I was told was that Laura would be charged as well, without any knowledge of the facts regarding her, let alone the truth or possible defenses we could mount.

Petrillo thought we could win at trial, but the Southern District had made it clear that they were going to freeze and move for forfeiture of all my assets, to the tune of more than $50 million. If I wanted to proceed, I needed to immediately wire $1 million to Petrillo's escrow account as a retainer. He also said I should reach out to friends to prepare to borrow several million dollars to cover his fees and living expenses.

Petrillo explained that there was allegedly unreported income from my New York City taxi medallions, as well as interest on a loan that I'd made to a private individual. All of the money had gone into local NYC banks, and I'd given all the records to my accountant—whose job it was to reconcile my books and records, I believed. I had two three-ring notebooks tabulating my accounts in monthly order, but by that time the FBI had taken those files.

Laura was crying by now. I had tears running down my face.

"You have to let me know what you want to do," Petrillo said, in a voice devoid of the milk of human kindness. "But just know that they intend on convicting you."

This was the American justice system at work. My lawyers had continually stated that they didn't see any charges coming, but the truth in this country is that if federal prosecutors want to get you, they will. No matter who you are. No one reading this book should think for a second that they're immune to these gangster tactics that have been so widely publicized, but continue unabated and unapologetically. I was in the grip of the conviction machine. I was the ham sandwich, and I had been indicted.

I looked at Laura, I took her hand, and I said, "I will never let anything happen to you."

"No, I don't want you to go to prison," she said. "Let's fight this."

"I'm not going to put you in harm's way," I told her. "I cannot take that risk, based upon their actions."

I knew that the Southern District would be ruthless. I knew that they'd stop at nothing to convict me and my wife, who is the furthest thing from a criminal you can imagine. She's the personification of sweetness and innocence, and they were threatening to put her behind bars?

Petrillo said it was unlikely that I would go to prison, based on the charges I had to plead guilty to, but that I'd face significant monetary penalties. I made up my mind to plead and took Laura home, both of us in a state of shock. Petrillo called me later that afternoon to discuss the money amounts on the tax-evasion allegation, and I told him that the IRS had made an error in their calculations by more than half a million dollars. It turned out that the businessman managing my taxi medallions, Evgeny "Gene" Freidman, had defrauded hundreds of medallion owners, as well as the city of New York, for more than $20 million. He was facing serious prison time, but he didn't do a day behind bars because he'd talked to the FBI and testified against me.

The next day, I was told that the plea was being moved to Tuesday. The reason? Petrillo said that there was better media coverage on Tuesdays, that they needed an extra day to prepare their media material to display at the press conference. On Monday, Petrillo showed me the allocution that I was to read, word for word, as I stood in court. Three counts had turned into eight counts. Instead of one tax charge, they'd separated it into five different charges, one for each year from 2012 through 2016. They'd also added Karen McDougal's payment to the Stormy Daniels payment for the campaign finance fraud count, along with a final count of misrepresentation to the bank about the use of my line of credit to pay off the porn star on behalf of Donald J. Trump.

My head was spinning. I said there was no tax evasion. How could there be a misrepresentation to the bank regarding the use of the line of credit, when the bank never asked what I was doing with the money? I had millions of dollars in that bank, and I'd never had any trouble. By now, I was shouting at Petrillo that I was barely involved in the McDougal payment; that was between David Pecker and AMI and Donald Trump.

"Are we pleading guilty, or not?" Petrillo yelled at me. "If we're not, I need that money sent to my account right now."

"There were supposed to be three counts," I replied. "Now there are eight."

"This is their offer, take it or leave it," he said. "You know what the ramifications will be if you elect to fight."

The next day, I stood before the court and I took responsibility for all the counts. I read the allocution word for word. I was told to return in sixty days for sentencing, and the rest, as they say, was history. The prosecutor's memorandum criticized every aspect of my life, ignoring the forty letters I'd submitted in support of my good nature and character. As I stood before the judge, after I received the sentence of thirty-six months, as I heard the gasp from the packed courtroom and the sobs from my family, I had to ask Petrillo if I'd heard the judge correctly. I had.

Chapter Eighteen

Otisville Federal Satellite Camp

On May 6, 2019, I took a friend's car upstate to Otisville Federal Satellite Camp, in the Catskill Mountains near the Hudson River. As I arrived at the winding road leading to the mountaintop camp, there were four or five helicopters in the sky, as well as a mass of people lining Two Mile Road, with satellite trucks, TV reporters, onlookers, and police cruisers. Some of the crowd were holding placards saying, "Stay Strong" and "Down with Trump."

It was like I was Al Capone, or El Chapo, not a corporate attorney railroaded into prison by federal prosecutors who'd since gone on to high paying white-shoe law firms, with my conviction as their signature achievement at the Southern District. Otisville was on complete lockdown, meaning that no movement was allowed by any of the inmates. Processing started with photographs and fingerprinting, and then I was stripped naked and issued khaki prison clothes, including socks and underwear. I wasn't afraid, as it turned out, as the people who processed me were very professional and decent.

The low security Otisville camp was like the worst summer camp you can imagine your parents sending you to. Otisville has a kosher diet available, as almost half the camp are Jews, with many Hasidic Jews. The camp is all white-collar crime, with accountants, doctors, lawyers, bankers, and Wall Street tycoons all mixed in together. The first bunk I got was the worst in the facility, located between two toilets, with the scent of locked-up inmates performing their ablutions, no matter which way you turn your head, but I was soon reassigned to 28 Lower, a decent location. I was bunked with the head orderly, a longtime inmate who was a forensic accountant, and we got along well as I described all the bullshit accounting I'd been through with the Southern District.

There was a tennis court painted on the parking lot, and my eating seat was next to Michael Sorrentino—the "Situation" from *The Jersey Shore*—while behind me was Dean Skelos, the former Senate Majority Leader in New York, and nearby was Joe Percoco, Governor Andrew Cuomo's longtime Chief of Staff. It was quite a scene. I came in with a lot of fanfare, and I was immediately accepted. It was prison, but if you're going to be in prison, it wasn't as bad as it could have been.

I'd never been away from my wife and children before, so that caused melancholy, along with the fact that I truly didn't believe that I belonged there. Talking to family was difficult because we only got 300 minutes a month of phone calls, which diced down to ten minutes a day, and visiting was complicated because the meeting room often became overcrowded.

There was a saying in prison: The days go by slow, but the weeks go by fast. Every Friday night, there was a Sabbath dinner, which I attended, so that was a good way to measure time. But there was another reality, as I developed serious hypertension problems, leading to my hospitalization twice, accompanied twenty-four-hours-a-day by two prison officers. The hospitalizations, along with pre-existing blood clotting conditions from years earlier, eventually provided the basis for my early release during the COVID-19 crisis.

But first I had to go through the William Barr Department of Justice kangaroo-court process. As the virus spread throughout the country, including the petri dishes that constituted prisons in a time of plague, I was moved to solitary confinement to quarantine for release on furlough to convert to home detention. As the date for my release neared, though, Bill Barr changed the criteria for release and seventy inmates were returned to the camp, leaving a dozen of us in solitary. It felt like Barr's sudden amendment of the rules was aimed at me, at the direction of President Trump, which speaks volumes about the nature of the rule of law in this age.

During these days, I truly did believe the President of the United States wanted me dead. It felt like I was receiving a death sentence, by proxy. A lot of the guards disliked me intensely, because they were big Trump supporters, and they followed his words when he attacked me on TV and Twitter, giving them license to be unusually cruel to me. As I tried to sleep, they'd flash a light in my eyes every half hour; they'd kick my door; they wouldn't let me get hot water from the machine for my coffee. These might sound like petty things, but when you're in solitary in a facility raging with COVID-19 it really is like psychological torture.

I was the last prisoner released from solitary, on May 21, 2020. Thirty-five very long and difficult days, being let out of the cell for a mere thirty minutes per day.

Remember at the beginning of this book, I told you that the President of the United States does not want you to read this book. Here's your proof: as news leaked out that I was completing this book, my lawyer was served with a Cease and Desist letter from the Trump Organization, threatening a lawsuit should I decide to publish. The letter alleged that I had signed a confidentiality agreement with the Trump Organization, which explicitly prohibited me from writing this book. It also said that I was forbidden by attorney-client privilege to tell my story.

But this story is all I have left for my wife, my children, and the country I love so much.

As I write from my apartment in New York City, I can see his lawyers using the same old tricks I did on behalf of the Boss for all those years. He's no different than the man on the 26th floor of Trump Tower, marching around like a robot imitating Barack Obama and mocking how easy it is to fake being presidential. No words ring more true for me than when Michelle Obama stated, "Being President doesn't change who you are, it reveals who you are. . . ."

Please remember what I testified to Congress, the second time: There is a serious danger that Donald Trump will not leave office easily, and there is a real chance of not having a peaceful transition. When he jokes about running again in 2024 and gets a crowd of thousands to chant "Trump 2024," he's not joking. Trump never jokes.

You now have all the information you need to decide for yourself in November.

Epilogue: Retaliation

On the morning of Thursday, July 9, 2020, I reported to the federal courthouse at 500 Pearl Street in Lower Manhattan, as required by the Department of Probation. The appointment was supposedly to perform a technicality, changing the terms of my COVID-related release from Otisville prison in upstate New York from furlough to home confinement. The only meaningful difference would be that I would serve out the rest of my sentence wearing an ankle bracelet to allow the DOP to electronically monitor my whereabouts, or at least that was what I'd been told.

Earlier in the week, I had talked to my probation officer about the transition. I'd originally been scheduled to report to a halfway house in the Bronx to sign papers and then have an ankle monitor attached, like all the other prisoners who'd been released. But the probation office had changed their rules, telling me first that they would come to my apartment in Manhattan to do the paperwork and install the ankle bracelet. Two days later, they said that I now had to report to the federal courthouse, a development that seemed strange and suspicious and that the official with the ankle monitoring company said he'd never heard of after decades in the business.

Why was I being treated differently? I'd asked my probation officer, Adam Pakula. He'd said it was just a random circumstance, reassuring me that I hadn't been singled out by the government.

"I hope I'll be allowed to work," I'd said. "I'm working on my book."

"We encourage you to work," Pakula had replied, reassuringly.

A few days before, I had appeared unexpectedly on the front page of the *New York Post*. The headline was "You Call This Hard Time?" and the paper reported that I had had dinner at a restaurant with another couple on the Upper East Side. The photograph showed me at a table, smiling, next to my wife Laura, as we had a quiet meal a block from our home. I was upset at the image in the *Post*, and the intrusion into my privacy, and I wondered if Le Bilboquet had called the tabloid, looking for a bit of free publicity for the restaurant, or if someone from the paper had been following me.

But I was also aware that I hadn't broken the terms of my furlough release, so I'd shrugged off the press coverage as meaningless at the time. I knew it risked catching the attention of the President, but I was pretty sure I'd already attracted a serious amount of his interest after I'd announced on social media that I planned to publish a book that included my time with Donald Trump. In hindsight, I can now see how the report in the *New York Post* falsely claiming I was in breach of the terms of my home confinement by dining out, and the many subsequent reports on Fox News about my case, sowed just enough confusion about the pretext for what was about to unfold. I'm not a conspiracy theorist, despite working for more than a decade for the king of conspiracy theorists, but that is how propaganda is practiced by Trump-allied people like the *Post's* owner, Rupert Murdoch. What followed had nothing to do with my meal at a restaurant, or any other bone-headed action on my part. I was ambushed, plain and simple.

That morning, my son Jake drove me to the federal courthouse, the imposing home of the offices of the Southern District of New York, to meet with my probation officer, as directed. I was accompanied by a childhood friend, Jeff Levine, an attorney in New York with his own small firm; he was there because of the suspicious ways the probation office had kept changing the rules for me, and my belief that I might need a lawyer, even though Jeff doesn't truly practice criminal law.

In the office, probation officer Pakula and a supervisor presented Jeff and me with a two-page document, consisting of the terms to have my status altered to home confinement, and assuring me it was the standard form for all released inmates.

I carefully read all eight provisions. The document was amateurish, with elisions and bad grammar, and it generally looked like it had been thrown together at the last moment. But it was the first provision which astounded me. This is exactly what the first paragraph required me to agree to:

"No engagement of any kind with the media, including print, tv, film, books, or any form of media/news. Prohibition from all social media platforms. No posting on social media and a requirement that you communicate with friends and family to exercise discretion in not posting on your behalf or posting any information about you. The purpose is to avoid glamorizing or bringing publicity to your status as a sentenced inmate serving a custodial term in the community."

Looking up, I shook my head.

"I don't know where to start," I said. "The first term is overbroad and a violation of my First Amendment rights. It prohibits me from the work on the book I told Mr. Pakula about a few days ago."

Jeff intervened, trying to keep the meeting on an even keel.

"Let me handle this," he said to me.

Jeff politely pointed out that I couldn't force my friends and family to not to talk to the press, and that I could be in breach of the agreement—and subject to being put back in prison—for things that I couldn't control. Jeff asked if the language could be changed or modified to make it less broad and in line with the stated intention of not glamorizing my status as a prisoner, a promise I could easily agree to. The probation officers suggested we go through the remaining seven paragraphs of the document and they would take the request "up the chain of command" for a decision on the language designed to kill my book.

"Was the first provision drafted specifically for me?" I asked, finally.

The probation officers replied that it was standard.

"It looks like it was drafted specifically for me," I said. "And it was probably drafted in Washington. The next time you speak to Attorney General Bill Barr, tell him I say hello."

With that, the two probation officers requested we leave their office and take a seat in the waiting room; which we did for more than an hour and a half. We watched the news, oblivious, and wondering what changes would be made to the document. But as time passed, I should have started to wonder what was going on behind those closed doors.

Consider the context. That same morning, New York City District Attorney Cy Vance had announced that the Supreme Court had ruled 7-2 that the President had absolutely no right to refuse to disclose his financial records to prosecutors looking into tax-fraud charges—precisely the kind of crimes I had been convicted of. It had been widely reported that I had met with prosecutors from Vance's office, and there was a press gaggle outside the building waiting for my comment on the devastating Supreme Court decision.

"No citizen, not even the president, is categorically above the common duty to produce evidence when called upon in a criminal proceeding," Chief Justice John Roberts wrote.

Worse for Trump, even the two justices he had appointed agreed with Roberts. Justice Brett Kavanaugh wrote, "In our system of government, as this court has stated so often, no one is above the law. That principle applies, of course, to a president."

Trump had reached for his Twitter, the one I used to post on for him all the time, to express his outrage. "This is all a political prosecution," Trump wrote. "I won the Mueller Witch Hunt, and others, and now I have to keep fighting in a politically corrupt New York. Not fair to the Presidency or Administration."

In recent weeks, Attorney General Barr had also very publicly tried to fire the United States Attorney for the Southern District of New York, attempting to replace Geoffrey Berman with the Chairman of the Securities and Exchange Commission—who, not coincidentally, was a golf buddy of the President and almost completely inexperienced in criminal law. Jay Clayton of the SEC was exactly what Trump and Barr wanted: a lackey. But Barr had failed, and Berman had relented, but only after an experienced and independent replacement prosecutor was named to the post.

The reason the President wanted a new head prosecutor in the Southern District, I knew better than anyone, was so that while in office, he could arrange to be federally indicted. In the event he loses the election in November, he could then pardon himself, as he's long claimed to be his right. The reason behind that unprecedented and serpentine thinking was that Trump knows perfectly well that he is guilty of the same crimes that resulted in my conviction and incarceration. He also knows that I would be a star witness in that case, and my book a fundamental piece of evidence for his guilt.

Without the immunity from prosecution granted to the president, Trump will also almost certainly face New York State criminal charges. He would likely be convicted on both the Federal and State charges and face serious prison time. That is Donald Trump's greatest fear in life, believe me, and if he fails to get reelected, that will be his fate—and he knows it—so silencing me was an essential part of his overall plan to evade the law and avoid that outcome.

Sitting in the waiting room, three United States Marshalls entered, carrying handcuffs and shackles.

"Mr. Cohen, please stand up and face the wall," the lead Marshall said.

"What are you talking about?" I asked.

The two probation officers then walked in and issued me with a remand document, stating that I had refused to sign the home confinement release and was therefore being taken back into custody. They seemed delighted, even thrilled, despite the fact that the document was premised on false information.

"I never refused to sign the document; we are waiting for their superior's determination," I said. "I'll sign it right now."

"This is ridiculous," Jeff sighed.

"It's out of our hands," probation officer Pakula said with evident pleasure. "We're not involved anymore."

"This cannot be happening," I said.

But it was. I was handcuffed and shackled and taken to the bowels of the building, where I was stripped naked and issued a brown jumpsuit. Within hours, I was returned to prison in upstate

New York, placed in solitary confinement, and left to the mercy of the raging COVID-19 and the possibility of dying behind bars with my underlying heart and respiratory health issues.

Let me say for the record: I was never really given the chance to sign the home-confinement document. I was imprisoned because I refused to sign away my rights under the Constitution of the United States. It was a surprise attack. By presenting me with terms they knew would be impossible for me to agree to, they were springing a trap, as might happen in any authoritarian country, a country where individuals lack the rights of due process and freedom of speech.

Within days, my wife found Danya Perry, a former prosecutor and a true criminal lawyer. Danya filed a writ of habeas corpus and an emergency restraining order, joined by the American Civil Liberties Union. At a hearing ten days later, Judge Alvin K. Hellerstein had little patience for the case made by the Southern District prosecutors. He asked if I'd been given the opportunity to negotiate the terms of the home-confinement document I'd been presented, dismissing the idea I'd been "combative." The judge said he'd never seen any clause that matched the first provision, taking away my First Amendment rights. The naked attempt to silence me in a gulag in Trump's America had failed.

"I make the finding that the purpose of transferring Mr. Cohen from furlough to home confinement to jail is retaliatory," the judge said. "And it is retaliatory because of his desire to exercise his First Amendment rights to publish a book and to discuss anything about that book or anything else he wants on social media and with others."

In the beginning of this book, which I publish in full and with a full heart, I wrote that the President of the United States doesn't want you to read my story. Now I have actual proof of how desperate he is to silence me and prevent the world from hearing this story and the truth about Donald J. Trump—the real real Donald Trump.

Michael Cohen
New York, New York
August, 2020

Appendix: Documents, Tweets, and Photos

INJUNCTION ORDER FROM JUDGE ALVIN K. HELLERSTEIN.

UNITED STATES DISTRICT COURT
SOUTHERN DISTRICT OF NEW YORK
-- X
MICHAEL D. COHEN,   :
                                               :
                          Petitioner,   :   **ORDER GRANTING**
              v.   :   **PRELIMINARY INJUNCTION**
                                               :
WILLIAM BARR, in his official capacity as :   20 Civ. 5614 (AKH)
Attorney General of the United States, MICHAEL :
CARVAJAL, in his official capacity as Director of :
the Bureau of Prisons, and JAMES PETRUCCI, in :
his official capacity as Warden of the Federal :
Correctional Institution, Otisville,   :
                                               :
                          Respondents.   :
-- X

ALVIN K. HELLERSTEIN, U.S.D.J.:

Upon the findings and conclusions stated on the record at oral argument

conducted telephonically on July 23, 2020, Petitioner Michael D. Cohen's motion for injunctive

relief, *see* ECF No. 4, is granted as follows.

The Court finds that Respondents' purpose in transferring Cohen from release on

furlough and home confinement back to custody was retaliatory in response to Cohen desiring to

exercise his First Amendment rights to publish a book critical of the President and to discuss the

book on social media. Accordingly, Respondents are hereby enjoined from any continuing or

future retaliation against Cohen for exercising his First Amendment rights. Respondents are

directed to provide Cohen with a COVID-19 test at his place of detention no later than tomorrow

morning, July 24, 2020, to report the results of that test to Cohen and to his Probation Officer

promptly when they become available, and to release Cohen from custody to any member of his

immediate family at the place of his detention at or before 2:00 p.m. tomorrow, July 24, 2020.

Upon Cohen's release, the parties agree, and I so order, that Cohen will be subject

to the eight conditions of release set forth in the Federal Location Monitoring Agreement, *see*

ECF No. 7-2, provided, however, that adherence to condition one, except for the last sentence, is temporary, subject to the parties' renegotiation of said temporary condition.[1] The condition shall be consistent with the First Amendment and legitimate penological limitations on conduct to which the parties mutually agree or the Court subsequently orders. The parties shall have one week to conduct their negotiations and will, unless an extension has been granted, file a proposed order to the Court by July 31, 2020. I reserve continuing jurisdiction to resolve any disputes in settling an order and enforcing same.

        This order, which codifies my extemporaneous ruling at argument, is intended to be final. A written decision providing a fuller statement of my findings and conclusions will follow when ready. The Clerk is instructed to terminate the open motion (ECF No. 4).

        SO ORDERED.

Dated: July 23, 2020   _____/s/_____
          New York, New York   ALVIN K. HELLERSTEIN
                            United States District Judge

---

[1] Condition one provides:

2

LETTER FROM GUY PETRILLO TO THE DEPUTY U.S. ATTORNEY FOR THE SOUTHERN DISTRICT OF NEW YORK.

PETRILLO KLEIN & BOXER LLP

655 Third Avenue
22nd Floor
New York, NY 10017
Telephone: (212) 370-0330
www.pkbllp.com

Guy Petrillo
Direct Dial: (212) 370-0331
Cell: (646) 385-1479
gpetrillo@pkbllp.com

CONFIDENTIAL

BY EMAIL

Robert Khuzami
Deputy U.S. Attorney
U.S. Attorney's Office
  for the Southern District of New York
One St. Andrew's Plaza
New York, NY 10007

Re: *Michael Cohen*

Dear Deputy U.S. Attorney Khuzami:

      I write on behalf of Michael Cohen to request a meeting with you and your colleagues to discuss the charge(s) the Office is prepared to present to the grand jury and an opportunity in short order (ten days or less) to return to the Office to present points relevant to the Office's discretionary decision to seek an indictment.

      On Tuesday, August 14, 2018, we were told by the Assistants assigned to the case that the Office would only accept a meeting on or before Friday of this week, and in substance that we should already know what the charges will be based on the public nature of the investigation. With all respect, the press concerning the referral from the Special Counsel and the Office's investigation, the search warrants, and the materials seized in the searches of Mr. Cohen's residence, temporary residence, office and bank safe deposit box in April 2018, do not manifestly announce the charge(s) the Office is actually prepared to seek. To take one example, over more than a decade, no financial institution that has dealt with Mr. Cohen has lost any money as a result. Many of the search warrant specifications refer to evidence pertaining to financial institutions, loans, *etc.* We are not presuming that the Office would seek a charge where no losses were incurred, but if it is, it would be fair to permit Mr. Cohen's counsel to be heard on more than a few days' notice.

      The son of a Holocaust survivor, Mr. Cohen, 51, has no prior convictions. He is married and has two children. He presents no risk of flight. Furthermore, Mr. Cohen has voluntarily presented himself for a full day's interview by the Office of the Special Counsel, and understands that his interview may continue on a date to be scheduled.

Hon. Robert Khuzami
Deputy U.S. Attorney

August 16, 2018

CONFIDENTIAL

    In the circumstances, and so that we, as counsel, may consider options including available alternatives to indictment, we request a confidential explanation of the charge(s) to be sought from the grand jury, and an opportunity, on a short but reasonable schedule, to discuss the same with the Office.

                                        Sincerely,

                                        Guy Petrillo

                                        Amy Lester

cc: AUSA L. Zornberg
       Chief, Criminal Division
    AUSA Carbone
       Chief, Public Corruption Unit
    AUSA A. Griswold
    AUSA R. Maimin
    AUSA T. McKay
    AUSA N. Roos

2

LETTER ORDERING ME TO PRISON.

UNITED STATES DISTRICT COURT
SOUTHERN DISTRICT OF NEW YORK
PROBATION OFFICE

New York, NY
February 15, 2019

P5291673

Michael J. Fitzpatrick
Chief
U.S. Probation Officer

Edwin Rodriguez Jr.
Sr. Deputy Chief
U.S. Probation Officer

Kyle Crayton
Deputy Chief
U.S. Probation Officer

Dawn Doino
Deputy Chief
U.S. Probation Officer

Ed Johnson
Deputy Chief
U.S. Probation Officer

Mr. Michael D. Cohen
502 Park Avenue
Apt# 10A
New York, NY 10022

As per order of U.S. District Judge William H. Pauley, III, you are scheduled to surrender to **FCI Otisville Satellite Camp on Wednesday, March 6, 2019, before 2:00 p.m.** FCI Otisville is located at Two Mile Drive, Otisville, NY 10963, telephone number 845-386-6700. Please contact the institution or visit www.bop.gov for instructions and directions. Your register number is 86067-054.

Very truly yours,

Yolette Leopold
U.S. Probation Administrative Assistant
212-805- 5095

cc: Andrea M. Griswold, AUSA
       Rachel Maimin, AUSA
       Thomas McKay, AUSA
       Nicolas T. Landsman Roos, AUSA
       Andrew D. Goldstein, AUSA
       L. Rush Atkinson, AUSA
       Jeannie S. Rhee, AUSA
       Guy Petrillo, Esq.
       Amy R. Lester, Esq.

New York City Office:
Daniel Patrick Moynihan
United States Courthouse
500 Pearl Street
New York, NY 10007
212-805-0040
212-805-0047 - Fax

White Plains Office:
United States Courthouse
300 Quarropas Street
White Plains, NY 10601-1901
914.390.4040
914 390 4055 - Fax

THE SENTENCING MEMORANDUM FOR MY CASE.

UNITED STATES DISTRICT COURT
SOUTHERN DISTRICT OF NEW YORK
- x

UNITED STATES OF AMERICA   :

           -   v.   -   :   18 Cr. 602 (WHP)

                               :   18 Cr. 850 (WHP)

MICHAEL COHEN,   :

             Defendant.   :

                               :
- x

**SENTENCING MEMORANDUM
ON BEHALF OF MICHAEL COHEN**

PETRILLO KLEIN & BOXER LLP

655 Third Avenue, 22nd Floor
New York, New York 10017
Telephone: (212) 370-0330

Attorneys for Michael Cohen

Dated: November 30, 2018

TABLE OF CONTENTS

PRELIMINARY STATEMENT 1

A SENTENCE OF TIME-SERVED WOULD BE WELL WARRANTED
UNDER 18 U.S.C. § 3553(a) 6

    A. Applicable Legal Standards 6

    B. Michael's Personal History and Characteristics 7

    C. The Nature of the Offense Conduct 13

    D. Sentencing Guidelines and Objections to PSR Guidelines Calculation 22

        1. The PSR's Calculation of the Guidelines Relies on a Flawed
           Grouping Analysis..22

        2. Under Section 3553(a), Mitigating Consideration Should be
           Given to Two Overlapping Guidelines Enhancements 25

    E. Deterrence Will Not Be Materially Promoted by a Custodial Sentence 26

CONCLUSION 29

i

TABLE OF AUTHORITIES

Cases   **Page**

Gall v. United States,
   552 U.S. 38 (2007)..7

Kimbrough v. United States,
   552 U.S. 85 (2007)..7

Nelson v. United States,
   55 U.S. 350 (2009)..7

Pepper v. United States,
   562 U.S. 476 (2011)..7

United States v. Booker,
   543 U.S. 220 (2005)..6

United States v. Cavera,
   550 F.3d 180 (2d Cir. 2008)..6

United States v. Dorvee,
   616 F.3d 174 (2d Cir. 2010)..6

United States v. Doxie,
   813 F.3d 1340 (11th Cir. 2016) 24

United States v. Gardellini,
   545 F.3d 1089 (D.C. Cir. 2008)...29

United States v. Gordon,
   291 F.3d 181 (2d Cir. 2002)..24

United States v. Jones,
   531 F.3d 163 (2d Cir. 2008)..7

United States v. Lenoci,
   377 F.3d 246 (2d Cir. 2004)..23

United States v. Ministro-Tapia,
   470 F.3d 137 (2d Cir. 2006)..6

United States v. Napoli,
   179 F.3d 12d Cir. 1999)..23

United States v. Olis,
   2006 WL 2716048 (S.D. Tex. Sept. 22, 2006) 28

United States v. Petrillo,
   237 F.3d 119 (2d Cir. 2000)...24

United States v. Ruiz,
   2006 WL 1311982 (S.D.N.Y. May 10, 2006) 28

United States v. Stewart,
   590 F.3d 93 (2d Cir. 2009)...27

We respectfully submit this Memorandum on behalf of our client Michael Cohen in connection with his sentencing proceeding scheduled for December 12, 2018. On August 21, 2018, this Court accepted Michael's plea of guilty to Information 18 Cr. 602, charging him in eight counts with tax evasion, in violation of 26 U.S.C. § 7201 (Counts One through Five), making false statements to a financial institution, in violation of 18 U.S.C. § 1014 (Count Six), and campaign finance offenses, in violation of 52 U.S.C. §§ 30118(a), 30109(d)(1)(A) (Count Seven), and 52 U.S.C. §§ 30116(a)(1)(A), 30116(a)(7), and 30109(d)(1)(A) (Count Eight). On November 29, 2018, Michael pleaded guilty before the Honorable Andrew L. Carter, Jr. to a separate Information, 18 Cr. 850, charging him in one count with making false statements to Congress, in violation of 18 U.S.C. § 1001(a)(2).[1]

PRELIMINARY STATEMENT

Beginning before the entry of his plea on August 21, 2018, and continuing thereafter through late November, Michael participated in seven voluntary interview meetings with the Special Counsel's Office of the Department of Justice ("SCO"). He intends to continue to make himself available to the SCO as and when needed for additional questioning. He also agreed to plead guilty to an additional count, namely, making false statements to Congress, based in part on information that he voluntarily provided to the SCO in meetings governed by a limited-use immunity proffer agreement. The SCO is expected to submit a letter to the Court describing its assessment of Michael's cooperation, and the Office of the United States Attorney for the Southern District of New York ("Office") is expected to join with the SCO in presenting Michael's cooperation to the Court as a mitigating sentencing factor under 18 U.S.C. § 3553(a).[2] Michael's

---

[1] This case was transferred from Judge Carter to this Court for purposes of sentencing.

[2] In the November 29, 2018 Plea Agreement, the SCO "agree[d] to bring to the Court's attention at sentencing . . . the nature and extent of [Michael's] cooperation with [the SCO] on the condition

decision to cooperate and take full responsibility for his own conduct well reflects his personal

resolve, notwithstanding past errors, to re-point his internal compass true north toward a productive,

ethical and thoroughly law abiding life.

Michael has also voluntarily met twice with representatives of the Office, and responded to

questions concerning an ongoing investigation. In connection with this inquiry, he intends to

continue to make himself available as and when needed by the Office.

Michael has similarly met voluntarily with representatives of the New York State Office of

the Attorney General ("NYAG") concerning a state court action in which the NYAG has sued the

Donald J. Trump Foundation and certain individual defendants, including Donald J. Trump. He

also provided the NYAG with documents concerning a separate open inquiry. As above, Michael

intends to make himself available to the NYAG to provide any additional cooperation it may

request in these matters.

Michael, following his plea, additionally waived subpoena and met on an expedited basis

with the New York State Department of Taxation and Finance ("DTF"), and has cooperated

personally and through counsel and tax professionals with requests for information from DTF. His

cooperation has included a waiver that allowed DTF to forego the burden of issuing subpoenas for

materials, including the federal tax revenue adjustment report in this case.

Arising out of Michael's concern that his entry into a traditional cooperation agreement

would likely delay his sentencing, as investigations and trials unfold and conclude, he respectfully

---

that [Michael] continues to respond and provide truthful information regarding any and all matters
as to which [the SCO] deems relevant." Nov. 29, 2018 Plea Agr. at 4. In a supplemental
agreement executed the same day, the Office agreed that Michael's "provision of information to the
SCO is a factor to be considered by the Court pursuant to Title 18, United States Code, Section
3553(a)," notwithstanding that, by agreement between the parties, the Office is not filing a motion
pursuant to Section 5K1.1 of the U.S. Sentencing Guidelines. Nov. 29, 2018 Supplemental Agr. at
1.

2

declined to pursue conventional cooperation so that his sentencing proceeding would go forward as scheduled. This personal decision does not signal any intention on Michael's part to withhold information or his availability to respond to additional inquiry. To the contrary, he expects to cooperate further. But, following the execution of search warrants in this case, nearly every professional and commercial relationship that he enjoyed, and a number of long-standing friendships, have vanished. Thus, the necessity, at age 52, to begin his life virtually anew, including developing new means to support his family, convinced Michael to seek an early sentence date, fully understanding that this Court will determine the timing under which his efforts to rebuild will commence.

For what it says about Michael's fortitude and fundamental character, the significance of his cooperation with the SCO falls outside of the ordinary framework in which courts routinely assess cooperation in criminal cases. It states the obvious to observe that this matter is unique. Michael is cooperating in a setting in which the legitimacy of the SCO's investigation – and the rationale for its very existence – is regularly questioned publicly and stridently by the President of the United States. *See, e.g.*, John Wagner, *Trump Attacks Mueller Probe for Fourth Straight Morning, Asks if it will "Go on Forever,"* Washington Post (Nov. 29, 2018, https://www.washingtonpost.com/ politics/trump-attacks-mueller-probe-for-fourth-straight-morning-asks-if-it-will-go-on-forever/ 2018/11/29/96b204ec-f3c9-11e8-bc79-68604ed88993_ story.html); John W. Schoen, *Trump Is Tweeting "Witch Hunt" A Lot More Than He Used To, as Mueller Probe Grinds On and Manafort Goes on Trial*, CNBC.com (Aug. 1, 2018, https://www. cnbc.com/2018/08/01/ trumps-witch-hunt-tweets-are-getting-more-frequent-as-mueller-probe.html). The President routinely denounces the SCO investigation as politically biased and reliant on excessively aggressive prosecutorial tactics. *See, e.g.*, Kevin Liptak, *Trump Says Longstanding Legal Practice of Flipping "Almost Ought to be*

3

Case 1:18-cr-00602-WHP   Document 22   Filed 11/30/18   Page 8 of 33

Illegal," CNN.com (Aug. 23, 2018, https://www. cnn.com/2018 /08/23/politics/trump-flipping-outlawed/index.html); Eileen Sullivan, *Trump Criticizes Investigators, Citing "Unrevealed Conflicts of Interest,"* N.Y. Times, (May 7, 2018, https://www.nytimes.com/2018/05/07/us/politics/trump-special-counsel-inquiry.html). He also openly criticized his former Attorney General's recusal from the matter on the ground that the former Attorney General should have remained involved and limited or terminated the SCO's work. *See* Jennifer Hansler, *Trump's Twitter Attacks on Sessions: An Annotated Timeline*, CNN.com (Aug. 25, 2018, https://www. cnn.com/2018/08/25/politics/trump-sessions-twitter-timeline/index. html); Katie Benner, Nicholas Fandos, and Katie Rogers, *Trump Denounces Justice Dept. as Investigations Swirl Around Him*, N.Y. Times, Aug. 24, 2018, at A1; Matt Zapotosky, John Wagner, *Trump Blames Sessions for Russia Probe, Suggests He Could Have Shut It Down*, Washington Post (June 5, 2018, https://www.washingtonpost.com/politics/trump-blames-sessions-for-russia-probe-suggests-he-could-have-shut-it-down/2018/06/05/19023474-68b2-11e8-bf8c-f9ed2e672adf_story.html).

        In the context of this raw, full-bore attack by the most powerful person in the United States, Michael, formerly a confidante and adviser to Mr. Trump, resolved to cooperate, and voluntarily took the first steps toward doing so even before he was charged in this District. *See* Nov. 28, 2018 Plea Agr. at 8 (proffer agreement with SCO first executed on August 7, 2018). He took these steps, moreover, despite regular public reports referring to the President's consideration of pardons and pre-pardons in the SCO's investigation. *See, e.g.*, Sharon LaFraniere and Nicholas Fandos, *Trump Raises Idea of Pardon For Manafort*, N.Y. Times, Nov. 28, 2018, at A1; Carol D. Leonnig and Josh Dawsey, *Trump Recently Sought His Lawyers' Advice on Possibility of Pardoning Manafort, Giuliani Says*, Washington Post (Aug. 23, 2018, https://www.washingtonpost.com/politics/trump-sought-his-lawyers-advice-weeks-ago-on-possibility-of-pardoning-manafort-but-they-counseled-

382

Disloyal: A Memoir

against-it-giuliani-says/2018/08/ 23/17dce5c6-a70a-11e8-8fac-12e98c13528c_story.html). And, he

acted knowing that the result would be personal attacks on him by the President, a bevy of advisers

and public relations specialists, and political supporters of the President, *see, e.g.*, David Jackson

and John Fritze, *Trump Attacks Former Fixer Michael Cohen as "Weak" and Accuses Him of*

Lying in Mueller Plea Deal, USA Today, (Nov. 29, 2019, https://www.usatoday.com/story/news/

politics/2018/11/29/donald-trump-calls-cohen-weak-says-hes-lying-mueller-plea-deal/

21482334002), as well as threats to him. Although it is true that any decision to cooperate in an

investigation directly or indirectly touching a sitting President would be weighty and fraught for

any former confidante and associate, here, in the circumstances of this case, at this time, in this

climate, Michael's decision to cooperate required and requires singular determination and personal

conviction. He could have fought the government and continued to hold to the party line,

positioning himself perhaps for a pardon or clemency, but, instead – for himself, his family, and his

country – he took personal responsibility for his own wrongdoing and contributed, and is prepared

to continue to contribute, to an investigation that he views as thoroughly legitimate and vital.

***

We now turn to the additional factors relating to sentencing. Our comments below,

respectfully, are intended to be taken in the above-expressed spirit, in which Michael has

determined to proceed responsibly and candidly as the continuing investigations unfold. He accepts

full responsibility for the offense conduct, and we, as counsel, submit the below considerations in

this context. Thus, for example, where we discuss below the exceptionally *un*sophisticated tax

conduct before the Court, we intend not to minimize the significance of the charges, but merely to

contrast the case with others, with a view to placing it in the proper comparative perspective with

the criminal tax cases that this Court and others routinely adjudicate.

5

For the reasons set forth below, we respectfully request that the Court, based on (1) the cooperation Michael has provided, (2) his commitment to continue to cooperate, and (3) all of the remaining sentencing factors required to be considered under 18 U.S.C. § 3553(a), impose a sentence of time-served and restitution to the IRS.

**A SENTENCE OF TIME-SERVED WOULD BE
WELL WARRANTED UNDER 18 U.S.C. § 3553(a)**

A.   Applicable Legal Standards

Section § 3553(a) provides that the sentence be "sufficient, but not greater than necessary to comply with the specific purposes set forth at 18 U.S.C. § 3553(a)(2)." *United States v. Dorvee*, 616 F.3d 174, 183 (2d Cir. 2010) (quoting *United States v. Cavera*, 550 F.3d 180, 189 (2d Cir. 2008) (*en banc*); *see also United States v. Ministro-Tapia*, 470 F.3d 137, 142 (2d Cir. 2006). Those purposes are: (1) the nature of the offense and the history and characteristics of the defendant; (2) the purposes of sentencing, described in § 3553(a)(2) to include (a) the need to reflect the seriousness of the offense, promote respect for the law, and provide just punishment; (b) the need to afford adequate deterrence to criminal conduct; (c) the need to protect the public from future criminal conduct by the defendant; and (d) the need to provide the defendant with needed educational or vocational training, medical care, or other correctional treatment in the most effective manner; (3) the kinds of sentences available; (4) the Guidelines and their policy statements; (5) the need to avoid unwarranted sentencing disparities among defendants with similar records who have been found guilty of similar conduct; and (6) the need to provide restitution. 18 U.S.C. § 3553(a).

Concerning the Guidelines, post-*United States v. Booker*, 543 U.S. 220 (2005), it is "emphatically clear that the Guidelines are guidelines – that is, they are truly advisory." *Dorvee*, 616 F.3d at 183 (quoting *Cavera*, 550 F.3d at 189) (*en banc*). Although the Guidelines are to be

6

given "fair consideration" "before imposing" a sentence, "in the end, [the Court] must make an 'individualized assessment' of the sentence warranted by § 3553(a) 'based on the facts presented.'" *United States v. Jones*, 531 F.3d 163, 170 (2d Cir. 2008) (citations omitted); *see also Pepper v. United States*, 562 U.S. 476, 487 (2011) ("It has been uniform and constant in the federal judicial tradition for the sentencing judge to consider every convicted person as an individual and every case as a unique study in the human failings that sometimes mitigate, sometimes magnify, the crime and the punishment to ensue.") (internal quotations and citations omitted). Regarding this individualized assessment, "[t]he Guidelines are not only *not mandatory* on sentencing courts; they are also not to be *presumed* reasonable." *Nelson v. United States*, 555 U.S. 350, 352 (2009) (emphasis in original). Indeed, the Court "may vary [from the Guidelines range] based solely on policy considerations, including disagreements with the Guidelines." *Kimbrough v. United States*, 552 U.S. 85, 101 (2007) (quotations and citations omitted); *Gall v. United States*, 552 U.S. 38, 47 (2007) (court need not find "extraordinary circumstances to justify a sentence outside of the Guidelines range").

As discussed below, based on these factors, it is respectfully submitted that a sentence of time-served[3] would be well warranted in this case.

B.   **Michael's Personal History and Characteristics**

Michael, age 52, is a first-time offender. The sole provider for his family, Michael has been married to Laura Cohen for 24 years, and they have two children, Samantha, 23, and Jake, 19.

Michael is utterly devoted to his family. Truly, the greatest punishment Michael has

---

[3] Michael was taken into custody on August 21, 2018, the date on which he entered his plea before this Court. Again, on November 29, 2018, he was taken into custody before the entry of his plea before Judge Carter.

endured in the criminal process has been the shame and anxiety he feels daily from having

subjected his family to the fallout from his case. The media glare and intrusions on all of them,

including his children, the regular hate correspondence and written and oral threats, the fact that he

will lose his law license, the termination of business relationships by banks and insurers, and the

loss of friendships, are but some of this fallout.

Michael's father survived unimaginable horrors during World War II, including

"bombings, target shooting, hunger and disease, [the] gulags of Siberia, and persecution." Ex. 1

(Maurice Cohen).[4] He eventually arrived in Canada and later became a surgeon. He and his wife, a

surgical nurse, together raised four children. They both retired about five years ago. Michael

remains very close to his parents, speaking to them almost daily. PSR ¶¶ 84-85.[5] Michael's father

calls his son "the oxygen in the air that I breathe." Ex. 1 (Maurice Cohen).

Michael describes his children as his "heart" and "soul." The family is very close-knit, and

Michael and Laura have never spent any extended period apart. PSR ¶¶ 93-95. "Michael is first

and foremost deeply committed to his family," Ex. 17 (Faisal Hassan), and has always worked

hard to make sure his wife and children are well-cared for. See Ex. 34 (Steve Weatherford)

("[T]he honor, adoration, and respect he shows his wife Laura, and two children, Samantha and

Jake, set the example I strive every day to attain."); Ex. 30 (Penny Sherman) ("When Michael says

family first he truly means it in every sense of the word."); Ex. 25 (Valerie Rosenwasser)

("Michael represents the true essence of a family man – extremely devoted, dedicated, a loving

---

[4] Letters in support of Michael submitted with this Memorandum as Exhibits are referred to by
author name.

[5] "PSR" refers to the Presentence Investigation Report dated November 13, 2018. We understand
that the Probation Department is preparing an amended PSR based on Michael's plea to
Information 18 Cr. 850.

husband and father.").

His children's education has always been of the foremost importance to Michael, and
"[d]espite his busy work schedule, Michael never missed an opportunity to participate in his
children's academic lives." Ex. 24 (Beth Rosenthal); *see also* Ex. 33 (Marea Wachsman) ("I saw,
first hand, Michael's devotion to his family and his children as he is determined to see them excel
in school, participate in numerous extra curricular activities and give to their community."); Ex. 9
(Erik Ekstein) ("I have never known Michael to miss anything that involves his children.").

Michael has both supported, and used his considerable fundraising skills to urge others to
support, Columbia Grammar and Preparatory School, which both of his children attended and
where he served on the Board of Trustees, "work[ing] tirelessly on the School's behalf." Ex. 36
(Andrew Zaro). In that role, Michael "went out of his way to ensure that children who[ ] were
qualified to have successful academic careers but were not able to afford the tuition were granted
[the] necessary financial aid," serving as "a true advocate for children and families in need." Ex.
10 (Brian and Amy France). As one of his fellow Board members describes, "[i]t was purely
[Michael's] drive and determination to raise as much money as possible that ensured that the
[School's] scholarship fund was fully capitalized," a task he undertook "purely to help the children
relying on these scholarships." Ex. 6 (Rona Davis).

Michael's care for children has fueled his support for numerous other charitable causes,
such as St. Jude's Children's Research Hospital, "where he has committed many hours of
charitable work and has enlisted the help of his children," Ex. 2 (Andrew Albstein); "Operation
Smile," "a humanitarian mission to aid refugee children in Jordan in need of surgical
intervention," in order to "enjoy a normal childhood and a better life," Ex. 17 (Faisal Hassan); and
his friend Steve Weatherford's foundation, through which Michael has "coordinated and assisted

9

in the execution of speakers, professional athletes, and role models to speak to students in the city

of Manhattan," thus advancing the foundation's ability "to change the lives of thousands of

students in the Tri-state area." Ex. 34 (Steve Weatherford). Cathy Gottlieb Weiss also describes

how Michael provided support to her family when her oldest son, ███████████████

██████████████ was applying to college. "Michael's ongoing guidance led to a successful

placement at [her] son's first choice college," and after receiving his education, her son has

"continue[d] to thrive" because of Michael's "invaluable" assistance. Ex. 35 (Cathy Gottlieb

Weiss). Similarly, when his friend Lauren Salerno's daughter █████████████████████

█████████████ Michael was one of the very first people to contact [her], sit with [her], offer his

shoulder to lean on, and help [her] ████████████████████████████." Ex. 26 (Lauren

Salerno); *see also* Ex. 19 (Felix Karafin) ("Michael was the first person to help when my daughter

██████████████████ and he was there for my family every step of the way."); Ex. 32 (Marc

and Sandy Taub) ("When our daughter was ████████████████████████████████,

Michael was there to help make a connection to the right doctor and insure she received the best

possible level of care."); Ex. 22 (Sara and Ken Pilot) ("[W]hen a beloved Housekeeper's child

██████████████ and could not afford it[,] Michael, without hesitation not only paid ██████████,

but visited the child in the hospital and made sure the doctors were the best and most

experienced.").

Michael's friends attest to his aid and generosity in assisting them with their own business

endeavors. Kelly Gitter recounts that when she was struggling to make a living as a real estate

broker in the aftermath of the financial crisis, "Michael was the first one to help me by putting me

in contact with a friend of his," eventually resulting in a successful purchase. When she attempted

to take Michael to dinner as a means of thanking him, "Michael flatly refused and instead

Case 1:18-cr-00602-WHP   Document 22   Filed 11/30/18   Page 15 of 33

suggested that if I were to do anything on his behalf, it would be to make a donation to St. Jude's

Children's Hospital," which she says "taught [her] in that moment what it was to have integrity,"

and that "there is nothing more authentic than paying it forward." Ex. 13 (Kelly Gitter).

Kimberley Green also describes how, when she was starting up a new company, "Michael made it

his mission to find me the right people to be involved and that I could trust," so that her business

would succeed. Ex. 14 (Kimberley Green). In the same vein, when Laura Sanko was "trying to

pursue a career in sports television" but "wasn't sure how to go about it," Michael "immediately

began giving me advice on how I might be able to get my foot in the door," "made several

introductions on my behalf and played a key role in launching the television career that is now a

huge part of my life." Ex. 27 (Laura Sanko); *see also* Ex. 7 (Andrew Dworkin) (Explaining that

when he met with Michael to brainstorm about potential job opportunities, "Michael was

exceptionally generous with his time, listening to my personal journey with unusual empathy. He

went out of his way to better understand my situation, and then introduced me to a number of

people who might need a person of my talents, often showcasing me at events while selflessly

fading into the background."); Ex. 33 (Marea Wachsman) (Describing that when she was handling

a difficult legal case, "Michael made himself available to me to answer my questions, point me in

the right direction, and assist me in achieving a successful resolution, without asking or expecting

any renumeration [sic] for himself."); Ex. 8 (Robyn and Richard Ebers) (When Robyn Ebers "was

starting out in a relatively new business," "Michael was the only person who immediately reached

out with a helping hand," and was consistent with his "favorite" refrain: "'What can I do for

you?'"); Ex. 11 (Cozy Friedman) ("[W]hen I launched a new business 5 years ago [Michael] was

very eager to help me, took time from his incredibly busy schedule to read my business plan and

offer advice, as well as to make introductions that proved to be very helpful as I built up my

11

business.").

Among Michael's admirable qualities are his genuine respect for others and interest in
getting to know and helping those from different walks of life. As David McNeer explains, when
Michael saw a "60 Minutes" broadcast that featured the devastating effect of the Maytag
Company's decision to leave his hometown of Newton, Iowa, Michael reached out to him directly
to see how he could help. "Being from the Midwest I wasn't quite used to how direct Michael
was," Mr. McNeer states, "[B]ut I soon grew to appreciate it," as Michael assisted him in initiating
new opportunities for his small promotional products business. Ex. 21 (David McNeer); *see also*
Ex. 37 (David DeAngelis) (Describing how, when he reached out to Michael without any prior
introduction, Michael "took a personal interest in helping my business and placed me in contact
with several vendors. . . . He offered advice and never asked for anything in return."). Andrew
Albstein recounts having dinner with Michael at a restaurant where "Michael had a lengthy
conversation with one of the employees who sought business advice" from him. Ex. 2 (Andrew
Albstein); *see also* Ex. 23 (Kathy Presto) (Michael "actively seeks to help others, whether they are
a lifelong friend or someone he's just met."); Ex. 35 (Cathy Gottlieb Weiss) ("Michael treated
everyone the same regardless of what role they played in his life, from the Security Guard at the
school, to the homeless man on the street – Michael always had time for a warm greeting, and
always – a helping hand."); Ex. 19 (Felix Karafin) ("Despite his immeasurable success, Michael is
always relatable and makes others feel special."); Ex. 27 (Laura Sanko) ("I have had several
opportunities to observe how Michael treats those around him. From the receptionist at his office to
some of the most influential business leaders in the nation, Michael is beloved by many and
deservedly so."); Ex. 3 (Sara Armet) ("I am indebted to Michael Cohen for showing me that
whoever you are, wherever you come from – we all have a story to share. Michael takes the time to

12

know your story."); Ex. 15 (Melissa Greenberg) ("I can't tell you how many times for as long as I have known Michael that our dinners, lunches and get togethers would be punctuated with calls from friends and mere acquaintances seeking Michael's help and guidance in their careers or with other personal problems. And Michael was there for *everyone*, tirelessly and genuinely."). His friend Jackie Harris describes Michael as "a true gentleman [who] deeply cares about those whose path he crosses, no matter what the relationship. He treats everyone with the same respect and concern and is very well regarded and beloved by so many people." Ex. 16 (Jackie Harris).

C.   The Nature of the Offense Conduct

Information 18 Cr. 602: Counts One to Five (Tax Evasion)

Counts One through Five charge tax evasion in the years 2012 through 2016. Michael reiterates his personal responsibility for this conduct and apologizes for it to this Court and his family.

As the Court considers this offense conduct for sentencing purposes, we respectfully set forth several observations directed at a comparison of the specific conduct before the Court with the complex and sophisticated offense conduct that characterizes many of the criminal tax cases prosecuted in this and other federal courts. In so doing, neither we nor Michael minimize the seriousness of tax evasion in any form. Rather, we respectfully submit that the nature of the instant conduct suggests that, on a comparative basis, it warrants relatively less punishment than cases where sophisticated means and schemes are employed. Indeed, we submit respectfully that little, if anything, separates the offense conduct from conduct that is routinely pursued through non-criminal enforcement.

As an initial matter, Michael did not find himself in the criminal justice system facing tax charges after audit, an unsatisfied or obstructed demand by the IRS, an investigated history of sophisticated tax maneuvers and deceptions, or the discovery by the government of offshore or

nominee accounts or bogus deductions. Nor was there any meaningful pre-charge process in this

case. Michael was notified through counsel of the government's intention to bring criminal tax

evasion charges only approximately three or four days before he was told they would be filed. The

usual practice of review with counsel and an opportunity to be heard by the Tax Division within

DOJ as to the filing of criminal charges was omitted by decision of the government.[6]

In comparison, numerous allegations of unpaid tax are routinely asserted by the IRS outside

of the criminal context and addressed through assessments, liens and penalties. On the merits, such

an approach could readily have been taken here, because other than the unreported income itself, no

aggravating or "plus" factors are present. Thus, this case involves:

1. No allegation of unreported cash transactions, much less systematic ones;

2. No allegation of the use of offshore or nominee accounts;

3. No allegation of phony deductions or expenses run through a business or otherwise;

4. No allegation of false statements or obstructive or similar conduct during audit or IRS proceedings, or disingenuous tax-driven sham transactions;

5. No allegation that absurdly minimal tax was paid where substantial sums were actually due;[7]

---

[6] Title 6, Section 4.214, of the Justice Manual (formerly the U.S. Attorney's Manual) states that, "If time and circumstances permit, the Tax Division generally grants a taxpayer's written request for a conference with the Division." Even if the matter has already been forwarded to the U.S. Attorney's Office, the taxpayer may request a conference with that Office. During such a conference, "the Tax Division usually advises [the taxpayer] of the proposed charges, the method of proof, and the income and tax computations that the IRS recommended." The taxpayer may then "present explanations or evidence for the Tax Division to consider in reaching a decision regarding prosecution."

[7] Michael paid approximately $6 million in taxes during the tax years in issue in this case.

6.   No allegation of nonpayment of any penalties or unsatisfied audit assessment; and

7.   No allegation of false responses to a tax preparer's annual questionnaire (no such questionnaires were ever sent to Michael by his accountant).

The means involved here could not have been less sophisticated. Indeed, the Sentencing Guidelines calculation in the August 21, 2018 Plea Agreement includes no offense level adjustment for "sophisticated means," under U.S.S.G. § 2T1.1(b)(2). Notably, the Information's core allegation is that Michael "did not provide records that would have allowed Accountant-1 *to reasonably identify* [the subject] income." Information 18 Cr. 602 (WHP) ¶ 8 (bold added).[8] Accordingly, without minimizing the seriousness of tax evasion, no matter its characteristics or size, Michael's case stands out for comparative purposes in that a failure to reasonably identify all income to a tax preparer who received all client-related bank statements is quite different in kind from the sophisticated and complex schemes typical of criminal tax evasion cases. *See* https://www.justice.gov/tax/about-division ("The Criminal Enforcement Sections [of the Tax Division of the Department of Justice] are staffed with prosecutors who are particularly skilled at investigating, prosecuting and evaluating *complex* financial crime cases.") (emphasis added).

For example, in *United States v. Earl Simmons*, the defendant, a recording artist known as "DMX," engaged in a "brazen, multi-year scheme to fraudulently conceal millions of dollars in income . . . and avoid paying $1.7 million in taxes" by, among other things, (1) "[a]rrang[ing] for hundreds of thousands of dollars of musical royalties to be deposited into the bank accounts of his managers, and then had portions of that money disbursed to himself in cash or used to pay personal expenses," (2) "[r]eceiv[ing] half of concert performance fees into the bank accounts of his

---

[8] Every year, Michael provided his regular accountant with all bank account statements of his personal and business entities, separated by marked tabs, in organized three-ring notebooks.

15

managers, who then distributed cash to [him], and then typically receiv[ing] the other half himself

in cash," (3) demanding payment for his participation in a reality television show without

withholding taxes, (4) failing entirely to file personal tax returns during a period when he earned

more than $2.3 million, and (5) filing a false personal bankruptcy petition understating his income.

Gov't Sent'g Ltr. at 1, 2, ECF No. 35, 17 Cr. 172 (JSR) (S.D.N.Y. Mar. 23, 2018). In that case, the

Court imposed a one-year prison term where the advisory Guidelines range was 57 to 60 months.

In another recent case, *United States v. Lacy Doyle*, Judge Carter imposed a sentence of four years'

probation where the defendant engaged in a complicated offshore tax evasion scheme that

continued over a six-year period and during which she "established and maintained a sham

foundation to hold [over $4 million in] Swiss bank accounts in order to conceal those bank accounts

from U.S. tax authorities and evade U.S. tax obligations." Gov't Sent'g Ltr. at 1, ECF No. 110, 16

Cr. 506 (ALC) (S.D.N.Y. Oct. 26, 2018).

To be sure, Michael, as a prominent American and attorney, may have been selected for

criminal prosecution to set an example. But that decision was far from a foreordained exercise of

prosecutorial discretion. In cases of unsophisticated means such as this one, even when the

taxpayer is a well-known public figure, the government routinely makes its point through IRS

administrative, not criminal, action. The table below provides a sample of such cases:

Kaseem "Swizz Beatz" Dean	The music producer paid over $650,000 in back taxes without criminal consequences after the IRS filed liens for two tax years. *See* https://www.dailymail.co.uk/news/article-3906918/Alicia-Keys-tax-shy-husband-Swizz-Beatz-coughs-650-000-IRS-case.html.
Floyd Mayweather Jr.	The boxer paid $15.5 million in taxes only after the IRS filed liens against him for unpaid taxes over multiple years, but he did not face criminal charges. *See* https://www.businessinsider.com/ap-mayweather-has-history-of-tax-woes-7m-from-2010-unresolved-2017-7.

16

Case 1:18-cr-00602-WHP   Document 22   Filed 11/30/18   Page 21 of 33

Willie Nelson	The IRS claimed singer Willie Nelson owed $16.7 million, but he was permitted to settle for $9 million without facing criminal penalties. *See* https://www.rollingstone.com/music/music-country/flashback-willie-nelson-settles-irs-tax-debt-196254/.
Chris Tucker	The IRS filed a $2.5 million tax lien against the comedian as the result of a multi-year audit, and he was permitted to settle without facing criminal charges. *See* https://www.cnn.com/2014/09/01/showbiz/chris-tucker-tax-bill/index.html.
John Travolta	The actor settled with the IRS and agreed to pay $607,400 in back taxes for disputed losses he claimed over the course of two tax years. He was not required to pay the $500,000 in penalties sought by the IRS and did not face criminal charges. *See* https://abcnews.go.com/Entertainment/story?id=112661&page=1.

Given the absence in the offense conduct of any aggravating facts and circumstances, we respectfully submit that the disparity in treatment that brings Michael before this Court on criminal tax evasion charges while so many others are pursued non-criminally for conduct similar to or more sophisticated than present here, should be considered by the Court in fashioning an appropriate sentence.

Information 18 Cr. 602: Count Six: False Statements to a Financial Institution

Michael and his family had banked with Bank-3[9] for more than a decade, and at the time of the offense conduct Bank-3 held a first mortgage on the Cohens' primary residence. In early 2015, Michael discussed with Gary Farro, the family's principal private banker, opening a $500,000 home equity line of credit ("HELOC") secured by his primary residence. At the time, the unencumbered equity value in the residence was more than 10 times that amount. Mr. Farro supplied Michael and his wife with a form for the HELOC application in which Mr. Farro had already completed certain lines of a balance sheet. Michael signed the form, without adding to the liability side of the balance

---

[9] In this Memorandum, we use the defined short-form names employed in the two filed Informations.

17

sheet a number of substantial obligations, none of which then encumbered his primary residence. After Michael drew down on the HELOC, he replaced the sums drawn in short order.

Michael's use of the HELOC caused no loss to Bank-3.[10] And, given the exceptionally favorable (to Bank-3) loan-to-value ratio, a very strong case can be made that Bank-3 incurred no realistic risk of loss during the period of the HELOC. Nonetheless, Michael recognizes that it was incumbent on him to meet the highest standards in his communications with banks. Thus, while we respectfully urge the Court to consider the relative significance of the misconduct in this case as a factor in mitigation of sentence, Michael does not distance himself from his conduct or its wrongfulness.

Information 18 Cr. 602: Counts Seven and Eight: Campaign Finance Violations & Information 18 Cr. 850: Count One: False Statements to Congress

We address the campaign finance and false statements allegations together because both arose from Michael's fierce loyalty to Client-1. In each case, the conduct was intended to benefit Client-1, in accordance with Client-1's directives. Michael regrets that his vigor in promoting Client-1's interests in the heat of political battle led him to abandon good judgment and cross legal lines.

Campaign Finance Violations

The details of the offense conduct captured by Count Seven and Eight are set forth in the charging instrument. Concerning Count Seven, as relevant here, Michael himself did not make the

---

[10] In his many years of dealing with financial institutions, Michael has never defaulted on a loan, except that in 2018, because he had been trying for *almost eighteen months* to gain Bank-2's focus on a proposed assignment of his medallions-secured loan to a prospective purchaser of his and his wife's taxi medallions, Michael, at wit's end, held back several monthly payments. Bank-2 finally then focused on the transaction and approved it. By this time, however, the prospective purchaser, having witnessed the decline in value of NYC taxi medallions over many months, decided not to close.

18

payment to Woman-1 called for by the agreement reached between Corporation-1 and Woman-1, but participated in planning discussions with Client-1 and the Chairman and CEO of Corporation-1 relating to the payment made by Corporation-1, including obtaining the commitment of Client-1 to repay Corporation-1. As the matter unfolded, the contract was profitable for Corporation-1, and Client-1's failure to reimburse Corporation-1 was ultimately not contested by Corporation-1.

Concerning Count Eight, Michael made a payment to the lawyer for Woman-2 in coordination with and at the direction of Client-1, and others within the Company. Michael was assured by Client-1 that he would be repaid for his advance of funds, and, later, again with the approval of Client-1, agreed to an arrangement conceived by an executive of the Company whereby Michael would receive reimbursement during 2017 in the form of monthly payments by the Company for invoiced legal fees.

With respect to the conduct charged in these Counts, Michael kept his client contemporaneously informed and acted on his client's instructions. This is not an excuse, and Michael accepts that he acted wrongfully. Nevertheless, we respectfully request that the Court consider that as personal counsel to Client-1, Michael felt obligated to assist Client-1, on Client-1's instruction, to attempt to prevent Woman-1 and Woman-2 from disseminating narratives that would adversely affect the Campaign *and* cause personal embarrassment to Client-1 and his family. In this sense, Michael's conduct was different in kind from recent campaign finance charges brought before this Court, in which the charged individuals used straw donors to make illegal campaign contributions. *See United States v. Dinesh D'Souza*, 14 Cr. 34 (RMB) (defendant sentenced to five years' probation for using straw donors to contribute to Republican Senate candidate's campaign); *United States v. Jia Hou and Xing Wu Pan*, 12 Cr. 153 (RJS) (defendants sentenced to ten months' and four months' imprisonment for involvement in scheme to use straw donors to raise money for

19

mayoral campaign of John Liu).[11]

False Statements to Congress

Michael's false statements to Congress likewise sprung regrettably from Michael's effort, as

a loyal ally and then-champion of Client-1, to support and advance Client-1's political messaging.

At the time that he was requested to appear before the Senate Select Committee on Intelligence and

House Permanent Select Committee on Intelligence, Michael was serving as personal attorney to

the President, and followed daily the political messages that both Client-1 and his staff and

supporters repeatedly and forcefully broadcast. Furthermore, in the weeks during which his then-

counsel prepared his written response to the Congressional Committees, Michael remained in close

and regular contact with White House-based staff and legal counsel to Client-1.

As such, he was (a) fully aware of Client-1's repeated disavowals of commercial and

---

[11] Michael's loyal service to his famous former client is well-known amongst his friends, as is that
the relationship has now led to a criminal case. *See, e.g.*, Ex. 8 (Robyn and Richard Ebers) (noting
"Michael's overwhelming loyalty" to Trump as well as the "destructiveness caused by Michael's
relationship with Mr. Trump."); Ex. 17 (Faisal Hassan) (Michael's "greatest weakness has been his
blind loyalty towards those who have misused his trust and his good name."); Ex. 2 (Andrew
Albstein) ("Unfortunately, because of his unwavering and zealous commitment to provide
excellence for his employer, Michael soon became the easiest person to blame, by those who
needed a person to blame."); Ex. 14 (Kimberley Green) ("Michael's greatest characteristic, yet also
on occasion his Achilles heel, is his staunch loyalty. When he is behind you it is unfaltering, at
times to his detriment."). Michael's friend Ethan Gerber, who is a practicing lawyer and former
President of the Brooklyn Bar Association, writes, "[a]s to his involvement in the Trump
Organization, to those who knew Michael outside of his current fame or notoriety, the assumption
is that if he erred in his representation it is because he was overly loyal and zealous on behalf of his
client. As a member of a Grievance Committee I have seen many attorneys succumb to the wishes
of a particularly persuasive client," and Michael "had a client whose extraordinary power of
persuasion got him elected to the highest office in the land." Ex. 12 (Ethan Gerber); *see also* Ex. 5
(Cory Colligan) ("His loyalty to Mr. Trump . . . was immeasurable. He spoke of him constantly. It
was obvious he was in CONSTANT contact with him running ideas, proposals, etc. by him for his
approval.").

political ties between himself and Russia, as well as the strongly voiced mantra of Client-1 that

investigations of such ties were politically motivated and without evidentiary support, and (b)

specifically knew, consistent with Client-1's aim to dismiss and minimize the merit of the SCO

investigation, that Client-1 and his public spokespersons were seeking to portray contact with

Russian representatives in any form by Client-1, the Campaign or the Trump Organization as

having effectively terminated before the Iowa caucuses of February 1, 2016.

Seeking to stay in line with this message, Michael told Congress that his communications

and efforts to finalize a building project in Moscow on behalf of the Trump Organization, which he

began pursuing in 2015, had come to an end in January 2016, when a general inquiry he made to

the Kremlin went unanswered. He also stated that his communications with Client-1 and others in

the Trump Organization regarding the project were minimal and ceased at or about the same time.

In fact, Michael had a lengthy substantive conversation with the personal assistant to a Kremlin

official following his outreach in January 2016, engaged in additional communications concerning

the project as late as June 2016, and kept Client-1 apprised of these communications. He and

Client-1 also discussed possible travel to Russia in the summer of 2016, and Michael took steps to

clear dates for such travel.

In the heated political environment of the moment and understanding the public message

that Client-1 wished to propagate, Michael, in his written statement to Congress, foreshortened the

chronology of events and his communications with Client-1 to characterize both as having

terminated before the Iowa caucuses. At the time, Michael justified his false summary of the matter

on the ground that the Moscow project ultimately did not go forward. He recognizes that his

judgment was fundamentally wrong, and wishes both to apologize and set the record straight.

21

D.   Sentencing Guidelines and Objections to PSR Guidelines Calculation

We respectfully submit two comments regarding the Guidelines calculation set forth in the

PSR issued in connection with Information 18 Cr. 602.

1. The PSR's Calculation of the Guidelines Relies on a Flawed Grouping
    <u>Analysis.</u>

Probation has calculated the total offense level as 24, resulting in an advisory Guidelines

range of 51 to 63 months, based on an analysis that groups all eight counts in Information 18 Cr.

602. For the reasons set forth below, this analysis is flawed and the correct offense level is 23,

resulting in a Guidelines range of 46 to 57 months.[12]

Pursuant to U.S.S.G. § 3D1.1, in a multi-count case, (i) "closely related" counts are grouped

under § 3D1.2; (ii) an offense level for each group is determined under § 3D1.3; and (iii) the

offense level applicable to all groups taken together is assessed under § 3D1.4. Counts are

considered "closely related" under the Guidelines when they involve "substantially the same harm."

U.S.S.G. § 3D1.2.

The tax evasion counts (Counts One through Five) do not involve money related to the false

statement (Count Six) and campaign finance counts (Counts Seven and Eight). As such, only the

false statement and campaign finance counts are "closely related" and should be grouped under §

3D1.2(d), because the "offense level [for both sets of counts] is determined largely on the basis of

the total amount of harm or loss" as calculated under § 2B1.1, and the offenses are "of the same

general type." U.S.S.G. § 3D1.2(d) comment. 6.[13]

---

[12] As set forth in the August 21, 2018 Plea Agreement, there is no stipulation between the parties
regarding the grouping of the tax evasion counts, on the one hand, and the false statement and
campaign finance counts, on the other. (*See* Aug. 21, 2018 Plea Agr. at 3 n.2).

[13] The parties agree that subsection (d) is the only applicable grouping provision. The tax evasion
counts are not subject to grouping with the false statement and campaign finance counts pursuant to

22

By contrast, for grouping purposes, the tax evasion counts should be viewed as completely

separate from the false statement and campaign finance counts. The unreported income that forms

the basis of the tax evasion counts did not arise from the conduct underlying either the false

statement count or the campaign finance counts. And, the amount of loss in respect of the tax

evasion counts is calculated under a separate table at § 2T4.1, which is different from the table at §

2B1.1. In this circumstance, grouping of all of the counts in Information 18 Cr. 602 under

subsection (d) is not appropriate. Nor is it mandatory, notwithstanding that the Guidelines

applicable to all of the charged offenses are listed in subsection (d).[14] *See United States v. Napoli,*

179 F.3d 1, 9 n.4 (2d Cir. 1999) ("We . . . reject the broad view that money laundering and fraud

counts can be grouped under subsection (d) simply because they both appear on its list of counts 'to

be grouped.'"); *see also United States v. Lenoci,* 377 F.3d 246, 252-53 (2d Cir. 2004) (noting that

grouping of Guidelines on the "to be grouped" list in subsection (d) cannot be automatic because

such a finding is inconsistent with the "careful [grouping] analysis" undertaken in prior cases and

the language of Application Note 6 of the guideline). Indeed, a contrary approach would be unfair

and unconvincing because it would afford undue weight to the application of two upward

adjustments – for special skill and sophisticated means – which relate factually solely to the

conduct underlying the campaign finance counts, not the tax evasion counts.

---

§ 3D1.2(a) or (b) because they do not involve the same victim or the same act or transactions, or a series of acts or transactions connected by a common objective or constituting a common scheme. Subsection (c), which covers grouping of one count that "embodies conduct that is treated as a specific offense characteristic in, or other adjustment to, the guideline applicable to another of the counts" with that other count, on its own terms does not apply to the counts in the Information.

[14] As set forth in the August 21, 2018 Plea Agreement, the applicable Guideline for the tax counts is U.S.S.G. § 2T1.1, for the false statement count, § 2B1.1, and for the campaign finance counts, § 2C1.8.

Notably, even where tax counts arise from the unreported proceeds of a fraud scheme –
which is not the case here – the vast majority of Circuit courts to consider the issue have held that
fraud counts and tax counts should not be grouped together, both because they use different loss
tables, and because they are not "closely related" as a factual matter. *See United States v. Doxie*,
813 F.3d 1340, 1345 (11th Cir. 2016) (collecting cases).

     United States v. Petrillo, 237 F.3d 119, 125 (2d Cir. 2000), is not to the contrary. There, the
defendant's tax and fraud offenses were properly grouped together under § 3D1.2(d), because "the
offenses [at issue] were both frauds, were part of a single continuous course of criminal activity and
involved the same funds." In addition, *Petrillo* was decided at a time when the tax table and the
fraud table "trigger[ed] substantially identical offense level increments based on the amount of
loss," which is no longer the case. *Id.* Moreover, in a concurring opinion issued after *Petrillo*,
Judge Newman noted that it is not clear whether even factually-related tax evasion and fraud counts
should be grouped, and he urged the Sentencing Commission to issue guidance on the topic.
United States v. Gordon, 291 F.3d 181, 198 (2d Cir. 2002) ("Ultimately, the Commission needs to
cut through this morass and tell us in plain English whether it wants tax offense group with the
offenses that produced the income on which the taxes were evaded.") (Newman, J., concurring).

     Accordingly, the tax evasion counts, on the one hand, and the false statement and campaign
finance counts, on the other, should not be grouped, resulting in a Guidelines range of 46 to 57
months' imprisonment.

     2. Under Section 3553(a), Mitigating Consideration Should be Given to
        Two Overlapping Guidelines Enhancements.

     The Probation Department and August 21, 2018 Plea Agreement applied two separate two-
level enhancements to the Count Eight offense conduct: (1) sophisticated means, under U.S.S.G. §
2B1.1(b)(10), and (2) use of a special skill, under § 3B1.3. *See* Aug. 21, 2018 Plea Agr. at 4. On

the facts of this case, the application of both enhancements results in an overstated total offense

level, and we respectfully request that the Court consider the same as a mitigating sentencing factor

under § 3553(a).

First, the two enhancements apply factually only to the campaign finance violation charged

in Count Eight of Information 18 Cr. 602. To the extent the government's view of the grouping

analysis were to be adopted by the Court – which, as we submit above, it should not be – these two

enhancements would have the effect of disproportionately reflecting Count Eight in the Guidelines

calculation.

Second, the two enhancements address overlapping conduct. The "sophisticated means" are

described as Michael's (i) use of a third-party entity – Essential Consultants LLC, incorporated by

Michael in 2016[15] – to make a $130,000 payment on behalf of Client-1, that was described in wire

instructions as payment of a "retainer" to Attorney-1, PSR ¶¶ 43-45, and (ii) at the request of

Executive-1 of the Company, the submission of "invoices" during 2017 purportedly for legal

services rendered, but really to obtain payment and repayment of amounts owed by the Company to

Michael, including the $130,000 payment. PSR ¶¶ 48-52. At the same time, the "use of a special

skill" is described as Michael's use of his status as an attorney to "facilitate and conceal" the

campaign finance offense in Count Eight by characterizing the payment and repayments as

payments for legal services. PSR ¶¶ 50-51. Thus, the facts underlying the special skill adjustment

are subsumed within the sophisticated means enhancement. *Cf.* U.S.S.G. § 3B1.3 (precluding

application of the two-level enhancement when a defendant's special skill "is included in the base

---

[15] Michael originally incorporated an LLC called Resolution Consultants LLC in September 2016,
but changed the name to Essential Consultants LLC in October 2016 after realizing that a friend
owned a business under the prior name. Michael did not attempt to conceal his role in or
relationship to the LLC; he was and is listed as its sole managing member.

offense level or specific offense characteristic."). Accordingly, application of both enhancements would cause an overstatement of the total offense level under the Guidelines.

E.   Deterrence Will Not Be Materially Promoted by a Custodial Sentence

In the circumstances of this case and defendant, we respectfully submit that a sentence of time-served would serve the purpose of deterrence.

With respect to specific deterrence, there is scant risk of recidivism in Michael's case; he has never had any prior interactions with law enforcement, other than a speeding ticket in 1985. Moreover, as publicly reported, from the time of the FBI searches through the culmination of this case, Michael has consistently shown his respect for members of law enforcement and their mission. And, his cooperation in numerous meetings with three different prosecutorial bodies demonstrates his commitment to set the record straight and assist in the government's various inquiries.

Moreover, from the time of the execution of the search warrants in early April of this year, this case has caused deep and lasting strain for Michael and his family. They have been subjected to daily public scrutiny and moral opprobrium in a media cauldron of exceptional heat and intensity. This scrutiny has been accompanied by threats of physical harm to Michael and his family, which have been referred to the authorities for investigation. All of this amounts to an alternative form of punishment that will act as a deterrent against future missteps. *See, e.g.*, Ex. 7 (Andrew Dworkin) ("I suspect the pain [Michael's] mistakes have caused his wife and children is a very real and incalculable punishment he must live with for the remainder of his life. I remain confident that . . . Michael will use this experience to become a better person, and continue living his life as a loving and devoted husband and father, supportive and valued friend, and meaningful and important positive contributor to society."); Ex. 26 (Lauren Salerno) ("We can only hope to

26

emphasize what a valued community member, parent and friend Michael is, and even while he is

dealing with these current and very publicized issues, he continues to be the most dependable,

supportive, and caring friend."); *cf. United States v. Stewart*, 590 F.3d 93, 141 (2d Cir. 2009) ("the

need for further deterrence and protection of the public is lessened because the conviction itself

already visits substantial punishment of the defendant").

Moreover, the letters submitted with this Memorandum on Michael's behalf provide

telling insight into his essential character. *See, e.g.*, Ex. 31 (Jan Sigmon) ("In the decades I have

known Michael, I have never known him to be anything less than kind, generous and giving of

himself to others."); Ex. 10 (Brian and Amy France) ("Michael has always and consistently

displayed an enormous level of kindness, humility, consideration and empathy for others,

including our family and our children."); Ex. 34 (Steve Weatherford) ("Michael has led me and

others by example every single day. His heart is one that desires to serve others, and acts upon

those desires over and over again."); Ex. 16 (Jackie Harris) ("Michael Cohen is a truly caring

person who does for others out of his huge heart and not because of anything he may receive in

return. . . . I am writing to ask that you consider the tremendous impact he has every day on his

family and his friends when deliberating his case."); Ex. 24 (Beth Rosenthal) ("After knowing

Michael for 40 years, it would take a novel for me to list all his good deeds, so I will close this

letter stating unequivocally that Michael is an upstanding, honorable, salt of the earth man and it

has been a privilege to call him a friend who is like family for all these years."); Ex. 14

(Kimberley Green ("Michael is a selfless caretaker. He gives of himself endlessly without

complaint and does not ask for anything in return. That is the way he has always been since I met

him 35 years ago."); Ex. 4 (Raffi Arslanian) ("The outstanding quality that I find stellar in

Michael is his selfless appetite to run to people's aid in time of his friends['] need. Michael does

27

not wait to be asked for the help or assistance.").

The observations expressed in these and other of the submitted letters provide every reason to believe that Michael will not re-offend, a conclusion only buttressed by his age, *see United States v. Ruiz*, 04 Cr. 1146 (RWS), 2006 WL 1311982, at *4 (S.D.N.Y. May 10, 2006) ("This Court and others have previously declined to impose Guidelines sentences on defendants who, like Ruiz, were over the age of forty at the time of sentencing on the grounds that such defendants exhibit markedly lower rates of recidivism in comparison to younger defendants."), his lack of any criminal history, and his substantial familial obligations. *See United States v. Olis*, 03 Cr. 217 (SL), 2006 WL 2716048, at *13 (S.D. Tex. Sept. 22, 2006) (granting significant downward variance where the "need to provide support for his family will provide adequate deterrence against any potential future criminal conduct").

A sentence of imprisonment is also unnecessary to further the objective of general deterrence. A reasonable person in the community viewing this case in full would understand its gargantuan cost to Michael, independent of any prison term. Aside from the enormous pain and stress this case has visited on Michael's family, including his son, who has just begun college, Michael (1) stands to lose his law license; (2) faces IRS civil penalties in addition to the restitution that is ordered by the Court; (3) will be named in a parallel tax case brought by New York State, with likely restitution, penalties and interest; (4) lost all of the business of his consulting firm; and (5) had numerous banking, credit card and insurance agreements canceled. Additionally, a number of long-term friendships have come to an end. No rational person would take any message from this case other than that similar conduct risks devastating, fundamentally life-changing results.

As important, the facts and circumstances surrounding this case are unique and

28

unprecedented, involving, among other things, the former personal attorney to the sitting

President, campaign finance violations centered on extramarital affairs of a presidential candidate,

and congressional testimony in an exceptionally heated political environment. Given this singular

context, there is little reason to conclude that general deterrence will be affected by the sentence.

See United States v. Gardellini, 545 F.3d 1089, 1095 (D.C. Cir. 2008) (rejecting government's

contention that affirming a probationary sentence imposed in criminal tax case would lessen

deterrent value of criminal law "because it elevates one § 3553(a) factor – deterrence – above all

others. As § 3553(a) makes clear, the district court at sentencing must consider and balance a

number of factors – not all of which will point in the same direction.").

CONCLUSION

For all of the reasons set forth above, we respectfully request that this Court

sentence Michael to time served.

Dated: November 30, 2018   Respectfully submitted,
    New York, New York

                    PETRILLO KLEIN & BOXER LLP

                    By: _____

                    Guy Petrillo
                    gpetrillo@pkbllp.com

                    Amy Lester
                    alester@pkbllp.com

                    655 Third Avenue, 22nd Floor
                    New York, New York 10017
                    Telephone: (212) 370-0330

29

THE STEELE DOSSIER.

COMPANY INTELLIGENCE REPORT 2016/080

US PRESIDENTIAL ELECTION: REPUBLICAN CANDIDATE DONALD TRUMP'S ACTIVITIES IN RUSSIA AND COMPROMISING RELATIONSHIP WITH THE KREMLIN

Summary

- Russian regime has been cultivating, supporting and assisting TRUMP for at least 5 years. Aim, endorsed by PUTIN, has been to encourage splits and divisions in western alliance

- So far TRUMP has declined various sweetener real estate business deals offered him in Russia in order to further the Kremlin's cultivation of him. However he and his inner circle have accepted a regular flow of intelligence from the Kremlin, including on his Democratic and other political rivals

- Former top Russian intelligence officer claims FSB has compromised TRUMP through his activities in Moscow sufficiently to be able to blackmail him. According to several knowledgeable sources, his conduct in Moscow has included perverted sexual acts which have been arranged/monitored by the FSB

- A dossier of compromising material on Hillary CLINTON has been collated by the Russian Intelligence Services over many years and mainly comprises bugged conversations she had on various visits to Russia and intercepted phone calls rather than any embarrassing conduct. The dossier is controlled by Kremlin spokesman, PESKOV, directly on PUTIN's orders. However it has not as yet been distributed abroad, including to TRUMP. Russian intentions for its deployment still unclear

Detail

1. Speaking to a trusted compatriot in June 2016 sources A and B, a senior Russian Foreign Ministry figure and a former top level Russian intelligence officer still active inside the Kremlin respectively, the Russian authorities had been cultivating and supporting US Republican presidential candidate, Donald TRUMP for at least 5 years. Source B asserted that the TRUMP operation was both supported and directed by Russian President Vladimir PUTIN. Its aim was to sow discord and

disunity both within the US itself, but more especially within the Transatlantic alliance which was viewed as inimical to Russia's interests. Source C, a senior Russian financial official said the TRUMP operation should be seen in terms of PUTIN's desire to return to Nineteenth Century 'Great Power' politics anchored upon countries' interests rather than the ideals-based international order established after World War Two. S/he had overheard PUTIN talking in this way to close associates on several occasions.

2. In terms of specifics, Source A confided that the Kremlin had been feeding TRUMP and his team valuable intelligence on his opponents, including Democratic presidential candidate Hillary CLINTON, for several years (see more below). This was confirmed by Source D, a close associate of TRUMP who had organized and managed his recent trips to Moscow, and who reported, also in June 2016, that this Russian intelligence had been "very helpful". The Kremlin's cultivation operation on TRUMP also had comprised offering him various lucrative real estate development business deals in Russia, especially in relation to the ongoing 2018 World Cup soccer tournament. However, so far, for reasons unknown, TRUMP had not taken up any of these.

3. However, there were other aspects to TRUMP's engagement with the Russian authorities. One which had borne fruit for them was to exploit TRUMP's personal obsessions and sexual perversion in order to obtain suitable 'kompromat' (compromising material) on him. According to Source D, where s/he had been present, TRUMP's (perverted) conduct in Moscow included hiring the presidential suite of the Ritz Carlton Hotel, where he knew President and Mrs OBAMA (whom he hated) had stayed on one of their official trips to Russia, and defiling the bed where they had slept by employing a number of prostitutes to perform a 'golden showers' (urination) show in front of him. The hotel was known to be under FSB control with microphones and concealed cameras in all the main rooms to record anything they wanted to.

4. The Moscow Ritz Carlton episode involving TRUMP reported above was confirmed by Source E, █████████████████████████████████, who said that s/he and several of the staff were aware of it at the time and subsequently. S/he believed it had happened in 2013. Source E provided an introduction for a company ethnic Russian operative to Source F, a female staffer at the hotel when TRUMP had stayed there, who also confirmed the story. Speaking separately in June 2016, Source B (the former top level Russian intelligence officer) asserted that TRUMP's unorthodox behavior in Russia over the years had provided the authorities there with enough embarrassing material on the now Republican presidential candidate to be able to blackmail him if they so wished.

5. Asked about the Kremlin's reported intelligence feed to TRUMP over recent years and rumours about a Russian dossier of 'kompromat' on

Hillary CLINTON (being circulated), Source B confirmed the file's existence. S/he confided in a trusted compatriot that it had been collated by Department K of the FSB for many years, dating back to her husband Bill's presidency, and comprised mainly eavesdropped conversations of various sorts rather than details/evidence of unorthodox or embarrassing behavior. Some of the conversations were from bugged comments CLINTON had made on her various trips to Russia and focused on things she had said which contradicted her current position on various issues. Others were most probably from phone intercepts.

6. Continuing on this theme, Source G, a senior Kremlin official, confided that the CLINTON dossier was controlled exclusively by chief Kremlin spokesman, Dmitriy PESKOV, who was responsible for compiling/handling it on the explicit instructions of PUTIN himself. The dossier however had not as yet been made available abroad, including to TRUMP or his campaign team. At present it was unclear what PUTIN's intentions were in this regard.

20 June 2016

COMPANY INTELLIGENCE REPORT 2016/086

RUSSIA/CYBER CRIME: A SYNOPSIS OF RUSSIAN STATE SPONSORED AND OTHER CYBER OFFENSIVE (CRIMINAL) OPERATIONS

Summary

- Russia has extensive programme of state-sponsored offensive cyber operations. External targets include foreign governments and big corporations, especially banks. FSB leads on cyber within Russian apparatus. Limited success in attacking top foreign targets like G7 governments, security services and IFIs but much more on second tier ones through IT back doors, using corporate and other visitors to Russia

- FSB often uses coercion and blackmail to recruit most capable cyber operatives in Russia into its state-sponsored programmes. Heavy use also, both wittingly and unwittingly, of CIS emigres working in western corporations and ethnic Russians employed by neighbouring governments e.g. Latvia

- Example cited of successful Russian cyber operation targeting senior Western business visitor. Provided back door into important Western institutions.

- Example given of US citizen of Russian origin approached by FSB and offered incentive of "investment" in his business when visiting Moscow.

- Problems however for Russian authorities themselves in countering local hackers and cyber criminals, operating outside state control. Central Bank claims there were over 20 serious attacks on correspondent accounts held by CBR in 2015, comprising Roubles several billion in fraud

- Some details given of leading non-state Russian cyber criminal groups

Details

1. Speaking in June 2016, a number of Russian figures with a detailed knowledge of national cyber crime, both state-sponsored and otherwise, outlined the current situation in this area. A former senior intelligence officer divided Russian state-sponsored offensive cyber operations into four categories (in order of priority):- targeting foreign, especially

western governments; penetrating leading foreign business corporations, especially banks; domestic monitoring of the elite; and attacking political opponents both at home and abroad. The former intelligence officer reported that the Federal Security Service (FSB) was the lead organization within the Russian state apparatus for cyber operations.

2. In terms of the success of Russian offensive cyber operations to date, a senior government figure reported that there had been only limited success in penetrating the "first tier" foreign targets. These comprised western (especially G7 and NATO) governments, security and intelligence services and central banks, and the IFIs. To compensate for this shortfall, massive effort had been invested, with much greater success, in attacking the "secondary targets", particularly western private banks and the governments of smaller states allied to the West. S/he mentioned Latvia in this regard. Hundreds of agents, either consciously cooperating with the FSB or whose personal and professional IT systems had been unwittingly compromised, were recruited. Many were people who had ethnic and family ties to Russia and/or had been incentivized financially to cooperate. Such people often would receive monetary inducements or contractual favours from the Russian state or its agents in return. This had created difficulties for parts of the Russian state apparatus in obliging/indulging them e.g. the Central Bank of Russia knowingly having to cover up for such agents' money laundering operations through the Russian financial system.

3. In terms of the FSB's recruitment of capable cyber operatives to carry out its, ideally deniable, offensive cyber operations, a Russian IT specialist with direct knowledge reported in June 2016 that this was often done using coercion and blackmail. In terms of 'foreign' agents, the FSB was approaching US citizens of Russian (Jewish) origin on business trips to Russia. In one case a US citizen of Russian ethnicity had been visiting Moscow to attract investors in his new information technology program. The FSB clearly knew this and had offered to provide seed capital to this person in return for them being able to access and modify his IP, with a view to targeting priority foreign targets by planting a Trojan virus in the software. The US visitor was told this was common practice. The FSB also had implied significant operational success as a result of installing cheap Russian IT games containing their own malware unwittingly by targets on their PCs and other platforms.

4. In a more advanced and successful FSB operation, an IT operator inside a leading Russian SOE, who previously had been employed on conventional (defensive) IT work there, had been under instruction for the last year to conduct an offensive cyber operation against a foreign director of the company. Although the latter was apparently an infrequent visitor to Russia, the FSB now successfully had penetrated his personal IT and through this had managed to access various important institutions in the West through the back door.

5. In terms of other technical IT platforms, an FSB cyber operative flagged up the 'Telegram' enciphered commercial system as having been of especial concern and therefore heavily targeted by the FSB, not least because it was used frequently by Russian internal political activists and oppositionists. His/her understanding was that the FSB now successfully had cracked this communications software and therefore it was no longer secure to use.

6. The senior Russian government figure cited above also reported that non-state sponsored cyber crime was becoming an increasing problem inside Russia for the government and authorities there. The Central Bank of Russia claimed that in 2015 alone there had been more than 20 attempts at serious cyber embezzlement of money from corresponding accounts held there, comprising several billions Roubles. More generally, s/he understood there were circa 15 major organised crime groups in the country involved in cyber crime, all of which continued to operate largely outside state and FSB control. These included the so-called 'Anunak', 'Buktrap' and 'Metel' organisations.

26 July 2015

RUSSIA/US PRESIDENTIAL ELECTION: FURTHER INDICATIONS OF EXTENSIVE CONSPIRACY BETWEEN TRUMP'S CAMPAIGN TEAM AND THE KREMLIN

Summary

- Further evidence of extensive conspiracy between TRUMP's campaign team and Kremlin, sanctioned at highest levels and involving Russian diplomatic staff based in the US

- TRUMP associate admits Kremlin behind recent appearance of DNC e-mails on WikiLeaks, as means of maintaining plausible deniability

- Agreed exchange of information established in both directions. TRUMP's team using moles within DNC and hackers in the US as well as outside in Russia. PUTIN motivated by fear and hatred of Hillary CLINTON. Russians receiving intel from TRUMP's team on Russian oligarchs and their families in US

- Mechanism for transmitting this intelligence involves "pension" disbursements to Russian emigres living in US as cover, using consular officials in New York, DC and Miami

- Suggestion from source close to TRUMP and MANAFORT that Republican campaign team happy to have Russia as media bogeyman to mask more extensive corrupt business ties to China and other emerging countries

Detail

1. Speaking in confidence to a compatriot in late July 2016, Source E, an ethnic Russian close associate of Republican US presidential candidate Donald TRUMP, admitted that there was a well-developed conspiracy of co-operation between them and the Russian leadership. This was managed on the TRUMP side by the Republican candidate's campaign manager, Paul MANAFORT, who was using foreign policy advisor, Carter PAGE, and others as intermediaries. The two sides had a mutual interest in defeating Democratic presidential candidate Hillary CLINTON, whom President PUTIN apparently both hated and feared.

2. Inter alia, Source E, acknowledged that the Russian regime had been behind the recent leak of embarrassing e-mail messages, emanating from the Democratic National Committee (DNC), to the WikiLeaks platform.

The reason for using WikiLeaks was "plausible deniability" and the operation had been conducted with the full knowledge and support of TRUMP and senior members of his campaign team. In return the TRUMP team had agreed to sideline Russian intervention in Ukraine as a campaign issue and to raise US/NATO defence commitments in the Baltics and Eastern Europe to deflect attention away from Ukraine, a priority for PUTIN who needed to cauterise the subject.

3. In the wider context of TRUMP campaign/Kremlin co-operation, Source E claimed that the intelligence network being used against CLINTON comprised three elements. Firstly there were agents/facilitators within the Democratic Party structure itself; secondly Russian émigré and associated offensive cyber operators based in the US; and thirdly, state-sponsored cyber operatives working in Russia. All three elements had played an important role to date. On the mechanism for rewarding relevant assets based in the US, and effecting a two-way flow of intelligence and other useful information, Source E claimed that Russian diplomatic staff in key cities such as New York, Washington DC and Miami were using the émigré 'pension' distribution system as cover. The operation therefore depended on key people in the US Russian émigré community for its success. Tens of thousands of dollars were involved.

4. In terms of the intelligence flow from the TRUMP team to Russia, Source E reported that much of this concerned the activities of business oligarchs and their families' activities and assets in the US, with which PUTIN and the Kremlin seemed preoccupied.

5. Commenting on the negative media publicity surrounding alleged Russian interference in the US election campaign in support of TRUMP, Source E said he understood that the Republican candidate and his team were relatively relaxed about this because it deflected media and the Democrats' attention away from TRUMP's business dealings in China and other emerging markets. Unlike in Russia, these were substantial and involved the payment of large bribes and kickbacks which, were they to become public, would be potentially very damaging to their campaign.

6. Finally, regarding TRUMP's claimed minimal investment profile in Russia, a separate source with direct knowledge said this had not been for want of trying. TRUMP's previous efforts had included exploring the real estate sector in St Petersburg as well as Moscow but in the end TRUMP had had to settle for the use of extensive sexual services there from local prostitutes rather than business success.

COMPANY INTELLIGENCE REPORT 2016/94

RUSSIA: SECRET KREMLIN MEETINGS ATTENDED BY TRUMP ADVISOR, CARTER PAGE IN MOSCOW (JULY 2016)

Summary

- TRUMP advisor Carter PAGE holds secret meetings in Moscow with SECHIN and senior Kremlin Internal Affairs official, DIVYEKIN

- SECHIN raises issues of future bilateral US-Russia energy co-operation and associated lifting of western sanctions against Russia over Ukraine. PAGE non-committal in response

- DIVEYKIN discusses release of Russian dossier of 'kompromat' on TRUMP's opponent, Hillary CLINTON, but also hints at Kremlin possession of such material on TRUMP

Detail

1. Speaking in July 2016, a Russian source close to Rosneft President, PUTIN close associate and US-sanctioned individual, Igor SECHIN, confided the details of a recent secret meeting between him and visiting Foreign Affairs Advisor to Republican presidential candidate Donald TRUMP, Carter PAGE.

2. According to SECHIN's associate, the Rosneft President (CEO) had raised with PAGE the issues of future bilateral energy cooperation and prospects for an associated move to lift Ukraine-related western sanctions against Russia. PAGE had reacted positively to this demarche by SECHIN but had been generally non-committal in response.

3. Speaking separately, also in July 2016, an official close to Presidential Administration Head, S. IVANOV, confided in a compatriot that a senior colleague in the Internal Political Department of the PA, DIVYEKIN (nfd) also had met secretly with PAGE on his recent visit. Their agenda had included DIVEYKIN raising a dossier of 'kompromat' the Kremlin possessed on TRUMP's Democratic presidential rival, Hillary CLINTON, and its possible release to the Republican's campaign team.

4. However, the Kremlin official close to S. IVANOV added that s/he believed DIVEYKIN also had hinted (or indicated more strongly) that the Russian leadership also had 'kompromat' on TRUMP which the latter should bear in mind in his dealings with them.

COMPANY INTELLIGENCE REPORT 2016/097

RUSSIA-US PRESIDENTIAL ELECTION: KREMLIN CONCERN THAT POLITICAL FALLOUT FROM DNC E-MAIL HACKING AFFAIR SPIRALLING OUT OF CONTROL

Summary

-   Kremlin concerned that political fallout from DNC e-mail hacking operation is spiralling out of control. Extreme nervousness among TRUMP's associates as result of negative media attention/accusations

-   Russians meanwhile keen to cool situation and maintain 'plausible deniability' of existing /ongoing pro-TRUMP and anti-CLINTON operations. Therefore unlikely to be any ratcheting up offensive plays in immediate future

-   Source close to TRUMP campaign however confirms regular exchange with Kremlin has existed for at least 8 years, including intelligence fed back to Russia on oligarchs' activities in US

-   Russians apparently have promised not to use 'kompromat' they hold on TRUMP as leverage, given high levels of voluntary co-operation forthcoming from his team

Detail

1. Speaking in confidence to a trusted associate in late July 2016, a Russian émigré figure close to the Republican US presidential candidate Donald TRUMP's campaign team commented on the fallout from publicity surrounding the Democratic National Committee (DNC) e-mail hacking scandal. The émigré said there was a high level of anxiety within the TRUMP team as a result of various accusations levelled against them and indications from the Kremlin that President PUTIN and others in the leadership thought things had gone too far now and risked spiralling out of control.

2. Continuing on this theme, the émigré associate of TRUMP opined that the Kremlin wanted the situation to calm but for 'plausible deniability' to be maintained concerning its (extensive) pro-TRUMP and anti-CLINTON operations. S/he therefore judged that it was unlikely these would be ratcheted up, at least for the time being.

3. However, in terms of established operational liaison between the TRUMP team and the Kremlin, the émigré confirmed that an intelligence exchange had been running between them for at least 8 years. Within this context PUTIN's priority requirement had been for intelligence on the activities, business and otherwise, in the US of leading Russian oligarchs and their families. TRUMP and his associates duly had obtained and supplied the Kremlin with this information.

4. Finally, the émigré said s/he understood the Kremlin had more intelligence on CLINTON and her campaign but he did not know the details or when or if it would be released. As far as 'kompromat' (compromising information) on TRUMP were concerned, although there was plenty of this, he understood the Kremlin had given its word that it would not be deployed against the Republican presidential candidate given how helpful and co-operative his team had been over several years, and particularly of late.

30 July 2016

COMPANY INTELLIGENCE REPORT 2016/100

RUSSIA/USA: GROWING BACKLASH IN KREMLIN TO DNC HACKING AND TRUMP SUPPORT OPERATIONS

Summary

- Head of PA IVANOV laments Russian intervention in US presidential election and black PR against CLINTON and the DNC. Vows not to supply intelligence to Kremlin PR operatives again. Advocates now sitting tight and denying everything

- Presidential spokesman PESKOV the main protagonist in Kremlin campaign to aid TRUMP and damage CLINTON. He is now scared and fears being made scapegoat by leadership for backlash in US. Problem compounded by his botched intervention in recent Turkish crisis

- Premier MEDVEDEV's office furious over DNC hacking and associated anti-Russian publicity. Want good relations with US and ability to travel there. Refusing to support or help cover up after PESKOV

- Talk now in Kremlin of TRUMP withdrawing from presidential race altogether, but this still largely wishful thinking by more liberal elements in Moscow

Detail

1. Speaking in early August 2016, two well-placed and established Kremlin sources outlined the divisions and backlash in Moscow arising from the leaking of Democratic National Committee (DNC) e-mails and the wider pro-TRUMP operation being conducted in the US. Head of Presidential Administration, Sergei IVANOV, was angry at the recent turn of events. He believed the Kremlin "team" involved, led by presidential spokesman Dmitriy PESKOV, had gone too far in interfering in foreign affairs with their "elephant in a china shop black PR". IVANOV claimed always to have opposed the handling and exploitation of intelligence by this PR "team". Following the backlash against such foreign interference in US politics, IVANOV was advocating that the only sensible course of action now for the Russian leadership was to "sit tight and deny everything".

2. Continuing on this theme the source close to IVANOV reported that PESKOV now was "scared shitless" that he would be scapegoated by PUTIN and the Kremlin and held responsible for the backlash against Russian political interference in the US election. IVANOV was determined

to stop PESKOV playing an independent role in relation to the US going forward and the source fully expected the presidential spokesman now to lay low. PESKOV's position was not helped by a botched attempt by him also to interfere in the recent failed coup in Turkey from a government relations (GR) perspective (no further details).

3. The extent of disquiet and division within Moscow caused by the backlash against Russian interference in the US election was underlined by a second source, close to premier Dmitriy MEDVEDEV (DAM). S/he said the Russian prime minister and his colleagues wanted to have good relations with the US, regardless of who was in power there, and not least so as to be able to travel there in future, either officially or privately. They were openly refusing to cover up for PESKOV and others involved in the DNC/TRUMP operations or to support his counter-attack of allegations against the USG for its alleged hacking of the Russian government and state agencies.

4. According to the first source, close to IVANOV, there had been talk in the Kremlin of TRUMP being forced to withdraw from the presidential race altogether as a result of recent events, ostensibly on grounds of his psychological state and unsuitability for high office. This might not be so bad for Russia in the circumstances but in the view of the source, it remained largely wishful thinking on the part of those in the regime opposed to PESKOV and his "botched" operations, at least for the time being.

5 August 2016

COMPANY INTELLIGENCE REPORT 2016/101

RUSSIA/US PRESIDENTIAL ELECTION: SENIOR KREMLIN FIGURE OUTLINES EVOLVING RUSSIAN TACTICS IN PRO-TRUMP, ANTI-CLINTON OPERATION

Summary

- Head of PA, IVANOV assesses Kremlin intervention in US presidential election and outlines leadership thinking on operational way forward

- No new leaks envisaged, as too politically risky, but rather further exploitation of (WikiLeaks) material already disseminated to exacerbate divisions

- Educated US youth to be targeted as protest (against CLINTON) and swing vote in attempt to turn them over to TRUMP

- Russian leadership, including PUTIN, celebrating perceived success to date in splitting US hawks and elite

- Kremlin engaging with several high profile US players, including STEIN, PAGE and (former DIA Director Michael Flynn), and funding their recent visits to Moscow

Details

1. Speaking in confidence to a close colleague in early August 2016, Head of the Russian Presidential Administration (PA), Sergei IVANOV, assessed the impact and results of Kremlin intervention in the US presidential election to date. Although most commentators believed that the Kremlin was behind the leaked DNC/CLINTON e-mails, this remained technically deniable. Therefore the Russians would not risk their position for the time being with new leaked material, even to a third party like WikiLeaks. Rather the tactics would be to spread rumours and misinformation about the content of what already had been leaked and make up new content.

2. Continuing on this theme, IVANOV said that the audience to be targeted by such operations was the educated youth in America as the PA assessed that there was still a chance they could be persuaded to vote for Republican candidate Donald TRUMP as a protest against the Washington establishment (in the form of Democratic candidate Hillary CLINTON). The hope was that even if she won, as a result of this CLINTON in power would be bogged down in working for internal reconciliation in the US, rather than being able to focus on foreign policy which would damage Russia's interests. This also should give President PUTIN more room for manoeuvre in the run-up to Russia's own presidential election in 2018.

3. IVANOV reported that although the Kremlin had underestimated the strength of US media and liberal reaction to the DNC hack and TRUMP's links to Russia, PUTIN was generally satisfied with the progress of the anti-CLINTON operation to date. He recently had had a drink with PUTIN to mark this. In IVANOV's view, the US had tried to divide the Russian elite with sanctions but failed, whilst they, by contrast, had succeeded in splitting the US hawks inimical to Russia and the Washington elite more generally, half of whom had refused to endorse any presidential candidate as a result of Russian intervention.

4. Speaking separately, also in early August 2016, a Kremlin official involved in US relations commented on aspects of the Russian operation to date. Its goals had been threefold- asking sympathetic US actors how Moscow could help them; gathering relevant intelligence; and creating and disseminating compromising information ('kompromat'). This had involved the Kremlin supporting various US political figures, including funding indirectly their recent visits to Moscow. S/he named a delegation from Lyndon LAROUCHE; presidential candidate Jill STEIN of the Green Party; TRUMP foreign policy adviser

15

Carter PAGE; and former DIA Director Michael Flynn, in this regard and as successful in terms of perceived outcomes.

10 August 2016

COMPANY INTELLIGENCE REPORT 2016/102

RUSSIA/US PRESIDENTIAL ELECTION: REACTION IN TRUMP CAMP TO RECENT NEGATIVE PUBLICITY ABOUT RUSSIAN INTERFERENCE AND LIKELY RESULTING TACTICS GOING FORWARD

Summary

- TRUMP campaign insider reports recent DNC e-mail leaks were aimed at switching SANDERS (protest) voters away from CLINTON and over to TRUMP

- Admits Republican campaign underestimated resulting negative reaction from US liberals, elite and media and forced to change course as result

- Need now to turn tables on CLINTON's use of PUTIN as bogeyman in election, although some resentment at Russian president's perceived attempt to undermine USG and system over and above swinging presidential election

Detail

1. Speaking in confidence on 9 August 2016, an ethnic Russian associate of Republican US presidential candidate Donald TRUMP discussed the reaction inside his camp, and revised tactics therein resulting from recent negative publicity concerning Moscow's clandestine involvement in the campaign. TRUMP's associate reported that the aim of leaking the DNC e-mails to WikiLeaks during the Democratic Convention had been to swing supporters of Bernie SANDERS away from Hillary CLINTON and across to TRUMP. These voters were perceived as activist and anti-status quo and anti-establishment and in that regard sharing many features with the TRUMP campaign, including a visceral dislike of Hillary CLINTON. This objective had been conceived and promoted, inter alia, by TRUMP's foreign policy adviser Carter PAGE who had discussed it directly with the ethnic Russian associate.

2. Continuing on this theme, the ethnic Russian associate of TRUMP assessed that the problem was that the TRUMP campaign had underestimated the strength of the negative reaction from liberals and especially the conservative elite to Russian interference. This was forcing a rethink and a likely change of tactics. The main objective in the short term was to check Democratic candidate Hillary CLINTON's successful exploitation of the PUTIN as bogeyman/Russian interference story to tarnish TRUMP and bolster her own (patriotic) credentials. The TRUMP campaign was focusing on tapping into support in the American television media to achieve this, as they reckoned this resource had been underused by them to date.

3. However, TRUMP's associate also admitted that there was a fair amount of anger and resentment within the Republican candidate's team at what was perceived by PUTIN as going beyond the objective of weakening CLINTON and bolstering TRUMP, by attempting to exploit the situation to undermine the US government and democratic system more generally. It was unclear at present how this aspect of the situation would play out in the weeks to come.

10 August 2016

COMPANY INTELLIGENCE REPORT 2016/136

RUSSIA/US PRESIDENTIAL ELECTION: FURTHER DETAILS OF TRUMP LAWYER COHEN'S SECRET LIAISON WITH THE KREMLIN

Summary

- Kremlin insider reports TRUMP lawyer COHEN's secret meeting/s with Kremlin officials in August 2016 was/were held in Prague

- Russian parastatal organisation Rossotrudnichestvo used as cover for this liaison and premises in Czech capital may have been used for the meeting/s

- Pro-PUTIN leading Duma figure, KOSACHEV, reportedly involved as "plausibly deniable" facilitator and may have participated in the August meeting/s with COHEN

Detail

1. Speaking to a compatriot and friend on 19 October 2016, a Kremlin insider provided further details of reported clandestine meeting/s between Republican presidential candidate, Donald TRUMP's lawyer Michael COHEN and Kremlin representatives in August 2016. Although the communication between them had to be cryptic for security reasons, the Kremlin insider clearly indicated to his/her friend that the reported contact/s took place in Prague, Czech Republic.

2. Continuing on this theme, the Kremlin insider highlighted the importance of the Russian parastatal organisation, Rossotrudnichestvo, in this contact between TRUMP campaign representative/s and Kremlin officials. Rossotrudnichestvo was being used as cover for this relationship and its office in Prague may well have been used to host the COHEN/Russian Presidential Administration (PA) meeting/s. It was considered a "plausibly deniable" vehicle for this, whilst remaining entirely under Kremlin control.

3. The Kremlin insider went on to identify leading pro-PUTIN Duma figure, Konstantin KOSACHEV (Head of the Foreign Relations Committee) as an important figure in the TRUMP campaign-Kremlin liaison operation. KOSACHEV, also "plausibly deniable" being part of the Russian legislature rather than executive, had facilitated the contact in Prague and by implication, may have attended the meeting/s with COHEN there in August.

Company Comment

We reported previously, in our Company Intelligence Report 2016/135 of 19 October 2016 from the same source, that COHEN met officials from the PA Legal Department clandestinely in an EU country in August 2016. This was in order to clean up the mess left behind by western media revelations of TRUMP ex-campaign manager MANAFORT's corrupt relationship with the former pro-Russian YANUKOVYCH regime in Ukraine and TRUMP foreign policy advisor, Carter PAGE's secret meetings in Moscow with senior regime figures in July 2016. According to the Kremlin advisor, these meeting/s were originally scheduled for COHEN in Moscow but shifted to

what was considered an operationally "soft" EU country when it was judged too compromising for him to travel to the Russian capital.

20 October 2016

COMPANY INTELLIGENCE REPORT 2016/105

RUSSIA/UKRAINE: THE DEMISE OF TRUMP'S CAMPAIGN MANAGER PAUL MANAFORT

Summary

- Ex-Ukrainian President YANUKOVYCH confides directly to PUTIN that he authorised kick-back payments to MANAFORT, as alleged in western media. Assures Russian President however there is no documentary evidence/trail

- PUTIN and Russian leadership remain worried however and sceptical that YANUKOVYCH has fully covered the traces of these payments to TRUMP's former campaign manager

- Close associate of TRUMP explains reasoning behind MANAFORT's recent resignation. Ukraine revelations played part but others wanted MANAFORT out for various reasons, especially LEWANDOWSKI who remains influential

Detail

1. Speaking in late August 2016, in the immediate aftermath of Paul MANAFORT's resignation as campaign manager for US Republican presidential candidate Donald TRUMP, a well-placed Russian figure reported on a recent meeting between President PUTIN and ex-President YANUKOVYCH of Ukraine. This had been held in secret on 15 August near Volgograd, Russia and the western media revelations about MANAFORT and Ukraine had featured prominently on the agenda. YANUKOVYCH had confided in PUTIN that he did authorise and order substantial kick-back payments to MANAFORT as alleged but sought to reassure him that there was no documentary trail left behind which could provide clear evidence of this.

2. Given YANUKOVYCH's (unimpressive) record in covering up his own corrupt tracks in the past, PUTIN and others in the Russian leadership were sceptical about the ex-Ukrainian president's reassurances on this as relating to MANAFORT. They therefore still feared the scandal had legs, especially as MANAFORT had been commercially active in Ukraine right up to the time (in March 2016) when he joined TRUMP's campaign team. For them it therefore remained a point of potential political vulnerability and embarrassment.

3. Speaking separately, also in late August 2016, an American political figure associated with Donald TRUMP and his campaign outlined the reasons behind MANAFORT's recent demise. S/he said it was true that the Ukraine corruption revelations had played a part in this but also, several senior players close to TRUMP had wanted MANAFORT out, primarily to loosen his control on strategy and policy formulation. Of particular importance in this regard was MANAFORT's predecessor as campaign manager, Corey LEWANDOWSKI, who hated MANAFORT personally and remained close to TRUMP with whom he discussed the presidential campaign on a regular basis.

22 August 2016

COMPANY INTELLIGENCE REPORT 2016/111

RUSSIA/US: KREMLIN FALLOUT FROM MEDIA EXPOSURE OF MOSCOW'S INTERFERENCE IN THE US PRESIDENTIAL CAMPAIGN

Summary

-   Kremlin orders senior staff to remain silent in media and private on allegations of Russian interference in US presidential campaign

-   Senior figure however confirms gist of allegations and reports IVANOV sacked as Head of Administration on account of giving PUTIN poor advice on issue. VAINO selected as his replacement partly because he was not involved in pro-TRUMP, anti-CLINTON operation/s

-   Russians do have further 'kompromat' on CLINTON (e-mails) and considering disseminating it after Duma (legislative elections) in late September. Presidential spokesman PESKOV continues to lead on this

-   However, equally important is Kremlin objective to shift policy consensus favourably to Russia in US post-OBAMA whoever wins. Both presidential candidates' opposition to TPP and TTIP viewed as a result in this respect

-   Senior Russian diplomat withdrawn from Washington embassy on account of potential exposure in US presidential election operation/s

Detail

1. Speaking in confidence to a trusted compatriot in mid-September 2016, a senior member of the Russian Presidential Administration (PA) commented on the political fallout from recent western media revelations about Moscow's intervention, in favour of Donald TRUMP and against Hillary CLINTON, in the US presidential election. The PA official reported that the issue had become incredibly sensitive and that President PUTIN had issued direct orders that Kremlin and government insiders should not discuss it in public or even in private.

2. Despite this, the PA official confirmed, from direct knowledge, that the gist of the allegations was true. PUTIN had been receiving conflicting advice on interfering from three separate and expert groups. On one side had been the Russian ambassador to the US, Sergei KISLYAK, and the Ministry of Foreign Affairs, together with an independent and informal network run by presidential foreign policy advisor, Yuri USHAKOV

(KISLYAK's predecessor in Washington) who had urged caution and the potential negative impact on Russia from the operation/s. On the other side was former PA Head, Sergei IVANOV, backed by Russian Foreign Intelligence (SVR), who had advised PUTIN that the pro-TRUMP, anti-CLINTON operation/s would be both effective and plausibly deniable with little blowback. The first group/s had been proven right and this had been the catalyst in PUTIN's decision to sack IVANOV (unexpectedly) as PA Head in August. His successor, Anton VAINO, had been selected for the job partly because he had not been involved in the US presidential election operation/s.

3. Continuing on this theme, the senior PA official said the situation now was that the Kremlin had further 'kompromat' on candidate CLINTON and had been considering releasing this via "plausibly deniable" channels after the Duma (legislative) elections were out of the way in mid-September. There was however a growing train of thought and associated lobby, arguing that the Russians could still make candidate CLINTON look "weak and stupid" by provoking her into railing against PUTIN and Russia without the need to release more of her e-mails. Presidential Spokesman, Dmitriy PESKOV remained a key figure in the operation, although any final decision on dissemination of further material would be taken by PUTIN himself.

4. The senior PA official also reported that a growing element in Moscow's intervention in the US presidential election campaign was the objective of shifting the US political consensus in Russia's perceived interests regardless of who won. It basically comprised of pushing candidate CLINTON away from President OBAMA's policies. The best example of this was that both candidates now openly opposed the draft trade agreements, TPP and TTIP, which were assessed by Moscow as detrimental to Russian interests. Other issues where the Kremlin was looking to shift the US policy consensus were Ukraine and Syria. Overall however, the presidential election was considered still to be too close to call.

5. Finally, speaking separately to the same compatriot, a senior Russian MFA official reported that as a prophylactic measure, a leading Russian diplomat, Mikhail KULAGIN, had been withdrawn from Washington at short notice because Moscow feared his heavy involvement in the US presidential election operation, including the so-called veterans' pensions ruse (reported previously), would be exposed in the media there. His replacement, Andrei BONDAREV however was clean in this regard.

Company Comment

The substance of what was reported by the senior Russian PA official in paras 1 and 2 above, including the reasons for Sergei IVANOV's dismissal, was corroborated independently by a former top level Russian intelligence officer and Kremlin insider, also in mid-September.

14 September 2016

COMPANY INTELLIGENCE REPORT 2016/113

RUSSIA/US PRESIDENTIAL ELECTION- REPUBLICAN CANDIDATE TRUMP'S PRIOR ACTIVITIES IN ST PETERSBURG

Summary

-   Two knowledgeable St Petersburg sources claim Republican candidate TRUMP has paid bribes and engaged in sexual activities there but key witnesses silenced and evidence hard to obtain

-   Both believe Azeri business associate of TRUMP, Araz AGALAROV will know the details

Detail

1. Speaking to a trusted compatriot in September 2016, two well-placed sources based in St Petersburg, one in the political/business elite and the other involved in the local services and tourist industry, commented on Republican US presidential candidate Donald TRUMP's prior activities in the city.

2. Both knew TRUMP had visited St Petersburg on several occasions in the past and had been interested in doing business deals there involving real estate. The local business/political elite figure reported that TRUMP had paid bribes there to further his interests but very discreetly and only through affiliated companies, making it very hard to prove. The local services industry source reported that TRUMP had participated in sex parties in the city too, but that all direct witnesses to this recently had been "silenced" i.e. bribed or coerced to disappear.

3. The two St Petersburg figures cited believed an Azeri business figure, Araz AGALAROV (with offices in Baku and London) had been closely involved with TRUMP in Russia and would know most of the details of what the Republican presidential candidate had got up to there.

14 September 2016

Kremlin-Alpha Group Cooperation Section deleted on purpose

COMPANY INTELLIGENCE REPORT 2016/130

RUSSIA: KREMLIN ASSESSMENT OF TRUMP AND RUSSIAN INTERFERENCE IN US PRESIDENTIAL ELECTION

Summary

- Buyer's remorse sets in with Kremlin over TRUMP support operation in US presidential election. Russian leadership disappointed that leaked e-mails on CLINTON have not had greater impact in campaign

- Russians have injected further anti-CLINTON material into the 'plausibly deniable' leaks pipeline which will continue to surface, but best material already in public domain

- PUTIN angry with senior officials who "overpromised" on TRUMP and further heads likely to roll as result. Foreign Minister LAVROV may be next

- TRUMP supported by Kremlin because seen as divisive, anti-establishment candidate who would shake up current international status quo in Russia's favor. Lead on TRUMP operation moved from Foreign Ministry to FSB and then to presidential administration where it now sits

Detail

1. Speaking separately in confidence to a trusted compatriot in early October 2016, a senior Russian leadership figure and a Foreign Ministry official reported on recent developments concerning the Kremlin's operation to support Republican candidate Donald TRUMP in the US presidential election. The senior leadership figure said that a degree of buyer's remorse was setting in among Russian leaders concerning TRUMP. PUTIN and his colleagues were surprised and disappointed that leaks of Democratic candidate, Hillary CLINTON's hacked e-mails had not had greater impact on the campaign.

2. Continuing on this theme, the senior leadership figure commented that a stream of further hacked CLINTON material already had been injected by the Kremlin into compliant western media outlets like Wikileaks, which remained at least "plausibly deniable", so the stream of these would continue through October and up to the election. However s/he understood that the best material the Russians had already was out and there were no real game-changers to come.

3. The Russian Foreign Ministry official, who had direct access to the TRUMP support operation, reported that PUTIN was angry at his subordinate's "over-promising" on the Republican presidential candidate, both in terms of his chances and reliability and being able to cover and/or contain the US backlash over Kremlin interference. More heads therefore were likely to roll, with the MFA the easiest target. Ironically, despite his consistent urging of caution on the issue, Foreign Minister LAVROV could be the next one to go.

4. Asked to explain why PUTIN and the Kremlin had launched such an aggressive TRUMP support operation in the first place, the MFA official said that Russia needed to upset the liberal international status quo, including on Ukraine-related sanctions, which was seriously

disadvantaging the country. TRUMP was viewed as divisive in disrupting the whole US political system; anti-Establishment; and a pragmatist with whom they could do business. As the TRUMP support operation had gained momentum, control of it had passed from the MFA to the FSB and then into the presidential administration where it remained, a reflection of its growing significance over time. There was still a view in the Kremlin that TRUMP would continue as a (divisive) political force even if he lost the presidency and may run for and be elected to another public office.

12 October 2016

COMPANY INTELLIGENCE REPORT 2016/134

RUSSIA/US PRESIDENTIAL ELECTION: FURTHER DETAILS OF KREMLIN LIAISON WITH TRUMP CAMPAIGN

Summary

- Close associate of SECHIN confirms his secret meeting in Moscow with Carter PAGE in July

- Substance included offer of large stake in Rosneft in return for lifting sanctions on Russia. PAGE confirms this is TRUMP's intention

- SECHIN continued to think TRUMP could win presidency up to 17 October. Now looking to reorientate his engagement with the US

- Kremlin insider highlights importance of TRUMP's lawyer, Michael COHEN in covert relationship with Russia. COHEN's wife is of Russian descent and her father a leading property developer in Moscow

COMPANY INTELLIGENCE REPORT 2016/134

RUSSIA/US PRESIDENTIAL ELECTION: FURTHER DETAILS OF KREMLIN LIAISON WITH TRUMP CAMPAIGN

Summary

- Close associate of SECHIN confirms his secret meeting in Moscow with Carter PAGE in July

- Substance included offer of large stake in Rosneft in return for lifting sanctions on Russia. PAGE confirms this is TRUMP's intention

- SECHIN continued to think TRUMP could win presidency up to 17 October. Now looking to reorientate his engagement with the US

- Kremlin insider highlights importance of TRUMP's lawyer, Michael COHEN in covert relationship with Russia. COHEN's wife is of Russian descent and her father a leading property developer in Moscow

Detail

1. Speaking to a trusted compatriot in mid October 2016, a close associate of Rosneft President and PUTIN ally Igor' SECHIN elaborated on the reported secret meeting between the latter and Carter PAGE, of US Republican presidential candidate's foreign policy team, in Moscow in July 2016. The secret meeting had been confirmed to him/her by a senior member of SECHIN's staff, in addition to by the Rosneft President himself. It took place on either 7 or 8 July, the same day or the one after Carter PAGE made a public speech to the Higher Economic School in Moscow.

2. In terms of the substance of their discussion, SECHIN's associate said that the Rosneft President was so keen to lift personal and corporate western sanctions imposed on the company, that he offered PAGE/TRUMP's associates the brokerage of up to a 19 per cent (privatised) stake in Rosneft in return. PAGE had expressed interest and confirmed that were TRUMP elected US president, then sanctions on Russia would be lifted.

3. According to SECHIN's close associate, the Rosneft President had continued to believe that TRUMP could win the US presidency right up to 17 October, when he assessed this was no longer possible. SECHIN was keen to re-adapt accordingly and put feelers out to other business and political contacts in the US instead.

4. Speaking separately to the same compatriot in mid-October 2016, a Kremlin insider with direct access to the leadership confirmed that a key role in the secret TRUMP campaign/Kremlin relationship was being played by the Republican candidate's personal lawyer Michael COHEN. ██████████████████████

Source Comment

5. SECHIN's associate opined that although PAGE had not stated it explicitly to SECHIN, he had clearly implied that in terms of his comment on TRUMP's intention to lift Russian sanctions if elected president, he was speaking with the Republican candidate's authority.

Company Comment

6. ██████████████████████████████████

18 October 2016

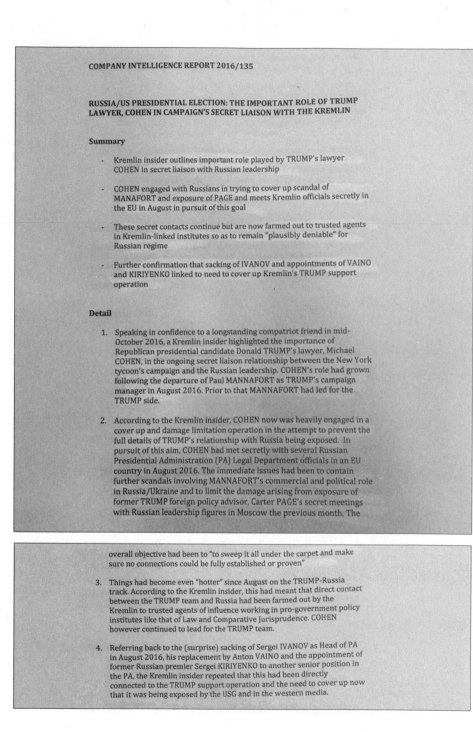

COMPANY INTELLIGENCE REPORT 2016/135

RUSSIA/US PRESIDENTIAL ELECTION: THE IMPORTANT ROLE OF TRUMP LAWYER, COHEN IN CAMPAIGN'S SECRET LIAISON WITH THE KREMLIN

Summary

- Kremlin insider outlines important role played by TRUMP's lawyer COHEN in secret liaison with Russian leadership

- COHEN engaged with Russians in trying to cover up scandal of MANAFORT and exposure of PAGE and meets Kremlin officials secretly in the EU in August in pursuit of this goal

- These secret contacts continue but are now farmed out to trusted agents in Kremlin-linked institutes so as to remain "plausibly deniable" for Russian regime

- Further confirmation that sacking of IVANOV and appointments of VAINO and KIRIYENKO linked to need to cover up Kremlin's TRUMP support operation

Detail

1. Speaking in confidence to a longstanding compatriot friend in mid-October 2016, a Kremlin insider highlighted the importance of Republican presidential candidate Donald TRUMP's lawyer, Michael COHEN, in the ongoing secret liaison relationship between the New York tycoon's campaign and the Russian leadership. COHEN's role had grown following the departure of Paul MANNAFORT as TRUMP's campaign manager in August 2016. Prior to that MANNAFORT had led for the TRUMP side.

2. According to the Kremlin insider, COHEN now was heavily engaged in a cover up and damage limitation operation in the attempt to prevent the full details of TRUMP's relationship with Russia being exposed. In pursuit of this aim, COHEN had met secretly with several Russian Presidential Administration (PA) Legal Department officials in an EU country in August 2016. The immediate issues had been to contain further scandals involving MANNAFORT's commercial and political role in Russia/Ukraine and to limit the damage arising from exposure of former TRUMP foreign policy advisor, Carter PAGE's secret meetings with Russian leadership figures in Moscow the previous month. The

overall objective had been to "to sweep it all under the carpet and make sure no connections could be fully established or proven"

3. Things had become even "hotter" since August on the TRUMP-Russia track. According to the Kremlin insider, this had meant that direct contact between the TRUMP team and Russia had been farmed out by the Kremlin to trusted agents of influence working in pro-government policy institutes like that of Law and Comparative Jurisprudence. COHEN however continued to lead for the TRUMP team.

4. Referring back to the (surprise) sacking of Sergei IVANOV as Head of PA in August 2016, his replacement by Anton VAINO and the appointment of former Russian premier Sergei KIRIYENKO to another senior position in the PA, the Kremlin insider repeated that this had been directly connected to the TRUMP support operation and the need to cover up now that it was being exposed by the USG and in the western media.

Company Comment

The Kremlin insider was unsure of the identities of the PA officials with whom COHEN met secretly in August, or the exact date/s and locations of the meeting/s. There were significant internal security barriers being erected in the PA as the TRUMP issue became more controversial and damaging. However s/he continued to try to obtain these.

19 October 2016

COMPANY INTELLIGENCE REPORT 2016/166

US/RUSSIA: FURTHER DETAILS OF SECRET DIALOGUE BETWEEN TRUMP CAMPAIGN TEAM, KREMLIN AND ASSOCIATED HACKERS IN PRAGUE

Summary

- TRUMP's representative COHEN accompanied to Prague in August/September 2016 by 3 colleagues for secret discussions with Kremlin representatives and associated operators/hackers

- Agenda included how to process deniable cash payments to operatives; contingency plans for covering up operations; and action in event of a CLINTON election victory

- Some further details of Russian representatives/operatives involved; Romanian hackers employed; and use of Bulgaria as bolt hole to "lie low"

- Anti-CLINTON hackers and other operatives paid by both TRUMP team and Kremlin, but with ultimate loyalty to Head of PA, IVANOV and his successor/s

Detail

1. We reported previously (2016/135 and /136) on secret meeting/s held in Prague, Czech Republic in August 2016 between then Republican presidential candidate Donald TRUMP's representative, Michael COHEN and his interlocutors from the Kremlin working under cover of Russian 'NGO' Rossotrudnichestvo.

2. ███████████████████████████████████████ provided further details of these meeting/s and associated anti-CLINTON/Democratic Party operations. COHEN had been accompanied to Prague by 3 colleagues and the timing of the visit was either in the last week of August or the first week of September. One of their main Russian interlocutors was Oleg SOLODUKHIN operating under Rossotrudnichestvo cover. According to ██████████████, the agenda comprised questions on how deniable cash payments were to be made to hackers who had worked in Europe under Kremlin direction against the CLINTON campaign and various contingencies for covering up these operations and Moscow's secret liaison with the TRUMP team more generally.

3. ███████████████ reported that over the period March-September 2016 a company called ███████████ and its affiliates had been using botnets and porn traffic to transmit viruses, plant bugs, steal data and conduct "altering operations" against the Democratic Party leadership. Entities linked to one ████████████████ were involved and he and another hacking expert, both recruited under duress by the FSB, ██████ ████████████ were significant players in this operation. In Prague, COHEN agreed contingency plans for various scenarios to protect the operation, but in particular what was to be done in the event that Hillary CLINTON won the presidency. It was important in this event that all cash payments owed were made quickly and discreetly and that cyber and other operators were stood down/able to go effectively to ground to cover their traces. (We reported earlier that the involvement of political operatives Paul MANAFORT and Carter PAGE in the secret TRUMP-Kremlin liaison had been exposed in the media in the run-up to Prague and that damage limitation of these also was discussed by COHEN with the Kremlin representatives).

4. In terms of practical measures to be taken, it was agreed by the two sides in Prague to stand down various "Romanian hackers" (presumably based in their homeland or neighbouring eastern Europe) and that other operatives should head for a bolt-hole in Plovdiv, Bulgaria where they should "lay low". On payments, IVANOV's associate said that the operatives involved had been paid by both TRUMP's team and the Kremlin, though their orders and ultimate loyalty lay with IVANOV, as Head of the PA and thus ultimately responsible for the operation, and his designated successor/s after he was dismissed by president PUTIN in connection with the anti-CLINTON operation in mid August.

13 December 2016

Randi Gleason

From:	Lois Weiss [lois@████████.com]
Sent:	Thursday, August 09, 2012 2:41 PM
To:	Randi Gleason
Subject:	Re: Newsmax article

DJ:
Wishing you would give a speech at the convention but What bugs me is how many people don't
seem to care that Obama may be lying about being born in this country and that a massive
coverup has taken place to conceal his Kenyan birth. I hope you have the Kenyan birth
certificate somewhere safe!
Lois
Lois Weiss

Please use email to:
Lois@████████.com

This message sent via BlackBerry

An email from a New York Post journalist shows how widely Trump's birtherism claims spread. © 2020 Michael Cohen

---

Rhona Graff

From:	David Crank <dc@████████.com>
Sent:	Monday, August 24, 2015 12:18 AM
To:	lee lipton
Cc:	Rhona Graff
Subject:	Re: Donald on the day you are ready to talk to BEN CARSON as you well know JUST ASK he is my BFF

This is absolutely brilliant!! You may be the smartest guy I know!

Sent from my iPhone

> On Aug 22, 2015, at 2:20 PM, lee lipton <leelipton01@████████> wrote:
>
> you already have the hispanic vote   you don't need hispanics to vote for you you are beatuing rubio in his state he cant do anything foir you either can CRUZ OR Martinez
>
> YOU NEED THE BLACK VOTE IT CAN BE DONE they hate Hillary !!!!
>
> BEN IS YOUR GUY
>
> HES PERFECT people love him he's not a politician HE LOVES YOU   HE respects YOU
>
>
> Please dont attack him save him as your VP!!!!!
>
> its too soon im sure he still thinks he s going to win   but when everyone realizes you are definitely the republican candidate maybe you campaign together fror the primary no one can beat that!!!!!
>
> BEN IS YOUR GUY!!!   and let him concentrate on every state If i were you dont get rid of NY and Calif with you and BEN its possible !!!!!!
>
> when you want to talk to Ben please allow me to set it up standing next to him on the podium is priceless Let HIM fix HEALTHCARE and VA HOSPITALS you do jobs and MILITARY!!!
>
> Its unbeatable team!!!!!!
>
> if you need me   call

"YOU NEED THE BLACK VOTE . . . BEN IS YOUR GUY!" © 2020 Michael Cohen

A SELECTION OF TRUMP'S TWEETS ABOUT ME, SHOWING HIS CHANGING OPINION.

Donald J. Trump ✔ @realDonaldTrump · Apr 21, 2018

The New York Times and a third rate reporter named Maggie Haberman, known as a Crooked H flunkie who I don't speak to and have nothing to do with, are going out of their way to destroy Michael Cohen and his relationship with me in the hope that he will "flip." They use....

Donald J. Trump ✔
@realDonaldTrump

....non-existent "sources" and a drunk/drugged up loser who hates Michael, a fine person with a wonderful family. Michael is a businessman for his own account/lawyer who I have always liked & respected. Most people will flip if the Government lets them out of trouble, even if....

9:10 AM · Apr 21, 2018   ⓘ

♡ 42.8K   ○ 16.5K people are Tweeting about this

Donald J. Trump ✔
@realDonaldTrump

Replying to @realDonaldTrump

....it means lying or making up stories. Sorry, I don't see Michael doing that despite the horrible Witch Hunt and the dishonest media!

9:10 AM · Apr 21, 2018   ⓘ

♡ 46.1K   ○ 24.9K people are Tweeting about this

← **Tweet**

Donald J. Trump ✔ @realDonaldTrump · Aug 22, 2018   ⌄

If anyone is looking for a good lawyer, I would strongly suggest that you don't retain the services of Michael Cohen!

○ 68.2K   ⟲ 59.6K   ♡ 132.6K   ⬆

Donald J. Trump ✔
@realDonaldTrump

"Michael Cohen asks judge for no Prison Time." You mean he can do all of the TERRIBLE, unrelated to Trump, things having to do with fraud, big loans, Taxis, etc., and not serve a long prison term? He makes up stories to get a GREAT & ALREADY reduced deal for himself, and get.....

10:24 AM · Dec 3, 2018   ⓘ

♡ 65.6K   ♡ 39.6K people are Tweeting about this

Donald J. Trump ✔
@realDonaldTrump

....his wife and father-in-law (who has the money?) off Scott Free. He lied for this outcome and should, in my opinion, serve a full and complete sentence.

10:29 AM · Dec 3, 2018   ⓘ

♡ 59.4K   ♡ 33.4K people are Tweeting about this

← **Tweet**

Donald J. Trump ✔ @realDonaldTrump · Dec 16, 2018   ⌄
Remember, Michael Cohen only became a "Rat" after the FBI did something which was absolutely unthinkable & unheard of until the Witch Hunt was illegally started. They BROKE INTO AN ATTORNEY'S OFFICE! Why didn't they break into the DNC to get the Server, or Crooked's office?

♡ 56.1K   ⟲ 34.8K   ♡ 112.5K   ↥

← **Tweet**

Donald J. Trump ✔ @realDonaldTrump · Feb 27, 2019   ⌄
Michael Cohen was one of many lawyers who represented me (unfortunately). He had other clients also. He was just disbarred by the State Supreme Court for lying & fraud. He did bad things unrelated to Trump. He is lying in order to reduce his prison time. Using Crooked's lawyer!

♡ 63.8K   ⟲ 32.5K   ♡ 118K   ↥

Trump and me with the Falwells. © 2020 *Michael Cohen*

Me with Trump. © 2020 *Michael Cohen*

Me at the White House. © 2020 *Michael Cohen*

Trump at my son's bar mitzvah. © 2020 Michael Cohen

Certificate of Dedication

In recognition of exceptional commitment and extraordinary generosity to the cause of American freedom, I do proudly award this Certificate of Dedication to:

Mr. Donald Trump

On this ___9th___ day of ___July, 2012___ .

This award is presented with great pride and humble appreciation by:

Senator Marco Rubio (R-FL)

Rubio gave Trump an award. You've read how we repaid him. © 2020 Michael Cohen